The Dead Walk

By
Andy Black
&
Steve Earles

Noir Publishing
10 Spinney Grove
Hereford
HR1 1AY
email:noirpub@dsl.pipex.com
www.noirpublishing.co.uk

Noir Publishing titles should be available from all good bookstores; please ask your retailer to order from:
UK & EUROPE:
Turnaround Publisher Services, Unit 3, Olympia Trading Estate,
Coburg Road, Wood Green, London. N22 6TZ
Tel: 0208 829 3000 Fax: 0208 8815088 www.turnaround-psl.com
Additional Specialist Distribution for The Last Snake Man:-
USA: Maryland Reptile Farm, 150 Bentz Mill Road, Wellsville, PA 17365
www.mdreptilefarm.com
SOUTH AFRICA
Stephan Phillips (Pty) Ltd, Unit 3, Old Brewery, 6 Beach Road,
Woodstock, 7925, Cape Town   www.stephanphillips.com
Other titles available from Noir Publishing:-
Necronomicon Book Three, Necronomicon Book Four,
Necronomicon Book Five - All edited by Andy Black
Once Upon A Fiend - By Ratfink & Pete McKenna
Shocking Cinema of the 70's - Edited by Xavier Mendik
The Last Snake Man - By Austin J Stevens
Flowers From Hell - By Jim Harper

The Dead Walk
By Andy Black & Steve Earles
ISBN 9780953656486
© Andy Black & Steve Earles 2008, all rights reserved
First published 2008 by:
Noir Publishing www.noirpublishing.co.uk
Copyright © Noir Publishing 2008

Photographs taken from the Noir Publishing Collection & reproduced in the spirit of publicity - any omissions to be corrected in future editions.
Cover Photo: Zombie Strippers! Back Photo: Evil Dead 2: Dead By Dawn

Authors Acknowledgements:
Many an individual has aided the production of this volume but special mention goes to Candy at Optimum Releasing, Gareth at Revolver Group, Almar, Farhana & Lisa at The Associates

British Library Cataloguing in Publication Data:
A catalogue record for this book is available from the British Library

The Dead Walk

Andy Black would like to dedicate this to the loves in his life, namely, Caroline, Aaron & Alex, Choca & Mocha, Aston Villa FC, fine films & even finer music!

Steve Earles would like to dedicate this with love and respect to his parents, Eileen and Gerry

CONTENTS

Introduction
Page 6

CHAPTER ONE
Into The Land of the Ton Ton Macoute
Page 8

CHAPTER TWO
The Monochrome Zombies
Page 17

CHAPTER THREE
A Plague On All Your Houses
Page 26

CHAPTER FOUR
When There's No More Room In Hell... The Zombie Films of George A. Romero
Page 35

CHAPTER FIVE
Into The Beyond - The Enigma That Was Lucio Fulci
Page 89

CHAPTER SIX
Raising The Dead
Page 104

CHAPTER SEVEN
God Bless America - (And Its' Zombie States)
Page 110

CHAPTER EIGHT
The Continental Cousin - Zombies Around The Globe
Page 136

CHAPTER NINE
Close Relations - Science Fiction Zombies
Page 168

CHAPTER TEN
Bandaged But Unbowed - The Mummy Lives!
Page 201

CHAPTER ELEVEN
Brave New Zombies
Page 214

Filmography
Page 252

Index of Films
Page 285

The Dead Walk
INTRODUCTION

When I first published *The Dead Walk* back in 2000, little did I realise that eight years later, we would find the zombie film to be in such rude, not to mention resurgent good health. With no obvious signs of decomposition, instead we have seen the renaissance of George A. Romero, coupled with a slew of vibrant new entries.

Given this fresh impetus in the genre, together with the ability to produce an entirely updated tome in colour, a new, improved *The Dead Walk* was born.

I make no apologies for adhering to the deliberately "fast and loose" definition of what constitutes a zombie film which is retained from the original edition. So, no tiresome serial killers or pure vampire films which have been done to, ahem, death, in other volumes. A resounding yes though to stretching the definition to include diverse entries from the science fiction genre, plus a number of surprises - *Jason and the Argonauts* may not be top of everyone's zombie list but it has certainly exerted a certain influence for which I feel it merits inclusion.

The enthusiasm contained within the first edition has also been augmented by the slightly "left-field", most certainly "outside of the box" contributions from Steve Earles. His fascinating behind the scenes details on key themes and films, together with a factual approach to incidental motifs such as the Knights Templars and the origins behind the viruses which pervade so many contemporary zombie films, adds a new dimension to this edition. For this Steve, I salute you!

There remains for me still, the unbridled joy of stumbling across a new *cause celebre* - be it the nihilistic zeal of *28 Days Later*, the inventive humour in *Shaun of the Dead*, the fearsome frissons evoked by *[REC]* or the audacious ambition in the simply riotous *Doomsday*.

Whatever your pleasure, I hope you have as much enjoyment reading the book as Steve and I had in writing it. So, dim the lights, settle into your seats and enjoy a phantasmagoria of horrific delights !

Andy Black (October 2008)

"WHEN THERE'S NO MORE ROOM IN HELL...THE DEAD WILL WALK THE EARTH...."

WELL...HELL MUST BE FULL TO BURSTING POINT!

It's ironic that the genre of horror that's most alive concerns the Walking Dead.

In a similar spirit, *The Dead Walk* tackles this singularly sanguinary genre.

Beginning with the true-life origins of zombie via voodoo, the truth being stranger than fiction, and progressing to monochrome classics like *White Zombie*, and of course, the 'Dead Sea Scrolls' of the zombie film as we know it today, Year Zero for the Reeks! - *Night of the Living Dead*. Like the undead themselves this, film has reached out and via optical infection- reproduced itself, for virtually all zombie films form this point onwards owe something to Romero's ground-breaking masterpiece.

Romero's masterpiece also owes much to Richard Matheson's *I Am Legend*, itself adapted for the big

Introduction

screen on numerous occasions.

The sheer variety of the Walking Dead is as myriad as the different facets of humanity itself.

Thus, we have the undead Knights Templars in the Blind Dead film. Space vampires in *Lifeforce*. The dark Lovecraftian masterpieces of Lucio Fulci. The slapstick mayhem of the *Evil Dead* Trilogy, and *Shaun of the Dead*. There are undead pirates roaming the ocean beds in *Pirates Of The Caribbean*, and stop-motion undead in *The Corpse Bride*. We've had a variety of computer games inspired by Romero's work, with disappointing results it has to said, but it shows how many media the zombies have infected. And not just computer games, bands, comics and books (particularly Max Brooks masterful "Zombie Survival Guide" and "World War Z", note to aspiring filmmakers (and Paul W Anderson!), read these books, and you'll build a better zombie movie).

Romero himself says he'll come back from the dead to keep making his beloved *Dead* films. To date, the Gore-Father has made five zombie films, and, who knows, may well return to keep his promise. Thus, he has explored consumerism gone wild in *Dawn Of The Dead* (with his protagonists 'trapped' in a Cathedral Of Consumerism as the world literally goes to Hell around them). *Day Of The Dead*, a masterful exploration of paranoia and distrust. *Land Of The Dead*, vividly reflecting the post 9/11 America, and *Diary of The Dead*, exploring the ramifications of the new media proliferation.

England's contribution to the zombie genre is not to be overlooked from Hammer's masterful *Plague Of The Zombies*, the incredible zombie on a train romp that is *Horror Express* (the best Hammer film that never was, complete with Cushing and Lee!) to the genre kick-starter that is *28 Days Later*, truly it can be said that Albion Reeks Triumphant!

But the zombie virus is world wide, with Ireland's *Boy Eats Girl* (a welcome return to the voodoo origins of zombies), Spain's *[REC]*, and Italy's *Demons*.

We are all fascinated by the undead. For, death is the one thing we all have in common, rich or poor, death is the great leveller, not caring of our colour or creed, an amoral equaliser that reduces us all to the same level. We all fear death to some degree, and not only death, but our 21st century is fuelled by fear. Advertising is driven by fear, fear of growing old (a pointless fear, it'll happen whether we like it or not, as Iron Maiden sang, "as soon as you're born, you're dying"), fear of being poor, fear of being unpopular, fear of being alone. Whatever happened to 'all you need is love'? We fear terrorism, viral diseases, global warming, recession….and the zombie genre reflects this.

In Romero's ode to consumerism gone wild, *Dawn Of The Dead*, Fran (Gaylen Ross) puts it best, "we're them, and they're us." They're our dark side, the part of us we would rather ignore and pretend wasn't there. Which is unhealthy and the zombie film provides a healthy catharsis. From humour to satire…no flesh is spared!

Long may they Reek!

Steve Earles (October 2008)

The Dead Walk

1

INTO THE LAND OF THE TON TON MACOUTE

The word "zombie" with all its varying connotations and connections with voodoo and magic, has spread far from its Carribean origins to have a continuing influence on Western culture. This has ranged from 1960's rock groups such as the "Zombies" to the staggeringly successful series of James Bond films of which the voodoo-inspired *Live and Let Die* (1973) has been one of the best. When the film's Baron Samedi (Geoffrey Holder) laughs eerily at the picture's end he is also, in effect, laughing in the face of all the sceptics who dismiss voodoo as a mere myth with no base in reality. Baron Samedi has also leant his name to such well-known idols in the music world as 10cc. Try these lyrics for size;

> *"Take a sip of dripping red,*
> *make it with the living dead,*
> *takes his cures from out the ground".*
> *"He's the one who can hypnotise,*
> *and you'll never believe your eyes,*
> *he can cause the dead to rise".*

The reticence by some to accept the existence of voodoo and its creation of zombies isn't shared by the official articles that constitute the Haitian Penal Code. For instance, Article 246 states: "Also to be termed intention to kill is the use of substances whereby a person is not killed but reduced to a state of lethargy, more or less prolonged, and this without regard to the manner in which the substances were used or what was their later results. If, following the state of lethargy the person is buried then the attempts will be deemed murder." Even more explicit is Article 249 which goes on to say that; "Also shall be qualified as attempted-murder the employment of drugs, hypnosis or any other occult practice which produces lethargic coma or lifeless sleep; and if that person has been buried it shall be considered murder no matter what result follows."

There was certainly no such lethargy on the side of the promoters of the very first voodoo film *White Zombie* (1932) as they used this Article to advertise their film.

The dictionary definition of a zombie is of a "corpse given the appearance of life by sorcery." There is a lot more to this than meets the eye, however. The actual origins of voodoo and the means by which a zombie is created are the result of an unlikely fusion between African and French religions. The roots of this alliance came from the 18th century and the French enslavement of Africans on the Haitian colony of Saint Dominique. At this time the French occupational forces presided over half a million slaves who worked in the numerous sugar cane plantations that yielded two-thirds of France's overall overseas trade. It seems incomprehensible that in 1801 Napoleon's army, the world's finest, was defeated by the ill-equipped African slaves. Various explanations

Into the Land of the Ton Ton Macoute

have been offered but all are tinged by the presence of voodoo.

The ritual magic of the African voodoo ceremonies, partly based on 18th century "grimoires" (French sorcery volumes), and the French Catholic religion, were both to stay resident in Haiti after the uprising. The proof of this can be seen today as catholicism is the official Haitian religion and that the system of government formed by the late "Papa Doc", Francois Duvalier, still relies heavily on the co-operation between voodoo societies and government members, in fact in some cases they are one and the same.

The Serpent & the Rainbow

Looking more closely at the voodoo ceremonies the central aim is to invoke the loa, the voodoo gods, by using drums, dance and sacrifice. The ceremony will end in the entrancement and possession of one or more of those who are taking part.

To start the proceedings the mambo (voodoo priest) will whiten his face using a pigment mixed from graveyard earth and human bone ash. It is intended to send the dead against any enemy. Spreading the powder outside the potential victim's door or on a path they regularly cross is enough to paralyse or kill. The actual creation of a zombie, a corpse revived by witchcraft to work doing simple, monotonous tasks, cannot be accomplished until the soul is displaced. The soul, according to voodoo religion, consists of two entities; the gross bon-ange and the ti bon-ange, or, the large and small good angels. The former is the essential soul, it forms a person's character whilst the latter forms their conscience. The soul is displaced during possession. Under normal possession the gross bon-ange will be restored by the hungan (priest), but if not restored the displaced soul may fall into evil hands and result in a zombie being formed.

In voodoo an alternative dwelling place for a soul could be at the bottom of a river, but during a special ceremony the hungan recalls it and places it in a jar. He then becomes an ancestral spirit who may advise and protect the family or mark down the dispossessed body for his own purposes. This depends on whether the priest is a benevolent one or alternatively, a bokor (sorcerer). In the latter case the likelihood is that the bokor will create a zombie. To do this he will

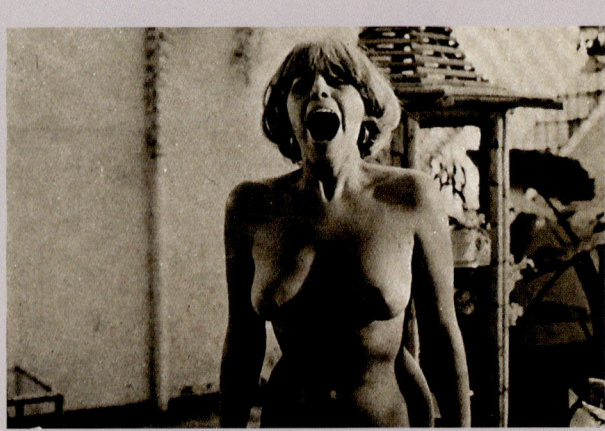

Jess Franco's "mediation" on the more carnal aspects of voodoo in Macumba Sexual

ride to the person who is about to die, reaching their house straddling a horse back to front. Then he puts his lips to the victim's door and sucks out the unfortunates soul, the gross bon-ange, and traps it in a cork bottle. The victim falls ill and dies.

At midnight on the day of the burial the bokor, with his assistant, will go to the grave and open it, calling out the victim's name. The now untenanted body has to answer. As the corpse lifts its' head, the bokor passes the bottle containing the soul under the copses nose. The reanimated body is then dragged from the tomb, chained at the wrists and beaten about the head until fully revived. It is Baron Samedi, the spirit of the graveyard to whom the zombie is dedicated. The newly-created zombie is then led past it's own house to ensure that it will never return there again and is then taken to the bokor's house or voodoo temple. There the zombie is given a secret drug, most probably an extract from the tropical belladonna plant. Such is the fear of becoming a zombie some Haitians bury their loved ones face down so that they can no longer hear the bokor's call. Others bury a weapon such as a machete with the corpse so it may fight off any evil hungans.

There have been many accounts in the past of people reputedly returning from the dead as zombies and this has provided the raw materials for various writers to launch sensational books on the subject. The first really influential of these books was William Seabrook's volume "The Magic Island" which later proved inspirational to the Halperin brothers who went on to bankroll the aforementioned *White Zombie* as a consequence. Almost as much mystery now surrounds Seabrook as the voodoo ceremonies he was investigating. He is said to have participated in such gatherings himself as well as eating human flesh. Whatever the truth, he committed suicide in 1945.

Into the Land of the Ton Ton Macoute

In his book Seabrook describes a bokor called Joseph who owned a group of zombies that his wife looked after. One day she gave them salted biscuits, (Salt being a substance equal to blood in voodoo folklore that can revive victims). To be certain the zombies did awake, only to walk away to the local cemetery and hurl themselves into their own graves.

A similar scenario is played out in films such as *The Terminal Man* (1974) and *Deathdream* (1972). The author of "Magic Island" also claims to have seen four zombies himself, working on the land "plodding like brutes, like automatons", their faces "expressionless" and described as being "unnatural" and "strange".

Another writer, Alfred Metraux in "Voodoo in Haiti" tells of a girl who rejected the advances of a powerful priest, who in return muttered that she would die as a consequence. Soon after the girl did indeed die and was buried in a coffin that was too small, meaning that her neck had to be bent to accommodate her body. During this, an overturned candle also burnt her foot.

Some years later people claimed to have seen the girl walking around, easily recognisable by her stoop and scarred foot. Local people maintained that the bokor had turned her into a zombie but, due to adverse comments from them, had set the girl free. Similar accounts can be read in anthropologist Francis Huxley's book "The Invisibles".

Some more detailed descriptions can be found in the work by the American author Zora Hurston, who even managed to photograph some reputed zombies. Hurston mentions amongst others, the case of a girl called Felicia Felix-Mentor who had died in 1907. In 1936 her brother and husband identified her after seeing her alive in Haiti. Hurston saw the girl whose "eyelids were white all around the eyes as if they had been burned with acid".

She goes on to document the case of another victim, a society girl called Marie who was reported as dead in 1909. Five years later some school friends noticed her staring behind a house window in Port-au-Prince. When her grave was later opened, it was found to contain a rather too well decayed skeleton to have been the remains of Marie. Hurston concludes in rather dramatic terms that the very use of the word "zombie" in Haiti strikes terror into people's hearts, explaining that "the fear of this thing and all it means sweeps over the country like a grand, cold air".

A much later study in 1976 by the Haitian anthropologist Michael Languerre concentrated on the secret societies that are said to control the operation of voodoo across Haiti. He verified the existence of passports, ritual handshakes, secret passwords, special ceremonial

The mystique of voodoo remains popular in cinema even to this day

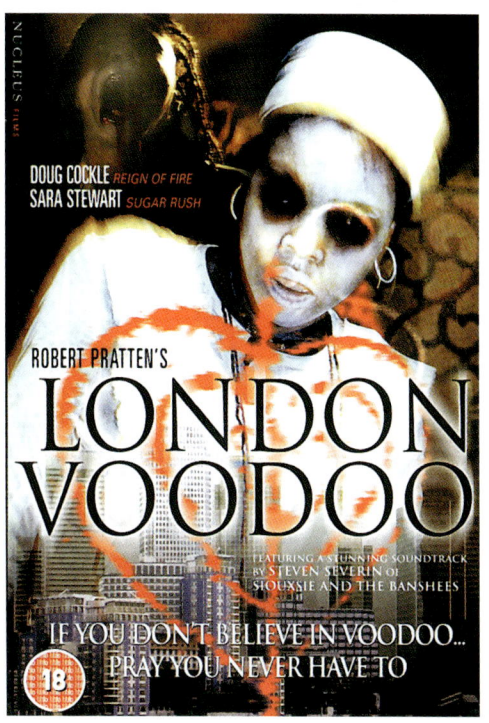

The Serpent & the Rainbow

uniforms, songs and dances.

He departed from Hurston, however, in that where she maintained that the secret societies were criminal, Languerre describes them as being a political wing of the voodoo society charged with the protection of the community. Hurston may have been somewhat disadvantaged by the fact that she had never attended any voodoo ceremonies herself.

The idea that these secret societies act as a political force in voodoo was given further credence during the reign of the former Haitian president Francois Duvalier, a mysterious figure rumoured to have used the power of voodoo to defeat his political enemies.

It is said that he once held a conference with all the voodoo priests in Haiti. His close liaison with such figures put him in touch with the Bizango society and its leaders, one of the main secret organisations in the country. Duvalier even had his own personal bodyguard, the "Ton Ton Macoute", which literally means travelling sorcerers, applied for personal vendettas.

It is two more recent studies though, that have come nearer to unearthing the secrets contained within the twilight world of voodoo. In 1985 a camera crew from the "20-20" magazine television show, headed by Geraldo Rivera, observed a voodoo ritual whilst filming in the Haitian jungle. The victims were rubbed with a skin-active potion derived from the tropical putterfish, which placed them in a death-like trance. The programme's doctor found that the potion contained a drug also used to relax the body during surgery. The victims were then buried alive for several hours or even a day and then exhumed. Most were still alive but left brain-damaged due to the lack of oxygen reaching the grave. It was this that produced the familiar blank-eyed "zombie look" and a person bereft of will-power. The condition was in fact inflicted upon law-breakers as a form of native justice.

All this and more appeared to be verified in a 1986 publication, "The Serpent and the Rainbow", a non-fictional account of Haitian voodoo and zombies written by an American anthropologist Wade Davis. His curiosity was aroused after hearing of what amounted to concrete proof that zombies actually existed and the suspected connection between certain toxic plants and zombie potions proved too alluring for Davis, a plant enthusiast, to ignore.

At the beginning of his investigation, Davis was shown the death certificate of one Clairvius Narcisse dated 1962, but now reported to be alive in the village of Artibonite Valley in central Haiti. His family claimed that he was the victim of a voodoo cult and, following his burial, was taken as a zombie. The most important fact here was that Narcisse died at an American directed philanthropic institution that kept precise medical records. Narcisse had been taken ill at the Albert Schweitzer Hospital at Deschapelles in the Artibonite Valley. The victim's elder sister, Marie Claire, had seen him die and affixed her thumb print to the official death certificate.

Narcisse was then buried near his home village in L'Estere. In 1980 Narcisse approached one of his other sisters, Angelina Narcisse, in L'Estere market place and introduced himself

Images from London Voodoo

MACUMBA SEXUAL

AJITA WILSON

con

CANDY COSTER

ROBERT FOSTER / JESS FRANCO

Guión: JESS FRANCO   Fotografía: JUAN SOLER COZAR
Música: JESS FRANCO y PABLO VILLA

un film de JESS FRANCO

CINEMASCOPE / EASTMANCOLOR   CLASIFICADA "S"

Into the Land of the Ton Ton Macoute

to her using an intimate boyhood nickname that only he could know. He then went on to claim that his own brother had been instrumental in having Clairvius turned into a zombie in an argument over land.

Haitian law states that all land must be divided equally between male offspring. Narcisse had refused to sell off his part of the inheritance, and so was punished by voodoo "law". After his resurrection, Clairvius claimed that he had been led away by a team of men to the north of the country where he worked as a slave for two years. When the bokor was killed, the zombies were set free. Narcisse had spent the intervening sixteen years lying low until hearing of his brother's death.

As a result of this, a film documentary of his story was made by the BBC in 1981. The outcome of this was that Narcisse correctly answered questions on his childhood and Scotland Yard detectives verified that the thumb print on his death certificate had been that of his sister, Marie Claire. Davis himself also interviewed Narcisse and found that he had been in various disputes with his brothers and had "compromised" many women without accepting any responsibility for his actions.

This in itself is interesting, as in Haiti there are seven codes of behaviour that should not have been contravened; any diversion from these codes can result in being turned into a zombie. Narcisse had broken the code as he had made excessive material advancements at the expense of his brothers and had also, according to his brother, stopped his family from working the land that Clairvius owned. His misdemeanors with the female fraternity had also led to his "punishment".

Davis also that you could be "sold" to a secret society to mete out punishment, as was the case of Clairvius whose brother "sold" him using the land dispute as a reason. Davis' main breakthrough however, was like Rivera in finding the main "zombie poison" to be an extract from the lethal puffer-fish of which there are two main types; the fou-fou or Diodon hystrix and the crapaud der mer.

These, along with the sea toad, Sphoeroides testudineus, all give out a highly poisonous tetrodotoxin which is five hundred times more potent than cyanide. This poison has been captured memorably on film in a James Bond picture, not the voodooesque *Live and Let Die* surprisingly, but the earlier *From Russia With Love* (1964) where an overzealous Russian General tries to kill 007 with a poison-coated knife concealed in her shoe.

Tetrodotoxin itself can induce a physical state where a person is alive but paralysed, with the appearance of being dead. This state has no doubt been confused with the disease catalepsy which also emits the same symptoms. It also dominates the macabre writings of horror author Edgar Allan Poe, who himself had a morbid fear of being buried alive. His ornate prose and the claustrophobic aura surrounding it, played on the very real fears of the period with such classic works as "The Premature Burial" and the "Fall of the House of Usher". His own character was summarised in one of his own stories as being someone who "talks of worms, of tombs and epitaphs."

There are numerous stories from all over the world that tell of graves being opened only to find blood on the occupant's hands as they have tried to escape. The most effective film materialisation of this instance can be seen in Lucio Fulci's *City of the Living Dead* (1981)

Such instances still occur today, though often the result of careless diners eating pufferfish, considered a great delicacy in China and Japan. People "dying" in these circumstances

The Dead Walk

are not buried until three days later for obvious reasons !

Davis sent samples of tetrodotoxin to the New York State Psychiatric Institute who in tests on animals found that the drug would give the specimens the appearance of being "dead". The way that the drug relaxes the body without affecting the heart seems conclusive proof of its usefulness as a tranquilliser in medicine. The anthropologist also discovered four different types of preparation that could create zombies; the Tombe leve, the Retire Bon Ange, Tue and Leve. Some cause skin to rot, some cause instant death and some make the victim waste away slowly. All contain crapaud de mer, the most toxic of the puffers to be found in Haitian waters.

He also identified a special paste given to zombies when risen from their graves. Its ingredients included sweet potato, cane syrup and Datura Stamonism, also known as the zombie cucumber, and categorised as a psychoactive plant drug.

What these various studies clarify is that zombies are not merely created "for the hell of it", to roam the countryside as marauding, mindless monsters, but created as a punishment, a catharsis for society and reinforcement of its penal code. More a case that the threat of being turned into a zombie can be used as a form of social control, underlining the political elements already discussed. It is similar to telling our children to be good or the "bogeyman" will get you. The link between secret societies, government and voodoo has now been more clearly established as well.

For the moment though, we are restricted to stories from film makers such as Wes Craven, of filming in Haiti (his version of *The Serpent and the Rainbow*), and being privy to fiery displays of ritual dancing and the ceremonial slaughtering of animals to act out voodoo rites. There are also tales of crew members having to leave the island after only four days due to the "weird", intimidatory atmosphere that pervaded the land.

The problem, as Davis and others have found, is that in order to open up the hitherto hidden mystique and magic of voodoo, one has to actually join a secret society and live out that lifestyle and its experiences to the full, something considered too dangerous for western explorers to undertake up to now, even if they were to be permitted entry into this clique.

For the moment at least, much of the supernatural aura surrounding voodoo lies intact, clouded in mystique, as yet impenetrable to the clawing hands of western man and modern science. The power of the loa and its continuing influence remains supreme in the Haitian voodoo society of today.

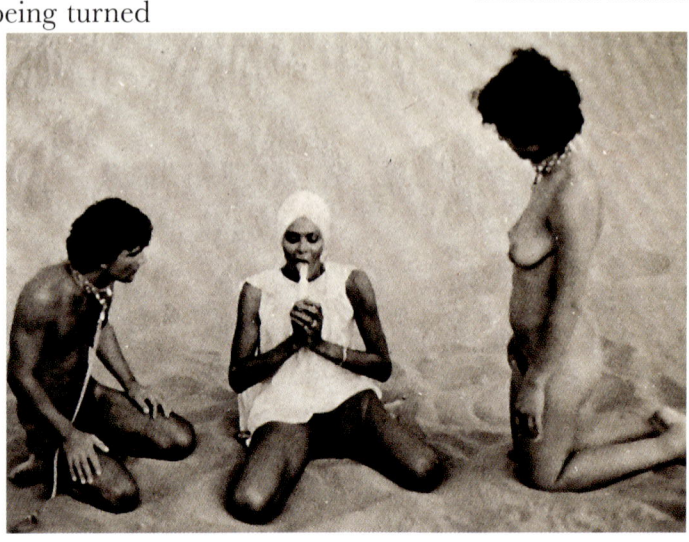

Macumba Sexual

2
THE MONOCHROME ZOMBIES

The very first genuine zombie film to exploit the voodoo connection to the full was Victor Halperin's *White Zombie* which, along with Jacques Tourneur's *I Walked With A Zombie* (1943), were among the finest of the early zombie appearances on film. In previous years the nearest cinema audiences had got to seeing zombies were titles such as Robert Wiene's *The Cabinet of Dr. Caligari* (1919) with Caesar (Conrad Veidt), the film's lead, literally sleepwalking through his role as an intended somnambulist murderer.

In reality however, the film owes more to German Expressionism with its penchant for distorted shapes and chiaroscuro lighting, coupled with political statement suggesting a parallel between zombiehood and the meaningless slaughter of millions in World War One, than it does to the zombie genre. The use of zombies as political metaphor was taken still further in later years, namely in the films of George A Romero, though often his social criticisms are laced with liberal helpings of sardonic wit.

White Zombie, inspired by Seabrook's sensational written account of zombies in Haiti, "Magic Island" (1929), took that novel's voodoo roots to heart and utilised them fully so that they formed an integral part of the film's story. Bela Lugosi, fresh from his screen success as *Dracula* (1931), played the part of Murder Legendre, owner of a Haitian sugar mill who uses zombie workers to run his plantation. He gives an impressive performance, capturing an inner intensity that is rarely displayed in his other films.

Legendre is a man obsessed with a rival plantation owners fiancee, Madeline (Madge Bellamy). He uses his voodoo powers to put her into a death-like trance. The unfortunate heroine is then buried alive, only to be revived by Legendre relentlessly pursuing his own compulsions. Despite the fact that one critic called it "a horror film for idiots", there is a lot to admire here; from the opulent sets previously seen in *Dracula* (1931), *Frankenstein* of the same year and *The Hunchback of Notre Dame* (1930, so no, not the Disney version !), to the effectively repellent zombie make-up fashioned by Jack Pierce.

Many scenes appear as a kind of visual poetry, such as the zombies' first appearance - lurching into view, black silhouettes amidst the sugar cane or the voodoo doll wrapped in Madeline's scarf that is then plunged into a candle flame, accompanied by the sound of a shrieking vulture. There is also artistry in the carefully composed frames as Legendre and Madeline glide into view glimpsed through apertures in walls and staircases. Zombies parade behind ornamented windows, their very silence echoing the figures seen in the old "silent" films whose influence shines through *White Zombie*, from its' creaking production values to its use of simple musical motifs.

The film's dreamy qualities

A series of pictures from the seminal White Zombie starring Bela Lugosi

are also reminiscent of the classic Carl Dreyer film *Vampyr* (1931). The enormous wheel that drives the sugar mill in *White Zombie* is taken from the flour mill in *Vampyr*. Madeline's "funeral" is dwelt on in the film as the coffin sounds harshly on the flagstones whilst being put into place, and is similar in tone and style to Dreyer's earlier masterpiece. The rapidly receding light that is obscured by the lowered coffin is also reprised in Brian De Palma's convoluted modern thriller *Body Double* (1984).

The juxtaposition of birth and death that the horror film so often revolves around is used here, represented by the shroud-like wedding dress that Madeline wears and the film's conclusion as Legendre plunges over a cliff, along with his followers. Their death allows Madeline to revive and so recapture her life. The zombies, referred to by Legendre as "The Angels of Death" have no more managed a foothold on Madeline's soul than the precarious earth on the cliff's edge that has led them to their doom.

White Zombie, though primitively made, is convincingly executed by a competent cast, led mesmerisingly by Lugosi whose character is a pot-pourri of jealous necromancer and malevolent dictator. The first film zombies may have fallen, but they left behind an indelible impression on future film makers.

The film to compare most favourably with *White Zombie* is the luridly titled *I Walked With A Zombie* from 1943. Despite its sensationalist name it is a subtle, expertly crafted film from the director/producer team of Jacques Tourneur and Val Lewton, who had previously collaborated to good effect on *Cat People* (1942). The catchpenny title was primarily conceived by Lewton after reading a series of Sunday supplement articles written by Inez Wallace giving evidence of the existence of zombies in Haiti. The film's literary inspiration however, owes more to Charlotte Bronte whose "Jane Eyre" it is, that has now been transported to the West Indies.

The film has a young nurse, Betsy (Francis Dee) starting work on the island of San Sebastian in the West Indies. She has been allotted the task of looking after a sugar plantation owner's wife, Jessica Holland (Christine Gordon). Her husband Paul (Tom Conway) believes his expressionless wife to be suffering from a fever, but the natives believe her to be a voodoo incarnation of the undead. This conflict between native voodoo beliefs and Christianity is further complicated by the actions of Conway's mother who is revealed to

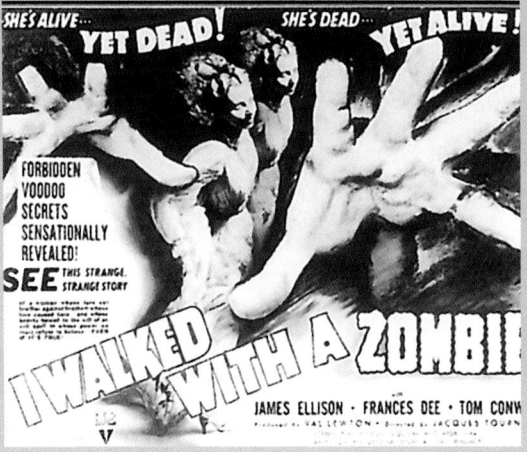

Poster art and eerie tableau from I Walked With A Zombie

be posing as a voodoo priestess and in fact turned Jessica into a zombie after hearing of her planned elopement with Conway's half-brother, Wesley (James Ellison). The way that the mother's matriarchal pride supersedes all other humane feelings, as she turns Jessica into a zombie, is in sharp contrast to the generous love Betsy shows for Conway. Despite falling in love with him, she is still prepared to do all she can to find a cure for his motionless wife.

Betsy is the one vibrant character in the film, a young impressionable girl who still retains her humanity in a strange and forbidding land. Others such as Conway have long since lost the luxury to be optimistic. This is shown early in the film as he takes Betsy across the island in his boat. Her joy at the flying fish is coldly crushed by Conway who explains that they are simply escaping from predators below. The cynical attitude of the mother, using voodoo regalia to exploit native superstition and encourage them to use modern medicine, has spread to her son.

The film's continual wavering between the cynical and the naive is finely presented in the film's most memorable scene. After being summoned at night by a voodoo priest, pulling a miniature doll in Jessica's image towards him on a piece of string, Betsy and Jessica take a nocturnal walk to the voodoo ceremony that is being staged that night. The image of the tiny doll being pulled and manipulated, clearly shows that Jessica is merely as a puppet under the control of the voodoo puppet master. Their walk to the ceremony through the field of sugar cane is full of lurking danger.

The swirling wind rustles through the cane as if whispering and Jessica's diaphanous gown glows through the darkness. Gradually, the voodoo drums can be heard as the two protagonists, followed by Tourneur's ever-tracking camera, move nervously past the intimidating but motionless zombie guard. The spiritualist chanting and frenetic dancing all enhance the realism of the voodoo ceremony. Jessica's eventual death, at the hands of her distraught lover, provides a strangely down-beat ending to the film. Here, Wesley, with Jessica in his arms, walks into the foaming spray of the beckoning ocean and both are immersed by the waves. The on-looking negro zombie stands silhouetted against the shining, rippling water and the dying sunset.

It is very much a film where you have to draw your own conclusions. In *White Zombie* much is decided for us, but here we can choose to

The Dead Walk

believe in voodoo or not. The modern, supposedly civilised characters are presented in a somewhat negative light. The white, clinical clothes they wear, as exemplified by Jessica, are much different from the warmth generated by the natives, both in their singing and dancing and in the brotherly spirit they show to one another. The mute figure of Jessica, who moves through the entire film as if just a floating body, is profoundly shown at the conclusion to be just that, as her body literally floats into view as the natives are searching the water for fish. The fiery flames of the wooden torches they hold aloft are in bold contrast to the lifeless figure below the waves whose own life flame has long since been extinguished.

The conflict between different cultures and religious beliefs later furnished film makers with the necessary background in which to make excessively graphic cannibal movies such as *Cannibal Ferox* (1981) and *Cannibal Holocaust* (1979), where western man is arbitrarily tortured and killed for his trespasses into hitherto uncharted territory. In the light of films such as these, Edward Cahn's *The Four Skulls of Jonathan Drake* (1959) on a similar theme, is a modicum of decorum.

Cahn's picture follows a policeman, Rowan (Grant Richards) who is investigating a curse placed on a family 180 years before when their ancestors massacred a tribe of headhunters in Ecuador. Of the two surviving brothers, one reaches 60 years of age and then dies, leaving the similarly aged Drake (Eduard Franz) remaining.

This is some source of discomfort to him as the curse causes all the family members to die by decapitation (!) on reaching the age of 60. Dr. Zurich (Henry Daniell) plays the film's malevolent head shrinker, whose growing supply of exhibits are brought to him by his tall, long-haired servant whose own mouth has been sewn shut. Besides being a considerable inconvenience to him, it also gives the unfortunate impression that he is continually eating cans of spaghetti ! The skulls themselves are hoarded in a cupboard in the family vault, forming a rather eccentric trophy collection.

The plot wrinkle here however, is that Zurich is really a 200 years old man whose head has been sewn onto the body of a witchdoctor. We never do get to find out if the missing head and body meet up, but we do know that the witchdoctor is responsible for placing the curse.

Drake, after surviving an attack by an Ecuadorian zombie, finally, and ironically, kills Zurich by decapitating him whereupon he crumbles to dust.

Despite somewhat pedantic direction, the film does boast a highly original if unlikely plot, and its main strength is the way that it integrates various voodoo elements into the story, along with its concurrent theme of "uncivilised" cultures taking their revenge on meddling westerners.

It was certainly an improvement on Cahn's previous zombie production, *The Zombies of Mora Tau* (1957), about adventurers diving for sunken treasure off the African coast. To their dismay they find it guarded by amphibious zombies who are the dead sailors left from the sunken wreck. The film does feature some effective underwater sequences but is let down by some tiresome acting. The most notable member of the cast is in fact Alison Hayes, better known for her "big" part in *The Attack of the Fifty Foot Woman* (1958). Any gothic flair nurtured by Cahn is restricted to some cursory camera pans over randomly assembled tombstones. Cahn's imaginative premise for the film is offset by an obviously rushed production schedule.

The revenge motif associated with Cahn's pictures is more effectively staged in Massimo Pupillo's first feature, *Terror Creatures From The Grave* (1965) starring the horror film's own female icon, Barbara Steele. She plays Cleo, the widow of an occultist, professor Dr. Hauff, who summons up the bodies of the medieval dead that are buried beneath his castle, to avenge his murder. A lawyer, Brandt (Walter Brandi) discovers that Cleo, his employer, and other eventual victims of the revived plague-bearing zombies, were all guilty of murdering Hauff.

Brandt escapes with the only other innocent party, Corinne (Marilyn Mitchell) as cleansing rain exorcises the evil spell. The film benefits greatly from the suspense that leads up to each victim's death. This is eerily announced by the loudly creaking wheels of the approaching meat wagon that had previously been deployed to carry away the bodies of the diseased dead during the original plague.

Images from Mark Robson's effective chiller Isle of the Dead starring Boris Karloff

The gloomy interior of the castle is well evoked by a prowling camera and the ominous, recorded messages from Dr. Hauff, who has recorded both his research and his own death. This device is frequently used in horror films today from Lucio Fulci's *The Black Cat* (1981) and *The House By The Cemetery* (1981), to more mainstream films such as *Poltergeist* (1982) which use audio technology to record any ghostly presence, reaching its commercial peak with the phenomenally successful *Ghostbusters* (1984).

One of the less acclaimed zombie classics of the time, though no less worthy for that, was 1960's *City of the Dead*. This was a ground-breaking film for a number of reasons. It was the first production by Amicus who went on to rival (but not surpass) Hammer Films with their horror output, especially with anthology films such as *Asylum* (1972) and *Tales From The Crypt* in the same year. *City of the Dead* also helped to launch director John Moxey onto

The Monochrome Zombies

a long film career before turning his attentions to the potentially lucrative business of making TV films. The film is also one of the earliest screen incarnations to capture the haunted, witchcraftian world of noted horror author H. P. Lovecraft.

It is set in America in Whitewood, Massachusetts where Professor Driscoll (Christopher Lee) sends one of his students, Nan (Venetia Stevenson) there to research into the local witchcraft legends. In fact, Driscoll is the leader of a coven of witches there and he uses his pupil as a human sacrifice. The village itself is a striking affair, populated by roaming zombies dressed in monk-like robes and practising forbidden rites. The local inn is presided over by a resurrected witch played convincingly by Patricia Jessel. She is finally killed by Nan's boyfriend Bill, (Tom Naylor) brandishing a cross. Ironically, he dies with a knife in his back from Driscoll, a symbolic reference to the earlier fate that befalls Nan, who is sent to her death by the same man, literally stabbed in the back.

It is the ever present mist and dark shapes moving silently through the murky fog that ensure the viewer's rapt attention. This is lovingly captured by the roving camera of Desmond Dickinson, whose previous films had included Olivier's *Hamlet* (1948). Through the all encompassing vapours of mist we can perceive a work that combines both superstition and clandestine rituals with a more modern American way of life.

Although *City of the Dead* does owe a debt to *Psycho* (1960), with the early death of the heroine and the subsequent search by others to fathom out her disappearance, it has also proved the inspiration for many other films. The Salem Witch Trials alluded to here can also be found in *Three Sovereigns For Sarah* which stars Vanessa Redgrave and in Tobe Hooper's *Salem's Lot* (1979). The monk-robed zombies appeared with great frequency in Amando de Ossorio's series of films featuring the Knights Templar, and similar creations are glimpsed in *The Omega Man* (1971) and more remotely in the sequels to the successful *Planet of the Apes* (1968) saga.

Moxey's film is one of those rare films that feature British actors who give convincing American accents to add to the realism. A minor point, but one that illustrates the attention to detail and meticulous thought and planning that went into the piece to create a work brimming over with dreamy imagery forged from a fertile world of rich Lovecraftian imagination.

Another minor masterpiece that lends itself to the zombie genre is *Isle of the Dead* (1945). Directed by Mark Robson, renewing his partnership with Val Lewton - they had previously made *The Seventh Victim* (1943) amongst others.

A painting by Arnold Boecklin provides the basis for the story that sees Boris Karloff playing a Greek Army General (Pherides), who is stranded on a remote island during the Balkan wars where he and his less illustrious survivors are left to fight off the threat of a wind-carried plague.

To make matters worse, the group are haunted by malevolent demons called vorvolakas. One member of the party, Mrs. St. Aubin (Katherine Emery), is known to be subject to cataleptic attacks and after one such occurrence, is buried, presumed dead. However, in the next sequence we see her to be very much alive as the camera closes in on her face to capture a slight movement.

It then *s-l-o-w-l-y* tracks up to her coffin, only dripping water can be heard, then it pulls unflinchingly back and away just as an ear-piercing scream breaks out and scrambling finger nails scratch the casket. Aubin,

The Dead Walk

once revived, is found to be possessed by the aforementioned demons and then proceeds to decimate the remaining survivors, impaling them with a trident. These scenes with Aubin really justify the whole film and it is on the strength of this that the film's reputation has been secured.

Otherwise, it is a plodding picture, listless in its conception and execution, as a brace of magnificent scenes do not a complete masterpiece make. If anything, Robson is guilty of being almost too subtle, too understated in his attempt at filming a restrained horror film. It was though, one of the earliest films to mention possession by demons, a subject that has since hypnotised horror film makers over the years; witness the plethora of such like-minded films as *The Exorcist* (1973), *The Evil Dead* (1982) and *Demons* (1986), which noticeably lack the restraint found in Robson's film.

To depart from the more serious zombie films mentioned above, there have also been numerous attempts at zombie comedy such as *Zombies on Broadway* (1945), with varying degrees of success. The funniest of these is probably *The Ghost Breakers* (1940), adapted from a Paul Dickey and Charles W. Goddard play filmed in 1922 as *The Ghost Breaker*. Starring Bob Hope, the more lavish 1940's film was primarily conceived as a follow-up to the earlier *The Cat and the Canary* (1939) that also starred Hope. As in that film, here the combination of creepy gothic houses with secret panels and sliding doors with American humour works well.

In a plot that seems to have furnished countless *Scooby-Doo* cartoons for children, Hope plays a radio performer who joins forces with an heiress (Paulette Goddard) and together they investigate her reputedly haunted castle in Cuba, also the site of buried treasure. Once inside, the story glides comfortably between genuinely eerie moments, such as the discovery of a fog-laden pier that houses zombies in its shack, and moments of humour such as the priceless line where a valet, confronted by a shuffling clothes closet asks; "Zat you zom?!" We are also treated to an effective scene as Goddard is pursued through some dimly lit corridors by a wide-eyed zombie.

Overall, the film manages to provide the right quota of shocks and scares together with some wry wise cracks from the ever-exuberant Hope.

The film was remade some years later in 1953 as *Scared Stiff*, starring the then popular comic duo of Dean Martin and Jerry Lewis. Although it aspired to it, the film never attained the heights of the Hope vehicle.

The Voodoo Man (1944), though not strictly comedy does contain some humorous elements and one of those totally unbelievable plots concerning the archetypal "mad genius" doctor searching for the lost elixir of life - didn't he know coke adds life ?! Bela Lugosi plays Dr. Marlowe, a tormented soul who's wife has been left as a zombie for the last 20 years. He abducts young women and drains them of their "life essence" which he then injects into his wife in the hope of reviving her. This he fails to do and only succeeds in creating zombies out of his unwilling victims. They are kept imprisoned in basement cells, presided over by the much travelled horror regular John Carradine.

The nubiles finally obtain their release when Marlowe is shot and can no longer exert his will over them which he had previously done through his own voodoo ceremonies. The sight of Lugosi, adorning a robe decorated with esoteric mystic symbols is one of the film's finer images, but all in all it cannot rid itself entirely of its' B movie origins.

The film that ends this chapter is completely unique in both tone

The Monochrome Zombies

and style to the previous films and is rarely discussed by horror writers. However, *J'Accuse* (1937), by the French director Abel Gance is a strikingly imaginative work, all the more realistic and appalling, considering its' very real subject and the "actors" it uses. It was aimed by Gance as his own anti-war statement.

The picture begins as a soldier from World War One hears radio propaganda urging France to go to war again. Still remembering the carnage he saw on the battlefield then he calls on all his dead comrades to leave their graves and frighten the politicians out of creating another war. Finally, the dead emerge and appeal for peace. What made these scenes so realistic was Gance's use of real World War One survivors, some terribly maimed by the ravages of battle.

Like Tod Slaughter's *Freaks* (1932) before it, the film uses genuine casualties of life to hammer home its message, only here the importance of life itself is brought to our attention.

This is symbolised in a series of images in the film, birds fly away, flowers wither and die on the ground, a skeletal plane pilot with grinning skull flies over towns laughing at the looks of panic aroused by the sight of the other dead soldiers marching. The allegory of zombies and war that is only an undercurrent running through *The Cabinet of Dr. Caligari*, is more fully confronted in this cautionary tale of war and its' human victims.

3
A PLAGUE ON ALL YOUR HOUSES

Plague of the Zombies

A Plague On All Your Houses

Hammer Films, for some years the world's leading exponents of scream entertainment, took a surprisingly long time before venturing into zombie territory, and a rewarding if solitary exercise it proved to be.

The company's undoubted strengths in the horror genre had been its realisation that film was primarily a form of entertainment, so their horror films had to entertain as well as frighten. Hammer also recognised the need to make their films look expensive, big-budget productions, even if they were only made on a shoestring, which was frequently the case.

To this end, close attention to period detail was adhered to and enhanced by the imagination and resourcefulness of art directors such as Bernard Robinson. Previously, Hammer had taken popular but rather staid literary material such as Bram Stoker's "Dracula" and in particular, Mary Shelley's "Frankenstein" and revitalised them. Leading actors such as Peter Cushing and Christopher Lee taking on their roles with vigour and infusing them with an inner passion and sincerity that was to become the hallmark of Hammer productions. This, coupled with sparse, intelligent scripts, in this instance, Jimmy Sangster's, ensured a successful transition from book to film.

In light of this it is easier to understand Hammer's apparent reluctance to tackle the zombie genre. There were no such famous literary origins to plunder and base a zombie film around. The nearest that Hammer had got were the series of "Mummy" films they released, another sub-genre that had no literary basis as such but had blossomed after the discovery by Lord Caernarvon and Howard Carter in 1923 of Tutankhamun's tomb in Egypt, and the subsequent "mysterious" deaths of expedition members that followed, said to be the result of a curse placed on the "defilers" of the sacred tomb.

Hammer soon ran into the same problems that the Hollywood studios had encountered making "mummy" films during the 1930's and 1940's. The trouble was that once you had revived the mummy, there was little he could do and nowhere he could go, at least not very quickly. Hammer's own *The Mummy* (1959), with Christopher Lee in the title role was their first and best entry into this territory, and then only due to it recapturing some of the dream-like aura that pervaded the seminal *The Mummy* (1932), though the film's plot owed more to that of *The Mummy's Hand* (1940) and *The Mummy's Tomb* (1942). Here Lee reprised Boris Karloff's role from the original film, though both were fine actors it was difficult to reveal any kind of character concealed beneath the mummy's bandages, and the direction had passed from the talented Carl Freund to Hammer's equally impressive Terence Fisher. Hammer's subsequent "mummy" films declined in quality considerably, not helped by Lee's well-documented refusal to play the part again and Fisher's absence from the rest of the series. If ever his gothic imagination and flair for kinetic pacing and judicious cutting were needed, it was here. Instead the series shuffled zombie-like to an end with the interesting but over-rated *Blood From The Mummy's Tomb* (1971), which in turn was later embalmed by Mike Newell in 1980 as *The Awakening*, an ironic title given that the film was such a soporific exercise for most. (See chapter 10 for more detailed coverage of the whole mummy film sub-genre).

Despite the mileage that Hammer got from their "mummy" series, their single zombie film was to contain more genuine frissons than the "mummy" films could muster in their entirety.

The company's previously

The Dead Walk

mentioned dexterity was illustrated in that two films; *Plague of the Zombies* (1966) and *The Reptile* (1966) were both made back-to-back utilising the same sets, cast and director, John Gilling. He had previously written scripts for Hammer, his best for *The Gorgon* (1964) and he had also directed their swashbuckling adventures such as *The Pirates of Blood River* (1962) and *The Scarlet Blade* (1963). It was his feel for atmosphere and eye for memorable images, coupled with Peter Bryan's economical script that helped to turn an interesting idea into a screen triumph.

The oppressive, claustrophobic tone that permeates the film perfectly captures the cloying sickness from the voodoo curses that form an integral part of *Plague of the Zombies* story.

The film's first images are unsettling, a voodoo priest preparing a miniature doll with which to introduce a curse, intercut with the writhing body of a screaming girl who is the intended victim. The rampant tribal drums that sound and the noisy, monotonous title music menacingly score the scenes and reinforce the Caribbean influence that is at work here.

The story is set in a small Cornish village where the new young doctor, Peter Thompson (Brook Williams) has written in desperation to his mentor in London, Sir James Forbes (Andre Morell) about the villagers being "beset by mysterious

The horror of it all becomes apparent to Diane Clare as she discovers the body of her friend Jacqueline Pearce in Plague of the Zombies

The dead are truly about to walk as a zombie erupts from the earth in Hammer's superior Plague of the Zombies

and fatal maladies". Sir James sees this as more of an inconvenience than anything else, but is prepared to travel to Cornwall and indulge his daughter, Sylvia (Diane Clare) who wishes to visit the doctor's wife Alice (Jacqueline Pearce), an old school friend.

Upon their arrival in Cornwall, Sir James and Sylvia find a village that has been devastated by the death of twelve locals in recent months. The over-wrought young Peter has nearly reached breaking point due to his failure to find a cure for the mystery disease. His problems are compounded by the villagers who refuse to allow him to conduct any autopsies as "they don't want the bodies of their loved ones cut about." In turn, the locals refuse to accept the doctor into their close-knit community because of his failure to find a cure, their feelings summed up by one villager who challenges him; "you're a doctor and you don't know?" The doctor's anxiety is furthered by his wife

Brook Williams, Diane Clare and Andre Morell strike a pose

Masked mayhem ensues in Plague of the Zombies

who is also succumbing to the disease, introduced to her body through a cut forearm.

Sir James and Peter soon set about finding the cause of the sickness. They embark on a clandestine visit one night to the village graveyard in order to exhume a body and perform an autopsy. Acting like a benevolent Burke and Hare they are discovered by the police, but not arrested as the coffin they unearth is found to be empty. The horror is further accelerated as first Alice goes missing only to be found later, dead, and one of the villagers claims to have seen his brother alive when in fact, he has only just been buried.

The all-powerful village squire, Clive Hamilton (John Carson), an imposing figure who "acts as coroner and magistrate, judge and jury" then visits Sylvia who like Alice before her is "accidentally" cut by the acquire, in order for him to use her blood and place a voodoo curse upon her.

By now however, the truth is becoming clearer. Sylvia recognises the link between her wound and that of Alice. Sir James, helped by the local vicar's occult tomes, realises that the squire's formative years spent in the Caribbean were in fact his introduction to voodoo. He is now using his "powers"

to create a workforce of locals for the old tin mine workings in the village. One powerful image of the mines shows the "wheels of industry" to be turning again, quite literally.

The film's most celebrated and oft-quoted scenes occur as Peter and Sir James return at night to the graveyard only to find the now zombie-like figure of Alice moving menacingly towards them. In a highly-charged sequence Sir James decapitates Alice with a shovel, the splash of red blood contrasting vividly against her chalk-white pallor as Peter collapses into a nightmare fever "dream" which becomes reality. His dreams are shown through a green filter and tilted camera angles, reflecting his mental imbalance at this time. Bony fingers burst through the churchyard soil as the zombie living dead emerge from their graves and converge on Peter. Their leering faces and outstretched hands fade as Peter awakens, only to find that his nightmare has become all too real. His wife lies dead and the graveyard has given up its dead as all the tombs lie empty.

Plague of the Zombies climactic scenes take place underground in the once dormant tin mines, now a hive of activity as zombies are driven to work by the squire's sadistic henchmen. Peter

A grim discovery in Plague of the Zombies

Brook Williams and Andre Morell indulge in some clandestine grave digging

and Sir James use the old mine shaft to enter and save Sylvia, who, in a zombie trance, is about to be sacrificed under the knife of Hamilton.

They escape as the works becomes rapidly engulfed by flames, exiting by the mine lift again. Their release and Hamilton's subsequent imprisonment are perfectly captured in the memorable image of Hamilton's face pressed rigid with fear, up against the closed grill of the lift-cover, the lift rising to freedom as he is dragged back by his own flame-ridden zombies into the inferno blazing within.

Where *Plague of the Zombies* really succeeded was in tying up all the disparate threads of zombie-lore, returning to and utilising its Caribbean voodoo roots to create finely-honed piece of horror that really delivered some authentic scares.

Unlike the previous black and white zombie films here, in vivid colour, the zombies actually looked as if they had just been unearthed from their graves, complete with pasty faces and putrifying clothes. The pale, slightly gaunt faces of the zombies in films and series like *Invisible Invaders* from the 1950's, had now been replaced by properly decayed features and suitable crumbling clothes. The memorable dream sequence, full of heaving earth as the zombies claw their way to the surface from their resting places, has had an especially lasting effect on film-makers.

It has spawned countless imitations in later years, from AIP's *Count Yorga, Vampire* (1970), to Hammer's own hotchpotch mixture of Kung Fu and vampire genres, *Legend of the Seven Golden Vampires* (1973).

The dream sequence itself from *Plague of the Zombies* can also be glimpsed playing on a television set in *Fright* (1971). The fact that this is the most frightening and effective scene in the film only serves to underline the paucity of ideas in *Fright*.

The fiery subterranean finale to *Plague of the Zombies* also seems to have served as inspiration to Italy's leading exponent of zombie films, the late Lucio Fulci; witness his *City of the Living Dead* (1980) as the film's zombies flounder in the heat of the enflamed catacombs.

Plague of the Zombies strict adherence to zombie-lore is personified by Hamilton who acts as the zombie master directing the operations of his zombie workers in much the same way as the Haitian sugar plantation owners would, only here, substitute Cornish tin mines for Haitian cane fields.

A zombie attack in Plague of the Zombies

The disparity between slave and master is also an important aspect of the film which admirably confronts the political polemics of the situation, showing the aristocratic arrogance and callousness to be responsible for the evil that spreads through the village.

This point is made early on in the film as Sylvia and Sir James view a fox hunt from their carriage window, whilst riding to Cornwall. Sylvia, defending the fox, points out that it hunts "for food, not for bloodlust" unlike the fox hunters.

The hunters' unconcerned approach is further illustrated when they recklessly career into a funeral procession taking place in the village, causing the coffin to fall into a river and expose the cadaver. The garish red of their hunting jackets brazenly flouts the solemnity of the occasion. Sylvia later encounters the hunters again as they chase and surround her, as they had done to the fox before, eventually drawing cards to decide if she can be released.

Here, Sylvia is treated as if she were an animal, but conversely, it is the hunters who are portrayed as the real animals. To them, life has no sanctity but instead can be sacrificed upon the altar of selfish frivolity typified by their corrupt social values and the malicious zeal inherent in their cruel hunting games. The village locals may be "simple country folk, riddled with superstition" but at least they are honest and loyal to each other.

The character of Alice is called into question during the film as she assesses Hamilton to be a good man on the basis that he owns "a big house and a lot of money". She cares not how he got the money - by exploiting the local villagers, and in this context it is easy to see why the close-knit community resents the presence of "outsiders" and their materialistic values, as shown in their mistrust of Peter.

The political overtones in the relationship between slave and master have still been left somewhat neglected by horror film makers. It has been

The hunt is very much on in Plague of the Zombies

left to more overtly science-fiction orientated films such as *The Stepford Wives* (1974) and *THX 1138* (1970), to explore similar themes set in the future. The horror genre has dwelt more predominantly on the encroachment by city life on rural life, as seen in *The Texas Chainsaw Massacre* (1974) and *The Hills Have Eyes* (1977), and non-genre films such as *Deliverance* (1972) and *Southern Comfort* (1981).

The influence of *Plague of the Zombies* however, still seems to be with us today only in George A Romero's *Day of the Dead* (1985), the tin mine lift has been supplanted by a lift serving an underground missile silo. Here, the lift, instead of allowing a means of escape, is used as a means of entrapment by bringing zombies into the silo and effectively sealing it off.

In view of the fact that Hammer moulded such a successful zombie story to outstanding cinematic images, without neglecting areas of social and political concern, it is still a disappointment that no further zombie films followed. A sequel was probably felt to be out of the question due to the conclusive ending as all the zombies perished, but then death was never an obstacle when it came to resurrecting the careers of both Count Dracula, or, Baron Frankenstein and his monstrous creation.

In later years the zombie genre was to be revived even further by films more politically overt and graphically realistic in their violence, something that Hammer would have been loathed to copy. The influence of *Plague of the Zombies* on future zombie film-makers cannot be ignored and it is interesting to speculate how

far the stunning visuals and keenly-wrought social and political metaphors went on to inspire a young American director of the time who, two years later, made the most famous zombie film of them all.

Left: Andre Morell and Diane Clare

Below: Jacqueline Pearce is the unfortunate victim in Plague of the Zombies

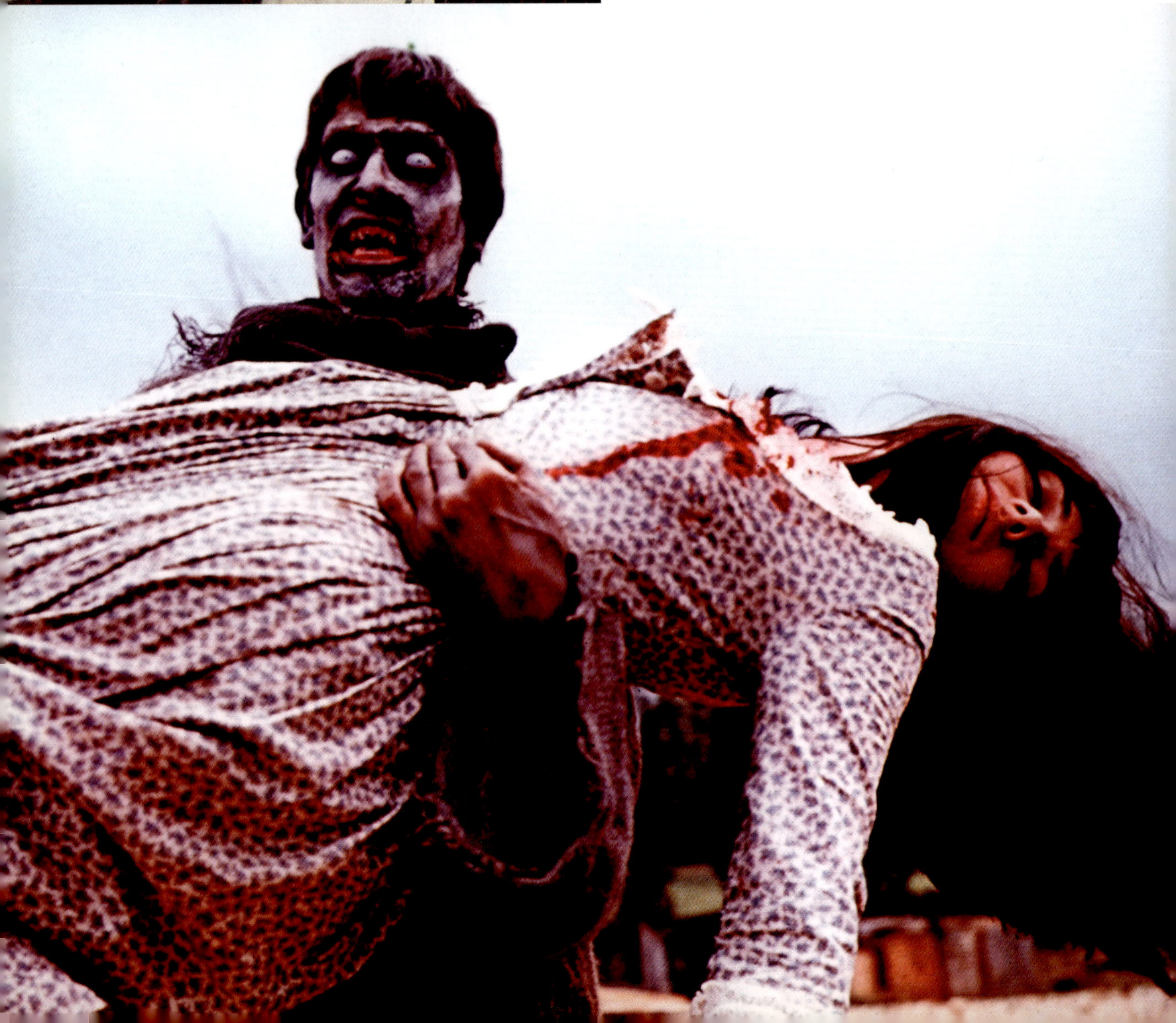

4
"WHEN THERE'S NO MORE ROOM IN HELL....." THE ZOMBIE FILMS OF GEORGE A. ROMERO

Land of the Dead

The Dead Walk

"I don't think younger kids really knew what hit them. They had seen horror films before, but this was something else. This was ghouls eating people - you could actually see what they were eating. This was little girls killing their mother. This was being set on fire. Worst of all, nobody got out alive, even the hero got killed." **(Robert Ebert article from "Readers' Digest")**

Had Mr. Ebert just viewed *I Spit on Your Grave*? *Last House on the Left*? *The Evil Dead*? *Cannibal Ferox*? *Zombie Flesh Eaters*?

No.

The above quotation refers to none of these films, however likely it may seem. It is one critic's outraged reaction to a seemingly innocuous, small budget film from 1968. Yet this is the reaction from some quarters that greeted the release of George A. Romero's *Night of the Living Dead*. From the film's opening scenes when Barbara (Judith O'Dea) and Johnny (Russell Streiner) visit a desolate graveyard as a mysterious figure lurches towards them, to Johnny joking "They're coming to get you" and being "gotten" himself, Romero could not have possibly imagined the importance of the film he had actually made. It was hailed by some as a classic and has since been in constant circulation to this day, gaining a place in the prestigious American Film Institute Museum, yielding a soundtrack album some 14 years after the film's original release and spawning a plethora of often poor imitations that have nevertheless helped to keep the zombie to the forefront of the horror genre.

Romero himself has experienced a meteoric rise to fame, beginning with a simple 8mm movie camera before forming his first production company called "Latent Image". After making various commercials, including one for Calgon washing detergent where a "tiny sub" was sent into a washing machine a la *Fantastic Voyage* (1966), Romero had enough money to buy a 35mm Arriflex camera. The logical step for "Latent Image" was to make a film so they decided on horror as a subject, due to its enduring audience appeal and relatively low budget cost. Originally titled "Night of the Anubis", *Night of the Living Dead* surfaced in 1968, made on a shoestring by a mostly amateur cast culled from friends of the film makers.

The film concerns the emergence of flesh-eating ghouls, caused by a radioactive venus probe returning to earth, and the ensuing struggle for survival between the zombies and the film's remaining humans who seek safety from the ghouls in an isolated farmhouse. From the very first scenes, when Barbara and Johnny's car travels along a deserted road to the accompaniment of unnerving, unearthly music, the film is a complete tour de force in creating tension, despair and a dislocating cinematic style.

The irony is not lost as they enter the nearby graveyard (the stars and stripes of the American flag waving in the wind), to pay their respects to their late father, Johnny complaining to the dutiful Barbara; "Five minutes to put the wreath on the grave and six hours to drive back and forth". He begrudges both the trip and losing an hour from the time change. He can't even remember what his father looked like. His selfish indulgence continues as he scares his sister, telling her that the figure in the distance lurching ominously towards them is out to get her. This is the signal for the jokes to end and the real horror to begin as the stumbling stranger does in fact make a grab for Barbara. Johnny, in the resulting struggle is felled by the zombie, cracking his head fatally

When There's No More Room In Hell....

against a tombstone that is now, in effect, his own.

Barbara is left with no choice but to leave her brother and flee, reaching their car but finding the ignition key is missing. She eventually has to release the handbrake to escape the clutches of the clawing zombie who is frantically continuing in pursuit of his would-be prey. After crashing the car, Barbara runs to a deserted farmhouse and locks herself in, where she eventually meets Ben (Duane Jones), who saves her from a reckless charge into the hands of the zombies who are amassing outside. The remainder of the film relentlessly tracks their hopeless battle against the walking dead, all within the confines of the claustrophobic farmhouse.

They are joined by a selfish and cowardly husband, Harry (Karl Hardman), and his young wife Helen (Marilyn Eastman), along with their sick child and a young married couple. Ben, the most resourceful of the protagonists soon discovers that his battle isn't just with the zombies outside but with Harry inside. Whereas Ben argues they should all stay upstairs, Harry decides on the cellar and their mutual distrust of one another is never resolved.

In a final, desperate bid for survival, Tom (Keith Wayne) and Judy (Judith Ridley) make a dangerous run to a truck that is parked just outside the house, aided by a gun-toting Ben. Upon reaching the nearby fuel pump to fill up with petrol, the truck tragically catches fire, barbecuing both Tom and Judy who are still inside. Ben makes it back to the house, only to find that he has to break down the door as Harry has locked it.

In their climactic confrontation with the zombies, Barbara sacrifices her own life to save Helen. Meanwhile, Ben is forced to shoot Harry who is then killed off by his flesh-eating daughter, Karen (Kyra Schon), who also slaughters her mother. *Night of the Living Dead*'s final ironic twist has the hero Ben, shot like a dog at the end on the orders of the "gung-ho" Sheriff McClelland (George Kosana) who relishes carving up the local zombies and so satisfies his personal lust for glory.

What really sets Romero's film apart from previous horror films is its unrelieved depiction of an apocalyptical struggle for survival. Here, there really is no escape from the marauding zombies, there is no convenient "happy ending", as even the film's inventive hero Ben is mercilessly killed, not by the zombies but by his fellow men. If you add to this, Romero's penchant for hand-held camera shots and weird angles, together with a realistic grainy black and white documentary or cinema verite style to the whole picture, you have all the ingredients for not just a horror classic but a total original.

In many respects this is why the film's opening sequence is so shocking.

Sleeve art for George A. Romero's first zombie film

The Dead Walk

George A. Romero's seminal Night of the Living Dead (1968)

Johnny's futile fight in the cemetery is filmed from tilted, disorientating angles as is Barbara's kinetic-paced flight to the farmhouse. she is tracked as unflinchingly by the camera as she is by her ghoulish attacker. We are right there with her, courtesy of the camera lens, as she struggles to escape in her car and then slips and falls whilst running towards the house. There is absolutely no release from the all-consuming terror that holds the film in thrall and is continued in the enclosed interiors of the farmhouse, accentuated as much by the diametrically opposed attitudes of the humans as from any danger from the zombies outside.

It is the realism in the characters that helps give the film its hyper-charged atmosphere. Ben is the resourceful, caring coloured man, it is he who provides the ideas to survive and to escape.

When he is not boarding up the doors and windows of the farmhouse, he is comforting the traumatised Barbara, or reflecting upon his own inability to help other victims of the zombies. He is the epitome of everything good that the cowardly Harry is not. Harry is purely concerned with his own instinct for survival, most importantly his survival. To him it matters not who lives and who dies but that he is proved right in thinking that the cellar is the safest place to stay in. He is left a wimpering coward, plagued by his own indecision at the most crucial times, as in his failure to unlock the door for Ben that nearly results in the man's death. His attitude is summed up when in vain he tries to justify his selfish behaviour in not rushing to Barbara's aid earlier after hearing her scream. Instead, he prefers to remain in his "safe" place in the cellar, unwilling to endanger his own life just to "save someone else's."

The other realistic characterisation that we see is of Barbara who throughout, remains in a state of shock, barely able to carry out the simplest of commands and often resorting to child-like states as

When There's No More Room In Hell....

she recounts memories of her brother to help calm her own nerves. Besides having these fears to confront she also has to face, along with Helen and Harry, the complete breakdown of the family unit. Barbara's eventual consignment to the ranks of the "living dead" is at the hands of her zombiefied brother who comes back to claim her.

Helen and Harry are eventually butchered by their ghoulish daughter in her own triumphant act of genocide. Here, what parents had been saying for many years was actually being proved true, that their children really were monsters! The film has been termed as the "literal depiction of America devouring itself" and it seems particularly appropriate here.

There are a number of influences that Romero has drawn upon to further embellish his own creative talents. There is an undeniable trace of Hitchcock present in some scenes; from the stuffed animal heads that adorn the farmhouse walls and echo *Psycho* (1960) to Barbara's flight down an expansive, deserted road that recalls Cary Grant's escape from a crop dusting plane in *North By North-West* (1959). *Night of the Living Dead*'s conclusion is, in effect, a repeat of *The Birds* (1963) as the horror will still continue, only here it is the zombies that will live on as opposed to the malevolent title creatures from *The Birds*. Ben's own tenacity in barricading the house is also a mirror image of Rod Taylor's actions in that film.

The stumbling ghouls themselves are partially culled from a host of similarly grotesque characters made popular in the 1950's horror comics such as "Vault of Horror" and "Tales From The Crypt", pioneered by William Gaines, founder of EC comics. Many of the comics' graphic illustrations sprang directly from artists who had participated in wars.

More cine verite mayhem in George A. Romero's Night of the Living Dead

The Dead Walk

It's a partnership that has continued with Romero's use of Vietnam war photographer Tom Savini, to create the special effects for his films such as *Dawn of the Dead* (1978) and *Creepshow* (1982), itself a homage to the old EC comics.

One aspect of the film overlooked at the time but that has garnered more discussion in hindsight is its political stance. This is something that Romero has frequently played down. For him *Night of the Living Dead* was a low budget but highly effective first break into films. Nevertheless, considering the political climate at the time the film was made; wars, assassinations, government scandals and race riots, the picture was always destined to reflect the social upheavals of the period. The final freeze frame images of Ben, the black hero, casually being dragged away by the police in meat hooks, seemed especially poignant against a backdrop of racial unrest in America.

In reality though, *Night of the Living Dead* did more for the horror genre than it did for any wider areas, revitalising the film industry and doing for zombie films what Hitchcock's *Psycho* had done for its' countless imitatory "slasher" films.

Knowing Romero's appreciation for Hitchcock, this is something that he will find most satisfying. Even the more inventive of today's film makers such as David Cronenberg still use Romero's picture as a yardstick towards quality - witness the Canadian's first popular feature film *Shivers* (1975) which has scrambling hands reaching through walls to ensnare potential victims in much the same style as Romero's seminal film.

Romero's film was the first in his projected "zombie trilogy", but his next offerings dealt with completely different subjects; *There's Always Vanilla* (1972) was Romero's attempt at a Hollywood style film in the vein of

The Crazies

1967's *The Graduate*, but its uninvolving story about a rock guitarist's search to "find himself" failed miserably at the box office as did *Jack's Wife* (1973). This concerned a bored housewife's attempts to escape from marital drudgery through the supernatural, expressed somewhat vaguely in her dabblings with witchcraft.

His next film was an unofficial zombie film, *The Crazies* (1973), that deals with the equally disruptive effects of mass hysteria and martial law on the small town of Evans City. A military plane has crashed near the city, spilling its contagious bio-chemical load, code-named "Trixie" which contaminates the local water supplies to produce "the crazies" of the film's title.

The main difference between *The Crazies* and Romero's other zombie films is that here the "crazies" show few physical signs of their disease, catching it when still alive and it is only obvious in some of their actions. This causes problems for both the military, who attempt to cordon off the city and quarantine it, and the survivors led by David (W G McMillan) and his girlfriend Judy (Lane Carroll) who are continually tormented by the threat of catching the infection, and of being shot by the soldiers who pursue them.

The Crazies jerky, hand-held camera shots and frenetic pacing owe much to *Night of the Living Dead*, only that film's terror, produced by mounting

When There's No More Room In Hell....

claustrophobia, is expressed here in agrophobic terms. Much of the action occurs in lush green fields, rolling hills and countryside, as the film's protagonists flee the military.

The soldiers themselves clad all in white, anti-bacteria suits and black oxygen masks, cut imposing figures, compounded by their terse, unexplained commands, which are greeted with understandable suspicion by the local people. Scenes of soldiers bursting into homes in the middle of the night, snatching frightened children from their beds, and gatecrashing discos to herd people like sheep into the city's school, effectively convey the chaos resulting from the imposition of martial law. The panic touches everyone as the military argue amongst themselves, Dr. Watts (Richard France) struggles to find a cure for the contagion, frustrated by inflexible army regulations and the authorities squabble over whether to drop a nuclear device on the city or wait in the hope of finding a scientific cure. This total lack of human co-operation results in the "accidental" shooting of the local Sheriff and even more poignantly towards the end, the death of Dr. Watts, and with him, a life-saving antidote.

The effects of the virus, on infected townspeople and on "immunised" soldiers, are equally devastating. One victim of the virus, an old lady, calmly stabs a soldier to death with a knitting needle before returning to her rocking chair, all this time hardly dropping a stitch.

Incestuous longings are awakened in Artie (Richard Liberty) and after realising his misdemeanors with his daughter Kathy (Lyn Lowry), he hangs himself. The soldiers themselves become de-humanised both by their antiseptic body suits and uncommunicative face masks. The process is completed as they carry out their orders to burn the

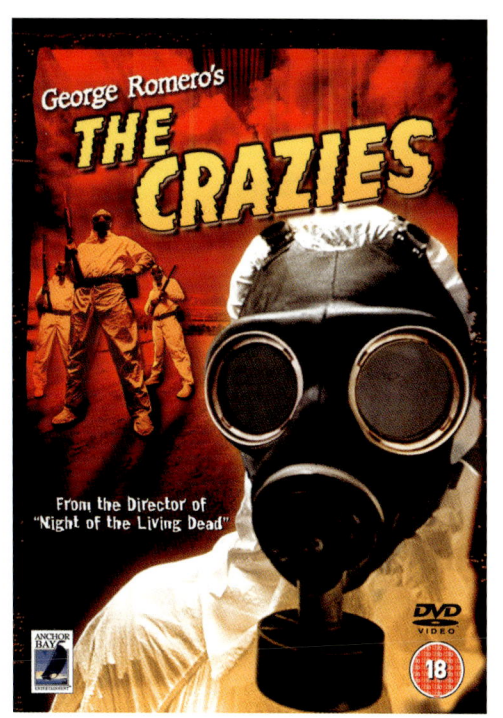

Sleeve art for The Crazies

bodies of the infected victims, stealing money from the corpses at the same time. The hysteria that is prevalent here is as much due to military intransigence as to any virus. This is most poignantly shown at the end of the film as, with the authorities still no nearer to finding an antidote, they refuse to spend time giving David an immunity check (in fact he is immune), so another chance of a cure is lost.

There are some prominent images here for those who are not too squeamish. The local vicar, having just seen his "flock" herded out of the church by the army, douses himself with kerosene before striking a match to become a burning religious effigy, his final defiant act of faith.

The battle scenes between the military and the victims of the virus take place in verdant countryside, almost an echo of the American Civil War as American fights American, one bemused woman "sweeping up the mess" afterwards with a broom. The silently falling helicopter that crashes, shot down by one of the survivors, is

Martin - a modern day vampire

Romero this time. His next work after *The Crazies* is widely regarded as one of his best. *Martin* (1976) is a modern updating of the vampire legend that subtly combines a young man's own ambivalent use of what may be the "supernatural", with a decaying industrial town milieu, devoid of any kind of hope or optimism, a situation in itself that may have helped to breed the fantasies that prevail Martin's mind. John Amplas' well-judged performance as the shy, sexually immature teenager who may or may not be a vampire carries the film extraordinarily well, especially in the inventive scenes where he seeks solace in that triumph of the twentieth century, the late night radio talk show. He cuts a lonely figure, seeking release from a drab industrial world (he fantasises that he is a movie star from vintage black and white films). His death becomes inevitable, though nonetheless shocking as his superstitious grandfather drives a stake through his heart in the time-honoured fashion.

This vampire casts a shadow - Martin

really the townsfolk's revenge on the military for their crashed plane that has unleashed the virus in the first place. Their lives and their environment have all been threatened by the army, best shown in one scene where freely-running sheep are herded back into line by the ominously marching soldiers who use the same techniques to capture and control their human quarry.

The film is certainly a worthwhile effort but the themes of human and social disintegration, coupled with slapstick comic-style violence were better employed in Romero's later zombie pictures. In keeping with the current vogue for remakes, *The Crazies* is due for just such treatment in 2010, although unlikely to be directed by

The blood splattered reality of Romero's second zombie epic, Dawn of the Dead

Fresh from the critical acclaim that greeted *Martin*, Romero went on to film the second instalment in his zombie trilogy. *Dawn of the Dead* (1978), which shifts the emphasis from an isolated farmhouse as in *Night of the Living Dead*, to a modern day shopping mall.

The opening sequences see a television reporter, Fran (Gaylen Ross) and her boyfriend Stephen (David Emge) escape the overrun city along with two S.W.A.T. troopers, Peter (Ken Foree) and Roger (Scott Reiniger). Romero's continuing theme of human breakdown and lack of co-operation is enforced in both the TV stations and the S.W.A.T. soldiers; it is everywhere.

Firstly, we are shown "media types" carrying out futile arguments amongst themselves and a TV station director who is more concerned with keeping viewers than preserving lives, as he broadcasts addresses of now obsolete rescue stations. The action then quickly cuts to the soldiers who

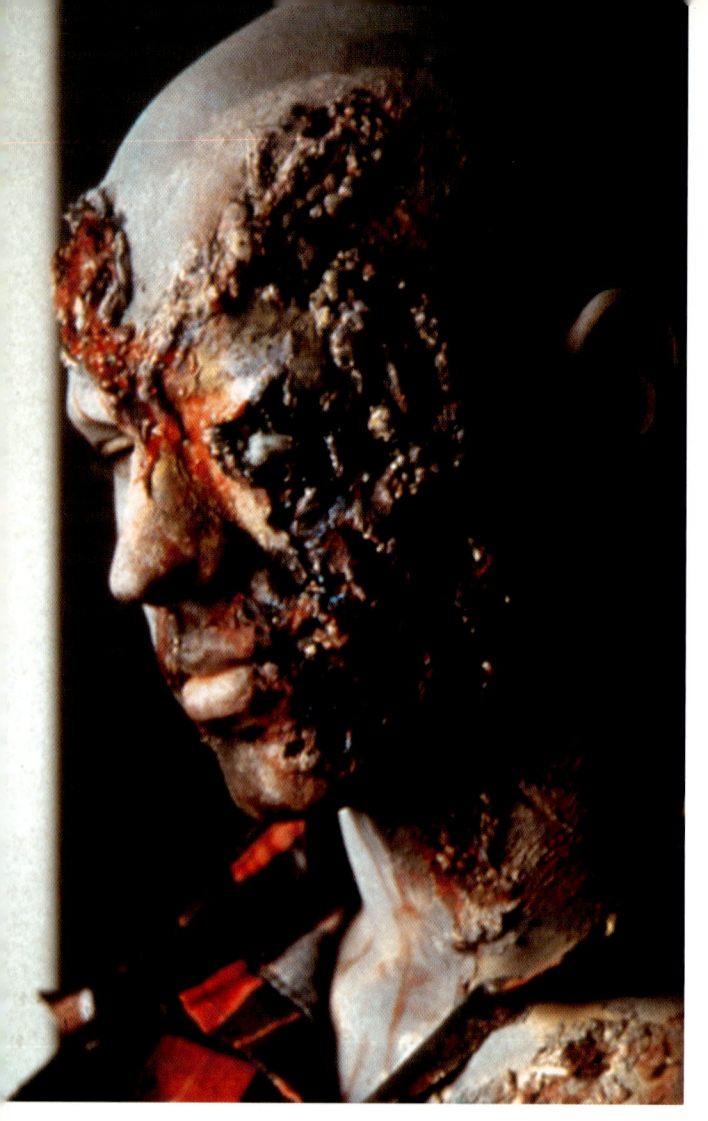

Beauty decidedly not skin deep in Dawn of the Dead

are flushing out zombies from a tower block ghetto. All around, humans are mentally disintegrating as one soldier overdoses on a killing spree and others kill themselves rather than face the horrors of the building that houses the now physically putrifying undead. The hands that lash out at the soldiers from behind wooden panels show that the horror from *Night of the Living Dead* is still very much with us.

Dawn of the Dead's most striking advance on its predecessor is that here it is often the zombies who are the victims, under threat first from the four survivors and then from the thrill-seeking gang of bikers who descend on the mall with military-style precision.

Here, the zombies are practically sympathetic characters. They lurch so slowly that if anyone is caught it is due to their own carelessness or over-confidence. Repeatedly, we see them as comical figures stumbling up and down escalators and falling into fountains, all to the accompaniment of insipid supermarket "muzak".

Peter and Roger's playful "shopping trips" to collect provisions in the store illustrate this as they push, shove and butt their way effortlessly through the swaying lines of zombies, before then beckoning them to amass at one chosen exit whilst they hurriedly escape from another. They can manipulate the zombies how and when they want. Roger's eventual lapse in zombiedom, bitten when blocking the mall exits with large haulage trucks, is directly due to his own flippant, carefree attitude, even when confronted by massive numbers of zombies.

Stephen also has numerous chances to escape during the film's climax but instead neglects to take them with the expected consequences. In the confrontations between the fast-moving bikers and the pedantic zombies it is again the zombies that elicit any audience sympathy.

The nauseating sight of bikers being arbitrarily disembowelled by swarming zombies is tempered by the fact that the bikers are still motivated by materialistic desires for televisions, hi-fi equipment and money, even though they are now meaningless symbols in a society where possessions now count for nothing next to the will to survive.

They are not alone in this out-dated reaction, as we see Fran dressing up in expensive clothes and jewellery, and Peter playing cards with Stephen for cash that won't buy their ultimate freedom. All these delusions are poignantly shattered when Fran rejects both Stephen's offered ring and his proposal of marriage. She realises that marriage is meaningless in a collapsed society without social order and values.

The mall itself stands as a concrete idol to the "seventies" craving for materialism that the film so dramatically destroys. It is equally a temple to mindless consumerism, now perpetuated ironically by the zombies who stay in the mall because of instinct; "it (the mall) was an important place in their lives". The parallel between consumerism and zombieism is one that Romero continually states and carries to the ultimate extreme as the dead zombies themselves are "packaged off" into the mall's freezer store like the endless rows of supermarket pre-packed meat that dominate the groaning shelves.

The main criticism that can be levelled against the film is that the zombies show little sign of development after *Night of the Living Dead*, and are often merely "easy targets" for the film's outrageous action scenes and graphic killings. There is, however, one exception to this as, the now zombified form of Stephen, leads the ghouls up to the roof of the mall at the conclusion, having remembered previously constructing a secret "fake" wall to hide the real entrance, when he was still among the living.

Romero's continuing admiration for EC comics surfaces again throughout the film in various comedy style scenes that occur. This is just as well considering the massive body count here and the quota of gore on show. The special effects of Tom Savini provide us with some suitably unsettling sights such as a screwdriver through one zombie's head, a decapitation as another zombie walks into the whirling blades of a helicopter, and a very grotesque zombie whose face has partly rotted away. Fortunately, the violence is so broad, so all encompassing, that it

Images from Dawn of the Dead

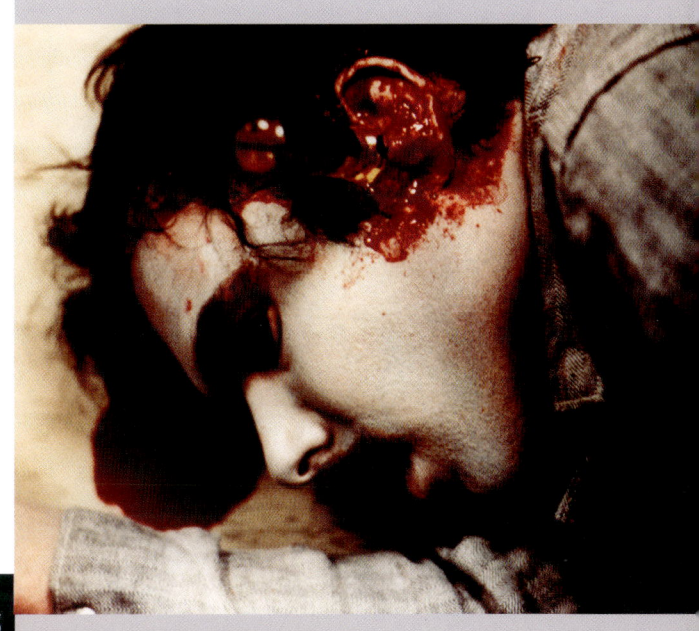

genuinely does translate as black humour if not exactly comic, cartoon style humour.

The tone of the violence is perfectly encapsulated in one scene where the zombies actually have custard pies pushed into their faces. Contrast this however, with some extremely frightening moments, none better than when Roger wakes up only to find himself now a zombie, his bed sheets sliding from his rising body to reveal a bone-white face and sunken eyes. *Dawn of the Dead*'s conclusion offers hope for the future amidst all the comic book carnage that has signalled societies collapse. Fran, who is pregnant, and Peter, both escape, Peter after surviving his own "crisis" and rejecting suicide. They, through their own efforts, have managed to remain alive and retain sane minds

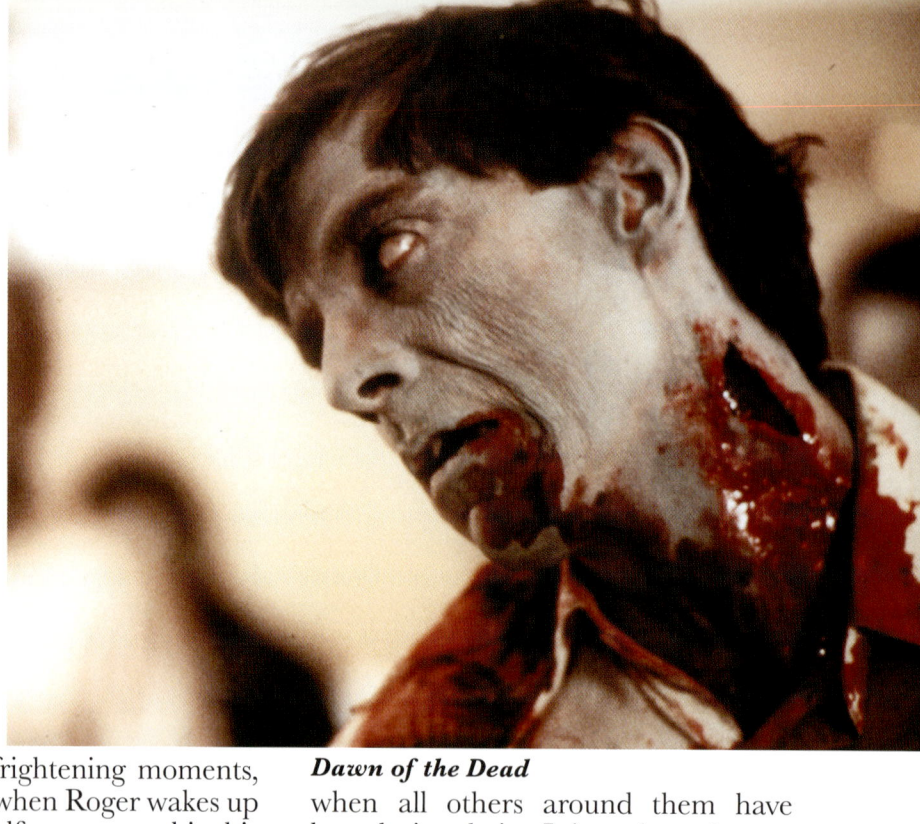

Dawn of the Dead

Dawn of the Dead

when all others around them have been losing theirs. It is to them that we look for a possible future and a more hopeful cause. They are the living example of Stephen's earlier prophecy that "We've got to survive. Someone's got to survive."

Outside his zombie trilogy, Romero's next films were *Knightriders* (1981) and *Creepshow* (1982), but each met with only limited success. *Knightriders* is the director's own modern interpretation of the Camelot myth, with jousts fought on motorbikes as opposed to horses. It's an endearing though rather overlong film and its' romance has, at times, worked against it in the fiercely competitive film world. Its release, in close proximity with John Boorman's examination of the same subject, *Excalibur* (1981),

When There's No More Room In Hell....

also accentuated the shortcomings.

Creepshow was more successful, accumulating all of Romero's various comic book influences and exhibiting them in one film, which itself is an anthology homage to the EC comics, complete with lurid lighting, animated sequences and ironic "twist" endings to each story in similar vein to Roal Dahl's "Tales of the Unexpected", Rod Serling's "Twilight Zone" and the "Alfred Hitchcock Presents" series.

There are two segments that deal specifically with zombies. "Father's Day" features Romero regular, John Amplas as Natham Grantham, a defiant zombie and "Something To Tide you Over", which has Ted Danson and Gaylen Ross returning from their watery graves as a final act of vengeance.

Both stories benefit from having accomplished casts; Viveca Lindafors appears in the former and Leslie Nielson in the latter, together with some effective Savini make-up, with Amplas looking particularly repulsive with skeletal face and muddied clothes, whereas Danson and Ross's signs of zombiehood include washed-out eyes and wrinkled skin. "Father's Day" especially showcases some fine camerawork as gravestones loom over us, apparently swaying to crush one character Hank Blaire (Ed Harris) and the sight of Aunt Bedelia (Lindafors) recoiling in horror as Grantham's decayed and bony hand bursts up from beneath the graveyard earth to grab her.

Despite moments such as these, there's a limit to what can be achieved in

Creepshow

only thirty-minute segments, so it was Romero's next full length feature that really showed his continually evolving talents as a film maker.

Day of the Dead (1985), the third part of Romero's envisaged zombie trilogy is not the film he wanted to make. His original idea of an elite, highly trained zombie corps engaged in zombie versus zombie warfare under human control had to be shelved due to budgetary restrictions. The final version of *Day of the Dead* however, is in no way a poor substitute, but a challenging, thought-provoking film in its own right, that shows further signs of zombie "development" and of human retrogression. The deserted farmhouse and expansive shopping mall around which the action is based

The Dead Walk in Day of the Dead

Zombies will not go hungry in Day of the Dead

in the earlier films is now supplanted by an underground missile silo in Florida. Once again, the cloying claustrophobia of *Night of the Living Dead* has returned to haunt us in *Day of the Dead*, most of the film being fought out within the confines of an underground complex and adjoining limestone caves.

Here, the attention is centred as much on the human survivors own arguments with each other as it is with their battles against the zombies. The collapse of civilised society is squarely laid at the door of the military, the scientists and to a lesser extent, those who choose to remain uninvolved.

Captain Rhodes (Joseph Philato) represents the military gone mad, as he embodies elements of megalomania that we all secretly feared were harboured by the army. To him, it is more important to arbitrarily kill and escape the zombies than to try and find out the reasons for their behaviour. He pays scant notice to his fellow humans and yet expects their rapt attention and obedience to his barked orders in return.

His complete lack of respect for his "companions" is best illustrated when he threatens to have Sarah (Lois Cardille) shot, just for refusing his command to sit down, and later he shoots another scientist in the head from point-blank range. It seems that the greatest threat to human survival comes not from the zombies, but from within, from Captain Rhodes.

Richard Liberty's Dr. Logan -"affectionately" referred to as "Frankenstein", is alternatively the representative of scientific madness. Like Rhodes he ignores the reasons why the zombies are created, preferring instead to further his own experiments in surgery in pursuit of his own "scientific glory". His grotesquely bizarre experiments include the use of the dead Major Cooper's body as "food treats" for the "star pupil", Bub (Howard Sherman). His laboratory, a surgery of spare parts, is a modern day equivalent of Baron Frankenstein's. Another soldier's head adorns one table, still being kept alive by Logan, whilst another table contains corpses in varying stages of surgery/mutilation, including one zombie whose entire face has been cut away and another whose internal organs have been removed.

Logan, in effect, has lost all grip on reality as humans no longer signify life for him, being reduced instead to nothing more than a continual source of experimental fodder and convenient guinea pigs. His "progress" with Bub amounts to teaching him (by reawakening his latent human memory), how to read books, in this

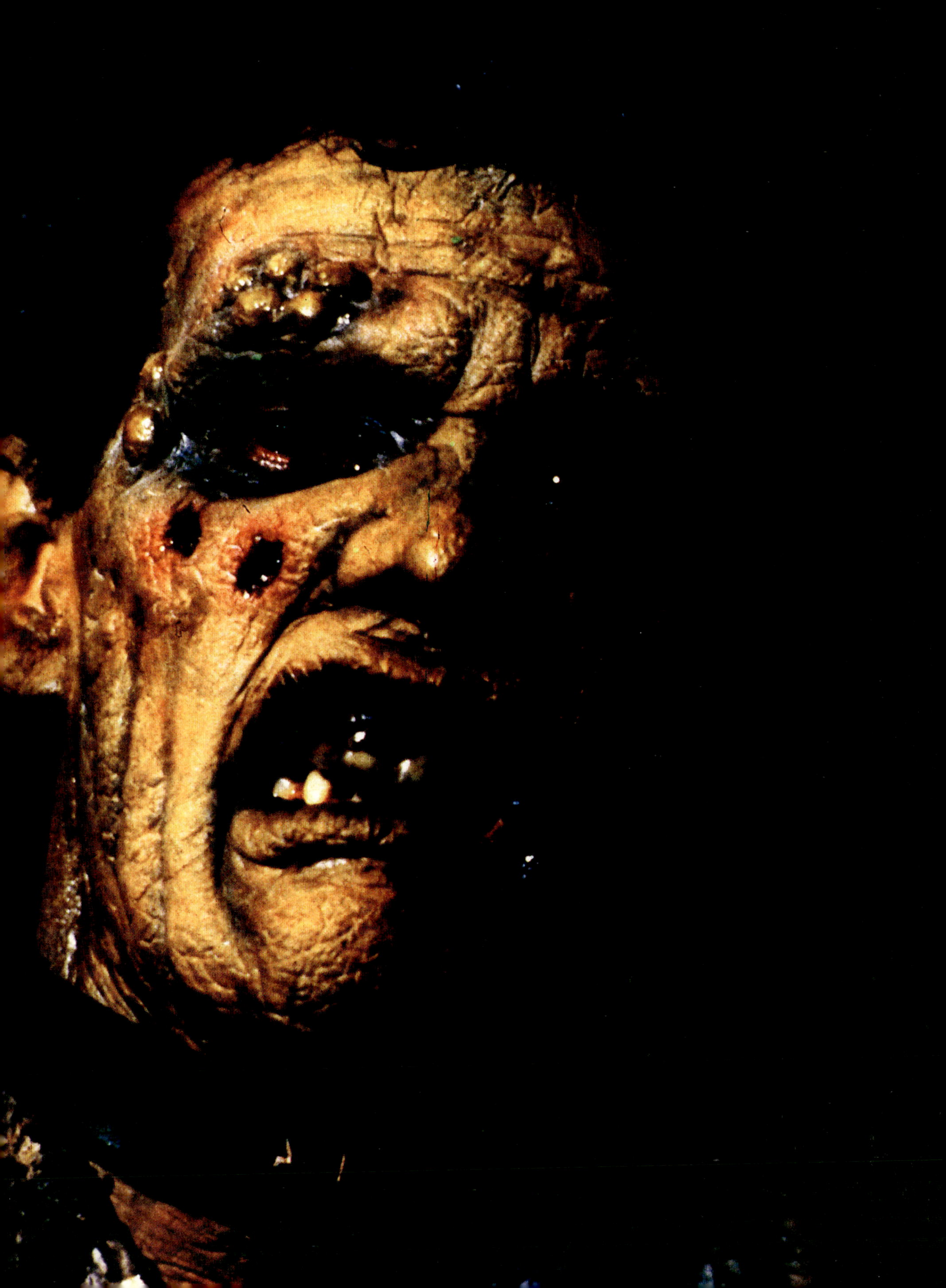

case Stephen King's "Salem's Lot", and to play tape cassettes. Logan's eventual demise is unsurprisingly at the hands of Rhodes, who mercilessly peppers him with machine-gun fire to put an end to his abbatoir-style practices.

The remaining group of survivors, radio officer McDermott (Jarlath Conroy) and John (Terry Alexander) both represent the apolitical strain of the human race. They try to remain distanced from the military and scientific arguments, their idealistic longing for a more peaceful and harmonious society is reflected in the painted Carribean back-drop that dominates their trailer home. The fact that it is John and McDermott who survive, along with the ever optimistic Sarah, isn't lost on the viewer. It seems that where there's a will there's a way. The tropical island they fly to at the conclusion is the nearest they will get to reaching their Utopia, and provides a vivid contrast to the prison-like corridors of the base they have now escaped from.

Romero shows himself to be increasingly at home with his zombie creations in this picture through his treatment of Bub and the numerously well-staged shocks that punctuate the film. These shocks burst quite literally through in the film's opening sequence as Sarah gazes dreamily at an idyllic picture of a green pumpkin field. The moment is shattered as zombie arms reach out from the sparse white wall behind and claw her. The action then cuts to the single most effective scene as Sarah, waking up from what has been a dream, finds herself in the helicopter with John and McDermott who are landing in the apparently deserted city of Fort Myers. They reconnoitre the rubbish-strewn streets, calling out in the hope of finding more survivors. The city remains ominously silent, only broken by the wind rustling through the buildings.

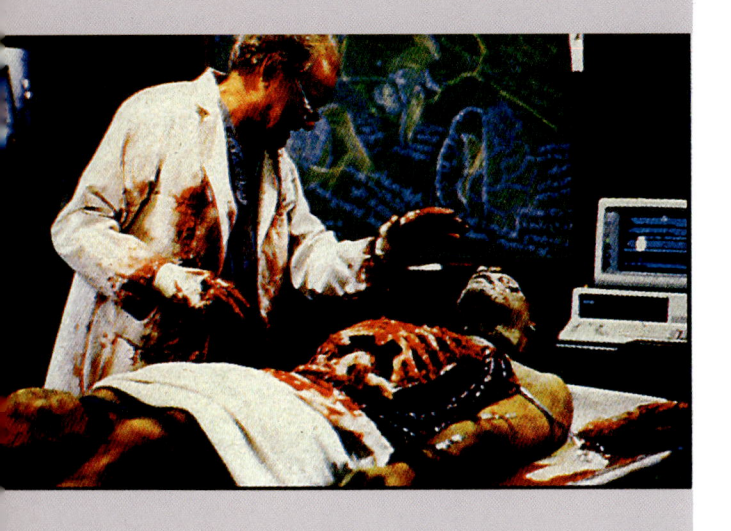

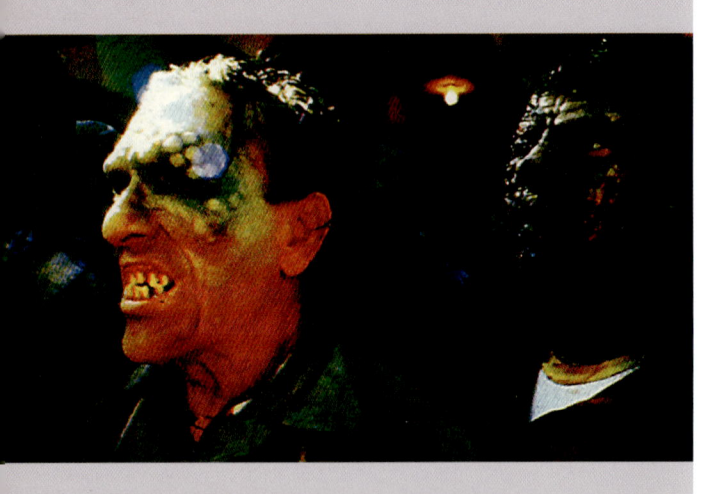

Images from Day of the Dead

Then, the tell-tale anguished groans signal the appearance, from every conceivable hiding place, of the city's zombies who have literally been "called to rise" by the unwitting helicopter team. A newspaper is blown open onto the apocalyptical headline "The Dead Walk" and zombies rapidly converge on the survivors. One jawless zombie is silhouetted ironically against the gleaming sun that shines brightly in the sky and the *Day of the Dead* is well and truly upon us.

You need guts to star in a Romero film as seen in both these pics from Day of the Dead

The mounting tension that pervades the members of the underground base is accentuated by the above ground scenes which show hordes of zombies constantly beating on the perimeter fence that guards the base. The zombies are now in the majority, outnumbering the humans by 400,000 to 1.

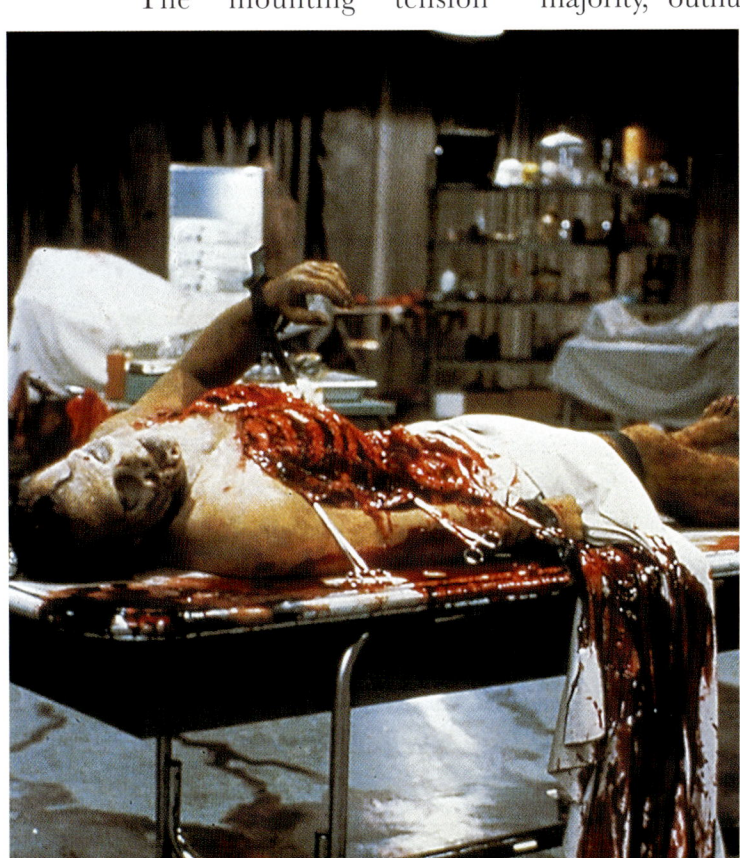

Inside the complex we see the increasingly dangerous attempts by the military survivors to capture zombies on which Dr. Logan can carry out his dubious experiments. They are caught by baiting the zombies and then rounding them up like cattle, trapping them in a narrow "cattle pen". We can almost imagine the strains of "Rawhide" scoring the action. The barbaric, gung-ho attitude of the soldiers is best illustrated in the hulking figure of the appropriately named Steele (G Howard-Klarr), who is all too prepared to also kill the civilian members of the team at the first opportunity, and even his own men. Most under threat is the emaciated figure of Miguel (Antone Diles), who is collapsing under the continual strain.

It has also invaded his relationship with his girlfriend Sarah, who constantly appears to be stronger both mentally and physically than him. To Miguel, the danger isn't so much from the zombies as from Sarah, who usurps any masculine dominance which he may have once exhibited. His final act of defiance occurs towards the end of the film as, having been bitten by one of the zombies, beckons the amassing creatures above ground onto the lift elevator and then takes them down into the underground base to run amok.

In the figure of Bub we have the first "real" zombie character, as he no longer sees humans as "lunch" and begins to remember his former life. In his scenes with the intransigent Rhodes, it is Bub who appears the more human, even down to his humorous army salute to an incredulous Rhodes, whose first reaction is simply to want to shoot Bub.

Tom Savini's incredible special effects however, steal the show at the conclusion as bodies are ripped apart by the ravenous zombies. Rhodes own grisly demise is saved until last when, after being wounded by Bub, he opens a door only to have hundreds of zombies spill forth onto him. The ever watching Bub refuses a chance to shoot Rhodes, preferring to let him die at the hands (and mouths!) of the hungry zombies, who gorge themselves on his body, pulling him apart to Rhodes cries of "Choke on 'em" as they tuck greedily into his entrails.

There are also obligatory scenes of zombies being shot through the head, bright crimson blood splattering against walls, and a particularly realistic decapitation as McDermott beheads one creature, only to see the still-twitching eyes on its head. Savini's creations here are grotesquely realistic as in the zombie corpse that rises from an operating table only to disgorge its' entire intestinal tract, and reach the pinnacle of achievement as far as Savini's profession is concerned, at least before the advent of CGI techniques, recalling the outrageous images conjured up in *The Thing* (1982), in both their bold impressiveness and convincing execution.

For some, if not all of these reasons, *Day of the Dead* stands as probably the best entry in Romero's original zombie trilogy (before his later renaissance with *Land of the Dead* (2005) and *Diary of the Dead* (2007). The realism of its effects and its astute character observations, coupled with a more fluid, sweeping camera style and imaginative compositions lend to it a quality and resilience too rarely seen in films today. In tone and characterisation it is very much a film of the 80's and a further enhancement in the zombie series.

(Now read overleaf for the full story behind Romero's original vision for Day of the Dead*).*

When There's No More Room In Hell....

DAY OF THE DEAD - UNSEEN, UNFILMED, UNCUT!

BACKGROUND

Romero originally wrote a sixty page story called *Anubis* inspired by Richard Matheson's *I Am Legend*, which paralleled some of Matheson's themes. It was the analysis of the three phases a society goes through when a revolutionary society overthrows the status quo: Insurgence, Equality, and Domination. The story was called *Anubis* after the Egyptian god who leads the dead to Judgement. Often represented as a jackal, it was the duty of Anubis to attend to the ritual preparation of bodies to weigh the heart of every person on the scale of justice, and to judge a person's good and bad deeds on Earth. It detailed the ideas used in Romero's first two zombie films, and core elements of the third. Romero said he 'originally wrote a sixty-page short story after I read Richard Matheson's *I Am Legend*, which I loved but found lacking in certain areas. It inspired me to create an allegorical concept about incoming and outgoing societies and a state of revolution without discussing specific ideologies, but rather examining the phenomenon of when a revolutionary society with a totally new morality deposes an operative societal structure. It happened in three stages right from the jump.

Stage One was the beginning of the phenomenon, which we covered in *Night Of The Living Dead*. At the end, the operative society was still in control, although the specific humans we were dealing with did die and we had a generally pessimistic outlook towards the future. Stage two was equal balance and that became *Dawn Of The Dead*. At that point it can go either way. In stage three, the zombie society is dominant, but in the denouement you find that even though the new society is the operative one, it's still under control of certain elitist humans. They fall right into the same pattern of human society being controlled by outside forces.

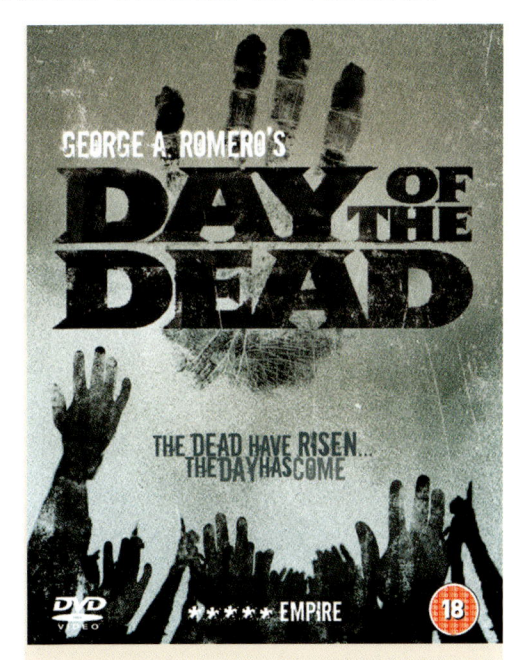

Romero would explore stage three with *Day Of The Dead* (1985). The film's production had been delayed by a plethora of 'spaghetti zombie' films. Hoping to rekindle the magic sparks of their *Dawn Of The Dead* collaboration, Romero and Dario Argento wrote a forty page treatment but their second zombie collaboration never materialised due to budgetary constraints, despite this Argento was optimistic-"I like the scenario, it will be very mystical and very good."

There were drastic alterations to the screenplay with eleventh hour-budget-slashing. In many respects this worked in the films favour, giving it an atmosphere of ever-increasing claustrophobia. The final budget for *Day* was quoted at $3 million, at the time no one would give the seven to eight million dollars required for an unrated film. In the sense of scope, *Land Of the Dead* is the film *Day Of The Dead* would have been. Tom Savini explained at the time- "with the budget cut way down, we couldn't do the original script, it was like *Raiders Of The Lost Ark* with zombies. It was incredibly large scale. George feels-and says-that this isn't the end (of the *Dead* series), because this isn't the film he had in mind to make."

Now, using that same un-filmed script, for the first time, we will see Romero's unrealised vision of *Day Of The Dead*!

Day Of The Dead would have begun with titles fading in one phrase at a time.

FIVE YEARS...

...SINCE THE DEAD FIRST WALKED.

FLORIDA-1987.

The un-filmed script begins somewhat similarly to the filmed version, the details are similar, the now useless banknotes blowing on the sea breeze, the garbage, the utter desolation. Instead of one alligator though, there are several, and there are many more zombies. The credits play over a mummified hanging corpse baring a sign: "TAKE ME, LORD. I LOVE YOU!" It's the first of many religious or mystical overtones in the script. The rope breaks, the corpses falls to the ground and shatters, it's sign blowing across to a marina, where a motorboat is coming in. There are three men and two women onboard. Romero describes them as looking like guerilleros from somewhere in Central America. One called Tony says it's just another dead place. Another, Miguel, says radio signals were coming from this area. Tony sticks to his guns, all the cities belong to the dead, life can only exist on the islands (a polar opposite to Romero's concept in *Land Of The Dead*, where humans only survive in their fortified cities.) The sight of this dead city has only brought the already strained Miguel one step closer to the edge: "Plenty of the time for the island. The rest of our lives for the islands. We gotta see if there are others here. We came all this way. We're gonna check it out."

One of the women Maria joins Tony in siphoning off fuel from the abandoned boats in the marina, while Miguel and the other two guerilleros, Sarah and Chico, make their way to the city. Miguel has an electronic bullhorn in one hand, an automatic rifle in the other. This is very similar to the scene at the start of the filmed version of *Day Of The Dead*. Miguel asks if there's anyone

When There's No More Room In Hell....

there. The Dead groan hungrily. The script describes it thus-"A MASSIVE WALL OF NOISE. The sound of hundreds-of-thousands of damned souls moaning in one solid voice-the sound of hell on earth."

Maria crosses herself and the leave the city to the Dead.

They make their way to a small private dock and begin scavenging. They have more luck this time and find fuel. Without warning a figure grabs Maria and puts a pistol to her head. Maria pulls a knife from her belt and stabs her attacker. She fires wildly, hitting Maria on the arm. Tony opens fire on her attacker, but two more gunmen appear behind him. Tony makes his way to Maria, while Miguel, Sarah and Chico draw their weapons and take cover in a boat shed. A pitched gun battle ensues between the two groups.

Tony rescues Maria and makes for open water.

Miguel has been firing through an open window on his side of the shed, when a zombie suddenly appears inside the open window "Biting Miguel's left arm-ITS TEETH TEAR A LARGE STRIP OF FLESH OUT OF THE ARM six inches above the wrist." Sarah puts three shots from a .45 into the zombie's head. In a scene that would appear in the filmed *Day Of The Dead* in a different context. Sarah takes Chico's Machette, and she and Chico knock Miguel unconscious. She then uses the machete to sever Miguel's bitten arm. Sarah destroys another zombie while looking for something to cauterise Miguel's stump. While Chico continues a lone fence, Sarah makes a torch from paint thinners and an axe handle and cauterises the amputated area.

It looks like their attackers will gain the upper hand, when Maria and Tony return, opening fire from their boat. Tony is wounded in return but then they kill the attackers. The battle over, Chico wants to leave Miguel, but Sarah threatens to shoot him-'help me or die.'

Later when they've left the dock, more zombies appear to devour the corpses. At sea, Tony dies from the wounds received in the battle. The seemingly recovered Miguel wants to put a bullet in his head to ensure he doesn't resurrect. Maria doesn't believe he'll come back-"It won't happen to him! You heard his prayer. His prayer will save him. He could never become one of...one of those devils. Miguel answers, "prayers have no power to save. The knife can save. It can cut the disease away. The bullet. It can shatter the brain where the evil takes seed. These are saviours…our new saviours…our only saviours.'

But Maria believes one day 'the curse will pass.' Miguel agrees, prophesising that "one day a dead man will refuse to return, And that man will be a saint. The first saint of our century. That's a prayer too. A catechism. Something the priests tell us to believe." Miguel is going mad! "He will rise and you…" he tells Maria. "You will die!"

They agree to wait. That night Tony does indeed return and attack Maria. Miguel could stop him but he merely grins and watches. Chico and Sarah open fire, destroying Tony, whose falling body drags Maria into the sea.

The following day they reach a place they will later discover is called Gaspirilla's island. Miguel is clearly not the man he was. The script describes him vividly: "MIGUEL is sweating profusely yet shivering as though cold. FLIES ARE BUSSING in a cluster around his WRAPPED STUMP. He's over the edge now, insane. And worse than that, the infection from the original bite is spreading. The amputation

The Dead Walk

was not done quickly enough to prevent the parasites from racing through his veins and to the brain and elsewhere."

On the island Miguel finds hundreds of subtropical plants, hundreds of them. Six feet tall and flowering. "Their red-gold blossoms are shaped like trumpets hanging with their bells down. He rants DATURA! DATURA METEL!"

Sarah knows what's happening and promises to shoot him when he dies. They make their way to the island's inner jungle. Sarah and Chico reach a clearing in the jungle. The find an enormous iron plate, fifty feet by ten, all painted in green and brown camouflage pattern. They speculate it may be a helicopter landing pad, when suddenly there's a "GREAT RUMBLING like the giant gears and pistons of a drawbridge being activated. The iron plate shudders and starts to move, downward into the earth."

The pair duck back into the jungle. Chico observes, "it's some kind of… elevator. There must be something under the ground here…maybe… military."

Romero describes the next scene brilliantly: "SEVERAL FIGURES are rising up into view, a dozen, maybe fifteen. Details are obscured by FOREGROUND FOLIAGE, but we can read helmets, heavy armaments, packs, utility belts. The impression is of a cadre of soldiers rising from hell. There are THREE SOLDIERS who do not move with the others. They are standing still with their shoulders slumped, their heads lolling listlessly from side to side. They have the body attributes of prisoners yet there is something menacing about them. WE HEAR A SERIES OF ELECTRONIC BLEEPS, something like computer bleeps, and, as though in response to that signal, the three slumped figures start to walk. They move slowly, stiffly, their feet shuffling, their arms dangling lifelessly at their sides."

Sarah and Chico are horrified!

Romero's description continues: "As we CUT IN CLOSER we see that the three slumped figures are ZOMBIES. They are wearing khakis and they are armed with RIFLES AND PISTOL BELTS. Their HELMETS have been painted an identifying bright RED and they wear slipover vests dyed a bright colour. All the others in the platoon are humans. They, too, wear vests but theirs are not red, but WHITE, with large ORANGE CIRCLES emblazoned front and back. Two of the men wield LONG ELECTRIC CATTLE PRODS for use should the zombies misbehave, but the creatures, amazingly, are shambling along, with the rest of the platoon voluntarily, co-operatively, even somewhat excitedly…the kind of excitement seen in a puppy that's just learned a new trick."

Chico can only ask, "are we truly in hell?"

The mysterious platoon begins setting up their equipment, which includes tripod machine guns. Two men don black rubber gloves and long black laboratory aprons. They strap large refrigerated cartons around their necks and open the sealed lids.

A siren sounds, calling zombies from the jungle. Some are wearing torn clothes, but others wear vests, the same type worn by the platoon. These are solid colours, some white, some blue. None are red and none have orange circles. The soldiers used the cattle prods to keep the more unruly ones in their place. They hand the zombies raw meat from the freezers. Chico and Sarah, watching, realise they could only be feeding the Stenches human flesh!

Then we meet an old 'friend' (or should that be fiend!) from the filmed *Day Of The Dead*. Romero's script description is bang on the money! "The man in command of the platoon is obvious, strutting around while others do his dirty work. This is CAPTAIN RHODES. He's conscienceless, the lowest of the low, and a weasely-looking guy to boot. He watches the operation almost hoping for trouble. (He loves to torture disobedient zombies). Behind him, their AUTOMATICS ready, are SEVERAL TROOPERS especially assigned to protect the captain. One of these troopers is TOBY TYLER, a good guy. TOBY is revulsed by the scene in the clearing."

Rhodes is amused by his discomfort. "Tyler. It's the only way. They don't bite the hand that feeds."

One of the wild reeks runs amok. A trooper with a long pole with a wire noose at the end captures it. (Another idea retained for the filmed *Day Of The Dead*!).

Wild zombies attack Sarah and Chico, who opens fire, alerting a delighted Rhodes. Using a remote control on his belt, he sends the three zombies towards the sound of gunfire. "Hah! If only the rest of you ladies would obey orders the way they do!"

Sarah and Chico destroy the wild zombies only to find themselves under attack from "THE RED COAT ZOMBIES, shuffling forward a breast in a line, have OPENED FIRE. It's a grisly parody of foot-soldiering. The creatures are unsteady on their feet, their hands shake when they squeeze the stiff army-issue triggers. BULLETS FLY this way and that, most of them grossly off targets."

Rhodes is delighted! "THAT'S IT, YOU WORM-EATEN SLIME! YOU FOUL-SMELLING, PUSS-FACED MAGGOTS! I TOLD YOU I'D FIND YOU REAL ACTION, DIDN'T I? YOU'RE GETTING BETTER…GETTING BETTER…GETTING BETTER, YOU SCUM!"

Two soldiers close in on Sarah and Chico, firing, wounding Chico in the chest. Then Miguel charges toward the clearing, firing at the soldiers, killing one, wounding another.

Miguel is hit and falls to the earth, he points his pistol at Rhodes, but it's hammer ringer hollow-it's empty. Rhodes uses his belt control to order the red coats to shoot Miguel, which they do, firing into him until they run out of ammo'. Chico panics and runs straight into the soldiers, who duly shoot him again. Sarah uses the confusion to escape.

Toby goes to give the badly wounded Chico a mercy killing, but Rhodes won't let him. "They can handle it, Tyler. We've got two dead. Cut the heads off and get the bodies underground to the refrigerators, fast. It's a hot day.

In the filmed *Day Of The Dead*, Rhodes kills 'Frankenstein', Doctor Logan, for feeding his fallen troops to tame zombies, but in the alternate *Day Of The Dead*, Rhodes not only approves but is the instigator. But it's only the troops he wants decapitated, he leaves Miguel to reanimate, hoping to get another shot at him later. Rhodes orders Chico to be tied up from a rope which is tied over a tall tree, his feet dangling ten feet off the ground. He begs Rhodes to kill him. Rhodes laughs, "After hanging up there for a few days you will be mad for food…crazed! You will lust for it. YOU WILL BE WORSE THAN ANY OF THEM!" Rhodes thinks that Chico is a 'rebel'. He won't believe Chico when he tells him he's alone and the Dead have inherited the Earth!

Bored with tormenting Chico, Rhodes turns his attention to the captured zombie struggling at the end of the noose. He shoves a hand grenade into the reek's mouth. The soldier wielding the pole releases the noose and the two soldiers run. The head explodes to the delight of Rhodes. Then someone puts Chico out of his misery and puts Rhodes back into a bad mood. He suspects it's Toby Tyler, and will deal with him later.

They return to their underground base. Described vividly in the script, "there's that GIANT SOUND again, the RUMBLE OF THE ELEVATOR. We're inside the place called THE CAVE, in a huge underground concrete bunker. TECHNICIANS AND ARMED GUARDS bustle around. Enormous hydraulic pistons are bringing the camouflaged iron plate down from the surface. Piling onboard, RHODES AND HIS PLATOON prepare to unload their paraphernalia."

We see that both the bunker and the sheer amount of cast are massively bigger and grander than the version of *Day Of the Dead* that Romero managed to film due to budget cuts. It's such a shame, it would have been Romero's *Citizen Cane*, the *Gone With The Wind* of zombie films

Outside in the jungle Sarah meets three humans. John a Caribbean Islander (he becomes the helicopter pilot in the filmed *Day Of the Dead*. There's Bill McDermott (who becomes the radio operator in the filmed *Day Of The Dead*) and a heavily-armed woman nicknamed Spider.

John explains the situation on the island to Sarah. "Bees. That's what we call the dead…the walking dead here on Gasparilla's Island. He was a pirate who sailed these waters long ago. His name is bein' borrowed these days by the long lost Henry Dickerson." Sarah recognises the name. "Governor Dickerson? Of Florida?" John confirms this. "That's the man. He's been holed up here ever since the shit hit the fan. Him and his family owned these islands around here. They was leasin' this one to the Fed. The whole underneath is dug out. There was missiles here and laboratories and bomb proof housing, nuclear power, all o' that. Now this here is Dickerson's…Gasparilla's…private fortress. Him and a bunch of his cronies from all the best golf courses in Tallahasse….and his private army….We been watching you since you landed. Couldn't help. I'm sorry for that. We ain't supposed to be outside. If we was spotted it could…well, it could be the end of everything."

They come across another hatchway leading from The Cave. Five soldiers come through followed by half a dozen zombies, followed by a woman and a man wearing lab coats. The woman is Mary Henreid, one of the top behaviouralists in The Cave. They leave the reeks outside and return through the hatch. The

When There's No More Room In Hell....

stenches then approach Sarah and her new friends. John explains that they've been trained to leave anyone wearing a vest with a circle alone. "It's the ones without colours you gotta watch for." Never the less a zombie attacks to be killed by John and Spider."

There's a moving moment when Sarah tells John, "the man I was with…until today…believed that praying was for blind men who couldn't see the truth." He asks, "how we gonna break the curse without a prayer or two?" She's puzzled. "Curse? It's a disease…a bug…a parasite that infects the brain." John doesn't see any distinction. "That sounds like a curse to me."

Sarah says the island is 'a worse nightmare' than anything she has seen yet. John agrees. "What's happening underground here is just what Lucifer planned for this sinful race o' man. But we're gonna beat Lucifer. We're gonna put an end to what's happening here."

Once again, mystical and religious overtones enter the script, as though the characters are part of a bigger, grander plan.

Sarah's had enough of fighting for what "feels like a hundred years." She takes off into the jungle. They move to follow her. Meanwhile Sarah is attacked by a zombie. John catches up with her, just in time to dispatch the creature.

The next scene is inside The Cave at night. We see zombies being conditioned and watch scenes of obedience on a video screen. There is also a communications centre. We Mary Henreid whom we briefly saw outside. In The Cave's zombie pen, Rhodes gives a human head to a zombie. Amazingly, Rhodes is behaving just like Logan from the filmed *Day Of The Dead*! Reflecting the larger scale of Romero's original vision, there are more zombies. Rhodes tells the one he's just fed, a zombie with large black beard, nicknamed 'Bluto'. "Remember who gives you favours" In other cells there are other nicknamed, tamed Red Coat Zombies-"Grumpy", "Tonto", "Fatso"….

…and of course "Bub"!

Rhodes is about to give the second head to Bub when Mary Henreid and her assistant Julie Grant enter. To their horror, they see that Rhodes has fed Chico's head to a reek called "Samson".

Mary is furious. "God…damn you, Rhodes!" Rhodes is amused at her words. "God has damned us all. Are my atrocities any worse than yours?" She's furious. "You have ruined weeks of work here! We've been trying to ween these specimens onto alligator meat." Rhodes is even more amused at this. "No wonder they're so hungry."

Then the remaining head reanimates! Rhodes shoots it. Mary takes the shocked Julie to her office. "I didn't realise. Those were de-caps! I didn't know that…de-caps…revived!" Rhodes takes great pleasure in telling her. "Any dead whose brains are intact will revive." She's horrified. "But…we bury the heads. Oh God! It must be torture for them." It's all academic to Rhodes…as long as it's not him! "They are brutes without feeling. Though I admit that I've requested cremation for myself. Burial is an archaic tradition. The purpose of decapitation is preserve as much…food…as possible. The purpose for feeding is to keep the beasts on our side. The fact that they can be taught to clean up our garbage or fire a gun is a convenient side benefit not the primary goal. The primary goal is to keep ourselves from becoming their supper, keep them fed and they behave. Keep them hungry and they revert back

The Dead Walk

into being the animal they always have been. You saw them in there." Rhodes also tells Mary he's had her boyfriend Toby Tyler assigned to his platoon, and that he's in trouble. Julie discovers Mary knew about the de-caps reviving, and it's clear she'll never trust her again-the knowledge has had some profound effect on her.

Mary goes to the place called The Residence. The part of the cave where people have their quarters. Rather like the City in *Land Of The Dead*. There she meets Toby. He wants to flee the island. She wants to continue her work. "For the good of mankind," he says scornfully. "That's what every monster-make says." His words cause her guilty anger. He tells her that if he gets sent to 'Stalag Seventeen', to stay in touch with him through his friend Tricks.

Sure enough, Toby is arrested, and taken to Stalag Seventeen- a prison camp/ghetto surrounded by zombies-very like the ghetto in *Land Of The Dead*. This place is a man-made hell-on-earth. Romero describes it as 'filled with the fury and desperation of man in his last days!' It's apathetic inhabitants lost in the pleasures of the flesh.

Outside John takes Sarah into a tunnel, and tells her about Stalag Seventeen. He says it's "home for us that don't make the grade. Us that ain't good enough to live inside The Cave. We live in our own filth, with bugs and snakes and disease and jungle fever…all the time waiting to become breakfast for the Bees."

We next see the horrific hospital in Stalag Seventeen. It's here that we meet Dr Logan from the filmed *Day Of The Dead*, very much the insane Dr Logan we know. A patient of his has just died. Logan says. "I have looked bad for four years. Everyone in the world has looked bad for four years. Thank God looks don't matter as much as they once did."

And this is where the tunnel John has been leading Sarah down leads. He takes Sarah to a place of relative safety.

The patient revives and Logan kills her expertly with his scalpel.

Sarah and John pass a structure with a sign that reads Joe's Corner Tavern. (Like the 'Stiff Drink' in *Land Of The Dead*.)

Sarah comments. "They seem to be havin' a good time. Some punishment." John answers knowingly. "You disappear in here, darlin'. You get a knife in the belly or two much shit in your veins. You get lost out here and nobody's gonna notice. Rhodes, he counts on that, it all makes food for the freezers."

They approach a hut with a sign that reads THE Ritz. (Another idea that survived into *Day Of The Dead*'s shooting script). This Ritz is different however. It's a Victorian-style doss-house on a large scale.

Back in The Cave, Two

When There's No More Room In Hell....

Red Coat zombies sit at a table attended by human technicians. One, Tonto, was a Seminole native American. In front of him is a plate of meat. Beside him is Bluto.

Inside a firing range a zombie is shooting (badly) at a target. Bub is there too, he's wearing western style gun belts similar to what Rhodes wears in the filmed *Day Of The Dead*. Bub salutes Mary. Then shoots his targets-he's actually a crack shot! Mary praises him much as Logan does in the filmed *Day Of The Dead*.

Next we see The Council Chamber in The Cave. Which Romero describes as "....a large Situations Room that is serving now as GOVERMENMENT HEADQUAURTERS. In a big, stuffed office chair behind a desk flanked with flags sits GOVERNOR HENRY DICKERSON (formerly of Florida, now of the world) AKA GASPIRILLA."

"At tables sit a dozen or so councilmen, his cronies from the old Doril Country Club, his friends, who were offered asylum in the private underground shelter and agree with everything he says."

His prosecutor Tommy Lee wants to sentence a soldier to death for stealing a radio. Gaspirilla changes the sentence to a year in Stalag Seventeen, to improve his image. The defiant prisoner would prefer to be shot. May enters the room, and the case against Toby Tyler comes up. It's clear Gaspirilla couldn't care less. It's Stalag Seventeen for Toby.

Later we see him resounding in bacchanalian splendour in his gymnasium. Indulging in every earthly pleasure while the Earth has turned to Hell! He is Nero on a massive scale! He says. "This here's the Capital O' The World! They came here...died...and went to hell....and the Devil sent 'em back as an army. Hah! General Gaspirilla's army. MY ARMY!"

Mary tells him other cities are surviving, such as Detroit and Philadelphia. He doesn't care. He wants to recruit a huge zombie army with himself at the head of it!

The following day Rhodes enters Stalag Seventeen and heads for the Ritz. He knows there's something going on and murders two people in their cots to prove he means business, and then kills the prisoner Gapirilla sentenced. Sarah tries to give herself up to stop the killings, but John stops here. He'll kill these people anyway, food for the reeks.

Toby has introduced himself to John and Sarah. He's getting Tricks to bring the equipment he needs to escape into the hospital marked with red crosses. They're afraid he's a spy but John trusts him.

In the hospital, Logan, his assistant Diesel, and Spider are leaching nitro-glycerine from dynamite. Logan is losing it badly, he has the shakes and nearly blows them up. They plan to blow up the powder magazine. A lot of different groups' schemes are about to collide violently. Logan plans to blow up the powder magazine, but Toby just wants to escape. He doesn't want to murder the two hundred plus people in The Cave, and the inhabitants of Stalag Seventeen that depend on them. This is a prime example of Romero showing both sides to the same situation-there are no clear cut Hollywood-style trite "good and bad" choices in Romero's world!

Logan however is lost in his own world of madness. He feels he's living in the biblical end-times. "We know what we must do, It is written for us in the bible-'They shall be driven from the land of the living down to the world of the dead. That is the fate of those who care nothing for God." Again, the theme of religion, good and bad, raises its head.

Given food for thought but Toby's sane humane words, John sees another way. "Datura Metel! The Devil's Trumpet. It's flower that grows on these islands. Where I come from the voodoo priests used it whenever they needed a Mickey Finn…in a sealed area it might be introduced through the ventilation system…The Devil's Trumpet blowin' the notes o' doom for the Devil's troops."

Until now they haven't been able to harvest enough plants, but Sarah remembers the place where Miguel spotted hundreds of them.

That night while making their plans, they discover that the fanatical Logan, Diesel, and Sarah have already left for The Cave. They realise their plans are compromised and they need to move tonight if Toby is to get Mary out. Now the pace really begins to speed up!

Insanely, Logan has surgically implanted the nitro-glycerine into the willing Spider to get into The Cave. On their way they meet a zombie with a hook hand (obviously lost while still warm), who wounds Logan. Diesel destroys it, and miraculously Spider doesn't explode.

Elsewhere, the other rebel group release the Datura through an air vent.

Meanwhile, Julie and an accomplice open a hatch to make their escape. Unfortunately they blunder into Logan's group, who kill her friend and take her prisoner. Logan sees this as the way in. But a guard sets off the alarm.

Gaspirilla has been having his usual party. When they hear the alarm, Rhodes takes some of his men to investigate. Gaspirilla goes back to partying as though nothing is wrong.

Tyler pretends to have captured his fellow rebels and gains access to The Cave that way. They disable the communications system which signals a general evacuation. In a system set up before the zombie uprising, all doors to the cave open so that nobody can get trapped. The Red Coat zombies are released, as are around fifty zombies from their cages in the pen. There is wholesale panic.

Outside Julie is attacked and killed. Logan, in the grip of religious mania activate the siren. This calls the wild zombies from the jungle, as they associate the siren with food. First on the menu is the crazed Logan.

There is a spectacular pitched battle between Rhodes' men and the zombies. Romero says, "for a moment he resembles Doc Logan, madness is bristling inside him."

Meanwhile, Spider and Diesel continue their suicide mission to blow the armoury. They don't want to escape the island. They want to blow it off the face of the earth.

The horde of zombies make their way into the gymnasium where Gaspirilla has been partying with his cronies.

Rhodes has spotted Mary and a nurse leading The Cave's children to safety. In a scene retained in a different form in the filmed *Day Of The Dead*, Rhodes orders his men to shoot them. Mary, and her band, walk into Bub and his Cadre of Red Coats. Amazingly, Bub simply salutes Mary, who salutes back and gives them their weapons, and changes their conditioning, so they can shoot at Rhodes and his men.

As Rhodes and his men burst in, a fire-fight begins, allowing the refugees to escape. There is a sad moment as Bub and Mary salute each other for the last time.

During all this, Gaspirilla and

When There's No More Room In Hell....

his cronies have been consumed. The party is finally over!

Diesel and Spider are still making their way to the armoury. Mary leads her party into the jungle where she meets Toby. Rhodes and his surviving men follow them, but they're cut to ribbons, and just like in the filmed *Day Of The Dead*, Rhodes is about to meet his Waterloo at the hands of Bub.

Making their way through the jungle, the rebels pass the corpse of Miguel. Sarah is amazed to find he hasn't reanimated. "Five days…and he hasn't risen." They make their way to the boat.

Back into the cave, the action is heading for an explosive climax. The confrontation between Rhodes and Bub remains much the same as in the filmed *Day Of The Dead*, save that Rhodes dies by gunfire alone. Diesel and Spider make their way to the powder magazine, where they're attacked by zombies who set off the volatile nitro-glycerine, igniting a chain reaction that sets off the powder magazine, and destroys The Cave, and much of the island with it!

On the boat, the children cheer as though they are watching fireworks. The top blows off the island like a volcano.

On the boat, Toby's friend Tricks has died from his wound. Toby moves to put a bullet in Trick's head so he can't re-animate. Sarah stops him, telling him to wait and see if its necessary.

The refugees make their way to another island to begin a new, more peaceful life. The survivors have embraced religion, and are baptised by John. They form a vigil over Tricks' body to see if he comes back. John says. "Satan ain't sent this man back. Not yet anyway, so we all hopin; that maybe he's up there with you, Lord. This might be the first decent soul we been able ta offer ya in quite a few years. We gonna pray that what seems to be happenin' here…is really happenin'…and I'm gonna take the chance and speak these words that I ain't been able to speak for so long…May he rest in peace."

They take it in turns to watch Tricks' body: "Forever" Till he turns ta dust and blows away on the wind."

With wry humour, Romero ends the unfilmed *Day Of The Dead* with the title: "THE END (I PROMISE)."!

Howard Sherman is Bub in Day of the Dead

1968, this remake is admirable. As an attempt to recreate a classic, this film is an abject failure. That is not to say that this is a particularly bad film, in fact it is a competent, at times engaging work, but alas, never inspiring. The real problem lies not with director Savini, but with the simplistic storyline which is basically a group of frightened individuals holed up in a farmhouse and fending off the advances of the zombie masses lurking outside.

It is a basic plot which doesn't lend itself easily to the remake treatment. The intrinsic restrictions are highlighted even more so as scene after scene is merely replayed from the original. Of the few changes made, Barbara (Tallman), is predictably transformed into a gun-toting Sigourney Weaver type role-model as opposed to her character's permanently catatonic state in the original, whilst only the subtle new ending and the alarming appearance of a graveyard zombie in the opening scenes, provide any germs of originality. At times you almost long for the jerky, adrenaline-pumping immediacy of Romero's hand-held camera from the original in favour of Savini's (too) carefully composed dolly shots.

Savin's remake shifts focus by supplanting the earlier film's 1960's race struggle motif with the 1990's gender struggle. Ben (Tony Todd) and

Pictures this page: Night of the Living Dead 1990 style

1990 was to be the next pivotal moment in the Romero zombie pantheon, albeit this time as writer as his then favoured special effects guru, Tom Savini, stepped up to the directorial plate for the first time. As an attempt to earn money to repay the "cheated" contributors to the original *Night of the Living Dead* in

Harry (Tom Towles) still argue as to whether they should stay barricaded upstairs in the farmhouse or retreat to the basement to avoid the zombies attacking outside. There's a key moment when, as the males argue the merits of each case, Barbara quietly discards her 'feminine' skirt in favour of some jeans and takes the initiative, unlike her character in the original. "They're so slow… we could just walk past them and we wouldn't even have to run" she observes of the zombies, injecting some practical common sense into the heady mix of testosterone.

In effect, the gender roles are reversed from the Hollywood stereotype as the women are represented as decisive, resourceful and independent, contrasting with indecisive, immature males who you feel are threatened as much by Barbara and her ilk as they are by the ravenous zombies swarming the farmhouse.

Curiously restrained in terms of violence, (perhaps because Savini was wary of simply being accused of directing special effects to the detriment of all else?), the closing stages feature the local rednecks pitting zombie versus zombie in mock fights and hanging zombies upside down and using them for target practise – the kind of human cruelty to be amplified later by Romero in both *Land of the Dead* and *Diary of the Dead*.

With screaming too often confused for emotion, especially with

Barbara (Patricia Tallman) takes aim in Tom Savini's Night of the Living Dead remake

Ben and Harry's protracted arguing, Richard Harrington writing in the Washington Post provides a germane summary – "This *Night of the Living Dead* is resurrected, but it's never brought to life."

After fourteen years of lying dormant with the assumption that Savini's competent but uninspiring entry had all but sucked the life from Romero's zombie series, step forward one Zach Snyder's *Dawn of the Dead* (2004), to breathe new impetus into the zombie cycle. The smart move by Snyder here was not to simply regurgitate a piercing critique of consumerism as with Romero's original *Dawn of the Dead* (1978), preferring instead to concentrate on greater action and considerably faster zombies as with Danny Boyle's *28 Days Later* (2002).

The opening scenes depict a convincing collapse of the social infrastructure as emergency TV broadcasts urgently warn about the 'plague' enveloping America. There's an incredible aerial shot – not of the expected urban sprawl but the leafy suburbs, the very heartland of the American Dream now shown to

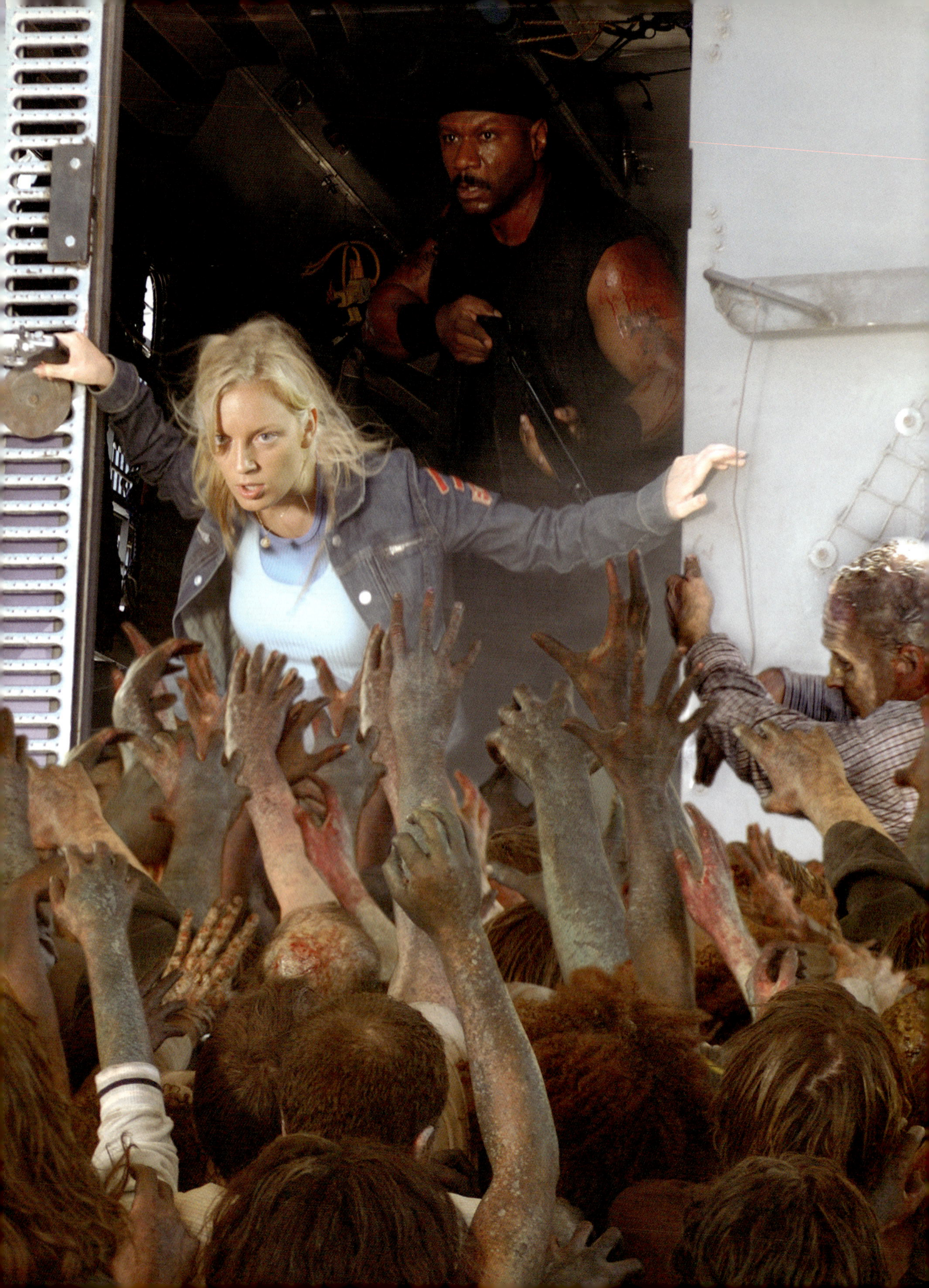

When There's No More Room In Hell....

be rapidly engulfed in flames and chaos. Everywhere people are running, shooting indiscriminately at anyone they suspect to be zombies as cars crash, homes burn and people die, all perforated with the incessant TV broadcasts now indicating this to be a global epidemic.

Whereas' Romero's original film delineates two groups of survivors fighting each other as well as the omnipresent zombies, to offer a further dynamic, Snyder reverts to pitting the human ensemble against the attacking zombies but, as Snyder has dispensed with the consumerism satire as well, the mall setting becomes almost incidental and our sympathies again turn towards the zombies who cannot be held responsible for their behaviour whereas' the humans most definitely can, and so reducing the impact of any inherent 'good versus evil' axis.

Snyder's new clique of survivors are in fact shown to have a diverse range of motives and personalities, embodying the Nietzschian concept of 'immorality' – where a good person can be a 'creator of values' as morality is dictated by human nature but this nature is not universal. One individual's nature is different to the next so people follow differing conceptions. The dying value systems depicted so convincingly in the opening anarchy, render there to be no virtue in obeying God so the fictitious promise of greater rewards in the next life cannot be used as an excuse for the subjugation of the spirit in this one any longer. The 'superman' or 'ubermensch' premise of Nietzsche rejects this in favour of carving out one's own place in the world.

As an original *Dawn of the Dead* survivor, Ken Foree's cameo here as a TV evangelist allows him to signal civilisations decline and also reprise his iconic lines from Romero's opus; "Hell is overflowing, and Satan is sending his damned to us. Why? God is punishing us. You have sex out of wedlock. You kill your unborn. You have man on man relations, same sex marriages. How do you think your God will judge you? Well, friends, now we know. When there's no more room in Hell, the dead will walk the earth." Glen (R.D. Reid), who we learn played the organ in church delivers his own doctrine; "It was just a job…I don't believe in God. I don't see how anyone could."

Those waiting to be judged, or perhaps aspiring to their own new ideals – "the lightning out of the dark cloud of man" as Nietzsche would have us believe, include; Michael (Jake Webber) who is a shrewd, intelligent protagonist, who deviates between recalling a life before zombies to being

This page & left shows Ana (Sarah Polley) - one of the main protagonists in Zach Snyder's revisionist Dawn of the Dead

The Dead Walk

shown as having the ruthless streak necessary to survive. Ana (Sarah Polley) a nurse, who is bright and composed rather than just the obligatory female screamer and Kenneth (Ving Rhames), an ex-marine now gun-toting cop who becomes the group's de facto leader.

Kenneth also supplies some of the film's bleak humour by communicating with Andy (Bruce Bohne), a gun store owner across the mall, who transmits messages by using a dry wipe board from the top of his roof. He also plays 'sniper' in shooting at the 'celebrity look alike' zombies below – "Tell him to shoot Burt Reynolds!"

In amongst this eclectic mix we are also introduced to Andre (Mekhi Phifer), a reforming street hustler whose hopes of redemption lie with his pregnant girlfriend Luda (Inna Korobkina) – ultimately proving to be false hopes with the subsequent birth of their 'zombie' baby in a well executed scene.

Completing, or should that be 'competing' with the survivors are the triumvirate of security guards CJ (Michael Kelly), Terry (Kevin Zegers) and Bart (Michael Barry) – CJ offering the couch potato outlook on humanity, detached from the collapse of the society he vicariously experiences via the banks of monitors he gazes into, in a numbing display on de-sensitivity. This trio, especially in the form of the selfish CJ, would prefer to keep the mall to themselves rather than risk letting in other survivors – the nearest Snyder comes to evoking the human conflict intrinsic to the original.

It is the sheer size of this ensemble, to almost soap opera proportions, which merely succeeds in dissipating the tension of the situation as there are simply too many characters on which to focus, diluting any personal interplay and dynamics. The racial divide so prevalent in *Night of the Living Dead* (1968) evolves here into a strictly class or cultural divide with both Kenneth and Andre as mixed race Americans, generating the most tension within the group and its' fractious, continually expanding factions.

There's a palpable sense of danger emitted from the scenes where first, the daring rescue of Andy from his store across the mall is attempted, and then subsequently, as the group raid his stock for firearms to use in the battle to come. The duo of customised 'battle buses' that the survivors embellish to aid their escape from the mall creates a compelling sequence as they finally

Dawn of the Dead (2004)

smash their way out of the mall, heading out on to the open road to temporary freedom while making for the nearby marina.

The complete lack of governmental presence, indeed of any authority figures or response in both *Land of the Dead* and *Dawn of the Dead*, is a factor perhaps unexpectedly addressed in the *Resident Evil* trilogy, whilst the "survivors" seeking sanctuary by boat on the ocean waves, draws a suitably nihilistic coda from Snyder as zombies emerge from the undergrowth of the 'deserted' island they pull into.

Bouyed by the almost universal critical acclaim which greeted the film's release, Snyder went on to direct the stylish Spartan army meets graphic novel concept of *300* (2006) and has recently announced the co-production with wife Deborah of the intriguing *Army of the Dead* (slated for 2009

The mall is once again home to a new group of survivors in Zach Snyder's Dawn of the Dead as shown in both pictures on this page

release), based on the premise of a father searching a zombie-ravaged Las Vegas for his daughter - all backed by the mighty bucks of Warner Brothers.

Whether Snyder can add to the vision shown in his *Dawn of the Dead* remake remains to be seen, but one thing is for sure, Romero has now shown his intent to embellish his own zombie mythos with his eagerly awaited return to the *Dead* cycle with

The Dead Walk

2005's *Land of the Dead*.

"THE DEAD SHALL INHERIT THE EARTH."

"His dealing with graphic violence started an entire trend in horror films. Before that point, horror films were usually about rubber monsters or hands groping in the dark. George revolutionised that."

John Carpenter

"Ethnically and sexually integrated, pro-feminist, gay-friendly, anti-macho and sceptical about capitalism. His work represents the progressive wing of a sometimes reactionary genre."

Baseline's Encyclopedia of Film

Land of the Dead is the fourth instalment in George A. Romero's highly influential saga that began in 1968 with *Night Of The Living Dead*.

BACKGROUND

It's fair to say that Romero, who's only experience in features at this time was as a nineteen year old grip on Hitchcock's *North by Northwest*, didn't expect *Night of the Living Dead* to be put on the American Library of Congress' prestigious National Film Registry, considering he shot the film with unknowns in thirty shooting days staggered over a seven month period. Even then he had a clear vision, he "meant to draw a parallel between what people are becoming and operating on many levels of insanity clear only to themselves."

Romero was influenced by pre-code E.C comics, such films as *The Invisible Invaders* (1953), *Carnival of Souls* (1960) and *Plague of the Zombies* (1966). He was also inspired by the way Orson Welles had used the reportage qualities of radio to scare a previous generation of Americans with his broadcast of *War of the Worlds* in 1938. His biggest influence was Richard Matheson's 1954 book *I Am Legend* (filmed first in 1964 with Vincent Price as *The Last Man On Earth/L'Ultio Uomo Della Terra*, and again in 1971 with Charlton Heston, as *The Omega Man*, most recently, to appear under the *I Am Legend* title with Will Smith in 2007.)

Romero has made no secret of his influences, "I like Matheson's books and was inspired by some of his novels. I had a similar idea. The old becomes the new and vice-versa, like the mentally disturbed becoming the rational ones instead. I decided that *Night of the Living Dead* was going to be a far more extravagant and fantastic plot, one step beyond the last human being in a society of vampires."

LAND OF THE DEAD

It would be almost two decades after *Day of The Dead* before Romero would return to his beloved zombie saga due to the resurgence in interest in zombie films, in a supreme irony brought about by films inspired by Romero's work such as *28 Days Later* and remakes of his world such as Zack Snyder's fine *Dawn Of The Dead* redux.

Land Of The Dead begins with the old Universal logo, in a nice nod to the studio that gave the world so many classic monsters, now with Romero's zombies on board the circle is complete! The atmospheric black and white title credits (which invoke happy memories of Romero's 1968 debut) lead into a montage sequence-'SOME TIME AGO' quickly establishing the background to the zombie uprising. Over monochrome scenes of zombies devouring flesh and general chaos, a series of voices merge together to give the story so far-"unburied human corpses are returning to life and feeding on the living.

This is not only a regional or

When There's No More Room In Hell....

Romero returns to the zombie genre with a smash in Land of the Dead

local phenomenon. Cities are under siege. If these creatures ever develop the power to think, to reason, even in the most primitive way…People are said to be establishing outposts in big cities, raiding small rural towns for supplies like outlaws…" Then we move from black and white to colour 'TODAY'. This an example of storytelling at it's best- quickly, stylishly and economically, Romero has set the stage, now it only remains for his rotting creations to take their places in this macabre dance of the dead.

We don't have long to wait. The first colour shot of *Land Of The Dead* is an arrow sign bearing the ironic word EATS! (Nothing more certain in Romero's post-apocalypse world-there are always the eaters, the eaten, and the wiley few, the survivors, in his dark world divided into the quick and the dead). Romero shows us a town of the undead-where the inhabitants are still going through the same motions they did in their 'warm' lives. It's their town, and is a scene of great pathos, these creatures are bothering nobody, and seem unaware of any outside threat. It's a scene we've seen on our television screens for real so often in recent years, innocent people going about their business, suddenly sucked up in carnage for the gain of others.

Thus, a zombie brass band tries to torture a tune from tarnished instruments, an undead couple stumble rather forlornly up the street, a re-animated cheerleader still carries her pom-poms, ready for a game that will never be played. Most significantly, we see the towering figure of a zombie gas-station attendant, whose overalls bear the name Big Daddy. Romero has often portrayed African-American characters in sympathetic roles, and Big Daddy (Eugenie Clark) continues that theme.

Then we see Riley Denbo (Simon Baker) watching the zombies with a colleague. He knows the zombies in this town are behaving differently to any he's encountered before, he comments the zombies 'used to be us, trying to learn to be us again." His friend is scornful, 'some germ or demon might have gotten those things us up and walking but they're not like us…it's like they're pretending to be alive." Riley replies cynically, "Yeah. Like what we're doing, pretending to be alive."

Romero then cuts to an awesome scene, a devastated wasteland, mountains of garbage, some burning. It's here we see Cholo DeMora (John Leguizamo), Riley's second-in-command, for the first time. Cholo spots a very decayed zombie, and puts a dart from an airgun into it. As Cholo and his companions add more rubbish to the mountains there already, we see blood flowing from one of the crates

The imposing Dead Reckoning armoured vehicle which nearly gave Land of the Dead an alternative title

they're tipping. Foxy comments "whole lotta trash', to which Cholo answers 'trick is not to get in it." Clearly, he's dumping more than household refuse for somebody.

Then Romero takes us back to the zombie's town, called Union Town before the zombie uprising.. We meet Riley's friend Charlie Houk (Robert Joy), for a second we think he's a "Stench" too, but he's living but badly scarred by fire. Riley tell him they're going to put "flowers in the graveyard", a reference to the fireworks they launch to distract the zombies while the humans raid. Charlie in his innocent fashion says, "these are sky-flowers." Riley replies "That's why I love you Charlie, because you still believe in Hell."

Then we see Dead Reckoning (one of *Land Of The Dead*'s alternative titles). It's an awesome, armoured, zombie killing machine, armed to the teeth with rockets and, machine guns. It looks like a refugee from *Mad Max*... Zombie killing is it's business…and business is good!

Having dumped the trash, Cholo joins the rest of the raiders, he finds the whole hellish situation a huge joke, "hey Riley, looks like God left the phone off the hook!" Riley tells Cholo it's his last night and he doesn't want anyone dying on his watch. Cholo tells Riley he's not dumping these "recycled delinquents on him" because it's his last night too. Both Charlie and Riley wonder why. Cholo takes the time to make fun of Charlie then he takes off to search for 'essential supplies.'

A barrage of fireworks distracts the zombies ("stenches can't take their eyes off of them"), then Riley's team move in to loot the town. Big Daddy tries fruitlessly to get his fellow zombies to take their eyes off the fireworks. Then the mercenaries cut a swathe of needless destruction through the town, because distracted by the "skyflowers", the zombies were no threat. This is

Picture opposite: Big Daddy (Eugene Clark) in Land of the Dead

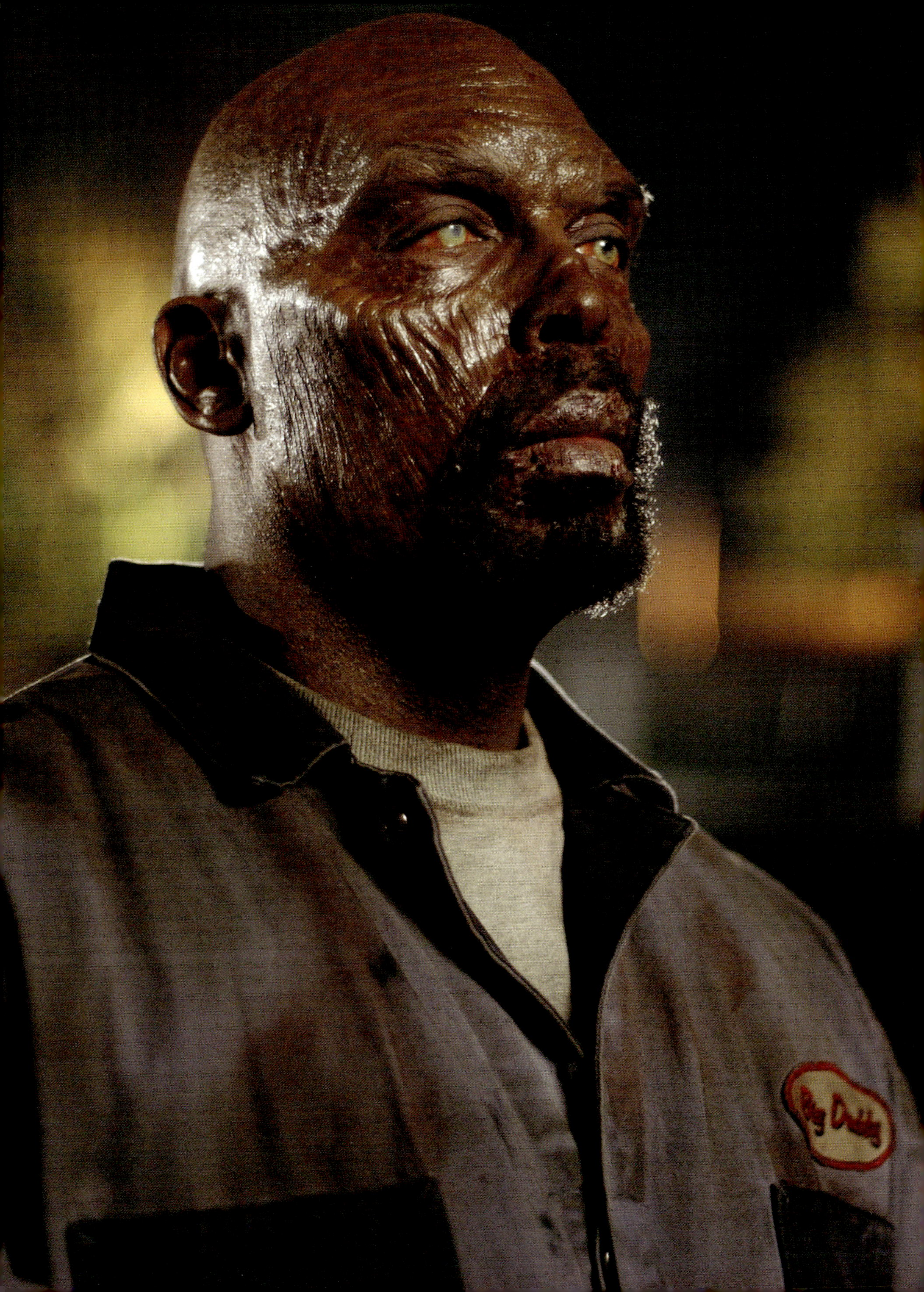
Big Daddy

The machiavellian Kaufman (Dennis Hopper) in Romero's Land of the Dead

film in Canada, the city is clearly Romero's beloved Pittsburgh). It's similar idea to John Carpenter's classic *Escape From New York* (One expanded to encompass an entire country in Neil Marshall's excellent *Doomsday*). Romero here merges two parallels, that of both post and pre 9/11 America. Pre-9/11 in Romero's wry comment on America's "shock and awe" tactics

Dead Reckoning is navigated by a character called Pretty Boy (Joanne Boland), who, while undoubtedly pretty, is certainly no boy. (In the original script, she wears a jacket with the words "Pretty Boy" on the back, having killed it's original owner for trying to make a pass at her! Feminism post-apocalypse style!).

We discover what Cholo's "essential supplies" are-cigars and booze to further his own ambitions. For this he gets an inexperienced kid killed! Contrast Cholo's behaviour with Big Daddy's grief at the unnecessary death's of his own people, and we truly see who the monsters really are.

Leaving the zombie's town devastated, the human raiders leave like so many times before…but this time things are different.

This time Big Daddy sees where Dead Reckoning is heading. He sees the neon glow of Fiddler's Green on the distant skyline and leads his people in search of vengeance.

The city Dead Reckoning is returning to is protected by water on two sides and an electric fence on another. (Despite shooting the the notion that, protected by both technology and water, no threat can penetrate the city. And post 9/11-in that the inhabitants of this city of the damned are ruled by fear. Anything goes for the powers that be, what options do the citizens have, tyranny within and the living dead without.

Back in the city, we see a video advertising the luxurious apartment block of Fiddler's Green. (It's name gives a hint of the shaky reality of the survivor's existence . Fiddler's Green was traditionally a pie-in-the-sky heaven for sailors, a fantasy that allowed them to get through their hard and drab existence).

Inside the city is a virtual police state. There is unrest in the ghetto. The gap between rich and poor mirrors the one that really exists in America today. Riley brings antibiotics for his friend Mulligan's son. Mulligan used to work for Riley before he realised what was going on, he refers to Riley as bringing in "toothpicks for the bastards to pick at their gums." Riley finds his deal for buying a car to take himself and Charlie to Canada has fallen through, and he goes to investigate the deal's broker, a dwarf who runs the city's "entertainments".

Unbelievably, the zombies are being exploited for entertainment. Simon Pegg and Edgar Wright, (whose fine zombie comedy was a big hit with Romero) cameo as photo zombies, chained up for the thrill-seeking rich to have their photos taken with. There are also zombies as paintball targets, as well as the more obvious alcohol, sex and drugs on sale. Everything possible in fact, to keep the people distracted from the reality waiting to devour them outside the city.

There is also a 'zombie pit', a 21st century version of the foul bear, cock, and dog fighting pits of previous centuries. Two zombies are selected for the pit, and coloured coded so the punters can take bets on them. Now, zombies don't fight each other (unlike the living humans), so usually an unfortunate dog or cat is on the menu, but tonight is different. Using methods of appeasing the mob that would have been familiar to the audience of a Roman arena, the zombies have a live human to fight over in the shape of Slack (the lovely Asia Argento, whose father Dario collaborated with Romero on both *Dawn Of The Dead* and the Poe-tribute *Two Evil Eyes*).

Slack puts up a spirited fight, clearly she's got great spirit, but she's unarmed save for her fists. Riley and Charlie save her, and end up being thrown into jail with her by the authorities. Slack tells her story, how she ended up in the pit for helping Mulligan and his friends, and that she had trained for the militia when the authorities decided she'd be better deployed as a hooker. Riley doesn't want to know, "everyone's got a story and I'm sick of them." She asks him what his story is and he replies "I don't have a story…nothing bad every happened to me." They are interrupted by the sight of the now-arrested Mulligan being dragged into a cell.

Meanwhile outside, the city, Big Daddy leads his people ever closer

This page & overleaf: Slack (Asia Argento) makes her presence felt in Land of the Dead

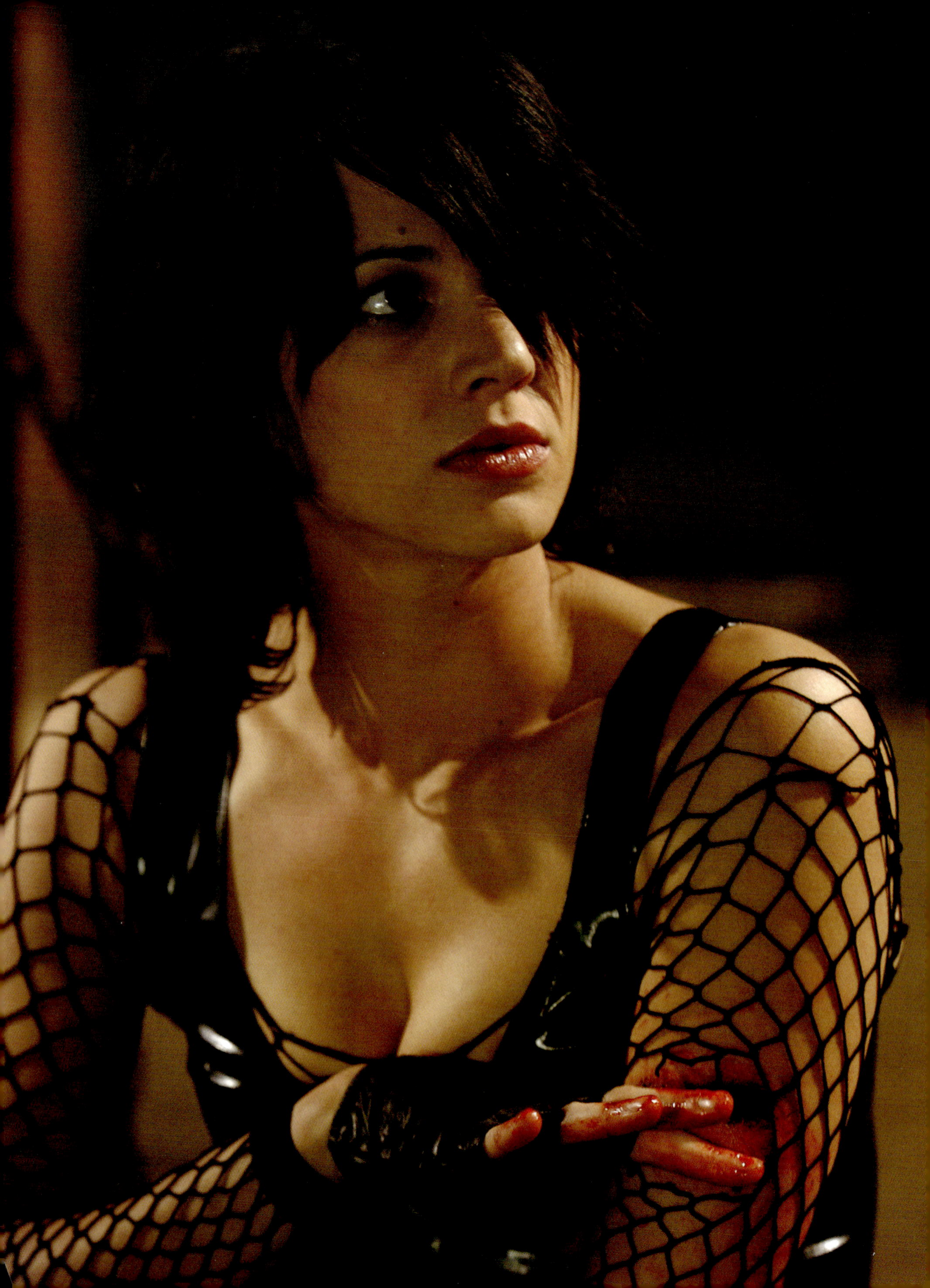

When There's No More Room In Hell....

to the promised land. There is a primal scream of horror from Big Daddy when he finds zombies used as target practise by the humans.

Meanwhile, Cholo has entered Fiddler's Green, to deliver the case of champagne that was paid for in blood to the city's ruler. Romero shows us the rich at play, shooting, enjoying fine food. It's hard to believe the other survivors live in a ghetto, while outside the city the dead walk. There a very poignant shot of a wooden bird in a cage. Even a gilded cage is still a prison. It's here, in a scene cut from the theatrical version, Cholo shows another side to his personality, when he rescues a woman from her recently resurrected husband. (Who had committed suicide-clearly even in Fiddler's Green, reality can make an appearance.)

Finally Cholo reaches the penthouse suite that is home to Kaufman (Dennis Hopper). From his Tower Of Spite, Kaufman and his rich cronies go about their everyday business as though everything is normal. Thus Kaufman survey's his kingdom, smoking a cigar and listening to classical music. Kaufman is clearly based on G.W Bush, using the (literal) fear of the enemy-at-the-gates to rule his kingdom of the blind like a Roman despot, right down to using games and vices to appease the masses.

Cholo hopes with the money he's made doing Kaufman's dirty work (He knows where the bodies are buried, after all, he buried them). It's a forlorn hope, nothing has changed, the same class system that existed before the zombie uprising is being maintained. Romero shows this cleverly by the simple act of Cholo pouring champagne into tumblers, and for Kaufman to pour his into a champagne flute. Kaufman turns Cholo down, he's good enough to do his dirty work but not live in the same place. Cholo threatens Kaufman with exposure, Kaufman couldn't care less, calling security and telling them simply, "I won't be needing this man anymore." Cholo however, overpowers the security guard, and gathering together Foxy, Mouse, and Pretty Boy, goes to take out Dead Reckoning.

There is a tense moment at the maintenance depot outside the city where Dead Reckoning is stored, the duty officer notices that Cholo's paperwork is from the day before. It looks like Cholo is going to shoot him, but he's saved the trouble by Big Daddy and his zombies who attack the depot en-masse. "That's our way out", Cholo tells Pretty Boy. The soldiers put up a good fight, but outnumbered, they're torn apart. Romero does not let the side down with the carnage, the zombies devouring the unfortunate

Chow down Romero style in Land of the Dead

The Dead Walk

soldiers in a variety of imaginative ways! Big Daddy calls a halt however, the City is his goal and he's had enough of human distraction.

Cholo phones Kaufman and threatens to shell the Green if he doesn't pay him $5 million dollars by midnight. A worried Kaufman ends the phone call. Asked by one of his cronies if there is trouble, Kaufman replies with classic understatement, "In a world where the dead are returning to life, the word 'trouble' loses much of its meaning." When told to pay Cholo off, he trots out a familiar line, "We don't negotiate with terrorists. We have other options."

In their prison cell, Slack comments to Charlie, "You take care of him", "He pulled me out of the fire. It was bad, just look at me, you can tell it was bad." One of Romero's great strengths is his characterisations, he lets the character develop organically, drawing from real life, rather than copying existing stereotypes.

Kaufman has Riley released from prison, we learn that it was Kaufman that prevented him leaving, "You're a popular man." It was Riley who designed the $2 million dollar Dead Reckoning, and Kaufman knows he's the best option for getting it back. Riley agrees, as long as Charlie and Slack can come with him.

In the meantime, Cholo has sent Mouse to the river to await delivery of the money Kaufman has no intention of sending.

Kaufman sends three of his own soldiers, Manolete, Pilsbury and Motown, along with Riley. They are there to ensure Dead Reckoning is returned to Kaufman. They make their way to the vehicle depot to get some transport. Riley tries to alert Kaufman to the problem the zombies pose telling him, there are "walkers, moving toward the city." Kaufman ignores the problem, "They're mindless walking corpses and many of us will be too if you don't stay focused on the task at hand." His message delivered to Riley, Kaufamn looks into the uncertain darkness and delivers the classic line, "zombies, man, they creep me out."

At the vehicle depot, Manolete is bitten. Riley tells Slack his brother was bitten, "less than an hour before he turned…I shot him." Surprised, Slack say, "you said nothing bad happened to you." "That was my brother." Realising what will happen to Manolete, she puts him out of his misery.

Kaufman makes preparation to move himself and the elite from the Green. When asked what about the others, he replies with obvious contempt, "All the others can be replaced by another." He will brook no arguments, praising his 'achievements'

"Alas poor Yorick"…. Land of the Dead has a "Bard" moment

with the city, "I took the people off the streets by giving them games and vices."

Outside the city Riley reveals to Slack he has a homing device hidden on dead reckoning. In a sad moment, Slack reveals she's not been out of the city "since it was a city."

Meanwhile the zombies, have found Mouse, who, in a manner reminiscent of Rhodes in *Day Of The Dead*, is torn apart while still living. The thousands of zombies stand in front of the river, it's an awesome scene, illuminated by the full moon. They're unsure of how to proceed from here. Then, seeing the reflection of Fiddler's Green in the water, Big Daddy takes a leap of faith and walks into the river. Of course being dead, he cannot drown! (Originally Romero planned to show the zombies walking across the river bed to the city, but a similar scene in *Pirates Of The Caribbean* put paid to that). The sight of the zombies rising from the water however is just as effective and awe-inspiring."

This page & overleaf: zombies rise from the depths in Land of the Dead

Riley has regained Dead Reckoning from Cholo, who, though wounded, laughs wryly at the sounds of battle coming from the city. Pilsbury has thrown his lot in with Riley.

The zombies tear through the city, allowing the imaginative kind of gore we've come to expect from Romero, including a soldier blown up by a grenade held in his own severed hand, a human wishbone, and an extreme removal of a body piercing. Cult hero and special effects guru Tom Savini makes a welcome appearance as an undead version of his character Blades from *Dawn Of The Dead*. Kaufman cannot accept what is happening, reality has intruded bloodily into his carefully constructed facade, "you have no right!".

Cholo is bitten, something he takes with black humour, "nothing ever works out." Foxy offers Cholo a mercy killing, but Cholo refuses, "I always wanted to see how the other half lives."

Dead Reckoning races towards the city, Riley needs to lower a drawbridge to gain access. While the zombies pick up everything they can use as a tool and head for Fiddler's Green itself, while Cholo makes his way for the Green too, to confront Kaufman. The zombies smash their way into the green, and the survivors run from the building, only to find themselves trapped by the electric fence. Riley lowers the drawbridge, decapitating the gatekeeper zombie (played Greg Nicotero, *Land Of The Dead*'s second unit director, make-up artist and special effects supervisor, he also played Private Johnson in *Day Of The Dead*, and the Surgeon Zombie in *Diary Of The Dead*) in the process.

The sound of undead nails scarping off Dead Reckoning's armour must have been as unbearable to Pretty Boy as it is to us because she takes the time to mow the zombies down (though one of them has crawled onto the roof. Dead Reckoning releases a barrage of firework but the shock and awe no longer works, and the zombies turn

on the surviving elite from Fiddler's Green. Kaufman intends to flee, but both Big Daddy and Cholo prevent him. Kaufman dies in a fiery explosion with his now-useless money.

Dead Reckoning arrives...too late, they put the zombie's victims out of their misery. There is a scene of quiet pathos, has it all being for nothing? Then they see the survivors emerge. Mulligan and his people emerge. Pretty Boy spots Big Daddy leading his zombies away, she's about to turn Dead Reckoning's guns on them, but Riley stops her, "they're just looking for a place to go, same as us."

Dead Reckoning fires its remaining fireworks and heads for Canada, ending *Land Of The Dead* on a high note, and leaving an opening for a sequel exploring what happens to the survivors.

GENESIS & THEMES

Reflecting the higher budget ($15 million), *Land Of The Dead* is Romero's first zombie film not to be cast entirely of unknowns. In the city there is potential anarchy on the inside and potential evolution on the outside. Romero calls it a society built on class. It's a familiar Romero theme, people not communicating, ignoring

Originally entitled *Twilight of the Dead*, then *Dead Reckoning* (after the Armoured vehicle the film's mercenaries use), the film became *Land of the Dead* at John Carpenter's suggestion. The film has been coming for a long time. Romero's original idea was to do a story that was further on from the zombie uprising, where there would be fewer people but fewer zombies too as they'd all have rotted away. The zombies would be wandering around like the homeless or A.I.D.S victims.

Back in the 90's, Romero had commented-"I don't know what zombies in the year 2000 will be like.

I had this dream, a nightmare rather, of the homeless walking through the deserted streets of an American metropolis. People were eating and drinking in restaurants, and paying no attention to what was going on in the middle of the street. If I were to make a fourth *Dead* movie, I might refer to this nightmare as a source of inspiration."

Romero sees his zombie films as a platform to comment on the decade they are made in and post 9/11, the drafts of *Land*'s scripts became more political, a comment on what was turning into America's new normal. A government that had thought it was protected by water. *Land of the Dead* is about a city that's protected on all sides by rivers, and the citizens are able to defend it by putting a barricade at the base of the river, and pretend that the zombies aren't a real threat.

The danger with the "new normal" is that it is far from normal. Romero thinks of the Fiddler's Green enclave as "Bush's America", ignoring the fundamental problem, living around it, almost profiting. The humans aren't communicating, the system is collapsing. Everyone is working to their own agenda, not willing to accept that the old world is gone. It's this theme that gives *Land* the punch lacking in most horror films. Romero knows that for horror to hit home it has to be personal. This, as in it's predecessors, is Romero's greatest achievement in *Land of the Dead*.

Given the relatively lengthy hiatus between *Day of the Dead* and *Land of the Dead*, Romero moved with some alacrity to bring the independently produced *Diary of the Dead* (2007) before us. This is a film which very much divides opinion due to the style of filming and has garnered a 'love it' or 'hate it' reaction from many audiences. By eschewing the avowedly studio-bound origins and production of *Land of the Dead* for a much more guerrilla style of filming Romero draws inspiration from *The Last Broadcast* (1998), *The Blair Witch Project* (1999), *[REC]* (2007) and *Cloverfield* (2008).

The dead are among us in Romero's latest zombie film, Diary of the Dead

With its' deliberately shaky, handheld camera and long takes, *Diary* is very much a contemporary film, rooted in the media-savvy age and with a deliberately documentary-style approach. As Romero himself explained to the expectant masses during the film's Hollywood premiere at Screamfest; "I loved doing *Diary*, it's really a liberating experience to make the film the way you want to. I got the idea because of the explosion of media out there. Everybody's a reporter; everybody's on *MySpace* and *YouTube*. There's all these millions and millions of voices and I wanted to do something that reflected that. So, anyway it's really one from the heart. I love it and I hope you do too".

Following the format of a "found" video diary, we are introduced to a group of student filmmakers who become embroiled in a real life zombie apocalypse whilst filming their own low budget horror film. Revolving around the premise of life and art imitating each other "this is the end of the world (filmed) as a home movie, both chilling and funny" as critic Philip French has observed. Very much behind the camera is aspiring director Jason Creed (Josh Close), his girlfriend Debra (Michelle Morgan), aided by an ensemble cast which includes special effects man Tony (Shawn Roberts), lead actor Ridley (Philip Riccio), scream queen and feisty Texan Tracy (Amy Lalonde), technician Eliot (Joe Dinicol), Winnebago driver Mary (Tatiana Maslany) and a cynical, booze-riddled professor, Maxwell (Scott Wentworth).

Romero alters the dynamics within *Diary* by rebooting his zombie series – not from the end point of *Land* but from the start point of *Night of the Living Dead*, as intermittent news reports play out the ensuing chaos of the zombie epidemic which now engulfs America and beyond. The truly global nature of the media is now fully integrated into the film as mobile phone video, TV news footage and internet film clips, are all incorporated by Jason into his 'The Death of Death' news documentary – at one point he ingeniously splices in CCTV footage of the group's arrival at a 'safe-house' populated by ex National Guard members, who seize upon the power vacuum created to install their own brand of lawlessness, an oligarchy based on looting, firearms and the mantra that possession equals ownership.

It is as the students begin their journey back from their film shoot and into the zombie-populated areas that the various character foibles begin to unravel. Whilst the traumatised Mary tries to kill herself after being unable to cope with running over zombies as she drives the Winnebago, Jason, in contrast, appears self-absorbed and desensitised in comparison. As they struggle to find medical help for Mary in a now deserted hospital (save for the assorted zombies they encounter),

When There's No More Room In Hell....

Jason's overriding concern is for charging his camera battery – "I can't leave without the camera – the camera is the whole thing" he pleads only to be admonished by Debra – "Getting help is the whole thing". Jason's apparent disregard for human life is mirrored by an earlier news clip where a reviving corpse on an ambulance trolley unduly flusters a TV news reporter – "She's supposed to be dead" is her withering response to the inconvenience of having to alter her live news report.

"It didn't happen if it didn't happen on film", Debra screams at one point – perfectly encapsulating the "celebrity culture" we now live in where even the most mundane "reality" TV shows are craved to somehow elevate our existence and give it 'meaning'. Likewise, Jason clamours for footage, to create content to counter the lies and misinformation disseminated via the mainstream media, in effect, creating his own 'truth'. His overzealous pursuit of this 'truth' is none better illustrated when his priorities at the safe-house involve getting online in order to edit and upload footage for his documentary, rather than trying to contact family members to see if they are still alive.

Jason's mistaken quest for the truth endangers Tracy, when having sought sanctuary in Ridley's sprawling family mansion estate, the still in-costume actor, swathed in mummy apparel but now decidedly zombiefied, chases the ingénue through the nearby woods in an ironic echo of *Diary*'s opening scenes showing the low budget horror film shoot. "See, I told you dead things moved slow" Jason shouts smugly, more concerned with hiding behind his camera lens, eyes clamped firmly to the viewfinder, rather than attempting to save Tracy, rendering him as heartless, ditto emotionless, as the zombies he continues unflinchingly to film.

This callous trait proves to be infectious however, as we also see Debra & Tony using the cameras at different stages to film the unfolding carnage – "Take this, it's too easy to use" Debra pleads at one point handing over her camera – a profound link to an earlier scene where Maxwell

And now the screaming starts - *Diary of the Dead*

The Dead Walk

discards a handgun uttering an identical comment. With both devices you point and shoot and the inference here is that the over enthusiastic pursuit of both can be equally destructive.

Jason's subsequent demise at the hands of the mummy, doesn't end the filming however as Debra and Tony take up the mantle, their almost robotic movements behind the cameras lending an icy conclusion to both the human condition and the film. Even without the aid of camcorders, the action can still be viewed inside the mansion via the ubiquitous security cameras which proliferate the building, whilst that particularly twenty-first century conceit, the panic room, is where the survivors hole up at the climax.

The most chilling image is reserved for the final moments as we see footage of some of the local rednecks out in the countryside, decapitating a zombie, hanging by a noose under a viaduct, by taking pot-shots with rifles 'just for fun'. As Debra ponders on the commentary "Are we worth saving? You tell me." Given recent events, be they the Iraq war and the ongoing prisoner mistreatment investigations, or the governmental atrocities perpetuated by the authorities in Zimbabwe, the message is loud and clear – that no matter how grave any given situation is, the human race always has the capacity to make it even worse.

Whilst the importance of media and media manipulation prays heavily on our minds in *Diary*, it is good to see that Romero still manages a vestige of black humour amongst the mayhem on show. There is the children's party clown who tears into a victim after zombification (shades of the custard pie fight in *Dawn of the Dead* perhaps?), the deaf Amish farmer who communicates by message cards – also overcoming his peaceful nature in order to help decimate the zombie hordes who attack his farm. There's also the zombie 'goldfish' who stand motionless in the mansion swimming pool like static members of a synchronised swimming class!

It is also good to see that Romero still manages to pull out his requisite array of outré death scenes in *Diary*, ranging from one zombie whose brains are fried in literally eye-popping fashion courtesy of an A&E ward defibrillator, the double-cleaver demise of the farmer and zombie recalling Mario Bava's inventive double-spearing in *Bay of Blood* (1971), and the acid-rotting dispatch of one zombie before our eyes. Romero also contributes a neat inversion on his celebrated night-time farmhouse scenes in *Night of the Living Dead*

Tony (Shawn Roberts), Debra (Michelle Morgan) & Eliot (Joe Dinicol) with the ever-present camera in Diary of the Dead

as the zombies lay siege to the occupants, only in *Diary*, the equally voracious attacks happen in broad daylight.

Although the much vaunted use of the handheld camera is far from groundbreaking news here – it is even somewhat trailing in the wake of the flawed but inveigling UK entry *The Zombie Diaries* (2006), the intriguing aspect is how little we actually see of the main protagonist, Jason – he is almost permanently fixed to his camera lens as if it is an extension of his body *a la* the homicidal Carl in *Peeping Tom* (1960) – we see the action literally via his own POV shots.

Suicidal tendencies played out in Diary of the Dead

In fact, if there is a criticism here, it would be that the remainder of the ensemble are in no way as clearly defined as Jason, save for his self-assured girlfriend Debra, who emerges as perhaps the most confident and sassy heroine of the entire *Dead* series. That said, the notion that a survivor would calmly and dispassionately shoot, assemble and edit footage of their friends being slaughtered, then reanimated, all set to music cues and voiceovers, may be a stretch too far to contemplate and the sporadic narration itself which informs the film, also veers towards the intrusive.

In essence, the grim conclusion simply begs the question that as we stare squarely at the death of civilisation, is there any reason to want to survive? *Diary* most probably raises more questions on this core theme than provides answers. With a sequel already announced for a 2009 release, you do begin to wonder as to whether now what we really need to see is not a paired-down entry in the style of *Diary* but an altogether more ambitious final chapter on a grander scale, encompassing grander battles yet still integrated with the twenty-first century milieu and where the *final*, conclusive answer is provided as to who survives – the zombies or us?

With a genre heritage of varying success, ranging from *Friday The 13th Part 2* (1981) and the equally average *House* (1986), to the adequate *Halloween H20: 20 Years Later* (1998) and the impressive *Lake Placid* (1999), director Steve Miner may not have been the most obvious choice to direct 2008's remake of *Day of the Dead*. There again, given the success of Zach Snyder's *Dawn* redux and Romero's own renaissance, it would be asking too much of Hollywood not to try and ride on the wave of renewed popularity engulfing the zombie genre at present.

To this end, Miner's 'interpretation' of *Day* involves jettisoning the calustrophobic setting

A very different Captain Rhodes appears in Day of the Dead 2008 style

of the subterranean missile silo and bunker, to a small Colerado town. Likewise, although a number of characters survive from the original into Miner's film, any similarities are purely accidental and their characteristics have been changed to implicate the culpable!

Not so much a case of 'shock and awe' as 'shocking, oh no!' Sarah, played by Mena Suvari in Miner's film, is a shadow of the original Sarah – lacking the fiercely independent spirit that so typifies the character. Likewise, the misguided but essentially philanthropic Dr. Logan, one of the main characters in the original – is relegated to a peripheral role here, his white medical coat replaced here by a suit as the new Logan (Matt Rippy), equally misguided but decidedly misanthropic, becomes merely a sharp-suited 'lounge lizard'. The restrained but utterly convincing performance by Howard Sherman as Bub in Romero's opus is transformed here to Bud (sic) (actor Stark Sands) – a 'sympathetic', vegetarian (!) zombie. This, in keeping with his character whilst alive, as we are informed that the zombies still retain some part of their former self, even in their new existence.

Most disappointing of all however, is the treatment of Captain Rhodes - a pivotal figure in Romero's original, finely developed before the outré pay off with his particularly visceral, yet strangely satisfying (not to mention humorous) demise. In Miner's film, besides an irrelevant ethnicity

When There's No More Room In Hell....

change, Rhodes (Ving Rhames of *Dawn* remake fame), is killed way before the halfway stage stymieing any attempt at character development. He also provides the most ludicrous moment in the film - leaping with Olympian prowess up into an air vent to chase Sarah, even though being rendered virtually limbless from previous zombie attacks on him. His coup de grace however, remains when he plucks his dangling eyeball from his cheek and eagerly devours it!

Set in the small town of Leadville, Miner replaces the isolated army base locale which served the original so well, with a kind of small town claustrophobia as most of the action occurs at night as we see the effects of a flu like virus begin to sweep through the locals. It creates a race of super - strength zombies – rabid and rapid, they speed through the darkened streets, running, jumping, crawling up walls and climbing onto ceilings. Mayhem reigns supreme as cars collide and windows smash as the zombies wade through the carnage to claim new victims, eagerly devouring their flesh.

Sarah, along with Dr. Logan, Bud and fellow squaddie Salazar (Nick Cannon), are forced to barricade themselves into a store room in the medical centre, to escape the chaos – everywhere frenetic zombies are rampaging, accompanied by continual screaming. It is as if the frantic action and wailing victims are meant to bombard the senses and perhaps disguise the blatant plot inadequacies and creative vacuum.

The group's eventual escape from this urban nightmare leads them into the isolated countryside and a military bunker where they discover the truth behind "Project Wildfire" – a chemical research project Dr. Logan is involved in with the aim of disabling enemy troops in the battle theatre by using a virus which attacks the central nervous system.

Aided by Sarah's bother Trevor (Michael Welch) and his girlfriend Nina (AnnaLynne McCord), the survivors embark on their very own seek and destroy mission to eradicate the zombies amassed below, before they encounter the infected Dr. Engel (Pat Kilbane) whose previous intellect now transforms him into the zombies' leader.

The resulting fire-fight and conflagration sees the zombies extinguished whereupon Sarah, Trevor and Nina drive away to 'safety' only for the obligatory 'shock' ending sees a surviving zombie burst into close-up to roar his defiance – but hopefully not

Zombies Steve Miner style in Day of the Dead

The Dead Walk

the prospect of a sequel!

Besides sharing a title and some surviving character names, Miner's entry is a remake in name only, discarding the key elements which helped to elevate the original *Day* to the exalted position it occupies in Romero's zombie canon, as noise and speed simply disguise a multitude of sins here. At one point in the film, the local DJ (Ian McNeice),'threatens' a soldier with the unedifying prospect of playing a Celine Dion CD – simultaneously giving us the most humorous and horrific moment Miner's film.

With its military conspiracy theories and Dr. Logan's clandestine figure, Miner's film shares a more symbiotic relationship with the *Resident Evil* series rather than Romero's zombie cycle, and it is to the former that its' aspirations would appear to lie, rather than laying down any definitive treatment to the latter.

Sarah (Mena Suvari), menaced by Dr. Engel (Pat Kilbane) in Day of the Dead

5
INTO THE BEYOND – THE ENIGMA THAT WAS LUCIO FULCI

City of the Living Dead

The Dead Walk

It is quite appropriate considering the converging links between voodoo and the Roman Catholic religion that the Italian director, Lucio Fulci, should have become as closely identified with zombie films as his illustrious American counterpart George A. Romero. Like him or loathe him, Fulci has managed to acquire a large group of admirers and has enjoyed international recognition and success in the world of horror. This popularity however, conceals a long and relatively unsuccessful career in the cinema that has spanned practically every genre.

After studying at the Experimental Film Centre in Rome under such celebrated directors as Michelangelo Antonioni (*Blow Up* 1966) and Luchino Visconti (*Death in Venice* 1971), Fulci embarked on a varied career which included work on comedies, television pop music shows, rock and roll films, westerns and a spell as assistant to Marcel Lherbier on the *Last Days of Pompeii* (1950) and to Stefano Steno on *Times Are Hard For Vampires* (1959).

In the 1970's he turned to psycho thrillers such as *Don't Torture A Duckling* (1972), *Schizoid* (1971) and *A Lizard in a Woman's Skin* (1971). By 1979 Fulci had directed over 30 films but it was the release that year of *Zombie Flesh Eaters* that proved to be the commercial breakthrough he had been striving for.

One of the prevailing themes running through Fulci's zombie films stems from his own religion, as his work contains a kind of perverted catholicism with the resurrection of the flesh carried to its utmost extremes, epitomised in the horrific walking dead who dominate his films. This, coupled with Fulci's own unique style of filming,

German poster art for Lucio Fulci's Zombie Flesh Eaters

refusing to follow traditional narratives and pacing in favour of a more personal approach involving his much maligned reliance on the zoom lens to create intensity and claustrophobia, and his atmospheric rendering of "Lovecraftian" underground caverns, caves and gloomy cellars.

In this respect *Zombie Flesh Eaters*, despite being Fulci's most successful film financially, is also his least satisfying aesthetically, containing little of the atmosphere and style that *City of the Living Dead* (1980), *The Beyond* (1981) and *The House By The Cemetery* (1981) all offer in abundance.

The main reason for this is that *Zombie Flesh Eaters* was primarily conceived as a "cash-in" on the overwhelming success of Romero's *Dawn of the Dead* before it. The American title for Fulci's film, *Zombie 2*, was even a blatant nod in the direction of the American title for Romero's film which was *Zombi*. The film, in fact, sets itself up as a prequel to *Dawn of the Dead*, showing how the zombies came to infect America.

Zombie Flesh Eaters is set in the voodoo heartland of the Caribbean, as Fulci himself comments; "I wanted to recapture the moody atmosphere of witchcraft and paganism that must have been prevalent when the Europeans first settled in the Caribbean during the 1700's." "That's when the concept of zombies, human slaves brought back from the dead - first became popularly known to western civilisation."

The film's pre-credit sequence, set in New York harbour, gives the film an intriguing start as a police launch vessel investigates a mysteriously drifting, apparently deserted boat. From the moment that the two cops board the boat we know that something is very wrong and the alarming appearance of an overweight and ravenous zombie from the ship's hold, confirms our worst suspicions. He proceeds to make a quick lunch of one of the cops before

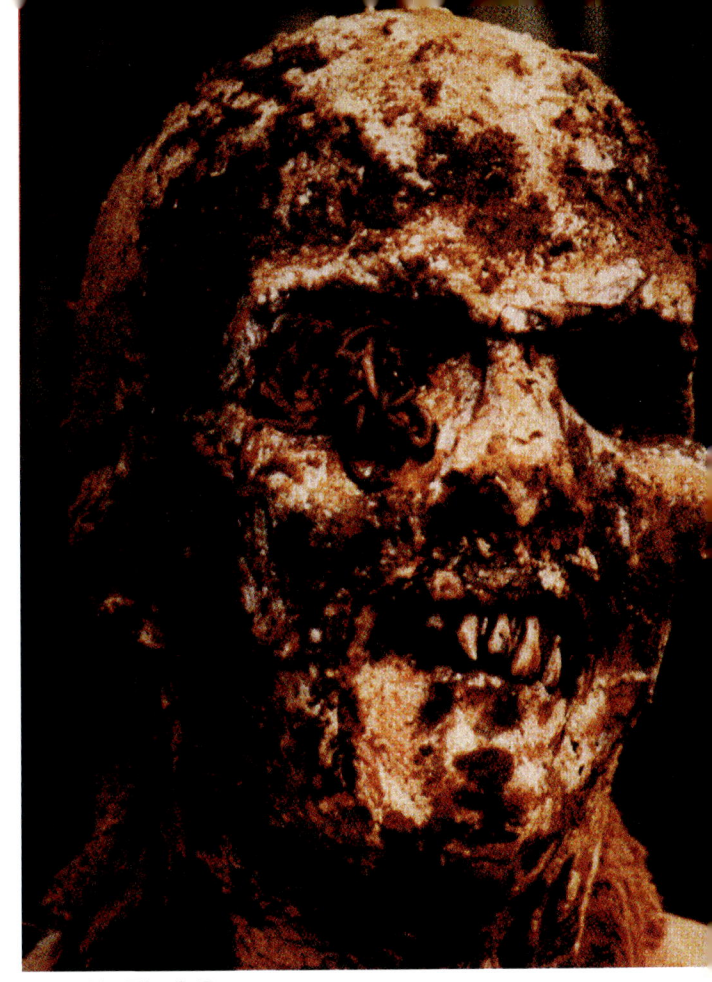

Zombie Flesh Eaters

being shot and the horror has very firmly begun.

The appearance of the boat, concealing impending doom on the calm water is similar in tone to the early vampire classic *Nosferatu* (1922), later remade by Werner Herzog in 1979 with Klaus Kinski as the titular vampire. The plague of rats and that film's scourge of vampirism are here replaced by the threat of a zombie epidemic causing ripples in the calm waters of civilisation.

Then we are rapidly transported to the tropical island of Matoul where Dr. Menard (Richard Johnson) is busy experimenting and as a result, unwittingly raising the dead. An intrepid reporter played by Ian McCulloch, and Menard's daughter (Tisa Farrow) spearhead an investigation into the evil events occurring on Matoul. Along the way the decorative Auretta Gay finds herself sandwiched between an amphibious zombie and a marauding shark in an electrifying underwater sequence. She escapes only because the zombie chooses to lunch on a quick shark steak, obviously no respecter of the synonymous villain of *Jaws* (1975).

Having survived this, the quartet, including Gay's boyfriend (Al Cliver - Pier Luigi Conti), head for the dry land of Matoul only to find that even worse horrors lie in wait. They encounter a village riddled with disease and rife with voodoo superstition. In the film's most infamous scene, the very unwilling Mrs. Menard (Stefania d'Amario) is slowly impaled, eyeball first, by a zombie with a penchant for sticking wooden stakes where he shouldn't. The non-too special effects of Gianetto de Rossi here are improved upon later as the search party, in an impromptu "picnic", are besieged by zombies rising from their graves. Unfortunately Gay, having learned nothing from her previous underwater battle, "gets it in the neck" as the remainder of the party escape.

The climactic scenes take place in the village hospital as the survivors, along with Dr. Menard, barricade themselves in, a la *Night of the Living Dead* style, as the zombies converge on them from outside. In the ensuing melee zombies are shot and "torched" with molotov bombs as they try to break into the hospital, and Dr. Menard himself receives some of his own medicine as he is bitten by a zombie and condemned to walk the ranks of the living dead.

As McCulloch and Farrow escape the burning hospital they see Cliver, now confronted with the sight of his zombified girlfriend Gay. As he debates the finer points of past love and future survival, she gives him a rather over-zealous love bite to remember. He is eventually rescued by the others, and after swiftly dispatching Gay, they are next seen sailing back to America, Cliver locked in the hold and betraying signs of zombiehood.

The real irony is that they are, in fact, sailing back to the same horror, as the final, puerile radio announcer, screams of zombies now attacking suburbia. The final image of zombies streaming over the Brooklyn Bridge shows that the "Big Apple" is now rotten to the core.

Whereas the film lacks the up front social satire inherent in *Dawn of the Dead*, it does contain an underlying statement on the western world's willingness to "meddle" in the third world and under-developed countries' affairs. This is exemplified in the film by the forlorn figure of Dr. Menard, infected by his own living dead creations. Also the bizarre appearance of grotesquely decomposing zombies set against the vibrant tropical sunshine looks unnervingly like the horrific news reports that are beamed back to the "civilised" world from starvation-torn nations such as Ethiopia.

In its entirety, *Zombie Flesh Eaters* is probably the most visceral

Into the Beyond - the Enigma That was Lucio Fulci

of all Fulci's films. Like most of his work it features exceptional make-up but very unexceptional special effects. Also, because it is the least personal of Fulci's zombie films, it lacks any real style or visual identity. The long camera takes echo the wide-open exteriors in which the story is predominantly filmed, as Fulci eschews any attempt at real directorial identity. For this reason, *Zombie Flesh Eaters*, despite its high graphic content, is probably the most accessible and watchable of Fulci's films.

For the same reasons however, it is also the least satisfying artistically, lacking the stylised Fulci trademarks that his later films contain. Of these, the most identifiable is his absolute willingness to interrupt any semblance of logical thought and so turn his films over into the realms of nightmares. Often his gore scenes are agonisingly slow-paced, and yet it is the very illogicality of such scenes that helps us to suspend our disbelief and reinforce the nightmarish atmosphere he has so lovingly created.

His next zombie film, *City of the Living Dead* (1980), incorporates many of these elements. Fulci has called it; "a visual rendering of the metaphysical side of bad dreams." Certainly the nightmare begins immediately as Father Thomas, the priest of Dunwich, a town built on the site of the Salem Witch Trials, hangs himself in the town's cemetery in renunciation of his religion. The sight of the rope being lashed around the tree is a throwback to the numerous crop of spaghetti westerns that left such a strong impression on Fulci. The image of the pale priest swinging amidst the autumnal colours of the graveyard is not easily forgotten. This acts as the signal for various decaying zombie heads to erupt from out of their earthen graves.

It is left to a reporter (Christopher George) and a medium (Catriona MacColl), jokingly called Mary Woodhouse (sic), to lay the restless priest's spirit before All Saints Day, when all the dead will rise. The most intriguing twist here is that before this can happen, MacColl must first be rescued, having been buried alive. This is a knowing reference to Edgar Allan Poe who is one of Fulci's main inspirations as shown in his filming of the Poe tale *The Black Cat*.

This one scene is probably the most memorable and expertly realised of all in Fulci's work, as George lingers in the cemetery, half-thinking that he can hear a voice screaming from within MacColl's coffin. It's a moment that perfectly captures that murky grey area in between knowing and not knowing if something feels right.

This is similarly alluded to in *Night of the Living Dead* as Barbara's brother taunts her in the graveyard. George's indecision is intercut with shots of MacColl trapped in her tomb, gasping frantically for air and clawing desperately at the coffin lid. Fulci, although not famed for his

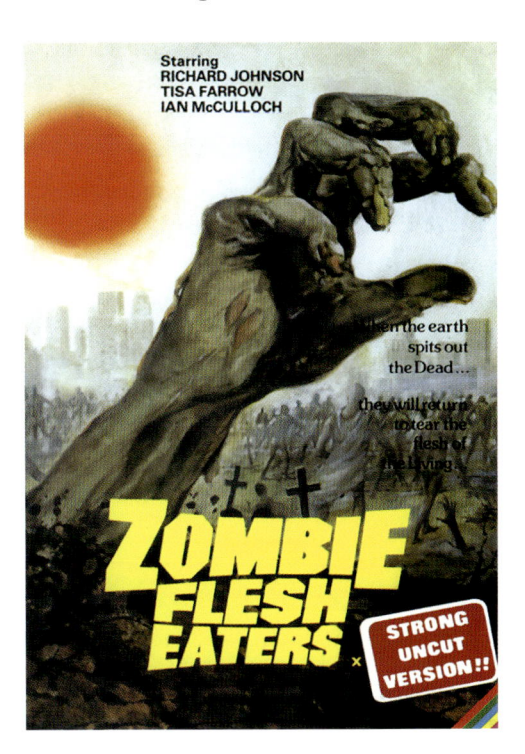

City of the Living Dead - Lucio Fulci's Lovecraftian masterpiece

subtlety, shows a deft touch here, betraying his gothic flair by showing the flower clasped in MacColl's hand wilt symbolically as her life is being gradually snuffed out. It is like the fly that puts out the flame from Eustacia's candle in Thomas Hardy's "The Return of the Native".

After what seems an agonisingly long time, George finally realises that MacColl has indeed been buried alive and rushes to her coffin. He commandeers a handily-placed pickaxe and then proceeds to rain blow after blow upon the coffin lid.

Simultaneously, as the axe cuts breathing holes in the lid, it also cuts perilously close to the poor girl's face. Her life is saved, but only by her life being further endangered in the process. The two protagonists then join forces with a Freudian psychiatrist (Carlo de Mejo) and his patient Sandra (Janet Agren), to defeat the priest and his undead disciples.

The endlessly repeated tracking shots down darkened streets and enclosed alleys, creates a feeling of tension, along with the swirling wind that skirts the outer reaches of the town. Despite this creation of atmosphere and suspense, there are still some extremely gruesome scenes offered up, such as the girl

Into the Beyond - the Enigma That was Lucio Fulci

who vomits up her intestines under the menacing gaze of the priest and various other victims have their brains ripped out by clawing zombie hands that lurch into the frame.

There is also a knowing reminder to the horror audience as in one scene the priest literally rubs a victim's face into some gore, and Fulci's own "mugging" of a scene from Dario Argento's *Suspiria* (1976), as the four would-be zombie fighters are bombarded by a non-too convincing "maggot-storm".

There is also some on-shore drilling as the local village idiot is given a crash course in the intricacies of a Black & Decker lobotomy by one irate girl's father. This scene echoes Fulci's own criticisms of middle class intolerance, it is "a cry he wanted to launch against a certain type of fascism." The film's closing sequences take place in an underground vault, full of genuinely eerie, cobwebbed caves and labyrinth tunnels that come the closest yet in the cinema to evoking a "Lovecraftian" other world.

It is here that George meets his end, and Agren, now returned as a zombie has to be unceremoniously run through with a cross by de Mejo, along with the still-glaring priest, just as the zombie hordes are about to close in for the kill. The two remaining survivors flee the now enflamed zombies where they see a child run towards them - only to be freeze-framed into a piercing scream. It is an unsatisfactory conclusion but then here the narrative is more an incidental than a primary concern. The ghostly sight of the pallid priest, appearing and disappearing irregularly, creates a real sense of fear and expectancy, adding to the hauntingly macabre ambience that permeates the film's entirety.

This is Fulci's "mood" picture, with tension totally supplanting any attempts at characterisation which here, even for Fulci, are purely perfunctory. Given that the creation of atmosphere is the film's main goal, it has to be judged as a success as Fulci accomplishes this admirably, including some powerful images along the way.

The themes and ideas put forward here are even further explored in *The Beyond* (1981), the most overtly surreal and image-conscious film in all Fulci's *oeuvre*.

It is, according to him, "an absolute film, with all the horrors of our world. It's a plotless film, people and dead men coming from "The Beyond". There's no logic, just a

Escape is in sight in Fulci's City of the Living Dead

The Dead Walk

succession of images." This is certainly the case as the "plot", or what exists of it, concerns a girl Lisa (Catriona MacColl), who inherits the "Seven Stars Hotel" in modern day New Orleans. Unfortunately for her, it has in fact been built upon one of the Seven Gates of Hell (a similar premise to *The Sentinel* - 1977).

Its' previous owner Schyke, an artist, is the hotel's own sentinel who is gruesomely dispatched in the film's opening sequence (set in 1927), as a local lynch mob give the unfortunate painter an acid wash down. His malevolent presence haunts the hotel whose guardianship is also shared by a blind girl, Emily.

It is interesting here to note Fulci's pre-occupation with the human eye - the "window of the soul". In *Zombie Flesh Eaters* it is skewered, in *Manhattan Baby* (1982) it is removed by birds and in *The Beyond*, it is pushed out by nails or filmed over, Fulci's reasoning here being that "sight has no *raison d'etre* any more in this lifeless world."

The irony here is that the film boasts some of Fulci's most memorable images, the numerous picturesque scenes on show are drawn from the artistry of the devil-worshipping Schyke, whose own canvassed vision of Hell provides the film with the most imaginative and satisfactory ending in all the Fulci series.

The most remarkable of these mise-en-scenes is the moment when Fulci jump-cuts to the solitary figure of Emily, standing silhouetted against an isolated causeway that is set amidst an expansive lake. The timeless theme created here can also be glimpsed in another scene when Emily runs through an open doorway, only for the same action to be repeated in slow motion. The apparently meaningless and arbitrary inclusion of this is typical of Fulci, who at least is prepared to step out of the ordinary in his attempts to conjure up another world, a Beyond where the edges between reality and dreams are blurred. A similar technique can be seen in Harry Kumel's interesting but barely fathomable *Malpertuis* (1972).

The Fulci trademark of sluggishly-paced gore scenes is also present here. Most effective is the morgue sequence where a young girl watches her mother fall and become smothered in acid. The garish red pool of blood that results, moves gradually towards the girl who runs from door to door amongst the plastic-shrouded

Into the Beyond - the Enigma That was Lucio Fulci

corpses, only to find each exit blocked. The last door she opens is guarded by a zombie. The next time we see the girl is at her mother's funeral, the blank, motionless eyes signalling her transcendence into the ranks of The Beyond.

The secret to the hotel is discovered by the town librarian as he reaches onto his shelves and picks out the "Book of Eibon", an ancient tome which explains the hotel is, in fact, one of the seven gateways leading to Hell. His find is shortlived as, falling from a ladder, he lies dazed on the ground only half-seeing the supernatural spiders that have emerged and now set about slowly biting him to death.

The denouement sees Lisa and a hospital doctor McCabe (David Warbeck) escape a zombie-besieged hospital via some underground steps that by chance, connect to the hotel cellar.

The geometry may be similar to *City of the Living Dead*, but here Fulci creates a more original finish, as, after various tussles with the zombies, the duo walk into The Beyond, which is the landscape depicted in Schyke's painting of the desert of Hell where they will "face the sea of Darkness and all therein that may be explored." The two survivors turn to face the camera whereupon we see the now familiar blank eyes etched onto their features.

The ending here is as welcome as it is unexpected. The importance of Schyke, or his ghost, haunts the characters throughout the film and is followed through to the film's conclusion as his painterly image of Hell does indeed become a passageway into another world. It is vintage Fulci in the way that it combines both the supernatural and the fantastic with unsettling scenes of outre violence.

The Dead Walk

The only disappointment here is that Fulci, who has shown that he has the talent and vision for creating a unique world of horror, still finds it necessary to constantly crib from other sources. *The Beyond*'s murderous dog can also be found in Dario Argento's *Suspiria* (1976), and the film's random plotting reminds one of both *The Sentinel* (1977) and *The Shining* (1980). The mysteriously ringing bells from the hotel rooms, supposedly unoccupied, again recall *The Shining*.

In comparing the two however, Fulci's film ranks as no mean achievement as his flair for atmospherics and highly original visual compositions surpasses the master craftmanship of Stanley Kubrick on this occasion. His arbitrary plotting works against *The Shining* whereas the absolute plotting found in *The Beyond* is intrinsic to fashioning that film's identity.

The one sustained highlight of Kubrick's film, its beautifully photographed chase through the snow-covered maze, cannot compensate for the "emptiness" that has gone before. The somewhat "empty" characters who populate *The Beyond* are unimportant, surpassed by the ingenious ideas and phantasmagorical images that pervade the film, both being integral to the film's success. *The Beyond* is a blinding flash of light. We may lose our sight but not our humanity or soul which remain unaffected. It is a film that deals with man coming to terms with his own corruption. In Fulci's language "every man chooses his own inner Hell, corresponding to his hidden vices." The wasteland of Hell portrayed in Schyke's painting is something that we must all face eventually.

The continuing evolution of Fulci's film personality and style can be further charted in *House By The Cemetery* (1981). Whereas his previous zombie films earned him notoriety as opposed to critical approval, *House By The Cemetery* came the nearest to garnering

Lucio Fulci's House By The Cemetery

both. In fact, that most "English" of newspapers, The Sunday Times even praised the film for its "style and restraint." Part of the reason for this becomes apparent when studying Fulci's treatment of children in his films. They are continually placed in danger, witness *City of the Living Dead* as well as *House By The Cemetery* for examples, but on each occasion the children escape unhurt, however narrow the margin for error may be.

In *House By The Cemetery* children are of primary importance as opposed to adults. All the occurrences revolve around children, especially young Bob (Giovanni Frezza). The film begins with a brief history of the title house, charting a young girl's abrupt demise at the end of a knife, wielded by the insane Dr. Freudstein (Giovanni de Nava).

After a briefing by a city professor (Lucio Fulci in a cameo role), academic Norman Boyle (Paolo Malco) and his wife Lucy (Catriona MacColl) together with their son Bob, take up residence in the house. They learn that its previous owner, Dr. Peterson, killed himself and his mistress, not exactly the stuff house-warming parties are made of!

Here, any resemblance with the inhabitants of the very one-dimensional *The Amityville Horror* (1979) ends. The unsavoury experiments being conducted by Dr. Freudstein in the murky cellar of the house are never far from the mind, but it is the actions of young Bob that are of the most interest. Throughout the film he switches from the adult world to a child's world where he communicates with the ghostly figure of a young girl called May. She warns Bob of the dangers in the house and he in turn sees for himself the danger as a shop window mannequin "comes to life" and is decapitated before his disbelieving eyes. This, in reality, is a premonition of babysitter Anna Pieroni's death later in the film at the hands of the murderous Freudstein. The fantasy of this children's world is emphasised by the two young charges who "speak" almost silently to each other as if through some form of telepathy, though hundreds of yards apart.

Fulci however, is unwilling to relax the tension for long and most of the film's action takes place within the claustrophobic confines of the house. Even Fulci's exterior shots of the house add to the "enclosed" feel, his raking camera filling the screen with shots of the adjoining cemetery. After a torrid conflagration with some tenacious vampire bats from the cellar, it is time for Norman and family to confront Freudstein in person. The cellar, a

Danger is ever present in Lucio Fulci's masterful House By The Cemetery

charnel house of butchered corpses, acts as Freudstein's life-blood as he constantly grafts new body parts onto his own rotting frame, a process that has kept him alive for 150 years.

The gruesome appearance of this "mosaic of corpses" is as electrifying as anything that Fulci has produced. Freudstein also possesses super-human strength, being stabbed by Norman and yet still being fit enough to tear out the helpless man's throat. Mother and son make for the ladders that lead above to a cracked tombstone in the graveyard, their only hope of escape.

Lucy is dragged back down below to her death whilst Bob struggles to squeeze through the cracked opening. As Freudstein's hands reach for his legs, Bob, in a final surge of strength, leaps up to freedom (of a sort).

Instead, he finds himself in limbo occupying the childhood world of Mrs. Freudstein and her daughter, May. The film's final quotation taken from Henry James; "Are children monsters or would monsters be children", perfectly encapsulates the idea that anything can happen in a child's world.

Taken to its logical conclusion the events in the film may have purely been the result of Bob's imagination. Although the ending does provide a great deal of suspense, it is also a reprise of the Jorg Grau's earlier sanguinary masterpiece, *The Living*

Into the Beyond - the Enigma That was Lucio Fulci

Dead At The Manchester Morgue (1974).

This aside, there is still much to commend the film. It is interesting to note the parallel between Boyle and his predecessor Peterson, in that he is also prepared to endanger his own wife and son to solve the mystery attached to the house, in much the same way that Peterson had jeopardised his own loved ones. Someone in the town even insists that he has seen Boyle before he has arrived at the house, suggesting another link between Boyle and Peterson.

The character of Freudstein himself is an embodiment literally, of Frankenstein's ideal of creating life from dead bodies and of Freud's theories on personal development. The murderous doctor's will to survive encompasses much of the "self-preservative desire" that Freud alluded to. This, together with the film's dual child/adult world and the tombstone/rebirth finish suggests more than a passing reference to Freud.

Fulci could have expanded on these influences but it is questionable as to whether any further elaboration would have added anything extra to the film. The real horror in *House By The Cemetery* is that nothing is resolved by the film's conclusion; the house still stands ready and waiting to receive more victims. The nightmare world of Fulci remains intact, with no glimmer of respite or release.

The rich vein of inspiration that Fulci exploited in making these zombie films through the early eighties appears to have dried up soon after. He had been less than prolific in recent years (partly due to illness), making less imaginative films such as *Manhattan Baby* (1982) and the non-supernatural psycho-slasher gore exercise *The New York Ripper* (1982). The former is a pale shadow of what Fulci is really capable of producing, whilst the latter dwells uncomfortably on sado-masochistic thrills as a substitute for atmosphere and suspense.

Lurching between Italian, made for TV, films and other alternatively insipid/gore-drenched offerings, Fucli made the gore disco *Murder Rock* (1984) *Demonia* (1990), *Voices From Beyond* (1990) and *Door To Silence* (1991).

Voices From Beyond is not quite a return to those halcyon days of a decade ago for Fulci, but ample proof that there was still some inspiration, however stilted, remaining at this stage of his career. Fulci's obligatory cursory plot involves a finance magnate, Giorgio Mainardi, whose unexpected

Murder most foul in Fulci's House By The Cemetery

death proves to be no accident as he contacts his beautiful daughter Rose (Huff) from beyond the grave to expose his murderer. Some authentic frissons can be found amidst the longuers as a mist-enshrouded forest evokes the "return" of the magnate, from his limbo state, whilst elsewhere suitably cadaverous zombies engulf one character in an eerie crypt. Certainly no classic but, together with *Nightmare Concert* (1990) - an extraordinary, semi-autobiographical romp, as Fulci stars as a horror director Fulvio, orchestrating scenes of graphic carnage, surreal humour and nazi orgies, goes to prove the resonance of the late maestro's unique oeuvre.

As something of a departure, Fulci turned his attentions to utilising the same cadre as his zombie films, only replacing zombies with pasty-faced, blackened-eyed nuns with *Demonia*.

The film centres on Professor Evans (Brett Halsey) and Liza (Meg Register), heading up an archaeological team investigating the ruins of a Sicilian monastery. With the time-honoured genre staple of "digging up more than they bargained for", they succeed only in awakening the dead - much to the chagrin of the locals, who it transpires, are fiercely guarding a guilty secret.

With shades of *The Beyond* resonating through the film, we discover that angry villagers had crucified the nuns some five hundred years previously, deep within the catacombs of the monastery.

The nun's revenge is suitably gruesome, ranging from behadings, to a tongue nailing and with the obligatory eyeball gouging all thrown into the mix. The *piece de resistance* however, is reserved for one unfortunate victim who is tied between two trees and wishboned in half a la Ruggero Deodato's *Cut and Run* (1984).

Despite some atmospheric Sicilian surroundings, the lacklustre performances, uninspired photography and perfunctory music score all conspire to render *Demonia* merely average at best.

Fulci also started but failed to finish *Zombie 3* (1988) which was eventually completed by Bruno Mattei and Claudio Fragasso, before the maestro finally shuffled off this mortal coil on the 13th March 1996, aged 69 and having just spent the last three years of his life trying to get *Wax Mask* (1997) - as it was eventually called, off the ground.

His untimely death left the horror genre a decidedly more prosaic place, but the rich legacy of his imaginative oeuvre has assured Fulci his rightful place at the vanguard of fantastic cinema.

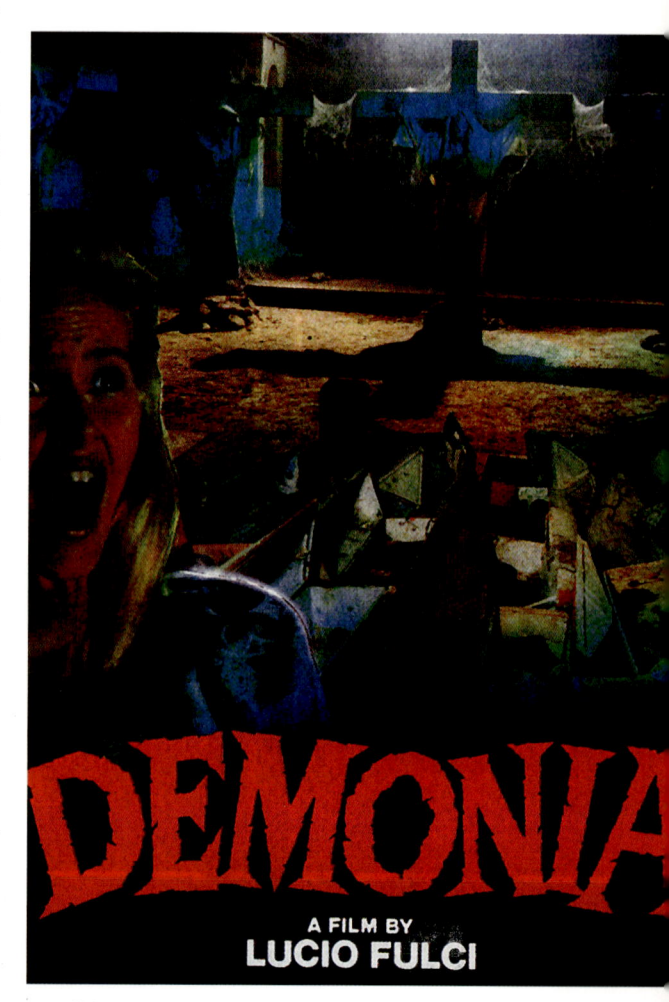

Pictures opposite from clockwise: The Beyond, Murder Rock, Nightmare Concert, Door To Silence & The New York Ripper

EL DESTRIPADOR DE NUEVA YORK

CK HEDLEY · ALMANTA KELLER · HOWARD ROSS · ANDREW PAINTER

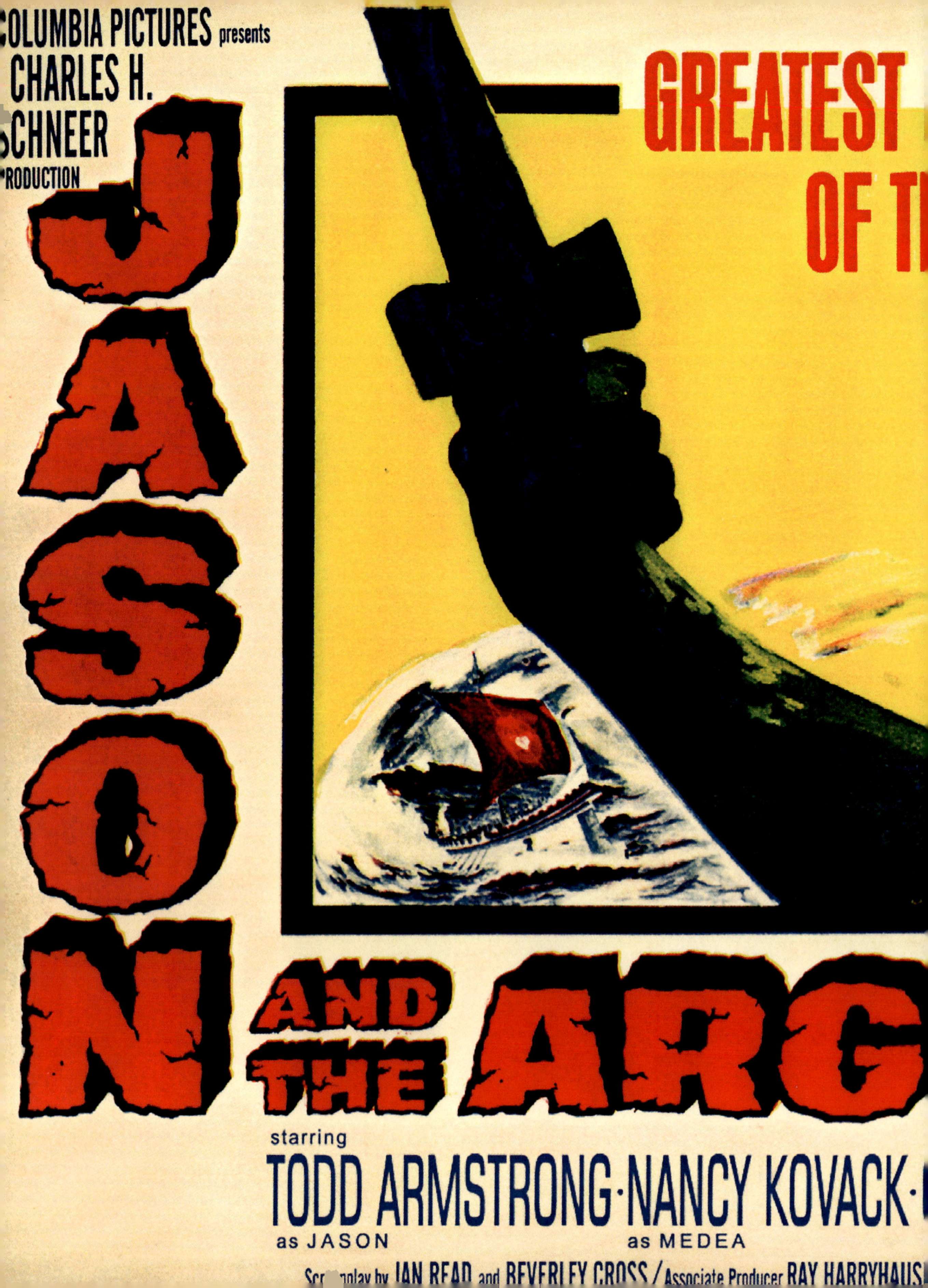
COLUMBIA PICTURES presents
CHARLES H.
SCHNEER
PRODUCTION
GREATEST
JASON
AND THE
starring
TODD ARMSTRONG
as JASON
NANCY KOVACK
as MEDEA
Associate Producer

YSSEY
AGES!

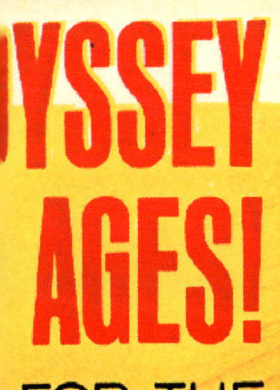

FOR THE
RST TIME
ON THE
SCREEN!

DNAUTS

starring
RY RAYMOND · LAURENCE NAISMITH

cted by DON CHAFFEY / A MORNINGSIDE WORLDWIDE FILM   EASTMAN COLOR

The Dead Walk

Following *Mysterious Island* (1961), Charles Scheer and Ray Harryhausen decided to film the story of *Jason And The Argonauts* (1963). At first titled *Jason And The Golden Fleece*, it's probably the most popular of Harryhausen's films. Budgeted at $3 million, and directed by Don Chaffrey with photography by Wilkie Cooper, it's a classic movie in every respect.

Jason, denied his rightful kingdom by the scheming King Pelias, can only gain his crown by seeking and retuning with the legendary golden fleece in the land of Colchis. A sailing vessel is constructed by Argos. Jason is aided by the goddess Hera (played by the beautiful Honor Blackman of Avengers and Bond fame). To provide balance, he is correspondingly hindered by Zeus (masterfully played by Niall MacGinnis). "Like toys to wanton children, are we to the Gods."

His ships built, Jason sets forth on his epic voyage with his Argonauts, amongst whom are Hercules (Nigel Green). Stopping to take onboard fresh water, they encounter the giant bronze creature Talos, who almost manages to destroy their ship, the Argo, and is only prevented in doing so, by Jason removing a stopper from it that releases its molten life fluids, ichor-the life blood of the Gods!

The Argonauts next encounter the harpies whom the gods have sent to torment the blind prophet Phineas (Patrick Troughton). In return for directions to the fleece, the Argonauts will incarcerate the foul creatures. Finally, they must voyage through the Clashing Rocks so they can reach Colchis. The Sea God Triton rescues the Agro from the deadly sea (Incidentally when Irish explorer Tim Severin recreated Jason's voyage in a replica of the Argo-he found this area of the ocean to indeed be perilous to a ship of this type!).

When they arrive in Colchis, Jason falls in love with the priestess Medea (Nancy Kovack). King Aeetes tries to stop Jason from taking the fleece, but once Jason has slain the hydra that protects the magical fleece, Jason escapes with Medea. Aeetes follows them. He calls on Hectate, Queen of Darkness, to avenge him, with the children of the Hydra's teeth, the Children of the Night. "Against the Children Of The Hydra's teeth, there is no protection!"

Fireballs rain from the sky and incinerate the flesh of the hydra, leaving only it's skeleton. (A fine special effect courtesy of Hammer stalwart Les Bowie). Aeetes gathers the teeth of the hydra which he hurls to the ground. Where the hydra's teeth fall, spring seven warrior skeletons are born from the Earth. With two of his men, Jason fights the children of the hydra's teeth.

Raising the Dead

Jason's two companions are slain, but diving off a cliff top, Jason escapes to rejoin the Argo, and be reunited with Medea.

This exciting sequence is fabulous to watch, and still amazes me as much today as when I saw it as a child. As to its' influence, you have only to watch Sam Raimi's *Army Of Darkness* (1992), with its' masterful and loving tribute to this (literally!) ground-breaking scene.

Jason and the Argonauts was actually filmed in Italy, due to its thriving film industry. It also had fine unused location, and even Greek temples, due to mainland Italy having being colonised by the ancient Greeks before the rise of Rome. In the legend it is decaying corpses that appear from the ground, and indeed, Harryhausen originally designed the creatures this way, but he and Scheer feared a certificate that would bar children and thus decided on seven skeletons, the same number as the hydra's heads. Harryhausen has commented that by today's standards, the decaying corpses would not just be accepted, but probably expected.

The degree of work Harryhausen put into his dynamation is staggering. Each of the model skeletons was between eight and ten inches high. Six of the seven skeletons were specially made for the sequence. The other was a survivor of *The 7th Voyage Of Sinbad* (1958), with some minor repainting to fit in with his new companions. (Incidentally all survive to this day, and Harryhausen brings one of them in a specially constructed box like a coffin with him on lectures!).

The bones were shaped from cotton wool soaked in latex, and allowed to harden. For the skeletons appearance from the ground, Harryhausen built a section of landscape from plywood, covered in with plaster, painted it, and cut seven holes. The holes were then covered with cork, and painted to match the area in front of King Aeetes and his soldiers who would appear in a rear-projection plate. Underneath each of the holes, Harryhausen built seven small platforms and attached the crouching skeletons to them. Each platform was fixed with a screw device, letting him slowly animate the skeletons rising up and breaking through the cork.

So that the cork could be animated in synchronicity with the models, he broke each disc into sections, when the skeletons broke through, it would appear as though lumps of earth had been pushed aside. Every section had copper wire passed through them, so that Harryhausen could animate them to look as though the skeletons had done the deed themselves. Also, some of the cork sections appear to roll away from the holes. These were animated using wax to hold them in place for the frame to be shot.

In the Scheer/Harryhausen films, their pre-planning was meticulous, thus very little was ever cut. However, there was a brief animation scene that was cut in the skeleton fight that was removed. It showed a skeleton on all fours, looking for its' decapitated skull. It had been intended as light relief. When the finished sequence was viewed, it was felt that it slowed the scenes pacing, and was removed for that reason, one of very few times any of Harryhausen's animation was removed. In the UK one scene where the skeletons charge towards the camera and a shriek is heard on the soundtrack, was removed for the film's release, the censor finding it unsuitable for a children's certificate. The scene would be reinstated in later years.

The intricacy of Harryhausen's animation was immense. There were three men fighting seven skeletons. Each skeleton had five appendages to move in each separate frame of film, involving a minimum of thirty-five animation movements to be synchronised to the actors movements. Sometimes Harryhausen produced just 14 or 14 frames a day-which amounts to less than one second of screen time for an entire day's labour. For him to finish the entire sequence took a record four and a half months to capture on film.

The concentration required to achieve this boggles the mind. Synchronisation between the models and human actors was crucial. For the skeleton fight, Harryhausen had to count every frame of film on the

Raising the Dead

rear projection plate so he would know precisely where the actor's sword, would appear on the plate, and where his skeletal opponents' sword would meet. The number of frames determines how long it would take for the skeleton to go from one point to another so that the swords meet at the right spot.

The number of frames also dictates what speed is required to get the skeletons arm in place, so that it can block the actors sword. The speed of the live-action photography would be 24 frames per second, so Harryhausen had to judge the movement speed for his animation to match this. Vital, so that the actors, both human and skeleton(!), appear to have been filmed simultaneously, sometimes moving the model approximately half a millimetre per frame so that it stays in synchronisation.

The live action choreography came courtesy of Fernado Poggi, a swordmaster who would also play one of the Argonauts in the skeleton fight sequence.

Harryhausen placed great emphasis on giving the skeletons human traits. One appears to be stunned, another wounded, It's these wonderful touches that give the character so missing from CGI. The illusion of reality is maintained by 'contact' between the live actors and the models. It was decided that the way to 'kill' the skeletons was to have them follow Jason over the cliff top.

In his book *An Animated Life*, Harryhausen says. "The sequence is one of my favourites, although I would never want to do it again. It was painful to the extreme. Hours and hours of the same movements wear a man down. But it was worth it. It is there on film for all to see, and no matter what technology is invented, it can never be reproduced. In stop-motion the whole scene has a supernatural quality that could only be achieved by the use of dimensional animation."

And in an earlier book, *Fantasy Film Scrapbook*, Harryhausen wrote. "The skeleton sequence was the most talked about part of Jason. Technically, it was unprecedented in the sphere of fantasy filming. When one pauses to think that there were seven skeletons fighting three men, with each skeleton having five appendages to move each frame of the film, and keeping them all in synchronization with the three actors' movements, one can readily see why it took four and a half months to record the sequence for the screen. Certain other time-consuming technical 'hocus-pocus' adjustments had to be done during the shooting to create the illusion of the animated figures in actual contact with the live actors."

Pics opposite page: the skeletons from Sam Raimi's Army of Darkness (bottom) - an obvious homage to the earlier Jason & the Argonauts (top)

7
GOD BLESS AMERICA
(AND ITS ZOMBIE STATES)

Army of Darkness

God Bless America (And Its' Zombie States)

Since the phenomenal world-wide success of George A. Romero's *Night of the Living Dead* in 1968, the American zombie film has grown from strength to strength, though the sheer volume of productions has been no indication as to their quality which has been extremely variable.

Two minor but interesting films managed to cast off the shadows from Romero's film, without quite generating enough imagination of their own to garner any major kudos. The first film *Sugar Hill* (1974), is an updated version of the voodoo revenge motifs that permeated the early zombie films. Diana "Sugar Hill", played by Marki Bey, enters into a pact with Baron Samedi after her boyfriend, the owner of the "Club Haiti" night club is beaten to death by a gang of white swindlers.

Her pact summons up an army of zombies to eliminate the murderers, but ingeniously, the zombies themselves are former slaves who died during a voyage from Guinea in the seventeenth century and were buried, still imprisoned in their shackles. They arise to defeat the modern day white exploiters who make up the gang.

The film's best sequence has the zombies rising from their muddied graves, cobwebbed and blank-eyed in similar style to 1966's *Plague of the Zombies*.

These zombies take no prisoners however, armed with machetes as they lurch forward in their leaf-covered clothes. Besides these unsettling images *Sugar Hill* also takes full advantage of a film climate that at the time, positively promoted race reversal pictures where black characters gained the upper hand over whites.

Witness the black heroes from *Blacula* (1973) and *Shaft* (1971) for example. *Sugar Hill* also stars genre favourite Robert Quarry whose career began in Hitchcock's *Shadow of Doubt* (1943) and included *The Deathmaster* (1972), *Count Yorga - Vampire* (1971) and *Madhouse* (1974).

The second film, *The Child*, released in 1977 is a combination of the zombie picture with the then thriving "Devil" films such as *The Exorcist* (1973), *Beyond the Door* (1974) and *The Omen* (1976).

Set in the 1930's, *The Child* features Laurel Barnett travelling to a remote woodland area where she is engaged by a widower (Frank Janson), to look after his daughter (Rosalie Cole). Unknown to the father, Rosalie has supernatural powers and for vengeance uses them to "summon" zombies from a nearby cemetery, who kill those she deems responsible for her mother's death.

The film's use of the deserted woodland, the subjective camera roving continually through it and the weird camera angles increase the "nightmarish" imbalance of the picture. The isolated family themselves evoke memories of the well-documented "Lizzie Borden" trial in America where a young girl was accused of murdering her parents. The finale, which has the zombies besieging the humans in a shed does recall Romero but not to the extent done by numerous other films.

Of the films that live more prominently in Romero's shadow, *Children Shouldn't Play With Dead Things* (1973) is one of the most effective.

It begins as five young actors and an effete company director, Alan, played by Alan Ormsby, travel by boat to a lonely burial island off the east coast of America. Alan wants to dig up a corpse and resurrect it by performing certain black magic rites.

The ceremony appears to fail but sure enough, amid all the wise-cracks and cries of derision, the earth begins to heave and spew forth its dead. Borrowing liberally from *Night of the Living Dead*, the survivors are eventually trapped in a decaying

The Dead Walk

This page & opposite: images from Children Shouldn't Play With Dead Things

cottage before perishing to the bloodthirsty zombies, who then board the sail boat at the film's conclusion, before presumably taking on the rest of America.

The film has a genuinely eerie, claustrophobic feel to it as all the action takes place under the darkness of night, the ever present gloom surrounding the actors ominously. The film's lead ghoul, Orville, is the best example of the effective make-up in the picture, (most of the chores being handled by Ormsby himself). The first half of the film is played for camp humour, particularly practiced by the company director, who is a remnant from the flowery peace movement of the 1960's.

The black humour, always prevalent, is slightly self-conscious but never descends into parody and is accentuated by the sparse cemetery set on which most of the action takes place. This jokey, irreverent humour, playing with rites to raise the dead and the "fake" resurrection of two "specially buried" actors finally dissipate in the face of the "real" appearance of the island's ghouls as the horror replaces the humour in the shock-filled climax. The film is all the more impressive considering that it was director Bob Clark's debut, made in only fourteen days for only $35,000 and financed by him and his college friends who also appear in the film. Clark went on to direct the excellent Sherlock Holmes - Jack the Ripper film, *Murder By Decree* (1978), before going on to such inane American school comedies as *Porkys* (1982). Ormsby followed him into directing with the equally well made *Deranged* (1974), as well as writing the remake of *Cat People* (1982).

Another first-time director, Fred Dekker's *Night of the Creeps* (1986), shows where his inspiration lies as it features characters with surnames such as Cronenberg, Craven, Hooper and Romero. In reality it is an amalgam of the 1950's science fiction films with the later zombie films of the horror genre.

The opening scenes show a dying alien release a canister from its space ship which then falls to earth. In a black and white tinted prologue we see it crash, interrupting a lovers' lane "necking" session, killing the girl and infecting her boyfriend who is turned into an axe-wielding zombie. He is caught and taken to the "Corman" University where he is placed in

God Bless America (And Its' Zombie States)

suspended animation, cryogenically frozen in a test tube coffin. He is released as a "dare" by a student who wishes to join the most prestigious campus fraternity. The zombie then unleashes slug shaped brain parasites which gradually turn the rest of the campus population into zombies. It is left to a detective (Tom Atkins) to defeat the alien menace.

Night of the Creeps captures so many diverse elements; the prom dance climax from *Carrie* (1976) and *Prom Night* (1980), the slug creatures from *Shivers* (1975) and *Brain Damage* (1987), combining them all with considerable gusto and integrating them into the film's slasher rock and roll high school setting. Amongst the gory delights on show are a zombie dog, and an impressive scene where an axe-wielding zombie bursts in on an old lady who is watching television.

The film's continuing allusion to horror "stars", as in *The Howling* (1980), even extends to the inclusion of Roger Corman veteran Dick Miller in the cast, best remembered for his role in Corman's *Little Shop of Horrors* (1960). Dekker was also responsible for the screenplay to the 1985 horror comic, *House*. As *Night of the Creeps* ad lines had it; "The good news is your dates are here. The bad news? They're dead"! Dekker made his own date with horror here and it's certainly worth more than a one night stand!

The ghost of Romero (amongst others), rears its head in *Spookies* (1987), a virtually plotless film full of mayhem and superlative special effects that leave no room for minor details such as characterisation and narrative structure. Produced by the appropriately named "Twisted Soul Inc.", the action begins as a young boy runs away from home after his parents have forgotten his 13th birthday.

He tells the sob story to a strange figure in a gloomy forest and is promptly killed and buried by the man. It is left to six partying teenagers to continue the action as they arrive "in high spirits" (they soon will be!) at a nearby mansion house.

Once inside the impressive structure, they set about playing ouija board games which tell them that no one will leave the house alive. After making a swift exit from the house they then return, in a moment of madness, to confront the now rampant assortment of demons and ghouls that roam the house at will. This is the signal for some exemplary effects scenes which include a startling "girl to spider" transformation and an attack by some flatulent mummies called the "muck men"!

Amidst all this chaos, creepy characters such as the Bela Lugosi lookalike Count Kreon, search for new victims. The climactic chase through the graveyard adjoining the house is well staged too as Romero-esque zombies appear with alarming regularity. Despite the state of the art special effects though, the absence of any characters remotely worth caring for condemns the film to relative obscurity.

The idea that zombies can be both created and caused by wars is one that runs continually through American zombie films. In *The Supernaturals* (1986), it is the memory of the American Civil War that causes the dead to rise, Michelle Nichols, better known for her role as *Star Trek*'s Uhura, leaves behind warp factor five in favour of a walk in the country as she heads some modern day army recruits on manoeuvres in a dense wood.

The prologue establishes that the division had previously carried out random atrocities in the civil war, forcing Confederate troops across their own minefields whereupon they were duly massacred and dumped into mass graves. The dead troops are re-awakened by the yankees who have now set up camp on the site of the carnage.

Unfortunately, any anticipated zombie attacks fail to materialise as much of the film is taken up with lengthy exposition and moody woodland photography. The final scenes show the realistically frightening zombies suddenly emerging from out of the blue mist that clings to the woods, the effective make-up being provided by Mark Shostrom of *From Beyond* (1987) fame. The director, Armand Mastroianni, is no stranger to the horror genre having previously filmed *He Knows You're Alone* (1980), an inept slasher film in the *Halloween* mould. His casting of "Dynasty" star Maxwell Caulfield in one of *The Supernaturals*' supporting roles is ironic considering the film's sterile (in true TV style) end.

The American Civil War is replaced with the Second World War in Ken Wiederhorn's *Shock Waves* (1977), and here the zombies are amphibious as well as carnivorous. The cast is lead by horror stalwarts Peter Cushing, as a World War Two Nazi officer, and John Carradine, as the captain of a steamer ship.

The story centres around the re-emergence of a "zombie corps", created by Nazi experiments during the war. Their ship had been sunk by Cushing but an underwater disturbance has now revived the corpses who proceed to kill Cushing and the crew of the ship-wrecked steamer nearby, that is full of tourists. The sole survivor, Brooke Adams, is found to be insane, a climax that foreshadows the popular "downbeat" endings favoured by later horror entries such as *The Thing* (1982).

Shock Waves contains many captivating moments such as the black-goggled zombies emerging from the watery depths, and later stalking the shipwrecked survivors on the nearby island. There are numerous shots of the silent corps moving underwater, and the opening scenes of the steam ship looming on the horizon craves attention.

This was one of the first films to combine its zombie creations with Nazi atrocities from the war - a theme repeated in more spurious shockers such as the notorious *SS Experiment Camp* (1980). Wiederhorn himself has returned to the zombie genre since this, although keeping his feet firmly on dry land with *Return of the Living Dead 2* (1987).

Zombies combine with Vietnam in Bob Clark's *Deathdream* (1972), one of the first American films to approach, albeit limitedly, the contentious subject of that country's involvement in the war. Francis Ford Coppola's *Apocalypse Now* (1979), Oliver Stone's *Platoon* (1987) and Stanley Kubrick's *Full Metal Jacket* (1987) have since explored the war in human and military terms, but none with the horror-influenced trappings that are contained in Clark's film.

The opening scenes show a soldier (Richard Backus) being killed in Vietnam and his body being shipped back to America. He then appears on his parents' doorstep, white-faced and "hiding" behind dark shades.

The ubiquitous "Tall Man" (Angus Scrimm) from Don Coscarelli's Phantasm series

The family reunion is short-lived as his father (John Marley), becomes suspicious of his son's behaviour.

It soon becomes apparent that Backus is a zombie who needs continual supplies of food to service his condition. To obtain this, he kills the family doctor and his own pet dog, all culminating in his father's suicide. The inspirational ending sees the boy's still loyal mother (Lynn Carlin), drive him to the cemetery where he then digs his own grave and claws his way inside the tomb before the alerted police can close in on him. *Deathdream* is interesting for a number of reasons.

It is the soldier's parents who are partly responsible for his return and the eventual carnage that is caused as they had both "wished" him back alive. The ignorance of civilians to both the war and its participants is typified in a scene where Backus' "strange" behaviour in a drive-in cinema is blamed on the "war" by his girlfriend and her companions.

The moral disintegration of Backus is graphically reflected in his physical appearance as he degenerates throughout the entire film until he is literally left as a walking corpse. Our repulsion at the very sight of him is our renunciation of Hollywood's previously filmed Vietnam propaganda, as against this, all the more engaging, account. The illusion has finally been shattered.

The pill-popping generation of the 1960's and the early 70's is now the norm during *Deathdream*, illustrated in Backus' behaviour as he uses a syringe to obtain some of the nutrients he now requires for his survival. Life can be both enhanced and taken away, all by the power of the needle - a potent image not lost on the makers of *Nightmare on Elm Street 3 - Dream Warriors* (1987), whose film includes a scene with a syringe-wielding killer, Freddy Krueger.

Deathdream's message seems to be that you may survive a war, but loose the "moral" battle as your mind will be left permanently scarred by the inhumanity of killing.

Inevitably, in the aftermath of the west's campaigns in Iraq and Afghanistan, this theme is due to be updated in a redux tentatively titled *Zero Dark Thirty* - only with Afghanistan replacing Vietnam.

To move away from the images of war to a totally different dimension, one only has to look as far as Don Coscarelli's *Phantasm* (1978), which deals with some supernatural occurrences at

God Bless America (And Its' Zombie States)

the Morningside Mortuary.

The compelling premise here is that the "Tall Man" (Angus Scrimm), is making homuncule from the dead bodies of victims killed in the cemetery, lured there by the "voluptuous" Lady in Lavender (in reality the Tall Man in heavy disguise !!).

The film's main character, Mike (Michael Baldwin), passes through a space gate into another planetary system where he watches dwarfs struggle across the desert landscape there. The denouement sees Mike waking up and thinking that he has dreamt everything in response to the recent death of his brother in a car crash. However, who is waiting in the mirror in the next room but the Tall Man.

Phantasm is a wildly inventive and incoherent exercise in the surreal. Scene upon scene defies explanation, as in one instance where a severed finger metamorphosises into a tiny demon, only to be destroyed by the kitchen garbage disposal unit. The illogicality of nightmare is rendered

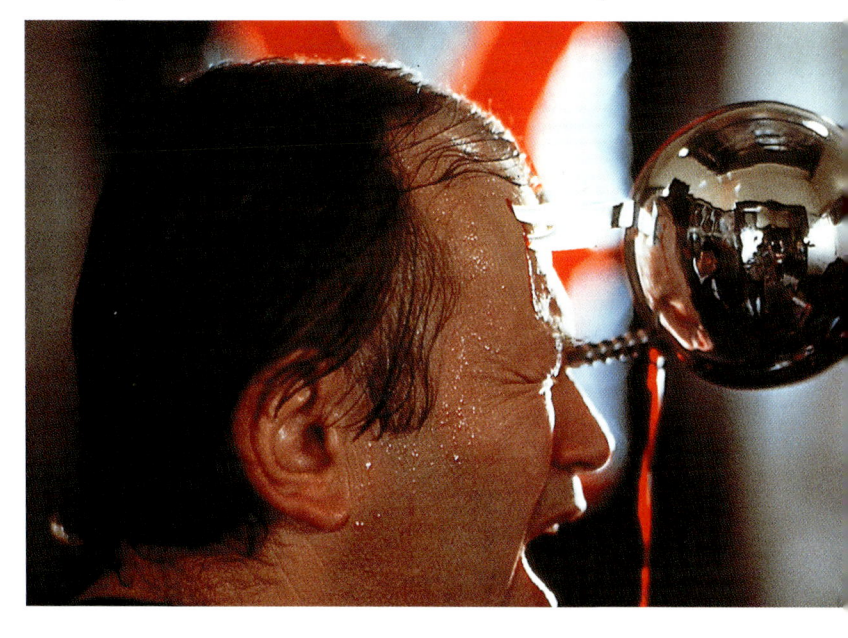

Silver balls & a Tall Man can mean only one thing - Phantasm!

conceivable as Mike flees at night from the mortuary caretaker, who is then killed by a spinning sphere that clamps itself to each victim's face and inserts a spike into the forehead ! This revolving sphere is symbolic of the ever-twisting "logic" that pervades the film as Mike somehow manages to impose his own meanings to the irrational occurrences he is faced with.

Phantasm, due to its' highly original pretext probably deserved its' sequel more so than the other "serialised" sequels which abound the horror pantheon, and yet the subsequent releases of parts 3 and 4 have likewise diluted the intital vision, with 5 muted for 2009 release with Coscarelli reportedly again at the helm. Coscarelli continued his inventive ways in *Beastmaster* (1982) which again explores another dimension.

The Dead Walk

An equally inventive, though less spectacular film is *Dead and Buried* (1981). Dan O'Bannon's fine script work on *Alien* (1979) is carried through onto this $ 6 million production, aided by Gary Sherman's no nonsense direction, as previously seen in *Deathline* (1972). *Dead and Buried* ingeniously suggests that Romero's extravagant city zombies in *Dawn of the Dead* may have had their roots in the small town zombies that populate insular communities such as this film's "Potter's Bluff", which as it turns out, is appropriately named.

An eye-catching start has a young photographer inveigled by a sultry siren to take pictures of her on the beach as she casually strips off her clothing to pose. The ensnared man is then attacked by a group of locals who violently beat him, then trussing him up in a fishing net, before tying him to a wooden stake and dousing him with kerosene, which is then set alight.

The whole sequence commands only a few moments of screen time but it is the emotionless, arbitrary nature by which the locals maim him that so shocks the viewer. The man's charred body is then later found in an upturned car. In a literally jaw-dropping scene, the man lets out a piercing scream as the town's Sheriff, Dan Gillis, investigates the debris.

Not buried yet but most certainly dead - Gary A. Sherman's captivating Dead and Buried

The barely-living photographer is then taken to hospital, wrapped head to toe in bandages due to the severity of the burns. Before he can inform on his assailants, he is fatally stabbed in the eye by the ingenue from the beach who appears now as a syringe-wielding nurse. (A similar fate lay in store for two other characters that year in both *Halloween 2* and *Dead Kids*).

As the plot thickens we learn (too early ?) that most of the townspeople are, in fact, zombies, reanimated by the deranged mortician Dobbs, played with manic glee by Jack Albertson. It is left to the sheriff to wage a lone war against them, tragically discovering his own wife's complicity in the conspiracy, by viewing a video of her in bed with an unknown lover, before stabbing him to death, urged on by the leering neighbours who are lapping up the spectacle by watching through the window.

The final showdown, in Dobb's mortuary, reveals the film's coupe de grace as Gillis (James Farentino), shoots Dobbs only to see him return to life again using his own resurrecting formula. The mortician's response; "Call it black magic, call it medical breakthrough, but I'll take my secret to the grave", is ironic as he will never need a grave.

His final revelation, as multi TV screens replay the video of the sheriff's wife in bed, is that we finally see that the victim of the stabbing is Gillis himself. He is also a zombie ! Call it original, call it outrageous, but it's certainly a startling denouement.

Dead and Buried uneasily combines the fog-laden seaside town, similar to John Carpenter's *The Fog* (1980) with some gruesome violence; there are numerous gory murders in the film and one man has his arm wrenched off. There is only Dobb's perverse humour to offset this, he prepares cadavers listening to loud jazz music, and is the forerunner to *The Return of the Living Dead*'s mortician who listens to classical music on a Sony Walkman !

Amongst the zombie killers is Robert Englund who later found fame as Freddy Krueger in the *Nightmare on Elm Street* film series, whilst the gross make-up is provided by the late, much lamented, Stan Winston who later worked on *Aliens* (1987). Despite these show stealing special effects, *Dead and Buried* still features enough originality, generating an eerie atmosphere and sufficient tension to successfully transfer Quinn Yarbo's source novel onto the big screen.

Whereas the previous quota of films have revelled in their splattery effects the following quartet of films have produced horror and humour in equal quantities, just as content to tickle the funny bone as they have been to chill the spine, resulting in some splendidly inventive work.

The most infamous of these has been the unjustly maligned *The Evil Dead* (1982), taken rather too seriously in some uninformed British quarters, where vociferous condemnation of the film led to the banning of the video from rental shops for 6 years.

In reality, *The Evil Dead* is an inspiring horror-comic with tongue firmly placed in rotting cheek. There is as much laughter here as there is horror, and the horror itself is so wildly imaginative and fantastical in its setting as to be rendered simply entertaining as opposed to nauseating.

It concerns five college students holidaying for the weekend at a tumbledown log cabin in the Tennessee wilds. Inside they find an ancient tome "The Book of the Dead" and whilst reading from it aloud they summon up some malevolent demons. The story couldn't be simpler but its' execution is what elevates the film above the ordinary.

We see repeated subjective point of view camera shots, but they are far removed from the all too familiar "mad-slasher" films that rely almost solely on such devices to

Dobbs (Jack Albertson) above & some seriously suspect nursing care below in Dead and Buried

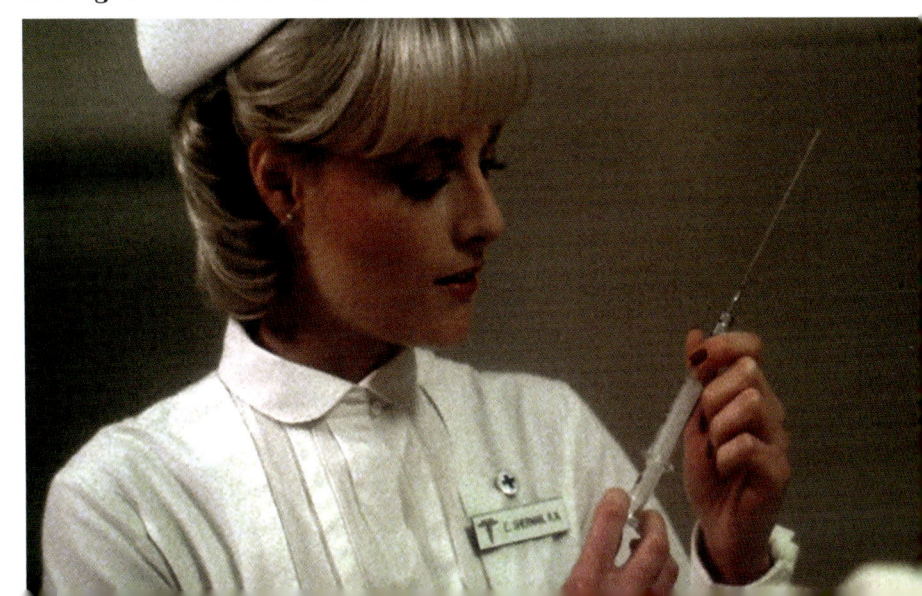

The Dead Walk

Sheriff Gillis (James Farentino) makes a grisly find in Dead and Buried

excuse scripts that are totally devoid of ideas. The improvised steadicam careers recklessly through tangled undergrowth and darkened forests, gliding over stagnant ponds as we, the viewers, share the "demon's-eye" view. The camera acrobatics do not stop here however. In one scene, the high-angled camera tracks the students' car as it bounces down a dirt road, to the accompaniment of a booming, crashing noise on the soundtrack. It is not just the camera though that creates the atmosphere here, there are many finely-judged moments that combine to create the required sense of foreboding. As they enter the cabin, a wooden sign outside swings continually to and fro, thudding into the cabin wall. It is like the swinging pendulum on which their own lives will be balanced later on in the film. The solitary wooden bridge that crumbles to dust and the fog that swirls increasingly around the shack are further signs of the impending doom they face.

Genre conventions are repeatedly taken and twisted into new forms during the course of events, Ash's (Bruce Campbell) descent into the dimly lit cellar generates suitable tension but without any audience "pay-off" as he surfaces again unscathed. It is here, amongst knowing references (a poster for *The Hills Have Eyes* lies in the cellar), that Ash discovers the tome that unleashes the demons as well as some creepy tape recordings from the cabin's previous tenant, a professor who had been investigating witchcraft and demonology.

It is the alarming transformations that the film is best remembered for however, as one by one, each of the youngsters, except Ash, are transmogrified into demons. In one instance, one of the girls (Ellen Sandweiss), is captured in the woods and raped by a virile tree as its' vines entrap her. It is as if John Wyndham's *The Day of the Triffids* (1955) has been taken to its logical conclusion; after all, if that living vegetation could move and kill like humans then surely it's not too much of a quantum leap for them to also function sexually ?! Eventually Ash is left the only "normal"

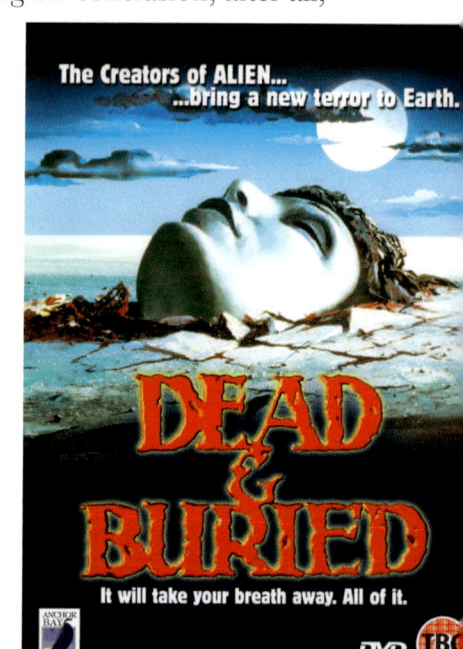

God Bless America (And Its' Zombie States)

human and has to fight off his now-zombiefied friends and kill them to escape from the demons that now control them. He can survive, but only at the expense of his companions. After decapitating one demon with a spade he sees two more disintegrate after he finally manages to push the tome into the fire, and so consign the demons to whence they came. Ash, by now bloodied but unbowed, is left the only survivor at the end, or is he, as in the final scene his retreat from the cabin is accompanied by the now familiar spiralling camera that rushes menacingly up behind him.

The virtuoso travelling camera invests the film with its "original" look, but it is the zombies themselves that provide the film's emotional core. There are many anomalies, though no less true to life for that; one of the girl demons develops a sense of humour once she has been turned into a zombie, laughing hysterically despite the fact that she is trying to kill Ash and vice versa.

In another (Sandweiss), the familiar human trait of cunning is accentuated as she tries to escape from the now locked cellar by pretending to be her "normal" self. The sight of her - a pasty-faced ghoul with glaring eyes and foaming lips, frantically trying to loosen the chained trap door is not easily forgotten.

Ash himself, when confronted with these horrors turns from a macho hero to a whimpering coward as again the frailties of human nature are exposed. The film's climactic scenes of zombies dissolving are the modern day apex of the disintegration scenes in earlier films such as Hammer's *Dracula* (1958).

One of *The Evil Dead*'s final twists however, is Ash finding a projector running onto a blank white screen that gradually becomes immersed in blood. It is the literal depiction of the now familiar argument that many horror films simply show the screen awash in blood at the expense of any vestige of characterisation. This, *The Evil Dead* avoids admirably as there is a very real raison d'etre for Ash's violence - he has to kill the demons to ensure his own survival. So, *The Evil Dead*, as well as exhibiting a wicked sense of black humour throughout, also develops the more emotional nuances contained within its pretext as well as being a compelling visual treat by virtue of its' devastating cinematography.

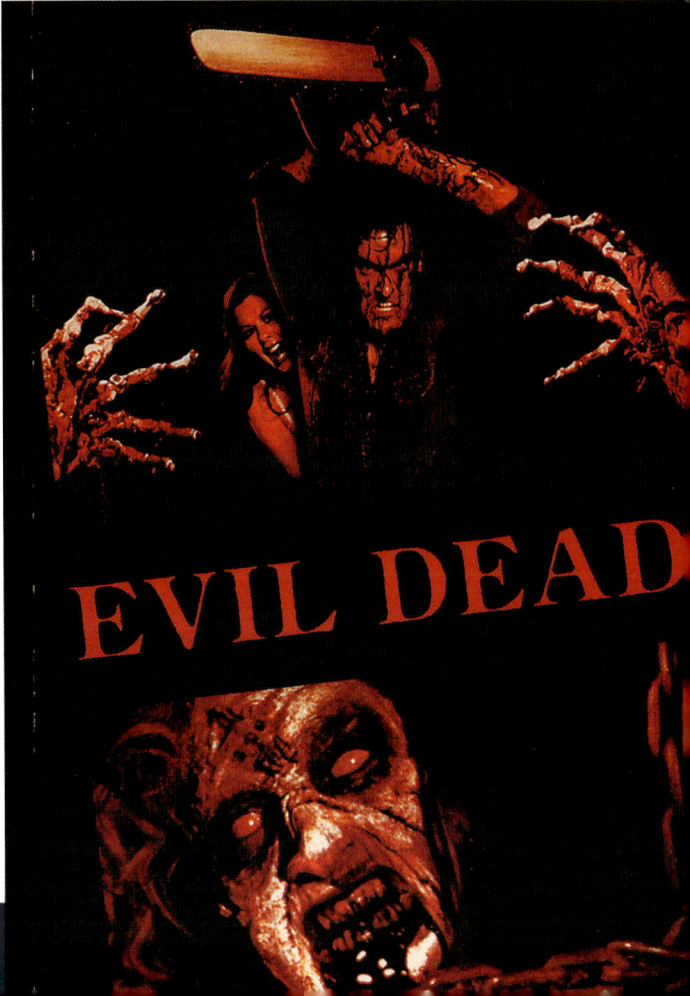

Evil Dead 2 (1986), directed like the original film by Sam Raimi, stands as one of the few worthwhile sequels made in recent years. Here, it is firmly the humour that is most gleefully placed to the fore (partly Raimi's response to the vitriol aimed at his earlier film). This, combined with some bloody but slapstick horror and an increasingly fluid camera, all go to contribute to the film's undoubted appeal.

The plot is basically a re-run of the former film as we find Ash again at the log cabin, only this time having to decapitate his girlfriend Linda (Denise Bixler). He is later joined in his battle against evil forces by Professor Knoby's daughter Annie (Sarah Berry), whose father had, in fact, previously owned the cabin.

The ensuing mayhem that is caused is also offset by the irreverent humour and superb comic timing that recalls the "Three Stooges" in parts.

This is no better illustrated then when Ash hallucinates that his girlfriend is performing a macabre pirouette and dance, with his own "severed" head bobbling around like a football. His nightmare really begins when he awakens to see her head bounce onto his lap and bite a chunk out of his hand!

This leads to Ash himself becoming possessed and having to eventually cut off his own hand, not before we witness the offending member smashing plates over his head and pull him along by the hair.

Even the eventual dismemberment takes place with a strategically placed copy of Ernest Hemingway's "A Farewell To Arms" in view. This manic slapstick works well within the confines of the film, surfacing again when a local redneck is captured and killed in the cabin cellar before reappearing as just a vile mass of blood that gushes out of the trap door like some bizarrely billowing geyser.

There is also an unforgettable moment when a rogue eye-ball flies across the room and into another open-mouthed recipient ! The gung-ho style of such playfully violent series as "The A-Team" and characters such as "Rambo", are wonderfully ridiculed when Ash, arming himself with guns, grenades, bullet belts and chainsaws,

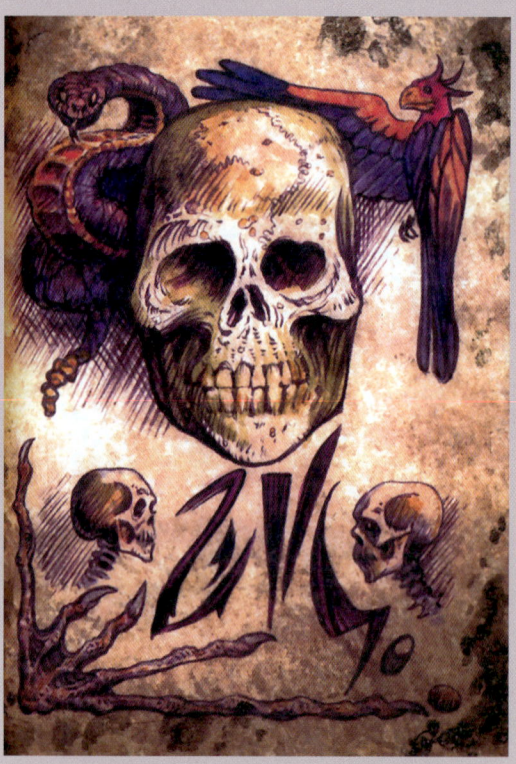

Images from The Evil Dead

stares wide-eyed into the camera and drawls "*Groovy !*"

This cartoonish humour is complemented by a flowing yet erratic camera that almost eclipses the first film. Even more so, we are treated to rolling, sweeping camera flourishes that usually finish up looking directly into the furrowed lines and staring eyes on Ash's tormented face.

In one breathtaking sequence we, the viewer, are picked up, hurled through the air only to land face down in a pool of water as Ash. In another scene, the camera relentlessly tracks Ash through the labyrinth style passageways that snake through the cabin. The ghost of "German Expressionism" is also evoked in the favoured scenes of twisted trees, contorted angles and fog-shrouded, fairytale bridges that pervade the film.

Evil Dead 2's concluding scenes reflect the film's changing emphasis away from straightforward horror to fantasy horror as first of all, Ash battles with a grue-covered monster from another dimension before later being transported back in time to medieval England, circa 1300 A.D., to fight flying terradactyl-type creatures of the Evil Dead.

Ash (Bruce Campbell) with a non too helping hand in Evil Dead 2

Once again it is the burning pages from the "Book of the Dead", bound in human skin, that signifies the defeat of the demons. Here, it is Ash who becomes part zombie, only to recover his humanity and so claim victory again. However, we know that the Evil Dead will return to fight another day - and they did, in *Army of Darkness - The Medieval Dead* (1992).

This spirited sequel sees Campbell as the ubiquitous Ash, once again combating legions of zombies, only this time in the 13th century - a kind of "Medieval Dead" film.

Whilst seeking out the Book of the Dead - the ancient tome with the power to return him to the 20th century, he has to defeat a variety of dead warriors, Conquistadors and Vikings who attack his castle abode.

Raimi's trademark humour is displayed at will - the camera panning down elongated lines of locals with eyes staring wildly in one direction, namely Ash's! Elsewhere, Ash finds himself

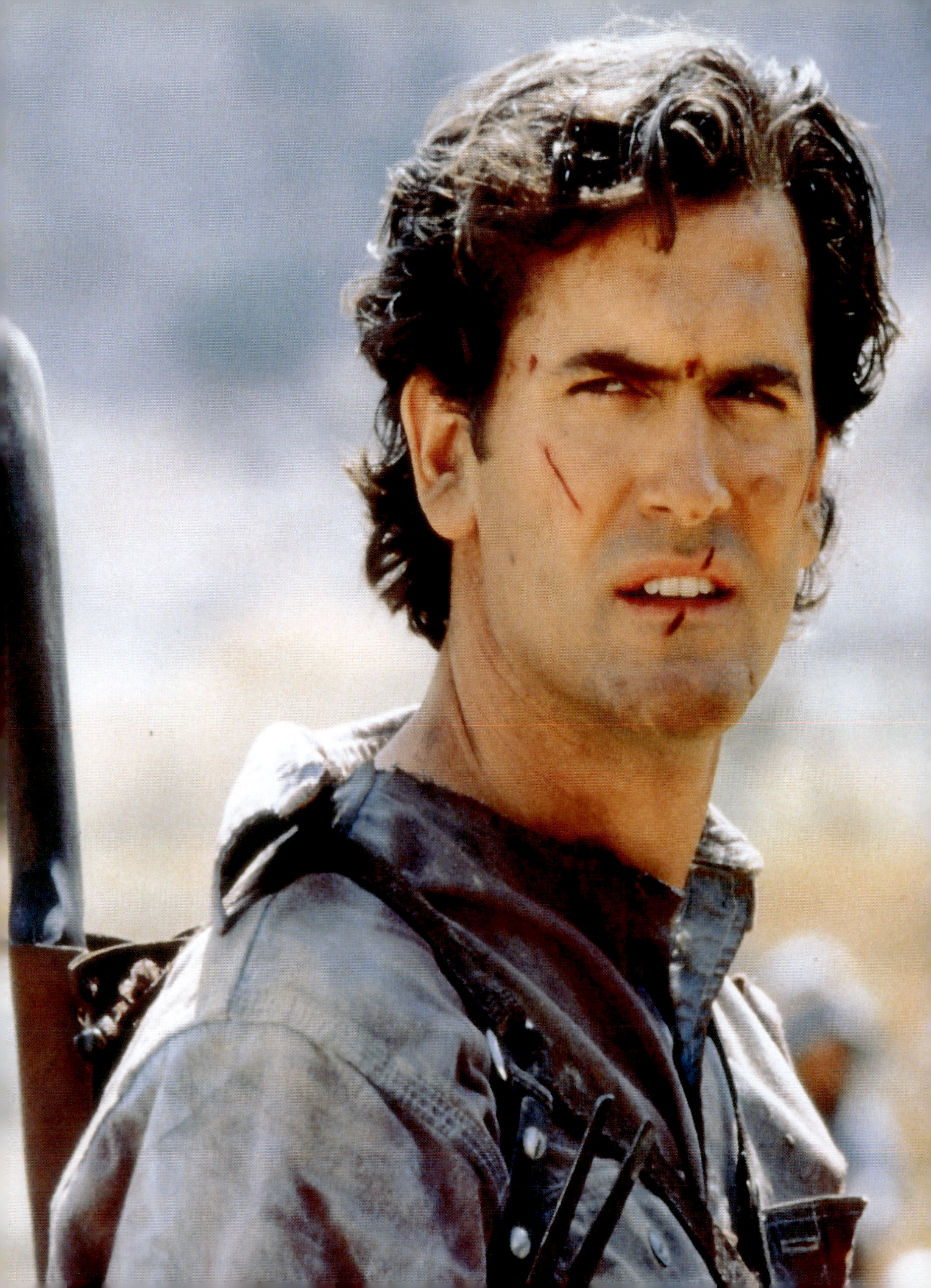

God Bless America (And Its' Zombie States)

tied down by mini clones of himself a la "Gullivers Travels" style, whilst the spooky cemetery yields skeletal hands exploding from the earth which then proceed to bang his head, punch his face and claw his nose. Is there no end to the indignities this man must suffer?!

At least the period setting lends the film an original touch, whilst Ash's skeletal adversaries evoke the memory of the superior fantasy *Jason and the Argonauts* (1963), whose "bone-a-fide" creations so captivated and inspired director Raimi as discussed in Chapter 6 of this book.

The film's original ending where Ash is trapped in a cave rock fall only to awake after seemingly an eternity, now complete with shaggy beard, reveals him gazing out onto a now apocalyptic, partially destroyed world uttering "I slept too long." This satisfies the fantasy elements within the story but the final cut features the alternative ending where Ash is transported back to his humble supermarket-worker origins to defeat a deadite monster and so claim a kiss from a female admirer.

There are no medieval monsters in *Re-Animator* (1985), but there are some age-old conflicts to resolve. The film's central theme, of scientists creating life from the dead owes much to Mary Shelley's "Frankenstein", as it does to its source story, H. P. Lovecraft's "Reanimator". Jeffrey Combs plays Herbert West, a doctor thrown out of Swiss medical school for his weird theories and unusual experiments. He later takes up residence at a New England hospital in Miskatronic University. He has been carrying on his experiments to make the dead rise; "We can defeat death, we can achieve every doctor's dream. We can live lifetimes", is his scientific aim. West is rented a room to stay in by his fellow student Dan Cain (Bruce Abbott), and his girlfriend Meg Halsey (Barbara Crampton). Soon they begin to regret their decision as the house cat goes missing only to turn up in West's fridge where he has killed it and then resurrected it with the life-giving serum he has formulated.

He then tries the serum on human corpses in the hospital morgue with tragic results, as the revived cadavers run amok, biting off Dean Halsey's fingers and then throttling him to death. West reanimates him for his daughter Meg's sake, but the Dean has to be locked up, now left a mindless zombie. West then kills the other

Opposite picture: Ash (Bruce Campbell)
Below: Sheila (Embeth Davidtz) - both in ***Army of Darkness***

zombie he has created with a bone drill through the chest.

It is now that West confronts the true zeal and jealousy of Dr. Hill (David Gale), the hospital's leading surgeon, who expels West when he refuses to reveal to him his secret formula. Hill tries to kill West, but it is West who eventually triumphs, decapitating Hill with a shovel. This acts as the signal for the film to move into overdrive, resulting in the climactic conflagration in the hospital morgue between West and hordes of crazed zombies.

There are some incredible scenes on show here, from the sight of the revived Dr. Hill's torso creeping up on West who is busily engaged talking to the doctor's head (!), to the scene where an enraged intestinal tract loops around and strangles a victim ! The

Dr. Herbert West (Jeffrey Combs) gets to the point in Re-Animator

perverse humour that pervades the film is best illustrated when the Dean's torso ties his daughter to an operating table, holding the salivating head of Dr. Hill next to her body in a very compromising position !

Quite simply, *Re-Animator* is an invigorating slice of the macabre, all the more so considering it was director Stuart Gordon's first attempt at horror.

He shows a great command of, and respect for, the genre, from the "Hammer" style orchestral strings in the score to the impressive production values and believable characterisations of West and Hill especially.

The perverse sex scene, that overshadows anything in *The Evil Dead*, and the plethora of splattery effects, rival any seen in the horror genre in recent years. This, coupled with the fluid camera and West's "noble" aim to create life contrasted with Hill's selfish pursuit

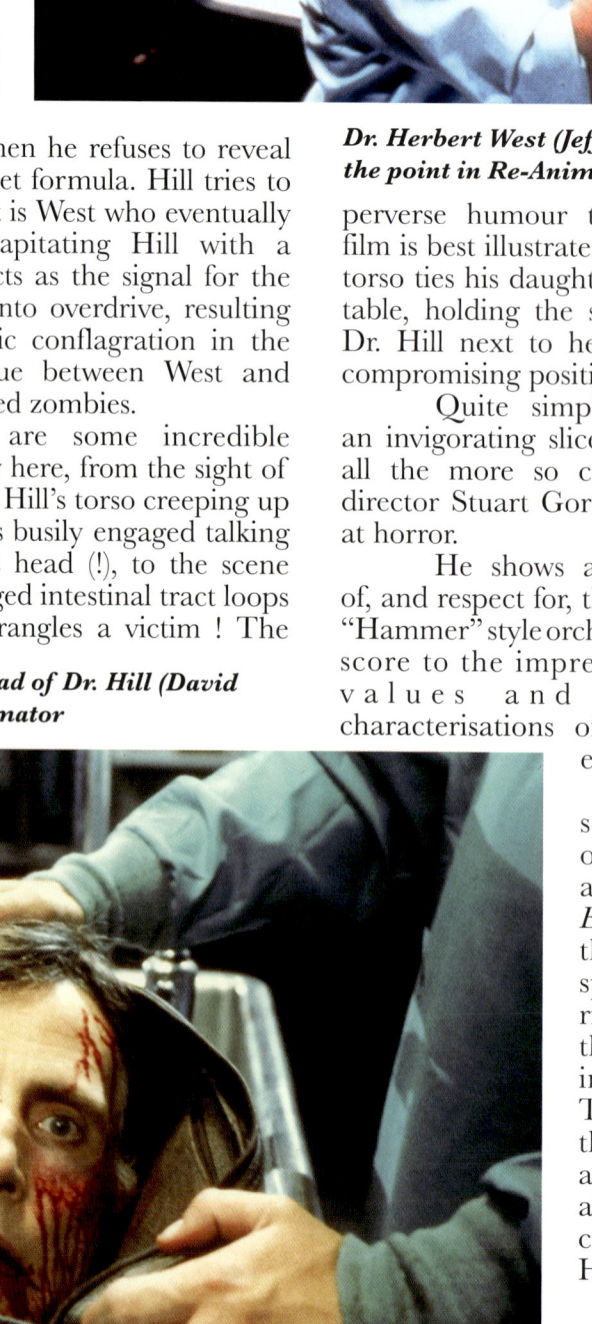

Bring me the head of Dr. Hill (David Gale) in Re-Animator

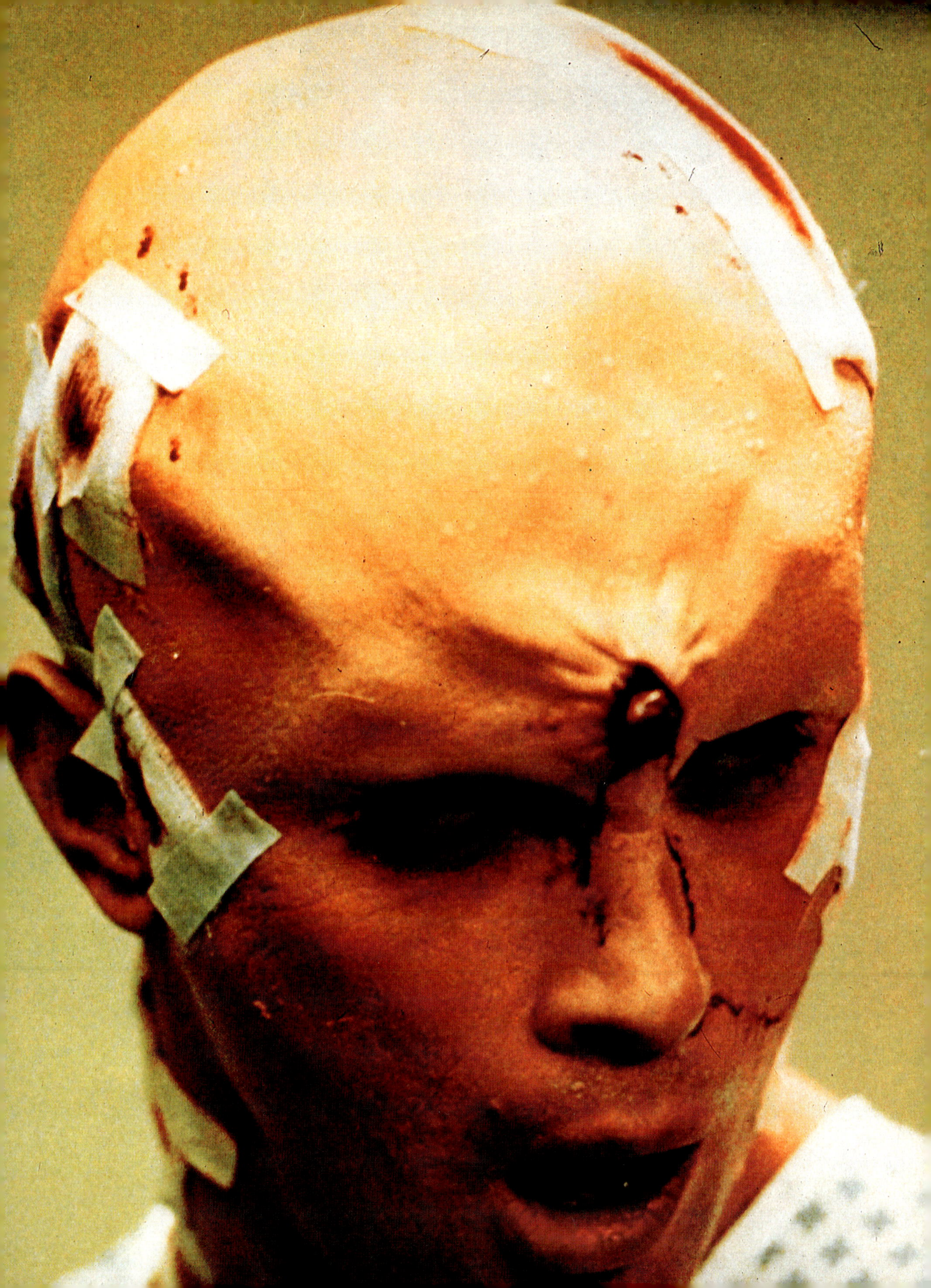

of medical recognition, help to further impress the viewer. Gordon has since taken these attributes to further projects such as *From Beyond* (1986), with another Lovecraftian theme, *The Pit and the Pendulum* (1990), *Castle Freak* (1996) and *Dagon* (2001).

From Beyond reunites Gordon with Combs as Crawford Tillinghast, Crampton as psychiatrist Dr. Katherine McMichaels and source material from H.P.Lovecraft again. The plot contrivance centres around the existence of space monsters occupying a parallel dimension to humans. It is the insane Dr. Pretorius (a nod to 1935's classic *Bride of Frankenstein*) who seeks to study the creatures by utilising his "Resonator" invention which works by stimulating the pineal gland and so allowing us to see the monsters.

He meets a particularly sticky end as one of his subjects eats him head first "like a gingerbread man" so Tillinghast helpfully observes. Also adding; "He (Pretorius) used to bring beautiful women here...eat fine meals, drink fine wine, listen to music...but it always ended with screaming."

Directed with Gordon's customary elan, *From Beyond* remains a fascinating offshoot to the whole Herbert West series.

Sequel to the impressive *Re-Animator*, *Bride of Re-Animator*, is scripted by Woody Keith, Rick Fry and Brian Yuzna, the same team that brought us *Society* (1989). The majority of the original film's principal players return here including the obsessed West (Combs), who takes his research one stage further this time - he attempts to create new life-forms as opposed to simply re-animating the dead. Once again the Miskatonic University Hospital is raided for body parts, only this time in order to rebuild Cain's (Bruce Abbott) girlfriend Gloria (Kathleen Kinmont). Also inspired by *Bride of Frankenstein*, this 'reborn' creature is "What no man's mind and no woman's womb ever dreamed of."

One thing West certainly didn't dream of is ending up behind bars but this is the very situation he finds himself in as Brian Yuzna's *Beyond Re-Animator* (2003), thanks to the evidence used against him by Cain.

West's 13 years incarceration has failed to nullify his thirst for scientific discovery, now aided by the similarly inclined prison director, Dr. Phillips (Jason Barry). This is especially so with the revalation that Phillips' sister was killed in West's last experiment before captivity.

Although West displays a more subtle intensity here given his own ageing, his relative lack of screen time and the introduction of a raft of new characters somewhat stymies the success of the film.

The most disappointing of all however, was the consignment to 'development hell' of Gordon's proposed satire on the George W.

Picture on previous page: From Beyond
Below: cover art for Re-Animator

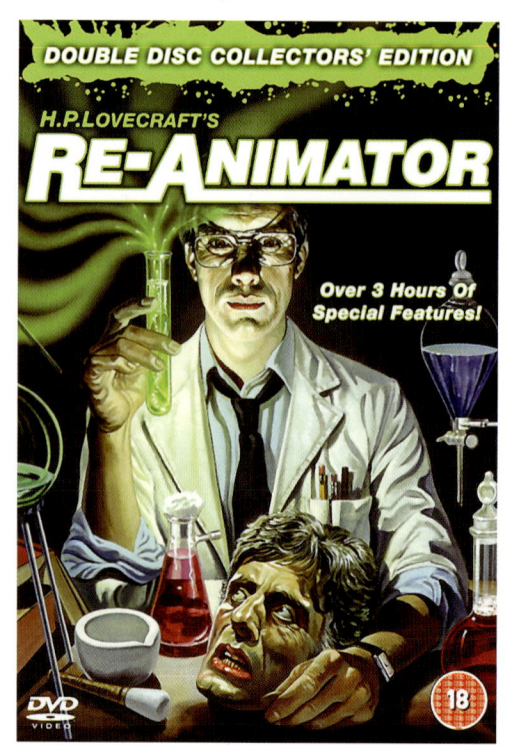

Bush presidency, *House of Re-Animator*. Set in the White House this would have reunited Combs and Abbott by reprising their roles from the original film, even down to Crompton returning as the First Lady!

The Return of the Living Dead (1985) may not feature rampant intestines and headless doctors but it definitely has the stomach for a cheeky and irreverent poke at the zombie films of the previous two decades. Written by *Night of the Living Dead*'s scriptwriter John Russo, it ingeniously takes for granted that the events in Romero's film happened for real!

Freddy (Thom Matthews), has just started work in the "Uneeda Medical Supplies"(!) warehouse in Louisville, and is shown around by his boss (James Karen). It transpires that some metal cylinders, which have been stored in the facility for twenty years, have now been accidentally broken by the two men, and the dead are starting to rise. This is where the film's humour comes into its' own as a frantic Freddy and his boss, joined by the stores manager (Clu Gulager), chop one zombie into pieces to kill it after an axe to the cranium has proved ineffective - "the movie lied" cries Freddy in disbelief. The wriggling limbs are then put unceremoniously into black plastic bags for cremation at the nearby morgue.

This proves to be a major error in judgement as the fumes from the burning zombie permeate the local "Resurrection Cemetery" and quickly revive the dead who are buried there, which is bad news for the punks who are partying in the self-same spot. The remainder of the action centres around the gang's fight for survival as they are forced to barricade themselves in the morgue, away from the zombies outside.

Some of the scenes owe more than a passing debt to Romero's influence - witness the zombiefication of

Herbert West (Jeffrey Combs) in Re-Animator

Dan Cain (Bruce Abbott) in Re-Animator

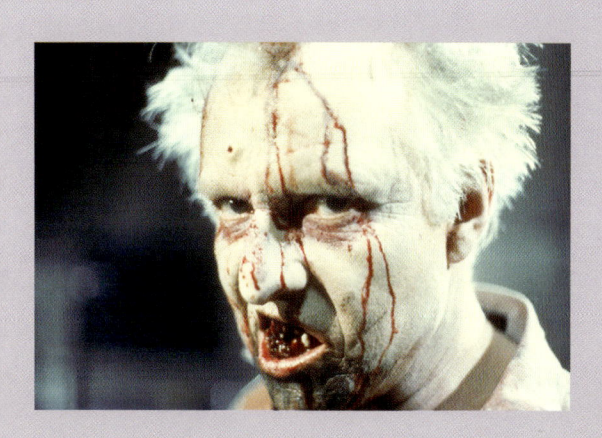

A zombie from Re-Animator

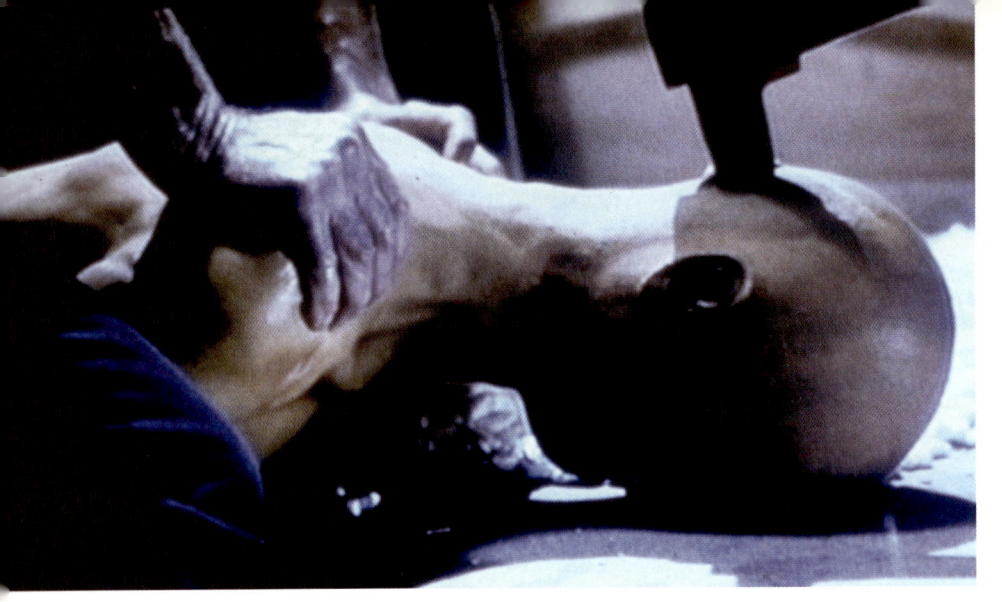

Both pictures on this page: Dan O'Bannon's hugely enjoyable spoof The Return of the Living Dead

one of the gang, Freddy, who gradually becomes one of the undead a la Roger in *Dawn of the Dead*, but on the whole, *The Return of the Living Dead* has enough ideas of its own to avoid any charges of merely "cloning" its predecessors. Take the zombies themselves, which give lie to the notion that zombies must be slow moving, shuffling and lobotomised in the tradition of Fulci and Romero.

Here, they are intelligent creatures in their own right, fast moving, communicative and cunning (in one scene they put out an SOS call to the authorities, "send more paramedics" (a name later appropriated by a Leeds metal band), having just devoured some helpless victims and commandeered their radio to set the trap). There are also liberal slices of off-beat humour such as Dan Calfa's nonchalant mortician, who listens to classical music on his Walkman and carries a revolver in his pocket, whilst going about his work. There is also a lengthy discussion between the gang and the half-body of one captured zombie that continues talking despite its' partial dismemberment.

The film also benefits from its enthusiastic punk soundtrack which features work from The Damned, The Cramps and Roky Erikson amongst others, and the skeletal jaw in the cemetery that lip-synch's "Let's Party" to welcome the 45 Grave track of the same title, is typical of the film's approach.

The only slight disappointment is that the punks with names such as "Trash" and "Suicide" seem to have been drawn from Hollywood's stereotypical model, even down to the arbitrary inclusion of Linnea Quigley's semi-nude antics in the cemetery, (she can also be glimpsed in a similar state of undress in *Night of the Demons* - 1987).

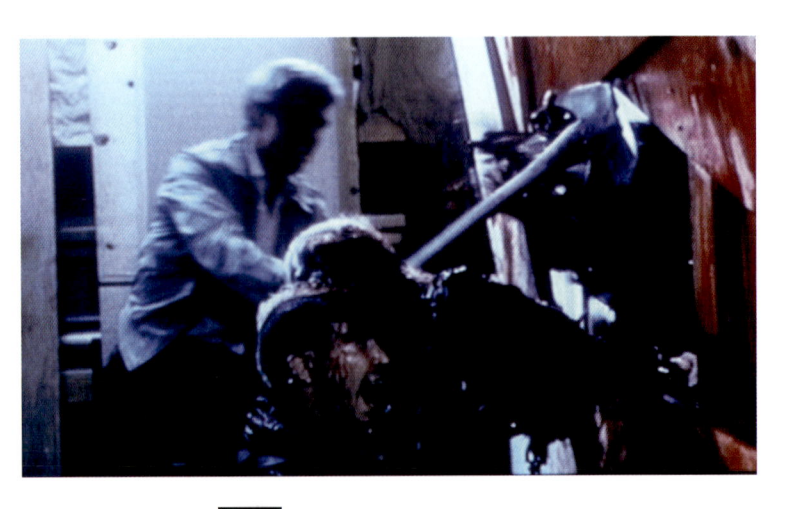

The film's generally impressive make-up creations, pounding music and director Dan O'Bannon's kinetic style certainly add to the film's superior quality, though it would have been interesting to see what the original choice of director, Tobe Hooper, would have made of the job.

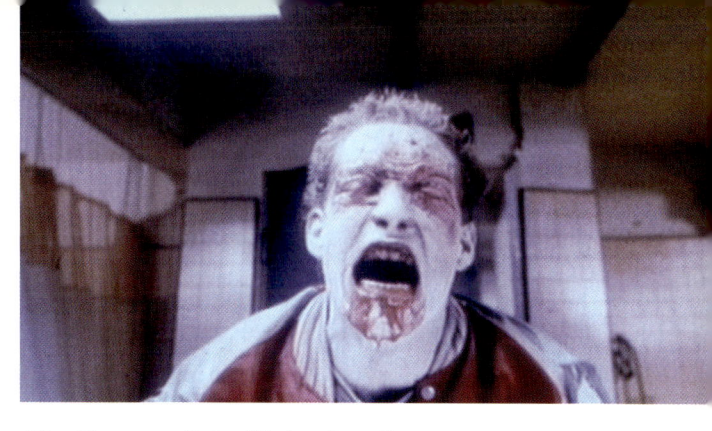

Needless to say, O'Bannon's film has begat further offspring - to date, *Return of the Living Dead 2* (1988), *Return of the Living Dead 3* (1993), *Return of the Living Dead: Necropolis* and *Return of the Living Dead: Rave to the Grave* (both 2005) !

One of the most bizarre zombie entries however proved to be Robert Zemeckis' big-budget *Death Becomes Her* (1992), whose big-name protagonists - an ageing screen icon Madeline (Meryl Streep) and her old college friend Helen (Goldie Hawn), in turn vie for the affections of a cuckolded plastic surgeon, Ernest, (Bruce Willis). Their 'battle of the bitches' culminating with Helen admonishing Madeline thus - "She married a brilliant surgeon and turned him into an undertaker."

Some startling special effects as Streep and Hawn are cursed to survive death, leads them to knock holes in one another, as even Streep's broken neck and Hawn's gaping stomach wound fail to dispel their passions as they strut their new-found zombiedom - "You're a fraud, Helen. You're a walking lie and I can see right through you" Madeline hisses.

The Return of the Living Dead

Very much more in the vein of the 1940's horror spoofs rather than the fast-paced action of *Back to the Future* (1985) as Zemeckis is known for, it is a very different approach to the typical low-budget zombie film, enhanced by the acidic script, plastic surgery satire and the leads' bravery in portraying such daringly unusual, ditto unsympathetic characters.

The ultimate irony here however, being that the film's satire on the slavish worship of the superficial by the beauty-obsessed movie industry by way of Beverley Hills and Hollywood, has now transcended its celebrity origins to be mirrored by an equally cosmetic-obsessed general public!

Given his proclivity for cosmetic surgery in *Death Becomes Her*, Bruce Willis' return to the zombie genre in Robert Rodriguez *Planet Terror* (2007), is all the more appropriate given the insistence on recreating the Grindhouse ambience of the seventies exploitation film scene. Only here, the cosmetic surgery is in reverse as the aim is to deliberately "doctor" the film stock to give the appearance of an older film complete with scratches, film grain, poor synching, faded colours and missing reels.

Originally slated as one half of *Grindhouse*, along with Quentin Tarantino's *Death Proof* (2007) - that director's intended homage, but ultimately, self-indulgent, conceit of running a double film bill with *Planet Terror* making up the spectacle, failed miserably at the box office. This may well have been in part due to Tarantino's own "talky" entry with Rodriguez supposedly more low profile offering, actually proving to be the most enjoyable and critically well received of the films by far. As Mark Kermode succintly noted in The Observer newspaper of Rodriguez film; "(it) lacks the self-congratulatory air (and interminably self-satisfied) dialogue of Quentin's wet dream."

Where Rodriguez scores in spades with *Planet Terror* is in not taking himself (or the genre) *too* seriously and yet still imbruing the film with enough gusto and affection to embrace its exploitation origins.

The strictly peripheral shlock-horror 'plot' sees Willis' renegade army chief Muldoon and a gang dealer Abby (Naveen Andrews) trade blows which result in the release of a biological weapons gas which, besides being highly contagious, also has the unfortunate side-effect of turning its victims into flesh-rotten, not to mention flesh-eating zombies.

Rose McGowan is a disaffected go-go dancer, Cherry, whose search for

Main picture: The deadly female is Cherry (Rose McGowan) in Planet Terror
Top picture: Cherry & Dakota (Marley Shelton) in Planet Terror
Bottom Picture: Dakota in Planet Terror

Wray (Freddy Rodriguez), Dakota (Marley Shelton) and Cherry (Rose McGowan) about to face the zombie hordes in Robert Rodriguez Planet Terror

a "new direction" only results in her seeking a new leg after a mass zombie chow down on her, only to be aided in her escape by one-time boyfriend Wray (Freddy Rodriguez). His ultimate solution to Cherry's predicament is to replace the limb with an M16 machine-gun instead.

With its mist-shrouded, near deserted highways and an eerie night-time ambience, the Texan locale serves as an effective backdrop to the prolific gun fights which rage between the survivors and the hungry zombie hordes.

In amongst this visceral mayhem, a minor emotional crisis resonates between the vindictive Dr. Block (Josh Brolin) and his physician wife Dakota (Marley Shelton) - her infidelity is revealed when her lover, Tammy (Stacy Ferguson) is brought into the hospital very much dead on arrival. Retribution spirals forth in a predictable face-off between the now infected Dr. Block against his wife and younng son.

Michael Biehn's turn as the hard nosed Sheriff Hague, "leading" the fightback is well observed, "aided" by the misfiring Deputy Tolo (played with relish by former Romero special effects guru, Tom Savini), whilst Quentin Tarantino himself is unable to resist a cameo appearance as a would be rapist, only for his illicit designs on the captive Cherry and Dakota to not be requited, courtesy of a particularly gross and appropriate demise, culminating with some severe genitalia melt-down - ouch!

Enlivened by the Carpenteresque synth score, the stylised icky green colour palette to evoke the B movies of the seventies as Rodriguez relentless pacing of the numerous firefights and explosions raises the spectre of Romero, Fulci and a multitude of Italian exploitationers that palpably fills the screen. The only irony being that unlike the aforementioned luminaries, Rodriguez has the monetary advantage of being able to spend millions in recreating the "dream" - which simply serves to reinforce the notion that you can't put a price on creativity and imagination and to pose the question as to when such attributes become compromised by corporate interference and financial expediency.

Above right pic: Bruce Willis as Muldoon in Planet Terror
Right pic: Cherry, Wray, Dakota & Abby (Naveen Andrews)

Wray (Freddy Rodriguez) with Cherry (Rose McGowan) riding shotgun (literally!) in Planet Terror

8
THE CONTINENTAL COUSIN – ZOMBIES AROUND THE GLOBE

Demons

The Continental Cousin - Zombies Around the Globe

Due to the reluctance of financial backers to subsidise the British film industry, the British horror film has become something of a rarity in recent years. This is surprising when considering the quality of films that have been made here, such as John Landis' humorously inventive *An American Werewolf in London* (1981), Neil Jordan's Freudian fairytale *A Company of Wolves* (1984) and Clive Barker's auspicious debut *Hellraiser* (1987).

From a country that once led the world in horror during the heyday of Hammer, it has been a sad fall from prominence. The worsening economic and employment situation led to a growth of British films that can loosely be termed "realist" in their portrayal of these factors and the accompanying social problems.

Of these films, *A Letter to Brezchnev* (1985) and *My Beautiful Laundrette* (1985) stand out, before the economic resurgence in the mid-nineties produced the comedy of *Four Weddings And A Funeral* (1994), hip-gangsters in *Lock Stock And Two Smoking Barrels* (1998) and the multi-cultural satire of *East is East* (1999).

Of the British films that have dealt with the living dead in one form or another, the James Bond adventure *Live and Let Die* (1973) reached the widest audience. Roger Moore, in his first Bond outing, is thrown against Yaphet Kotto's black villain who is intent on single-handedly turning America into a nation of drug zombies (he already appears to have had some success !), by flooding the "land of the free" with heroin to create a land of the enslaved.

It is a form of black retribution against the white race for their past colonialism. This revenge motif is effectively set against the backdrop of a Caribbean island immersed in superstition and voodoo regalia, all culminating in the well-staged voodoo ceremony where the suitably menacing Baron Samedi (Geoffrey Holder), rises up from the grave to instruct his obedient masses. Scare sequences such as these are interwoven with typical Bond fare such as Jane Seymour's beautiful tarot reading "Solitaire", who unfortunately, cannot see far enough into the future to realise the fate that she will suffer at the mercy of Bond's libido. An even worse fate befalls Kotto whose undignified exit has him filling up with air to balloon size before exploding, a feat emulated more humorously in the Monty Python team's *The Meaning of Life* (1983).

The interesting cast featuring J. W. Pepper's country clown sheriff, Dave Heddison's CIA agent (he had previously starred in the cult TV serial *Voyage to the Bottom of the Sea*) and Madeline Smith's vamp (she was a star in Hammer's 1971 entry *Twins of Evil*), inject the film with added vitality. *Live and Let Die* also boasts one of the finest Bond scores, the music here provided by Paul McCartney's "Wings". The half comic, half horror character of Baron Samedi holds the key to the film's success as Bond's gadgetry and innuendo take a back seat to the supernatural aura that pervades the film, embodied in the end sequence as

James Bond (Roger Moore) in a tricky situation in Live and Let Die

The tarot reading Solitaire (Jane Seymour) in 1973's Live and Let Die

a seemingly dead Samedi returns, sat atop the cow-catcher on Bond's fast moving train, and laughing creepily.

The part British, part Spanish production *Horror Express* (1972) is also set aboard a rapidly moving train, the Transiberian Express. The action is set in 1906 in China, as Christopher Lee's arrogant Professor Saxon discovers the fossilised remains of a neanderthal monster frozen in ice.

Saxon boards the train with a crate containing the animal, but not before the early demise of one inquisitive Chinese victim. Once on board the express the pace never falters, under the capable direction of Eugenio Martin. The neanderthal, who has a keen eye for a potential victim and a useful skill for picking up keys, escapes and begins to turn the majority of the train's passengers into zombies. This, he accomplishes by staring at the unwilling humans with his glowing red eyes that boil the brains and absorb the intelligence of his chosen victim.

The train's passengers include Peter Cushing as Dr. Wells - Saxon's professional rival, a spy, a Countess and a raving demonic priest (Albert de Mendoza) whose character owes more to Rasputin than Holy Orders.

Eventually, the creature is trapped and shot by police inspector Mirov, but not before one last, lingering stare from the creature, who transfers his "personality" and power to the now-infected inspector. It is then left to Wells and Saxon to defeat him, only after Telly Savalas' army of Cossacks have boarded the train to be arbitrarily reduced to zombies en masse. The final scenes, as the scarlet-coated, erubescent-orbed cossacks march to kill the remaining survivors, still trapped within the confines of the train, are classically frightening in a claustrophobic way. The Express speeds relentlessly towards its inevitable demise with the uncoupled carriageful of zombies careering off a cliff edge, with the survivors carriage halting just in time before the looming precipice.

The most notable features of the film are its breakneck direction, emulating the momentum of the locomotive, and its outrageous, though ingenious, science fiction explanation for the creature's existence. This has Saxon and Wells discovering that

Zombies on the loose in Horror Express

the neanderthal's eye retina contains images of earth from outer space and a history of the world as dinosaurs can also be glimpsed through the eye's image.

The central theme of an alien who can transfer from one body to another, taking over that form, is also the basis for Howard Hawk's *The Thing From Another World* (1951), and its special effects dominated remake, *The Thing*, by John Carpenter in 1982. The idea that the creature could be anyone, could even be standing next to you, works well within the cramped interiors of the train in *Horror Express*. The film plays as a supernatural "Murder on the Orient Express", only here substitute a mysterious creature for a mystery killer(s). Tom Gries' *Breakheart Pass* (1975) and the tense, *The Cassandra Crossing* (1976) create the same nervy tension by confining their action to on board a fast-paced train.

Martin also manages to suffuse his film with some nicely judged humour, as when Saxon and Wells themselves are accused of playing host to the creature they reply in unison; "But we are British !" For them the dilemma they face is the age-old horror conflict of scientific breakthrough set against endangering their fellow human beings. Saxon, who brought the creature back to civilisation and so does endanger his fellow men, but in pursuit of a greater goal, as the creature remarks; "Let me live and I will give you the power to end disease, war, famine." It's a trick but an attractive one. The time-honoured tempting by the Devil in "Faust" and more humorously *Party Animal* (1984) has been taken from a religious plane to a scientific one. It is the same temptation that Baron Frankenstein succumbs to in *Frankenstein* (1931 & 1957). Whereas the lure of say the vampire is immortality, the lure of this creature is world peace, an inviting trap to lay.

Images from Eugenio Martin's engaging chiller Horror Express

HORROR EXPRESS (1972)

When producer Bernard Gordon picked up Peter Cushing at Madrid Airport in December 1971, he received unwelcome news. Filming on *Horror Express* had begun the previous week, and Cushing scenes were to commence filming the next day. Cushing stated he did not want to participate in the film and that it was his intention to return to England. Cushing said that while he had approved of the first draft of the script, he did not approve of the final draft. It is much more probable that since *Horror Express* was to be his first film shoot outside of England since the sad death of his wife less than a year before, that he was suffering from both grief and homesickness.

Gordon asked Christopher Lee to help the situation. All three got together in Cushing's hotel sitting room. There, Lee proceeded to bombard his old friend with stories, jokes and anecdotes. He did not allow Cushing an opportunity to mention his departure. Lee wished Cushing a goodnight, and next saw him on the set of *Horror Express*! Cushing would tell Gordon a week later that he now really liked both the film and its script.

It's amazing to think that one of Cushing and Lee's finest collaborations, and certainly most innovative and interesting films, wasn't produced by Hammer, as might well be expected, but by a small independent company, Scotia International that usually made Euro Westerns. Financed by backers in London and to a lesser extent Hollywood, Scotia International's few films were shot in Spain under the guiding hand of Bernard Gordon, who had previously been a scriptwriter. *Horror Express*, ironically, was to be the company's last film. It's clever script works on a number of levels and benefits from sharp direction and editing. It's set design is impressive, and the film is beautifully photographed. All on a budget of approximately $350,000 on a 28 day shooting schedule. As often happens, quality and budget are not always in direct proportion.

The fine screenplay was created by Arnaud D'Usseau (first draft) and Julian Halevy (final draft) with scenes added and re-written during production by Bernard Gordon.

The bulk of the film takes place on the Trans-Siberian Express, which is being used to transport a 'missing link', a 'fossil' as Christopher Lee's character, anthropologist Alexander Saxton describes the creature he finds frozen in a cave in the Provincia de Szechuan in 1906 China. Once thawed, the creature breaks free and the alien life-force within inhabits one host after another (shades of *The Thing From Another World* (1951) and especially its' fine John Carpenter remake *The Thing* (1982)) as the Trans-Siberian Express speeds through the frozen tundra between Peking and Moscow.

The alien life-force is the sum of all the memories absorbed from its victims. For example, its absorbing the memories of an expert lock-pick enable it to escape from its locked crate on the train.

It has one single-minded (if you'll pardon the pun!) purpose- it wants to return home, and it's not using the 'E.T phone home'-method! Accidentally left behind on the Earth millions of years earlier, it has survived in a variety of creatures, a mental parasite hopping from host to host. It now knows that finally technology is fast approaching the point where it can return home, as it absorbs information from the scientist and engineer amongst its

The Continental Cousin - Zombies Around the Globe

victims.

To add further spice to an already imaginative and exotic concoction, there is Pujardov (Alberto De Mendoza), a Rasputin-like figure, who is spiritual advisor to two other passengers on the train-the Count Petrovski and Countess Irina. Before the creature is even stored in the train-he sees the corpse of the thief who attempted to pick the lock of its case-with eyes like those of a boiled fish. Instantly, he tried to inscribe a cross on the box but to no avail. He states prophetically-"Satan is evil. And where Evil lives there is no place for the cross."

Once the creature is loaded onto the train, the pace accelerates at the same paces as the speeding steam engine.

As the journey continues, so does the creature's knowledge. A gorgeous stowaway called Natasha (Helga Line), who is in reality an international spy, seeking Count Petrovski's formula for a steel harder than diamond. Absorbing her mind, the creature learns of the existence of the formula and seeks and possesses Police Inspector Mirov (Julia Pena) to make acquiring the formula possible. An engineer travelling on the train makes the deadly mistake of discussing his study of the rocket propulsion needed to escape the earth's gravitational field, becomes part of the Creature's mental library.

The creature must protect itself from discovery by rival British anthropologists Saxton (Christopher Lee) and Dr. Wells (Peter Cushing). After Mirov shoots it, causing the creature within to possess his body, Saxton and Well's draw fluid from the missing link's eye. Under a microscope they see images of prehistoric creatures and the Earth seen from outer space. They assume that an alien creature had inhabited the missing link's body and that it's memories are located in it's eyes, and also that the alien absorbs its victims memories through the eyes.

To protect itself, the creature must destroy the anthropologists and also Well's American assistant Miss Jones (Alice Reinheart) and the Countess Irina (Silvia Tortosa), all of whom saw the microscope images. To further complicate the creature's already complex life, Captain Kazan and his squad of Cossacks board the train to investigate the murders-subsequently becoming zombies at the hands of the creature.

The interplay between Lee and Cushing is a delight. Cushing's Dr Wells describes Lee's Saxton as a man "who dabbles in fossils and bones." Wells gets a private compartment without a reservation, "It's called 'squeeze' in China. The American's call it 'know how'." "And in Britain we call it bribery and corruption", Saxton states, before sweeping the ticket clerk's desk clear with his umbrella and gaining the required ticket.

Later Cushing comments to Lee that "you've got something alive in there. I heard it." Lee answers deadpan. "The occupant hasn't eaten in two million years." Cushing goes one better with. "That's one way to economise on food bills."

There is also a fun scene where Cushing offer to make the 'huge sacrifice' of sharing his compartment with the lovely Natasha only to have Lee unexpectedly join him. "Couldn't you double up with someone else?" Cushing pleads.

Despite their differing personalities a strong respect grows between Saxton and Wells.

Saxton's character has a great moment when challenged on his disinterest in the growing number of deaths by the Countess Irina. "You're right, madam, I don't care as much as I should." Later he will reject a tempting offer from the creature, showing how much he has changed since the conflict began.

The all-time classic line has to be, when the possessed Miroc suggested Cushing or Lee could be the creature. "Monster? We're British you know."

Eventually, Wells and Sexton save the remaining passengers by gathering theme into the baggage car and detaching it from the rest of the train, which speeds off a cliff top to explode into an inferno, destroying both creator and his zombie creations.

Bringing added flavour to a loaded smorgasbord is Telly Savalas' deranged Cossack Captain Kazan. Drinking vodka like water, whipping the mad monk and sacrilege… striking Christopher Lee. The Countess threatens to have him sent to Siberia, he amusingly replies he already is in Siberia

Eugenio Martin directs with confidence and verve, and uses the pace and isolation of the train to great effect.

The trains in the film were previously made for a previous Scotia International production *Pancho Villa* (1972). Indeed the trains inspired the genesis of *Horror Express* as Scotia needed a project to utilise their fine trains.

Alejandro Ulleas' photography is rich and multi-layered, adding veneer to an already classic picture.

John Cacavas soundtrack is particularly haunting, particularly the main theme, which is whistled in the film itself, and echoes of it can be heard in the later work of John Carpenter and Goblin. Peter Cushing describes it as "…exactly the right sort of thing, very tasteful and full of fun with dark chords in all the appropriate moments and prestos in their proper places. John Cacavas is a very talented man." (Interestingly, Cacavas would go on to be composer-music director of Kojak starring *Horror Express*'s Telly Savalas. He would also compose the music for such films as *Airport* 1975, *Airport '77*, and *The Executioner's Song* (1982).

The wrought iron train station we see at the start of the film was built in Spain by no less than one Alexandre Gustave Eiffel!

The monk, possessed by the creature looks most Satanic as do the zombies.

Cushing's first Christmas without his wife Helen was spent with Christopher Lee, his wife Gitte and Christina Lee.

MISCELLANEOUS

Cinema TV Today described the film thus on release-"Gothic Horror on wheels, highly sprinkled with in-jokes for the benefit of British audience who can enjoy the understated wit with which Christopher Lee and Peter Cushing portray stiff upper-lipped Englishmen coping with a lot of hysterical foreigners."

While…

Monthly Film Bulletin said "When a hairy monster arm snakes out of the crate after the murder of the baggage-car attendant, and begins to pick the lock with professional expertise to let itself out, one begins to sneer at the improbability; but then the tune the dead man was whistling is heard mysteriously continuing along the corridor, and it gradually dawns the creature learned its lock-picking from its first victim (the thief at the station), just as it picked up the whistled tune from its second victim.

In 1984 in American Film

The Continental Cousin - Zombies Around the Globe

Magazine's Halloween issue, director Joe Dante described it thus- "Cossacks, countesses, and mad monks abound, the plotting achieves astonishing complexity for a film of this type, and the level of humour is highly sophisticated. Cushing and Lee are especially amusing in a sort of Basil Redford-Naunton Wayne relationship. In short, it's a real treat."

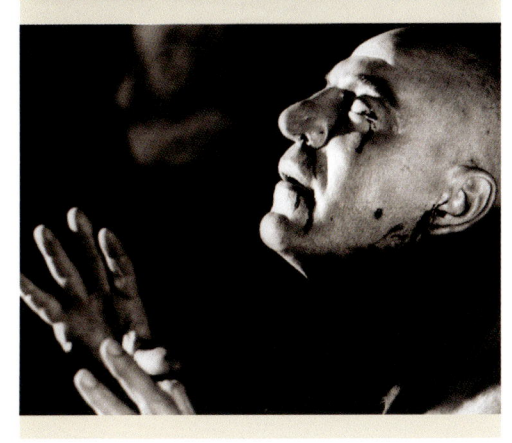

No such wider theorising in Hammer's bizarre mixture of the vampire and martial arts genre's, *The Legend of the Seven Golden Vampires* (1973), which owes more to the zombie than the vampire for its' thrills. The powdery faced Dracula (John Forbes-Robertson), complete with gaudy lipstick, is more camp than Count, lacking Christopher Lee's commanding stature and presence. Dracula returns to China to resurrect his vampire forces (the 7 Golden Vampires), who seek to terrorise the nearby village of Ping Kuei and it is these scenes of heaving earth that steal the show as all around the darkened graveyard, arms and heads burst up into view.

The slow motion scenes of the army of the dead charging towards the isolated village, and of the apocalyptic horse-riding vampires inject the film with its only real frissons. It's very much a case of Hammer robbing their own grave (*Plague of the Zombies*), but these sequences are still more effective than the rest of the film. It is left to Peter Cushing, reprising his Van Helsing role, and his young protege (David Chiang) to defeat the vampires.

Despite some well-staged martial arts battles, the action never really excites and the Chinese scenery is of more interest than the cast which includes the decorative Julie Edge. The film's one inventive moment sees Chiang impale both himself and Edge on the same stake for a unique double death. Dracula's expected demise, as Cushing plunges a metal spike into him, is also a reflection of the film's lack of ideas.

Director Roy Ward Baker fared rather better with his earlier Hammer entries; *The Vampire Lovers* (1970), and *Dr. Jekyll and Sister Hyde* (1971). *The Legend of the Seven Golden Vampires* is very much a case of a missed opportunity by Hammer. The idea of merging the western gothic with oriental, martial arts/action was a good one but both

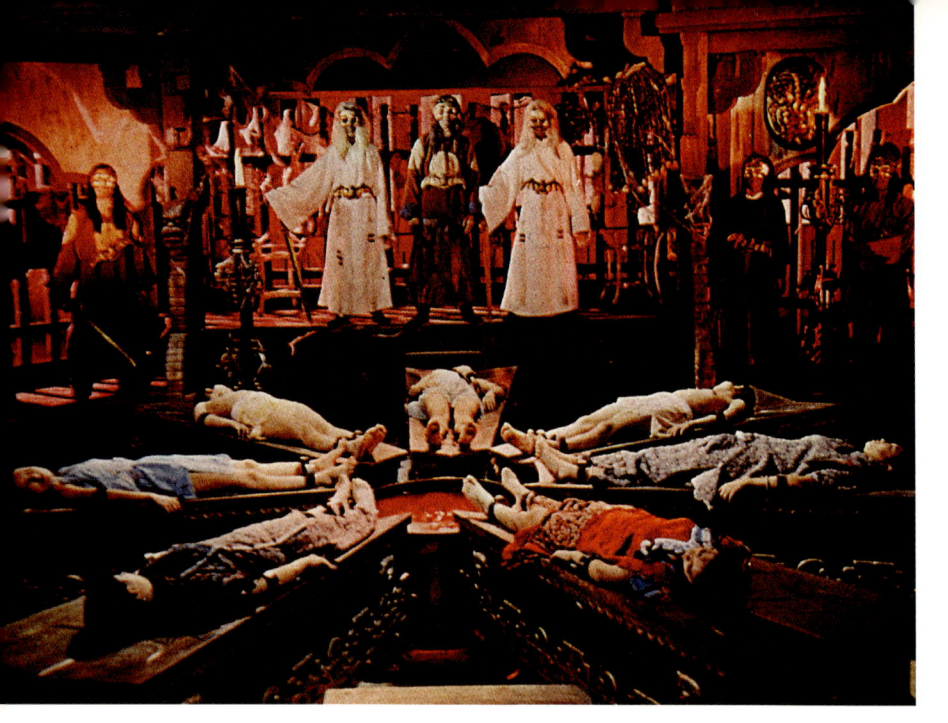

The Legend of the Seven Golden Vampires

elements needed to be more fully developed into a stylised formula and hung around a more original premise.

Director Amando de Ossorio has almost single-handedly been responsible for the creation of the Spanish zombie with his series of films based around the Knights Templar.

TEMPLARS ARISE!

"KNIGHTS OF THE BLIND DEAD!"

Spanish director Amando de Ossorio created horror films that, while deficient in many respects, particularly in their treatment of women (vile and unnecessary- as all such scenes are- I actually prefer the cut versions of the films with such foul misogyny removed- a rare example of positive censorship), they are noteworthy for the creation of the Blind Dead themselves, undead, sightless, Knights Templar, who hunt their prey by sound, their creepy movement not entirely part of our reality, enhanced by a fine score by Anton Garcia Abril.

The first of these films, *Tombs Of The Blind Dead* (1971), begins in a very boring fashion, the film only coming alive when a young woman, Virginia, leaves a train following a disagreement with her friends, Betty and Roger, and spends the night in a derelict monastery (as you did back in the 70s!). During the night, corpses arise from their graves and kill her. In the meantime her friends have become concerned. They start out for the monastery and begin to learn of the legends of the Knights Templar connected with the graveyard.

They are told by the police that their friend's body has been found. Virginia's body, while in the morgue, reanimates and kills the creepy mortuary attendant. Roger and Betty visit a medieval expert, Professor Cantal, who explains the Templars returned from the Crusades practising Satanism, they were executed for this, their bodies hung from trees so the birds could devour their eyes.

Betty's assistant Nina is attacked by Virginia, who is destroyed by fire. Roger and Betty meet Pedro, the Professor's son, who is a bandit leader whom the police believe is responsible for the killing. Pedro brutally attacks Betty. The Templars arise again and Pedro deservedly is killed, as is everyone except Betty. She makes her way to the train, as do The Blind Dead, who kill all the passengers save for Betty. When the train arrives, the Templars find fresh victims, and the film ends on an almost apocalyptic note. To say the film is poorly acted and badly plotted is an understatement. Loathsome in

The Continental Cousin - Zombies Around the Globe

it's treatment of women, the film is in fact very dull, save for the Blind Dead themselves. When they are on screen, the film comes alive, and one can only mourn that the entire film isn't of that quality. The Blind Dead, with their mummified faces, blank empty eye-sockets, and rotting monks cowls, are an awesome concept. A true medi-evil dead! Fast forward to the Templars and ignore the rest.

The next film *Return Of The Evil Dead* (1973) is the best of the four. Opening with a flashback to the Templars sacrificing a young girl, from the village of Berzano, in the medieval period. The local villagers however, have had enough of these evil priests, and rise up against them. (This gives this film a great resonance, symbolic of the power of the medieval church, which lived off the people it purported to serve, indeed, it demanded both money, servitude and blood during the Crusades, the Templars in particular, were hated and feared.

The theme of powerful overlords exploiting the peasants, is of course a strong theme in the Hammer Horror cycle, such as *Plague of the Zombies*. The villagers storm the monastery and put out the Templars eyes, so they can't find their way back from hell (a strongly symbolic desecration, the eyes being the windows of the soul in many cultures and times, and of course, an act of vengeance against an oppressive and wealthy church).

The action shifts to the present day. The citizens of Berzano prepare to celebrate the anniversary of the destruction of the Templars by burning them in effigy. A man named Jack arrives to set up fireworks for the celebration. He meets an old flame, Vivian, and they walk together to the ruined Templar monastery. They are met by a crippled man, Murdo, who tells them the Templars will arise this very night.

As the celebrations begin, the Templars do, as promised, arise! (though how they managed to have bodies to re-animate, or even be buried with, since they were incinerated (in-sin-erated?) at the stake, is never explained). On their undead steeds they ride into town (again, the question of where the horses came from is not explained either). All attempts by the villagers to escape or get help fail. The Templars slaughter the townsfolk, the people who laughed and mocked at what they thought was a myth are no longer laughing but screaming. The beautiful people are not beautiful anymore.

Jack leads a spirited defence, allowing his companions to barricade themselves in the church. They find Murdo already inside, he used a tunnel to enter the church. But when he and another survivor use it to escape, they are both killed. Everyone eventually dies save for Jack, Vivian and a little

The Blind Dead are on the march!

These muthas' may be blind but they still mean business!

girl.

After the night of the blind dead has passed, the Templars are still standing sentinel in the morning. They attempt to leave quietly, but the threat has passed, the Blind Dead have lost their power as the sun rises, and they crumple to the ground. Easily the best of all four films. Far more Templars, far less exploitation of women. Taut direction and a strong plot really make this a memorable film that still stands up well today. It owes a lot to *Night Of The Living Dead* but then all post-1968 zombie films do.

The villager's cruel treatment of Murdo is particularly affecting, and certainly de Ossorio is making subtle points about the corruption and disregard shown for ordinary people by the authorise, the Mayor being more like a feudal overlord. Franco still ruled Spain at the time, so de Ossorio had a deep well to draw inspiration from and the film is all the better for it. The medieval flashback is a fine notion, and really adds to the atmosphere of creeping death across the centuries And of course, the Templars are an awesome creation indeed, de Ossorio was a fine artist, and his conceptual paintings of the Templars have an incredible, otherworldly vitality.

It is a shame that technological and other considerations held him back from fully realising his vision. (When you think of the huge budgets wasted on dull films, remakes and the like, it makes the conditions de Ossorio struggled under particularly poignant, indeed it serves to remind one that whatever his films shortcomings, even making them was a great achievement, that he would create the Blind Dead is even more impressive.)

The third film in the series, *Horror of the Zombies* (1974), alas, showed a steep decline in quality, and, in the interests of honesty, much as one would wish it otherwise, is utterly dire. The plot, such as it is, concerns a pair of glamour models at sea (much like the viewer!), as part of a publicity stunt (the mind can only boggle, still it was the 70s so perhaps it felt like a good idea at the time!). Their boat is struck by a ghost ship. They radio for help and then enter the ghost ship. A group of people leave to search for them. They find the ghost galleon with the aid of a professor who has been investigating reports of ghost ship sightings in the area.

The professor believes they have entered another dimension (that's one way of putting it). The rescue party go aboard the ghost galleon, and one of their number is killed. The professor finds a logbook that says the galleon was captained by a Dutchman, bringing back Templars excommunicated for devil worship, and

The Continental Cousin - Zombies Around the Globe

apparently, the now undead Templars are guarding a horde of treasure on the ship. They find a hidden room with the said treasure, and a horned human skull, which the Templars apparently worship as an idol, and not a stage prop from Slayer as you might expect.

The Blind Dead, as is the way with the Blind Dead, arise once again, and attack their rather stupid visitors, who hold the Templars back with a burning wooden cross, driving them back to their coffins. They try to hail a passing ship but they are invisible due to being in 'another dimension'. They throw the coffins overboard, and swim for shore. The professor stays onboard as he cannot swim. The sockets of the horned skull glow red and the ship combusts. Only two survivors make it to the shore, where the Templars emerge from the water and kill them, (A grimly effective scene, would that there had been more like this).

Once again, de Ossorio's fabulous vision is hampered by his frugal budget. Once again, the treatment of women is loathsome. Even the Templars, removed from their horses, and hampered by the confines of the ship, lack the effectiveness and atmosphere they show at the end of the film. The sole positive outcome of *Horror of the Zombies* would be it's influences on John Carpenter's Lovecraftain *The Fog*.

Thankfully, the final film in the series, *Night Of The Seagulls* (1975), would be a fitting swansong to de Ossorio's creations.

The film begins with another medieval flashback. A couple are travelling by cart on a foggy night. The woman grows nervous and the man seeks shelter in a nearby house. He is surrounded by white-robed warrior monks who kill him, then abduct the women, whom they bring to nearby castle where she is sacrificed to a hideous idol.

Moving to the present day. A couple, Doctor Henry Stein and his wife Joan, travel to a Lovecraftian village to take over from it's retiring doctor. When they reach the cottage, they find the doctor cannot get away fast enough, curious, Henry joins the old fellow for part of his journey. Whilst Henry is away, Joan tends to the wounds of a misfortunate cripple (what did de Ossorio have against the handicapped, it's positively medieval, in those days people vilely believed that people's physical form was an indicator of their 'good' or 'evil', mind you, they also believed the earth was flat and that women were the spawn of the devil) named Teddy who was beaten by the sadistic (and doubtlessly inbred) villagers. Later, Joan and Henry see a young girl being led to the beach, what

Things don't look good for this young lady in Amando de Ossorio's Horror of the Zombies

The Dead Walk

they don't see is her being left for the Templars

Joan finds the villagers hostile, the local shopkeeper is reluctant to serve her (I almost expect her to tell her "this is a local shop, for local people, when did you last sacrifice a comely maiden to a group of undead optically challenged religious fanatics?"). Joan meets a young women named Lucy, who offers to do some housework for Joan.

That night a girl named Tilda runs to the doctor's house, but she is taken away by the villagers and sacrificed. Following Teddy's directions, Henry tries to discover Tilda's fate, but receives only lies as answers. Teddy is pushed from a cliff by the evil villagers and badly hurt. That evening, the villagers come to the doctor's house for Lucy, who leaves with them. Henry wants Joan to leave, as the seagulls howl overhead. Teddy makes his way to the house, returning to the only place he was ever shown kindness, to die. He tells Joan and Henry that for seven nights each year, seven young girls are sacrificed to prevent the Templars from destroying the village.

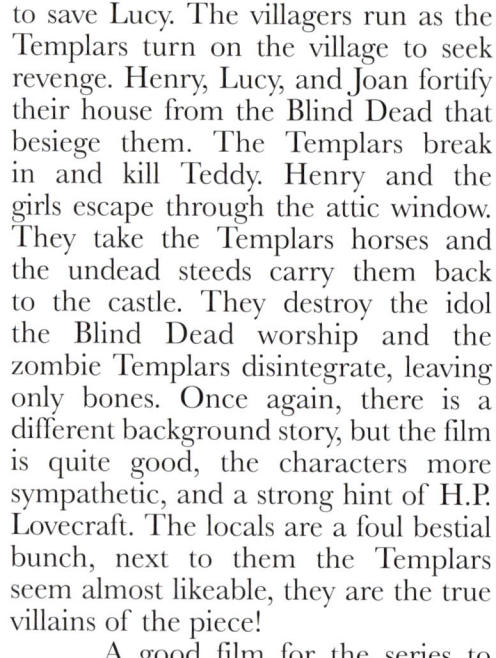

After death, the souls of the girls come back as seagulls. Henry goes to save Lucy. The villagers run as the Templars turn on the village to seek revenge. Henry, Lucy, and Joan fortify their house from the Blind Dead that besiege them. The Templars break in and kill Teddy. Henry and the girls escape through the attic window. They take the Templars horses and the undead steeds carry them back to the castle. They destroy the idol the Blind Dead worship and the zombie Templars disintegrate, leaving only bones. Once again, there is a different background story, but the film is quite good, the characters more sympathetic, and a strong hint of H.P. Lovecraft. The locals are a foul bestial bunch, next to them the Templars seem almost likeable, they are the true villains of the piece!

A good film for the series to end on. Looking on the positive side, making horror films in Franco's Spain was no easy task, and factoring in problems with infrastructure, budget, and the technology and expertise required to realise de Ossorio's vision, it's a remarkable achievement indeed. We can only feel for such an artist, full of visions he could never realise fully, his unrealised conceptual paintings are ample proof of this. I sincerely hope that with the renewed interest in both the Knights Templars and de Ossorio's work, that some enterprising filmmaker (Guillermo Del Toro would be perfect!) will one day realise fully, this man's unique creation and put the Blind Dead in a film his vision deserves.

The Knights Templars do their worst in The Return of the Evil Dead

*"That is not dead
Which can eternal lie
Yet with strange aeons
Even death may die."*

(H.P. Lovecraft)

The Continental Cousin - Zombies Around the Globe

THE KNIGHTS TEMPLARS

"KNIGHTS OF THE SWORD."

The Knights Templars were a religious and military order established in the Middle Ages. A kind of SWAT team for the Church. They fought in the Crusades, becoming famed for their ferocity in battle, they also became famed as one of the richest and most influential groups in the Christian world.

The order of Knights Templars was founded in Jerusalem in 1119. Several French Knights pledged themselves to defending the Holy Sepulchre. Under the leadership of Hugues de Payens of Champagne, they also vowed to defend Christian pilgrims in the Holy Land. The Knights Templars at first limited membership to nobles, who took vows of poverty and obedience.

The Knights Templars expanded quickly. We have to remember that, in the Middle Ages, Jerusalem is shown as the centre of the world. Baldwin, King of Jerusalem, gave the Knights Templars quarters in his palace, built on the site of Solomon's Temple. This was the origin of their name, Poor knights of the Temple. The Templars adopted the Benedictine rule. They wore white robes with red crosses. The order eventually came to have four classes of members. The knights and sergeants were the fighters. The farmers carried on the worldly affairs of the order. The chaplains took care of the religious needs of all the members.

The Pope took the Knights under his special protection, and following his lead, many European rulers granted them favours. They gained possession of property all over Europe. The Knights Templars played an important part on the battles of the Crusades. Thousands of Knights were killed while fighting in the Holy land. To promote the cause of the Crusades, the Knights Templars established local offices, or temples, in all the Christian countries. These offices encouraged enlistment in the crusading armies and took care of funds for the pilgrims. The Templars were drawn into the banking business and gained new power and influence. But, the ruling princes of Europe coveted the Templars' goods. Philip IV, (the so-called 'Fair' but in reality, anything but), of France, started an investigation of the order in the early 1300s. He ordered all the Templars in France thrown into jail, where they were tortured until they confessed to false accusations of heresy.

Templars in England, Spain, German and Portugal also stood trial, but most were acquitted. Pope Clemet V was persuaded to abolish the order in 1312. The Grand Master of the Templars, Jacques de Molay, confessed to false charges during the French trials. He later withdrew his confession, but was burned at the stake in 1314. The King of France stole most of the cash wealth of the Templars, while the Knights of Saint John received most of their lands.

The Templars moved quickly from reality to legend. The Templar Knight in Ivanhoe, Brian of Bois-Guilbert is "valient as the bravest of his Order, but stained with their usual vices, pride, arrogance, cruelty, and a voluptuousness, a hard-hearted amn, who knows neither fear of Earth, nor awe of Heaven." In Wagner's Parsifal, Templar-like knights appear as the chaste guardians of the Holy Grail.'

It is believed more recently that the Templars were initiated in the mysteries of ancient Egypt, which were passed on to the Free Masonic lodges of modern times. It is also said that they were infiltrated by the Cathars, that they have protected the bloodline of Jesus Christ and Mary Magdalene and were guardians of many holy relics, including the embalmed head of Christ, the Holy Grail, the Shroud Of Turin, the embalmed head of John The Baptist, and even an idol called Baphomet!

It is possible that the Templars brought new knowledge and customs back from the Middle East, which was far ahead of Europe in such practices as medicine, hygiene, mathematics and astronomy, this could have given ammunition to their enemies, jealous of their wealth and success. What we can be certain of, is the Templars were the first multi-nation, military and financial force, engaged in the defence of the Christian concept of a new world order.

Appropriately enough in Franco's Spain(!), the prolific Spanish film-maker Jesus Franco has made frequent forays into the zombie genre, some completely unmemorable such as *Virgin Among The Living Dead* (1982), but others such as the *Secret of Dr Orloff* (1962) are almost credible. This, the sequel to *The Awful Dr. Orloff* of the same year, bears little resemblance to the first film, save for the appearance of Marcelo Arroita Jauregui again, this time as a disciple of the evil titular doctor.

He develops a technique for controlling people's minds through the signal from a radio beam, a theme graphically revised and expanded to modern television in David Cronenberg's *Videodrome* (1982). Angered by his wife (Pirla Cristal) and her relationship with his brother (Hugo Blanco) he kills and transforms Blanco into a woman-killing zombie, Cristal numbering amongst his victims.

It is the zombie's daughter (Agnes Spaak), who alerts the police to the situation, whereupon the doctor orders his creation to kill Spaak, the zombie's own daughter. For Blanco, however, paternal instinct is still intact and he refuses, turning instead on his master before then vanishing into the woods.

He is finally lured back to the village by the authorities who use his daughter as bait. He is shot as he returns to see her, as she is held captive in the village square. It is a film refreshingly free from glib endings as Franco does try to explore the relationship between the zombie and his daughter, though admittedly, not to its furthest extent. It is still one of Franco's better films although his oneiric *Venus in Furs* (1969), featuring a suitably psychotic Klaus Kinski in the title role, remains the best in his prolific oeuvre.

The most memorable zombie film to originate from Spain (in title especially) is Jorge Grau's *The Living Dead At The Manchester Morgue* (1974), shot in England's scenic Lake District with a Spanish film crew. It remains one of the most assured films made in the "image" of *Night of the Living Dead*.

Here, the political emphasis is even further to the fore in the shape of Ray Lovelock's left-wing biker, Trendy George (the name says it all), and in Arthur Kennedy's ultra right-wing policeman, Sergeant McCormick. Filmed in colour, the exterior scenes are exploited to the full as the screen is awash with red splashes of blood that contrast vividly against the lush green, countryside surroundings. The graphic scenes that are on view here are made all the more so by the painterly backgrounds that they are set against.

The film's political tone is set early on as we learn that a Ministry of Agriculture machine that uses ultra-sonic soundwaves to kill pests (the question of insect or human is raised), is in fact making the bugs eat

Jorge Grau's superior The Living Dead At The Manchester Morgue

each other, symptoms that are soon prevalent in the human population. The opening shots of a busy city show the "zombiefied" commuters travelling uncaringly to work, set against a backdrop of billowing pollution clouds. A tramp inhabits a shop doorway and a naked girl runs through the streets unnoticed, as a radio announcer warns of "hysteria when confronted with ecological problems."

The action soon cuts to the picturesque Lake District where a holidaying George meets up with a young woman (Christine Galbo). As George leaves to ask for directions, so Galbo is left alone in her car as a recently reanimated tramp stumbles menacingly towards her. Narrowly escaping him, she takes George to her brother's house only to find that he has been viciously murdered. The two now face an uphill battle with both the zombies and the police who suspect them of being responsible for the murder. As McCormick tells George; "You're all the same. Drugs, sex, every sort of filth." George doesn't exactly engratiate himself by replying glibly that "Christ and the Saints are out of fashion" and that "Satan's very popular these days."

Free from the questioning they search the local cemetery for the grave of the tramp that attacked them. As they descend into the crypt the film's previously expansive outdoor scenes and open spaces are replaced by an overwhelming sense of claustrophobia, as corpses then begin to rise and attack George and Galbo. Only a climactic escape through an opening in the crypt roof saves them, a sequence imitated in Lucio Fulci's *House By The Cemetery* (1981). An investigating police constable isn't so fortunate and soon becomes a victim of the cannibalistic cadavers, the gaping wounds and viscera courtesy of Fulci's own make-up man, Gianetto de Rossi.

George and Galbo's continuing struggle for survival is once more overshadowed by the actions of the police who, despite hearing reports of new-born babies biting staff in the local hospital, send the helpless Galbo there to "convalesce". She is finally killed there by hordes of zombies, with George left stranded in a police cell. His eventual escape is too late to save her, but he does succeed in killing off the rest of the zombies by setting fire to the hospital.

The film's final irony however, has the hero George, shot "dead" by McCormick amidst the now blazing inferno - the cop's parting message to him being; "I wish the dead would come back to life you bastard because then I could kill you again!" McCormick does indeed get his "wish" as a revived "zombie" George returns to gain his revenge on the policeman.

For all its similarities to *Night of the Living Dead*, the film still offers enough originality to be considered a worthwhile addition to the zombie cycle. The political aspect is well handled, as throughout the film, George faces more danger from the police than he does from the zombies, as the authorities, with their own "plodding" misconceptions, thwart George in his attempts to save Galbo.

The film continued the movement of the horror film away from the almost "cosy" period horrors of Hammer, to a more modern day setting, reflected by the anxiety felt at the use of radiation to control nature. In this respect the film anticipated later nuclear danger films such as *The China Syndrome* (1979) and *Threads* (1985). The explicit violence - a policeman's chest is ripped open and his eyes gouged out, a woman has her breast torn off, was to be a major feature in later offerings in the horror cinema.

Grau's other forays into horror such as *Ceremonia Sangrienta* (1972) have lacked the visceral impact and mise en scene that are contained and so expertly deployed in *The Living Dead At The Manchester Morgue*, a film which still stands as the final word in Spanish zombie films.

One country that seemed to have been only marginally influenced by *Night of the Living Dead* was Italy, but it has since more than made up for lost time, especially so by exploiting the success in that country of Romero's *Dawn of the Dead*.

Part of the reason for the popularity of that film in Italy was due to the involvement of Italian director Dario Argento as the co-producer, and the use of his music maestro's "Goblin" to score the film. Argento's films such

Images from The Living Dead At The Manchester Morgue

A zombie from The Living Dead At The Manchester Morgue

as *Tenebre* (1982), *Suspiria* (1977) and *Deep Red* (1975) owe more to Hitchcock and Mario Bava than any Romero films, but nevertheless *Dawn of the Dead* was to prove the catalyst for a host of other would-be zombie films made by countless Italian directors.

Of these, some can roughly be termed as exploitation films with barely a minimal undercurrent of wider societal observations, the accent here is firmly placed on action and gore. *City of the Walking Dead* (1980) is one such example, directed by Umberto Lenzi whose other "restrained" films include a duo of cannibal "gut-munchers", *Eaten Alive* (1980) and the notorious *Cannibal Ferox* (1981).

This film, however, is more of a *Dawn of the Dead* meets *The China Syndrome* hybrid. It stars Hugo Stiglitz as a news reporter who, in the film's opening, is waiting at an airport to welcome an incoming professor. The plane lands, but as it does it disgorges a seething mass of zombies who proceed to take over the airport and surrounding area. It is revealed that the zombies have been created by a radiation leak that infected the professor, who in turn transmitted the disease to his fellow passengers, infecting all, with the need for fresh blood to survive.

The remainder of the film charts the progress of Stiglitz and his girlfriend (Laura Trotter), who attempt to escape the rampaging zombies. She is finally killed, falling from a helicopter rope ladder into the teeming ranks of zombies below. It is then that Stiglitz "awakens" from what has all apparently been a "nightmare". The circular conclusion however, sees him going to the airport to meet a plane.....

It's all a rather tame ending to a film that, besides featuring blood-lusting zombies, also attempts some cursory narrative structure as Stiglitz's tenacious reporter has his work censored by an authoritarian army General (Mel Ferrer). The ineffectual military "help" that is given to the reporter is as adequate as the unoriginal "it's all a dream, no it isn't"

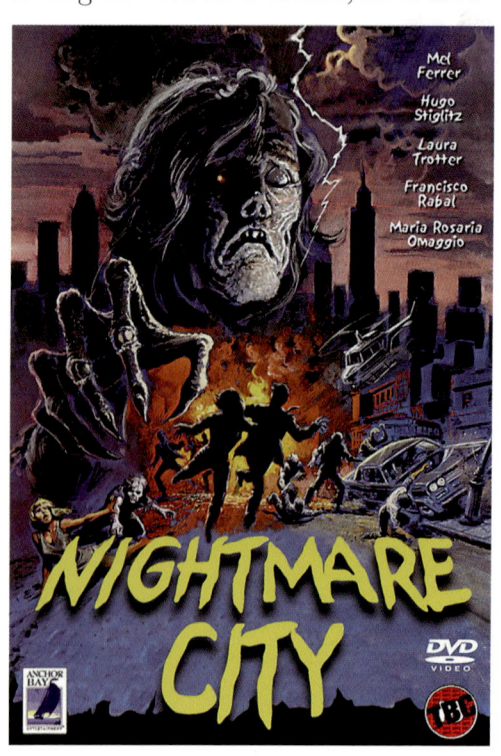

Sleeve art for Umberto Lenzi's City of the Walking Dead

HUGO STIGLITZ
LAURA TROTTER

LA INVASION DE LOS ZOMBIES ATOMICOS

The Dead Walk

conclusion to the film.

Bruno Mattaei's *Zombie Creeping Flesh* (1979) is marginally different in tone to Lenzi's film as it approaches the problems of Third World starvation in an almost "documentary" style at times. Shots of zombies are liberally inter-cut with realistic footage of natives in their villages, mixing food and performing other daily chores.

The action is set in Papua, at the ironically-named HOPE research station where a team of scientists are experimenting with synthetic food substances. After a laboratory accident, the workforce are transformed into flesh-eating zombies. A force of commandos, led by Franco Giraldi, are sent into the area to rescue a group of journalists trapped there, including Margit Evelyn Newton amongst their number. Gradually, the real purpose behind the research station's experiments becomes clear, as we learn that they have in fact been trying to eliminate overpopulation in the world by reviving dormant cannibalistic instincts in the natives via this newly developed synthetic food.

The zombie scenes owe much to *Dawn of the Dead* - even down to using the same Goblin soundtrack!

Bruno Mattei's Zombie Creeping Flesh

The perverse logic implied in the Third World/Western conflict - the Third World biting back literally here, isn't enough to bolster the ponderous "action" scenes, a sagging script and any attempts to "out-gross" Romero fall embarrassingly flat.

Frank Martin's *Zombie Holocaust* (1980) takes plagiarism even further being a copy of a copy, borrowing not from Romero's film but from Fulci's *Zombie Flesh Eaters* (although Fulci's film does stand up to analysis in its own right as previously discussed).

Zombie Holocaust even "boasts" the same star (Ian McCulloch), somewhat of an Italian horror film veteran having also appeared in Luigi Cozzi's *Alien Contamination* (1981). He plays a scientist who travels with a doctor (Alexandra Delli Colli), to the native island of Kito in the Pacific to investigate the suspected origins of some gruesome happenings in New York, where hearts have been ripped out of cadavers in a hospital morgue.

Once on the island they meet the depraved doctor of the alternative title (*Doctor Butcher M.D.*) - a Dr. Albrera who is practising Dr. Moreau type experiments on human victims and creating zombies whose alarming appearance contrasts vividly with the sight of Colli, who is eventually captured by the natives, stripped, painted and worshipped as an ancient goddess! Yes, they know a thing or two these natives!

She escapes as the cannibal natives capture and then kill the demented doctor, a novel twist, leaving McCulloch to flee the now burning laboratory. The

Apocalipsis Canibal

The Continental Cousin - Zombies Around the Globe

the actual film. This is one case of the cooking pot boiling dry and leaving us *Zombie Holocaust* as a burnt offering!

There are no native zombies in *Cannibal Apocalypse* (1980), as the zombies shown here are all the product of the western world. The film is one of director Antonio Margheriti's few excursions into the zombie genre, his other films ranging from the science fiction orientated *Planet of the Lifeless Men* (1961) to the gothic horror of *The Long Hair of Death* (1964).

Cannibal Apocalypse has John Saxon from *A Nightmare on Elm Street* (1985) fame playing a Vietnam veteran returning home to America. The opening scenes show the war at its height as Saxon discovers two American soldiers imprisoned in a bamboo covered pit, tucking into a Vietcong. As he offers them a helping hand, one of the G.I. cannibals sees it only as lunch and bites a chunk out of the horrified Saxon's arm.

film's raison d'etre is mainly to show numerous shots of Colli's semi-draped body, coupled with some grisly scenes such as when one helpless victim runs into a jungle trap and is impaled on a row of spikes, his writhing body greedily devoured by the natives.

In another scene, a maggot-infested skull adorns a bed along with the arbitrary inclusion of a half-clad female form in the frame, which sums up the film's exploitative attitude. The film's spirited advertising campaign - speaking of the doctor, ran "He is a depraved, homicidal killer and he makes house calls", along with a picture of a Salvador Dali-posed figure, only with a knife replacing the walking cane, unfortunately, being more inventive than anything contained in

Later, the three men meet up again in Atlanta, Georgia, where one of the survivors (John Morghen), goes on a killing spree after his release from a mental hospital. He bites a girl in a porn cinema and then "holes up" in a nearby shopping mall. He is saved from the police by a calm-talking Saxon.

This only paves the way for future bloodshed though as the zombies, led by the infected Saxon and Morghen, proceed to chomp their way through the remaining members of the

Born to be wild - mayhem in Lamberto Bava's imaginative riff on the zombie genre, Demons

cast, culminating in a final showdown with the authorities by the city sewers.

Now it is the G.I.'s who are hunted down and "torched" by soldiers wielding flamethrowers, a reference to earlier in the film to the fate that is meted out by the G.I.'s to the Vietnamese. Now we have turned full circle, the hunters have become the hunted. Only Saxon survives the encounter, to die with somewhat greater dignity later in a suicide pact with his wife. His "disease" lives on though, now in the shape of the young girl next door who Saxon had previously bitten, the victim's fridge now chock-full of human meat as man has now become the ultimate in packaged consumer goods.

Margheriti does little to show the affects of war on its survivors and on society as a whole; he is content to merely pile on one gory excess after another, lacking the style so freely exhibited in his earlier films. His one moment of inspiration here is the camera shot that is taken through the gaping hole in one man's chest, the closest the lens comes to actually breathing life into a character itself. This, and the humorously named G.I. Charles Bukowski (aka Charles Bronson) are the film's only imaginative elements.

An Italian zombie film that does succeed despite its lack of characterisation is Lamberto Bava's *Demons* (1986), a kinetic offering, high on style, low on plot, but fascinatingly escapist for all that. Bava's pedigree certainly goes unchallenged, being the son of the late and great Mario Bava, who was the director of such stylish gothic horrors as *Mask of Satan* (1960), *Planet of the Vampires* (1965) and *Curse of the Dead* (1965), as well as giallo films such as *Blood and Black Lace* (1964) and *Bay of Blood* (1971).

Lamberto garnered his first experience of directing on one of his father's final films *Shock* (1977), before his own creations; *A Blade in the Dark* (1981) and *Macabre* (1981). *Demons* atmospheric start has the two glowing eyes of a train peering out of the darkness at us, accompanied by Claudio Simonetti's synthesised variations on Prokofiev's music. Two girls, Sharel (Natasha Hovey) and Kathy (Fiore Argento), are given free tickets to a horror film preview at the ominously shadowed Metropol cinema in Berlin. At the screening, a black prostitute cuts herself on a promotional mask in the foyer, a neat echo of Mario Bava's *Mask of Satan*, which also features a spiked, satanic mask.

Inside the darkened theatre the action then cuts to a film within a film style narrative as the diverse audience watch a film about the discovery of the tomb of Nostradamus. Gradually,

The Continental Cousin - Zombies Around the Globe

the scenes on the cinema screen of demonic possession are duplicated in the cinema itself as the prostitute metamorphosises into a razor-teethed, gooey-eyed demon with taloned fingernails. As the cinema exits become mysteriously blocked, she bites her way through the others in the cinema who in turn become zombies. The remainder of the film is taken up with breathtaking action scenes inside the cinema; there is an indoor motor bike chase and a helicopter which crashes through the cinema roof at one stage.

Eventually the girls and their dates, George (Urban Barberini) and Ken (Karl Zinny), find their number infected by the demons, leaving only two survivors who escape using the helicopter winch cable to haul themselves up onto the cinema roof.

Despite the almost consistent lack of characterisation there is still plenty to admire in Bava's film. He certainly knows how to create tension in an original manner. An opening sequence sees one of the girls chased by a mysterious figure wearing a mask, in the menacing underground station, only to find him catch up with her, and merely give her free tickets to the Metropol.

The figure surfaces again during the film's climax as the survivors scramble on top of the cinema. His efforts to push them back down to the zombies below are thwarted as he is finally impaled, face down, on a metal spike. Bava makes good use of his locations, his camera ever prowling the gloomy corridors and corners of the eerily deserted cinema, with shafts of fluorescent light warning of the impending appearance of the demons.

The exteriors, shot in Berlin, also manage to capture some of the ambivalence and tension inherent in the all-pervasive East/West divide that then clouded the city. Bava infuses the film with bravura action sequences, with samurai sword wielding bikers slicing up legions of zombies in bloody fashion and manages to integrate the potentially troublesome film-within-a-film technique into the picture, which has thus been called *The Evil Dead* meets the *Purple Rose of Cairo*, (the latter, Woody Allen's cinematic screen comedy).

Bava's cinematic style betrays his father's influence, and he also shows admiring glances in the direction of various genre films. The cinema lobby in *Demons* sports a poster of Herzog's *Nosferatu* (1979) and the scenes where one of the heroes transforms into a fiery zombie, pleading for his friends to kill him, recalls Roger's agonised demise in *Dawn of the Dead*. The diverse cross-section of characters in the film's cinema audience which

Demonic possession at work in Demons

include a prostitute, a pimp, a blind man and a vampish usherette, are the type of people that we would expect to find in a Dario Argento film such as *Cat O' Nine Tails* (1971), not altogether surprising as he did in fact produce *Demons*. The film makes for compelling viewing as a tour de force for Bava's own fluid camera style, matched by his affinity for highly-paced, frenzied action sequences. The film's climax, as the demons can be seen sprawling over other parts of the city leaves us in no doubt as to the dangers to be faced in the sequel, *Demons 2* (1987).

The zombie may have crossed many continents and reached many oceans but New Zealand has certainly not been his favourite port of call. David Blyth's 1985 film *Death Warmed Up* goes some of the way to redressing the balance, being a cautionary tale of hospital brain operations that turn patients into zombies.

The film's numerous action scenes carry the narrative weaknesses in much the same way as the aforementioned *Demons*. Here we see a surgeon (Gary Day) programming a young man (Michael Hurst) to be mean to his parents, this he carries out with zeal as he proceeds to slaughter them to death. On his release from an insane asylum the blonde-haired zombie encounters the surgeon again and discovers that he is still carrying out his experiments on a remote island. It is left to the now reformed Hurst, to defeat the army of homicidal zombies that Day has created.

The graphic scenes on display here - heads explode a la Cronenberg's *Scanners* (1980) and an underground bike chase ensues, ride uneasily with the film's otherwise conservative viewpoint and ideal, in itself a by-product the less than prolific New Zealand film industry has nurtured. Its genre films have been few and far between with *Scarecrow* starring John Carradine being an interesting example from

Images from Demons

The Continental Cousin - Zombies Around the Globe

1983. In more recent times of course interest has exploded with the *Lord of the Rings* trilogy offering a spectacular opportunity to boost both the Kiwi film industry and the numbers of tourists Their close relations across the sea have fared better with *Picnic at Hanging Rock* (1975), *The Last Wave* (1977), *Patrick* (1978) and *Undead* (2003) all emanating from Australian shores.

The French have also been reluctant to delve into the explicit images of the zombie film, preferring instead a preoccupation with realism, surrealism and eroticism, elements which do not lend themselves easily to the zombie genre !

As a result, the French cinema has produced pictures such as Jean Luc Goddard's *Weekend* (1967) and Alain Resnais' *J'taime, Je T'Aime* (1967), coupled with his *Last Year at Marienbad* (1961) and Roger Vadim's *Barbarella* (1968) that all stress such qualities.

The French zombie film has been left almost exclusively in the hands of one Jean Rollin, whose previous horrors such as *Les Frissons des Vampires* (1970), *Requiem Pour un Vampire* (1971) and *Levres de Sang* (1975) had concentrated more on the implicit eroticism of the female form than on the fatal charms of the vampire. His *Pesticide* (1978), translated to *The Grapes of Death*, is the most commercially accessible of his films, owing to its American origins as opposed to Rollin's own unique brand of horror. The film's plotting recalls *Night of the Living Dead*, but its characters are based more upon the "cross-section of society" stereotypes found in innumerable American "disaster" movies, as in *The Poseidon Adventure* and *The Towering Inferno* from 1974.

Only here the "normal" world of the disaster film is jettisoned in favour of Rollin's own "fantasy" world as surely as Romero's claustrophobic farmhouse scenes are replaced with Rollin's agoraphobic use of wide open spaces. The film has Elisabeth (Marie Georges Pascal) travelling to Southern France to join her lover, when she is assaulted on a deserted train by what looks to be a corpse, (Romero's *Martin* also has the synonymous vampire praying on a lone girl train passenger in its opening sequence).

After escaping from other such corpses, Elisabeth teams up with two

The Dead Walk

apparently "normal" Frenchmen and they shelter in an overgrown vineyard after leaving the train. She then learns that the vines here have been infected with pesticide and are responsible for the zombie contagion that is spreading across the country.

The film's conclusion sees her realising with horror, that she too, will eventually succumb to the infection as she gradually begins to lose her sanity, accelerated by the gruesome sight of her former lover and friends being killed, their heads cut off and their torsos' impaled on pitchforks and crucified.

The sight of faces crumbling and disintegrating is indicative of Rollin's skill and style at manipulating the horror audience, and film, with his concept of France's national drink turning people into zombies, being an audacious one.

Rollin's *Zombie Lake* (1980) may not be as successful as it could have been but then this is mainly due to the late appointment of Rollin to direct the film, having taken over from the original choice, Jess Franco. The film features German soldiers returning as zombies to haunt the inhabitants of the village that had previously killed Nazi soldiers and dumped them all into the village lake. The opening scenes recall *Jaws* (1975), as a young woman swimming in the lake is caught by a zombie rising from the depths below. A battle between the zombies and the villagers ensues, culminating with the elimination of the German "dead" by a youngster who sets fire to the mill that has become the soldier's headquarters.

The boy has symbolically been the product of an affair between a local woman and a German soldier. Considering the short amount of time he was given to work on the film Rollin does a creditable job in reviving the zombie soldiers who look suitably repulsive with their green and putrifying faces and dishevelled uniforms. The film has been wrongly credited on occasions to director Alain Lesoeur who in fact made *L'abime des Morts Vivants* (1981) whereas Jess Franco went on to direct a similar piece to Rollin's, *El Lago de las Virgenes* (1981).

The Living Dead Girl (1982), one of Rollin's best films, has a plot faintly reminiscent of Georges Le Franju's *Eyes Without A Face* (1959), as a woman (Marina Pierro), seeks out potential victims for her friend (Francois Blanchard) as did Alida Valli in Franju's film. Blanchard, as the dead girl, is revived by earthquake gasses and then proceeds to consume more and more blood, haunting a castle in the volcanic

Jean Rollin's The Living Dead Girl

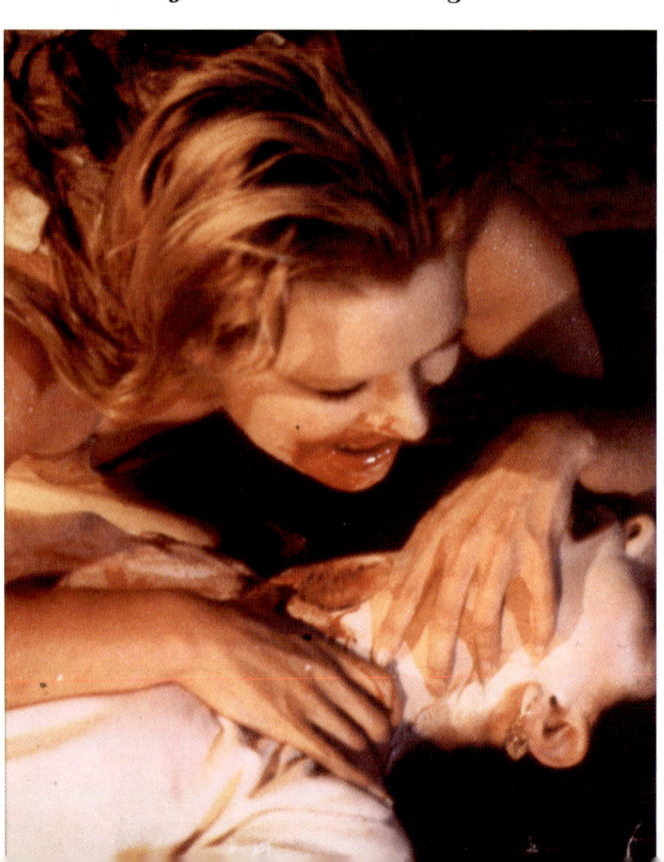

area of the Arvenge where she had once lived. Gradually, she finds her memory, and more importantly, her conscience, returning to her, including an awareness now of her "death" and "rebirth".

Pierro, as the devoted childhood friend, provides the victims with which Blanchard now satiates her bloodlust. Eventually, it is this all-consuming appetite that overcomes both love and death, culminating with her killing Pierro. The film is interesting in its creation of a zombie with "feelings" and emotions, no mindless automaton here. Despite this inner intensity however, the living dead character of Blanchard is still left a slave to her own suffering, she may maintain the appearance of life but it is death she longs for.

Her devoted friend, who teaches her to talk and to "live" again, is still cast unceremoniously aside in the end by an inconsolable Blanchard. Her revived memories of her old house and of childhood toys are simply icons of a past life that she can never reclaim. For her, death is an appealing release from the torment of a painful past life remembered and of a conscience that is of no consolation to her now. The surreal images of the billowing gases effusing from the earth are like the life-spirit that is now being sucked out once again from a rueful Blanchard.

Like the French, the Chinese cinema, and oriental films in general, have rarely diversified into the zombie genre, preferring instead "monster on the loose" pictures such as *Godzilla - King of the Monsters* (1954) and *Rodan* (1956), featuring atomically created mutations, a lingering influence from the atom bomb destruction that so devastated Japan. This range has extended to cover other horror genres such as the vampire film, with 1971's *Lake of Dracula*, but nowhere have the age old fixations of Chinese cinema been more inventively and excitingly

The Living Dead Girl

remoulded than in Ching Sju Tung's *A Chinese Ghost Story* (1987). Despite the title the film manages to utilise a phenomenal range of influences, from the stylised martial arts sequences, (a relic from Kurosawa's samurai epics such as *The Seven Samurai* - 1954), to the images of rapidly decaying zombies the like of which have populated Romero's films and *Ghost Story* (1981) amongst others.

The film itself has a very contemporary appearance, evoked through the graphic action scenes, loud pop music and fluid camera movements, all topped with some dazzling special effects. A collection of Ming dynasty, supernatural tales, forms the basis for the film's premise

The Dead Walk

A Chinese Ghost Story 2

Howling dogs roam the wood, silhouetted against the night sky, their eyes burning as brightly as the glowing lantern that lights up the tax collector's way. The fog-shrouded graveyard he visits has verdant green plant life sprawling amidst the dull grey tombstones, as bells toll ominously and skulls sit silently atop the headstones, a symbol of the gothic regalia that pervades the film.

The prowling camera that rushes through the forest in the opening scenes is clearly inspired by the electrifying *The Evil Dead* (1982), but takes the formula even further as the all-seeing lens circumnavigates the lake house before then exploding into the interior, where the ghost is making love to an unwilling victim, her "love" sapping his life. This action is all surrounded by the type of kaleidoscopic lighting that recalls early Mario Bava films. The ghost's next victim fares even worse - being reduced to a shrivelled zombie shell, that nevertheless has to be stabbed in the forehead and set on fire to kill it.

The film's numerous action scenes owe much to the director, a former martial arts sequence adviser, as lurid red blood splashes across the screen in the opening scenes where the bemused tax collector witnesses a samurai battle and is himself tainted with the blood of its participants. The blood continues to flow in the climactic confrontation with the tree demon. All around, foliage comes alive and soon the haunted temple is surrounded by spiralling tree branches and leafy tentacles which coil around the awe-struck characters inside. Tree stems

which follows a young tax collector who encounters a beautiful ghost whilst looking one night for a place to sleep.

At first, he resists her subtle charms but is gradually lured to her by the romantic sounding music with which she serenades him from her lakeside abode.

Little does he realise that she is, in fact, held in thrall by an androgynous tree demon, Lord Black. Despite warnings from the local people, he elects to stay the night at the haunted Lan Ro temple.

This acts as the catalyst for the dead zombies inside the temple to revive and begin to converge on the unsuspecting traveller.

The breathtakingly paced denouement has the tax collector, aided by the ghost and a swordsman priest, Yen, conspire to defeat the evil tree demon, resulting in a final battle in a ghostly-shrouded world of Hell. The tax collector and Yen escape, returning the ghost's ashes to her family estate in the nearby graveyard, to affect her spiritual release from the tree demon.

A Chinese Ghost Story is sumptuously filmed in an invigorating style. Old fashioned, creaking gothic images are revitalised here, especially so in the mist-laden forest that is densely filled with grotesquely twisted trees and an ever-moaning wind.

The Continental Cousin - Zombies Around the Globe

burst through trap doors and walls encircling the temple like the giant octopus straight out of *Warlords of Atlantis* (1978), rippling underneath the floor in much the same fashion as the creature from *The Thing* (1982).

The slimy tentacles pummel the collector about the face, submerging him under a sea of mucus as crocodile jaws emerge simultaneously with sinuous roots which further entrap the helpless victim. The film's puppet zombies are drawn from Ray Harryhausen's seminal skeletal creations in *Jason and the Argonauts* (1963), and it is around them that much of the film's charmingly innocent humour revolves.

In one sequence, the collector explores the temple cellar, completely oblivious to the zombies behind him that crumble instantaneously to dust as he pulls open some window shutters, so flooding the room with sunlight. He narrowly escapes the zombies clawing hands later on when he is dropped and then raised in yo-yo fashion by Yen over an open trapdoor as zombie fingers clutch at him from out of the darkness below.

The rich vein of humour that continues throughout the film is also well illustrated when the hapless collector is once again found bobbing up and down - only this time when concealing himself from Lord Black's female sirens by hiding in a bathing barrel full of water. He times his surfacing for air to perfection - grabbing an eyeful of the de-robed ghost who stands before him on each occasion.

This is typical of the film's approach and we know that despite the graphic deaths that pervade the piece, the innocent humour and fantastical fairytale atmosphere continually remind us of the fact that the main characters will remain free from harm if not danger. Although the film does draw heavily from a vast range of influences it has enough style and wit of its own, coupled with its unique joi de vivre, to elevate it above the purely imitative status that so many other films fall into.

A Chinese Ghost Story, together with its eventual sequels, emerges as a promising product from the "new wave" Chinese cinema which has spawned other films such as *In The Wild Mountains* (1986) and draws on such diverse entries as *Zoo Warriors From The Magic Mountain* (1983). The priest, played by Woo Mar is himself no stranger to the horror genre having directed horror comedies such as *The Dead and the Deadly* (1982).

In terms of China's oriental cousin, Japan, one of the main obstacles to having any meaningful zombie film entries lies in the cultural/religious issue of the majority of the dead being cremated, leaving little to resurrect!

This seemingly insurmountable problem is circumvented by the old "let's infect the living with radiation from a stray asteroid" ploy which is how Kazuo Komizu's seminal *Battle Girl* (1991) begins. Although the by-product of this is to turn the citizens of Tokyo into the walking dead, (the film is also known as *The Living Dead in Tokyo Bay*), Komizu's camera lens appears just as interested in the shapely charms of female wrestler Cutey Suzuki as the heroine Keiko.

Suzuki spends the majority of the film squeezed into a tight black

Atsushi Muroga's Junk (2000)

Naoyuki Tomomatsu's teenage zombie girl epic Stacy

PVC outfit and leading the survivors charge against the Self-Defence Forces who have turned against the civilians. Featuring probably the only scenes to date of zombies being wrestled to defeat (courtesy of Keiko's pro-wrestling skills), *Battle Girl* is also noticeable for the maniacal army general who tries to create his own zombie-human hybrid. This intended "super race" is characterised by their badly applied face paint and spiky shoulder-pads in true post-apocalyptic film fashion!

Tetsuro Takeuchi's *Wild Zero* (1999) also features an extra-terrestial theme with aliens from outer space landing on earth and turning the populace into zombies.

Takeuchi's opus plays an entirely different riff (literally) with its teenage punk hero, Ace (Masashi Endo) joining forces with Guitar Wolf, his favourite rockabilly band, in order to save the earth and find true love, though not necessarily in that order!

Ultra-violent, *Wild Zero* plays with a *Night of the Living Dead* meets *Spinal Tap* vibe with gun-shooting motorcycles and guitars, together with some incidental delights, including the bickering couple who actually become more likable once transformed into zombies and the object of Ace's desires revealed to be not quite what "she" seems?

Following hot on the heels of Takeuchi's entry is Atsushi Muroga's *Junk* (2000), only this time using gaijin or "foreigner" soldiers instead. Inspired by *The Return of the Living Dead* and the *Resident Evil* video games, the film revolves around US Army chemical weapons being accidentally uncovered and unleashed by some amateur bank robbers. That the thieves spend as much time squabbling with gangsters to keep hold of their loot as they do avoiding the newly created living dead, adds to the humour here, though the requisite lashings of gore are still spilled to reinforce *Junk*'s horror status.

Continuing with this almost spoof-like tone is Naoyuki Tomomatsu's *Stacy* (2001). Eschewing the need for any alien intervention it is the "alien" world of the teenager which is highlighted here as a number of girls aged between 15-17 years old are, after a brief period of ecstasy known as "Near Death Happiness", transformed into zombies or "stacies". With dismemberment by chainsaw the preferred option and the remains left for the refuse collectors to dispose of, it is as well that the Japanese local authorities appear more concientious in their waste collection than the UK's, with the current clamouring for fortnightly or even monthly collections!

Borrowing liberally from Romero's *Day of the Dead*, (the zombie cleansing operation is headed by "The Romero Troops") the film has a group of scientists who have captured some of the "stacies" in order to search for a cure for the teenage epidemic.

Based on a novel by former rock star turned writer Kenji Otsuki,

The Continental Cousin - Zombies Around the Globe

(who appears in the film peddling "Bruce Campbell's Right Hand 2" device for dismembering your daughter), Tomomatsu film is a diverse mixture of ambitious, over the top carnage, uneasily married with some surprisingly sentimental scenes which, whilst quite effective (and affecting), in no way compensate for the leaden pace and scatter-gun approach.

With the release of Ryuhei Kitamura's *Versus* in 2001, the Japanese zombie film genre reached its apex. A volatile hybrid of gore, martial arts and samurai influences, the frenetic pace and outre violence manfully disguise the obvious bugetary limitations. The intriguing premise sees Prisoner KSC2-303 (Tak Sakaguchi) on the run following his recent escape from prison. His "escape" appears short-lived however, as he encounters a gang of yakuza and their female hostage in the nearby woods.

As KSC2-303 continues his flight, now accompanied by The Girl (Chieko Misaka), their pursuers are joined by The Man (Hideo Sakaki) and his clique of smartly-dressed assassins. As if all this wasn't enough for audiences to chew on, Kitamura throws in the little matter of the woods being the Forest of Resurrection, conveniently positioned over the 444th gate into the world of the dead, with anyone dying in the forest doomed to return to (after) life.

In a final act of audacious revelation, we discover that the main protagonists are continually being reincarnated to fight a war that has in effect been raging for thousands of years - think *The Evil Dead* meets *Groundhog Day*!

Just like Raimi, the camera here is restless - all tilted angles and relentless pacing, supremely stylish amongst the broad stroke violence. Every scene counts here as a spirited cast combine to infuse the film with a wildly imaginative and entertaining foray into zombiedom. The gaping chest wound of one victim which provides the unlikely framing for one particularly nauseus camera shot, may recall the excessess of exploitation fayre such as *Cannibal Apocalypse*, but with shades of Raimi and Peter Jackson exhibited by Kitamura's work here, perhaps his eventual aim is far higher.

9
CLOSE RELATIONS - SCIENCE FICTION ZOMBIES

Invasion of the Bodysnatchers (1978)

Close Relations - Science Fiction Zombies

Since the earliest days of film, from Frenchman Georges Melies' magical box of tricks *Rocket to the Moon* (1896), to modern day efforts such as *Sex and the City* (2008), (which also, simultaneously, signposts the shift from "typical women's" film to sassy chickflick), film has reflected the fears and mores of contemporary society.

Thus, films of the 1940's expressed fears of man's own inhumanity to man, epitomised by the atrocities committed in World War Two. The 1950's reflected the birth of the atom bomb as numerous pictures were released dealing with mutations from normal life caused by radiation such as the rampaging spider that weaved a web of destruction in Jack Arnold's *Tarantula* (1955). The fashion-conscious 1960's spawned countless films that were primarily preoccupied with clothes, free love, free sex and free living in general, as seen in the "new wave" cinema by directors such as Michaelangelo Antonioni, whose own *Blow Up* (1966), incorporated most of these themes.

The increasingly violent society of the 1970's and 1980's, amidst a back-drop of the ever present threat of nuclear war and subsequent obliteration, furnished a flock of films that "thrived" on portraying greater violence, often mindless, as explicitly shown in the "psycho splatter" films such as *Friday the 13th* (1980), *He Knows You're Alone* (1980) and similar ilk where crazed killers reigned supreme, intent only on decimating as many as possible of the films' cast.

The gamut of media outlets and the easier access it has brought to "celebrity" and the fabled "15 minutes of fame" produced a plethora of Hollywood serial killer films in the 1990's including *Silence of the Lambs* (1991), *Dust Devil* (1992) and *Seven* (1995). Wes Craven's influential post-modern satire on the slasher film *Scream* (1996), dominated the latter part of the decade with *The Faculty* (1998) being one of the more interesting, not to mention outlandish variants on a theme.

With the approach of the new millenium, Hollywood turned to the old, with a proliferation of big-budget remakes and graphic novel inspired releases including *War of the Worlds* (2005), *Spiderman* (2002), with sequels in 2004 and 2007, plus the likes of *Hellboy* (2004) and *Hellboy 2: The Golden Army* (2008).

Even more recently, the influence of the Afghanistan and Iraq wars in particular, has permeated mainstream Hollywood with releases such as *Fahrenheit 9/11* (2004), *Redacted* (2007) and *In The Valley of Elah* (2008).

The zombie films more closely aligned to the science fiction genre split generally into two camps The mainly 1950's entries showing the threat from outer space and the later films that show the zombies to be "invaders from within", in which ordinary men and women become zombies of society.

OUTER SPACE ZOMBIES

Examples of the former films have become increasingly diversified as zombies from outer space have been replaced by big-budget space battles using fairytale motifs such as the *Star Wars* series or inhuman monsters seemingly housing limitless supplies of killing power, in an omnipotent show of force against the human race, such as the embryonic monster that hatches and later bursts into life in *Alien* (1979).

The best examples of extra-terrestial zombies are found in *It Came From Outer Space* (1953) and *Invasion of the Bodysnatchers* (1956). The former is the more overtly science-fiction orientated, not surprisingly considering that it was based on famed sci-fi author Ray

The Dead Walk

Bradbury's short story "The Meteor", and filmed by the aforementioned Arnold.

The story unfolds as a group of aliens crash land their spacecraft on earth, the ship closely resembling a meteorite in its appearance. An astronomer (Richard Carlson), witnesses the event, but like the exasperated James Stewart in Hitchcock's *Rear Window* (1954), finds that no one will believe his story. The aliens are also invisible and soon begin to "replace" the local people with their own "clones" who act similarly to their human counterparts. Their only inconsistency is the tell-tale zombie stare that they produce when not in human company, betraying their alien origins.

The aliens intentions are in fact shown to be non-violent as the humans are merely used as a silent workforce to repair the aliens spaceship. It is the aliens all-consuming need for more and more locals that finally draws peoples attention and hostility towards the unwelcome visitors, their lone human ally being Carlson who, on recognising the aliens benevolent nature, sides with them to help effect their eventual escape. This completed, the locals are returned to "normal" in what, until *Invasion of the Bodysnatchers*, was the obligatory happy ending.

The film concentrates on the more fantastical elements in the story as opposed to making any political statements, these were to come later. It benefits greatly from Arnold's taut direction, using the eerie expanses of wasteland desert to good effect, in many ways a forerunner to his later film *Tarantula*, which uses similar techniques and locations to create a foreboding atmosphere. In other aspects Arnold was no doubt helped by his art director Robert Boyle who went on to work on Hitchcock's *The Birds* (1963) and producer William Alland who had worked with Orson Welles on *Citizen Kane* (1941).

Miles Berrell (Kevin McCarthy) in Don Siegel's beguiling Invasion of the Bodysnatchers

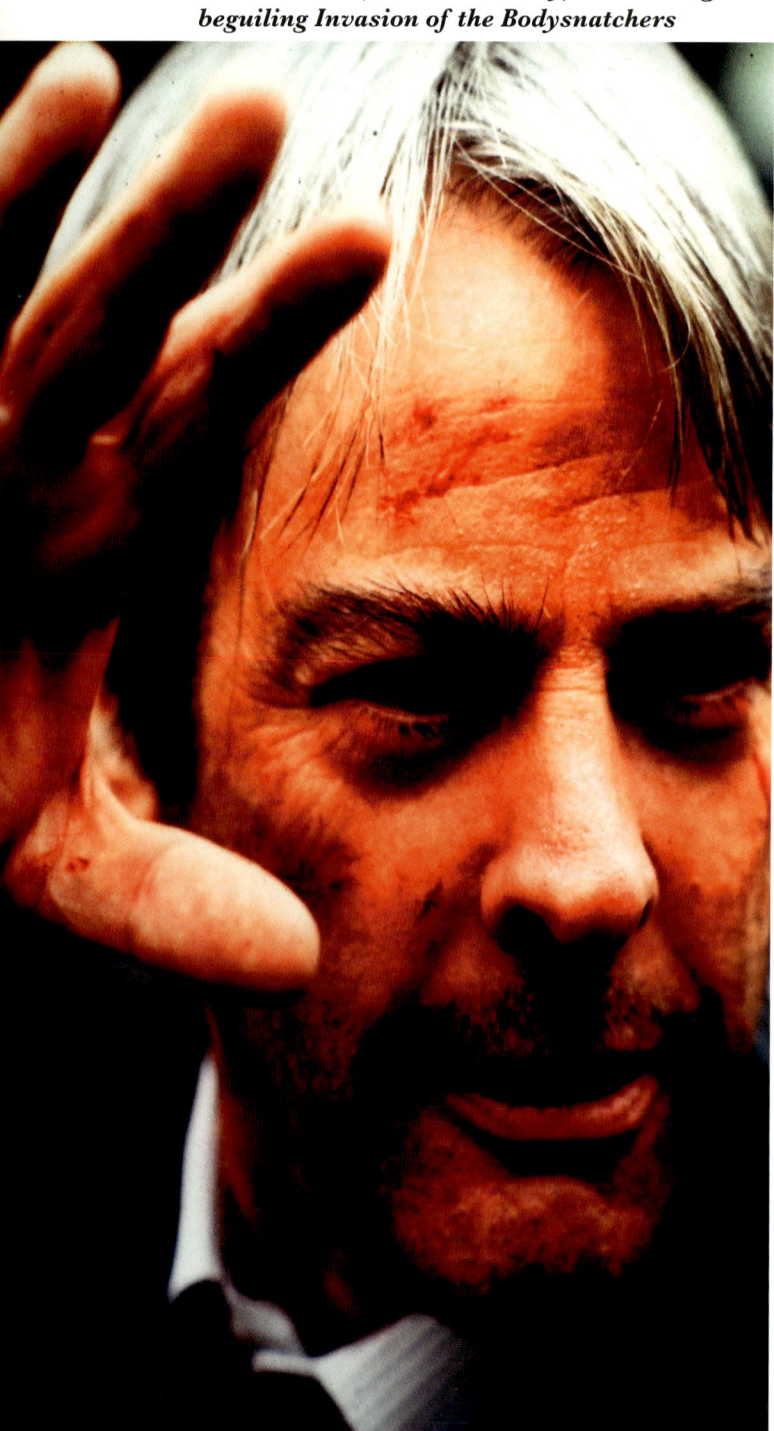

WHILE YOU SLEEP, WE DESTROY YOUR WORLD

The idea of alien forces penetrating human society was further explored in 1956's *Invasion of the Bodysnatchers* and expanded into a more rounded achievement by its allusion to the various psychological and political elements contained within its central theme. The relentless, kinetic direction by Don Siegel (he went on to make action pictures such as *Dirty Harry* -1971 and more thought-provoking studies of human relationships as in *The Beguiled* - also 1971), gave the film the necessary drive and inspiration so that these elements didn't "weigh" the film down with dour theorising.

The film, adapted from a Jack Finney novel, begins as a psychiatrist Miles Berrell (Kevin McCarthy) returns from a medical convention only to find that his home town of Santa Mira has changed disturbingly, though he is not sure how. He uncovers an alien invasion perpetrated through parasitic pods of the same appearance. The film carries a continuing sense of hopelessness as Berrell continues a lone battle against the invaders. Everyone he trusts and believes in capitulates to the aliens.

From the very start, when with friends, he discovers an unfinished pod on a pool table, he finds normality crossed by conspiracy and fear. His response after being shown the blank pod that will eventually become his friend Belice (King

Nicole Kidman as Carol Bennell in The Invasion

Donovan), is to make a frenzied attack on it with a pitchfork.

This scene is surprisingly difficult to watch as Berrell and Belice rain blows on the pod, all the more disconcerting for its almost embryonic, human immobility. The personal "hell" for Berrell however, is only reached later as his girlfriend is duplicated, and so he has now lost a major part of his life. This void is suitable increased by the film's memorable coup de grace as Berrell runs despairingly into the middle of the state highway, warning the unconcerned motorists *"You're next."* Despite all his efforts, the world still seems ready to embrace the aliens. He is left a solitary figure at the end, quite impotent, unable to change the course of events.

The real success of the film is in its portrayal of man's own paranoia and insecurity at losing his sense of identity and his emotions. Like Patrick McGoohan's alienated character in "The Prisoner" television series, Berrell is "not a number but a free man." He fights throughout the film to retain his personal identity whilst all those around him lose theirs, in a mindless pursuit for conformity. The film is the screen's most literal depiction of the fears of losing human feelings and responses, and the overwhelming strength of character needed to retain them in an "inhuman" world.

It is a universal fear that affects us all, showing also the "monster" that is within each of us, as the film's aliens are deliberate "clones" of ourselves, a sobering comment on the character of the human race. Because of the film's attack on conformity and lack of emotion, it has been seen as an attack on communism, the "enemy" within society. In fact, it is an attack on political extremism of all persuasions, as extremism and its inherent dogma deny both free will and individualism whichever political view is expounded.

Ironically, the film's own identity has sometimes been submerged under a prologue and epilogue, added later on, that give the film a "happy" ending. A similar fate befell *The Cabinet of Dr. Caligari* (1919), many years earlier. It is Siegel's ending that is best remembered though and it is the finish that is most "true" to the story and its themes. Unlike, *It Came From Outer Space*, here the implications of an alien takeover and its effects on the human race are fully investigated in Siegel's own, stylishly invigorating manner, his prominent use of low camera angles, shooting upwards into claustrophobic areas, reinforces the film's paranoia and tension.

Unfortunately, another part of the film "lost" is Sam Peckinpah's poignantly humorous dialogue, written for the film's earlier stages. Peckinpah himself is no stranger to censorship as many of his violently stylised films will testify, *The Wild Bunch* (1968), *Straw Dogs* (1971) and *Bring Me The Head Of Alfredo Garacia* (1974), being the prime examples. One of the most disturbing reactions to the film, however, is that the only sane reaction for Berrell, in the face of the overwhelming odds he is up against, is madness, the ultimate paranoia.

Philip Kaufman's 1978 remake of Siegel's classic *Invasion* loses some of the former's impact whilst still managing to retain enough character of its own to justify its existence. Here, the accent shifts from the original film's emotional politics to a villification of the 1970's "me generation" and the resultant urban alienation that takes place. Siegel is given a cameo as a taxi driver and McCarthy also reprises his earlier role here again by finding himself a lone voice against the invasion.

By tackling such a celebrated original, Kaufman may well have been playing with fire, but to his credit, he invests his version with some intriguing ideas of his own. By relocating the action from the small town environs of Siegel's film, Kaufman sacrifices the insidious horror of a small community gradually being transformed into strangers, but gains by ingeniously identifying with the social landscape of the time where people actively wanted to change their lives. While the film now lacks any real political/cold war inflections, it does harvest the appeal of the aforementioned "me" generation and of a certain conformity it can bring.

Donald Sutherland gives an assured performance as Health Inspector Matthew Bennell, an ordinary guy facing up to an unthinkable terror and is given good support by Brooke Adams as Elizabeth Driscoll in the female lead. Art Hindle as Dr. Geoffrey Howell is her now suddenly, emotionally detached boyfriend, whilst Leonard Nimoy's suave psychiatrist Dr, Kibner, is only too willing to analyse everything and everyone in order to

Close Relations - Science Fiction Zombies

offer a myriad of explanations.

Kaufman's prowling camera adds considerably to the tension of the creeping alien menace at work here, and only by lingering too long on the icky pod transformations and an extended car chase sequence towards the end, does he relinquish his otherwise steadfast grip on proceedings.

A noticeable change in emphasis informs the third entry, Abel Ferrera's *Bodysnatchers* (1993). Given that up to this point, Ferrera's reputation was built upon the notoriety of so called "video nasty" *The Driller Killer* (1979), it is no surpise to see the gore and special effects quota increased considerably here.

To indulge critic Roger Ebert's overview that the first film reflects the paranoia of the McCarthyist era, the second, the conspiracy of Watergate and evolution from "flower power" to "me" generation, then Ferrera's film reflects the uncertainty of the AIDS generation.(The most recent film, *The Invasion* (2007) incidentally, reflects the global tension of the post Iraq period).

The agoraphobic-based paranoia of an entire city being "invaded" which pervades Kaufman's film is replaced here by the strictly claustrophobic-based paranoia of an isolated army base which provides the sporing ground for the alien invasion in *Bodysnatchers*.

The enforced regimentation of this milieu lends a certain black humour to proceedings as it is often difficult to distinguish between the human soldiers and the pod clones, given that both thrive upon a regime requiring conformity of behaviour, attitude and appearance with rows of identical, uniformed ranks everywhere.

Following an ominous warning en route to the base - "They're out there" intones one squaddie, enter the Malone family, headed up by Steve (Terry Kinney), a biologist investigating toxic substances within the base. There'a neat parallel drawn between the "bodysnatching" and this typically (?) dysfunctional family where the fiesty teenager Marti (Gabrielle Anwar) harbours enough suspicion towards her stepmother Carol (Meg Tilly) to launch a multitude of conspiracy theories of her own. With some irony, Tilly's "imposter" rather than "foster" mum is the first victim to be cloned-her price for being substitute for Marti's birth mother and also for subverting the influence of her father.

This "enemy within, enemy amongst us" theme is none better reinforced than by the sight of the soldiers dispersing numerous (pod) containers throughout the base, including the family's own bedroom closet - cue the vivid scene later of Tilly's purtifying corpse lying on the

Carol (Nicole Kidman & Dr. Driscoll (Daniel Craig) in The Invasion

bed and being replaced by her pod clone emerging chillingly from the said closet.

With R. Lee Emery as General Platt, stealing a march as the pod people leader (he was also memorably the severe drill sergeant in Stanley Kubrick's *Full Metal Jacket*), Ferrera utilises the confines of the military base to good effect, as well as supplanting the decidedly "adult" neuroses of the first two films, with the avowedly teen-orientated angst of Marti this time around, which proves ultimately, to be less emotionally involving.

With *The Invasion* (2007), director Oliver Hirschbiegel brings the most recent version of the *Bodysnatchers* motif to the screen but with decidedly mixed results.

Perhaps dazzled by his stellar cast - Nicole Kidman's psychiatrist Carol Bennell and new Bond star Daniel Craig as her "good" friend Dr. Ben Driscoll, or, more likely, by the well documented studio interference from Warner's, with the Wachowski brothers hired to rewrite key scenes and James McTeigue to direct the revisions, *The Invasion* remains something of an enigma.

In this retooling we learn that a US Space-bus has exploded upon its return to earth - the scattered fragments containing an alien virus which recodes human DNA, to compound the collateral damage suffered here.

As Carol notices that her estranged husband Tucker Kaufman (Jeremy Northam) has begun to act strangely - suddenly wanting to contact their son Oliver (Jackson Bond) after four years of separation, she then embarks upon a mission with Driscoll and research colleague Dr. Galeano (Jeffrey Wright) to stop the now rampant "flu" pandemic which threatens the planet.

In effect, Hirschbiegel totally

Images from The Invasion

Close Relations - Science Fiction Zombies

reverses the plot dynamics of the previous entries by unleashing a "top down" conspiracy contagion here - it really is "government flu", spread by Kaufman in his prominent position as Head of the Centre for Disease Control. By "spiking" the flu "vaccine" the populace is urged to take, he manages to almost instantly endanger the entire population and facilitate the rapid spread of the virus, disseminated through governmental, police, media and other authority infrastructures.

There's also an interesting shift in approach here - the danger cannot be quantified in a physical "vehicle" - the pods from the previous films, but is an intangible, airbourne virus - a more modern and frightening proposition altogether?

One of the rather unfortunate side effects of this is the "projectile vomiting" which is one of the means of virus transmission now - in one scene Kaufman even vomits into Carol's mouth in an attempt to infect her.

Given the almost total lack of suspense, atmosphere, the dull characters that Kidman and Craig as forced to inhabit and the predictable studio attempts to inject some sanitised "family values" - Carol shouts at one point; "No one touches my child" as she "saves" Oliver by shooting several approaching replicants - nausea and sickness are also reactions the audience experience too!

Ultimately, *The Invasion* raises more questions than it provides answers to, introducing a variety of salient themes but lacking in any profound treatment of them. Having discovered that the virus spreads as people sleep, Carol and Driscoll indulge in some frantic pill-popping by downing amphetamines to stay awake - no such drugs were prescribed for audiences however!

This is paralleled with Carol's own occupation where she prescribes sedatives and all manner of other drugs to give unhappy patients a semblance of bearable normality in their lives. In a similar way, the alien virus pacifies those it infects - one of its by-products we glimpse via the news channels in the background, is that all wars and aggression throughout the world, are gradually being halted.

It's a persuasive argument - alien virus equals world peace, but the irksome suggestion that the Iraq war is simply a product of human nature is way too simplistic to even begin to ponder. The moral dilemma Carol and Driscoll face is whether to plunge the world back into war in order to protect their own emotional state and preserve their personal identities.

The notion that mankind is responsible for all wars simply states the obvious - to offer up an alien virus as a "cure" simply replaces the threat of physical violence with the threat of mental erasure instead. Some choice?

The Dead Walk

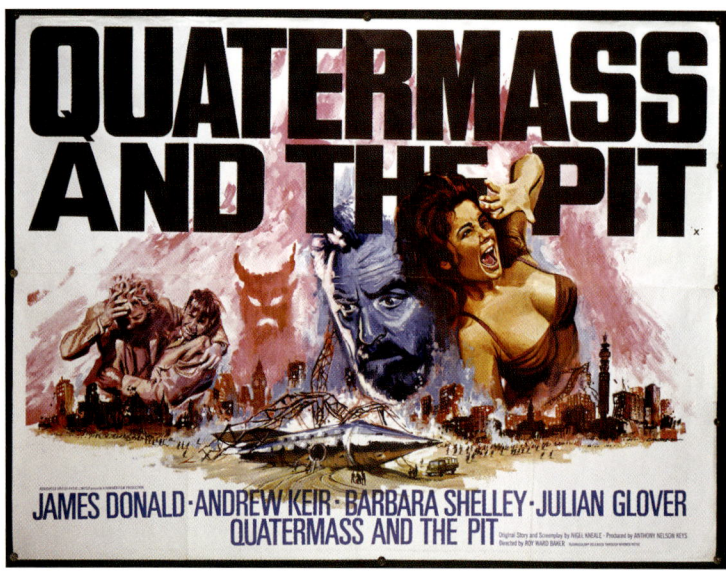

Ad mat for the final entry in Hammer Films' successful Quatermass series

The best British entry on this theme came, not surprisingly, from Hammer studios with their *Quatermass 2* (1957), the second in the trilogy of films to be based on Nigel Kneale's teleseries character Professor Quatermass, the others being *The Quatermass Experiment* (1955) and *Quatermass and the Pit* (1967).

Thames Television revived the character as late as 1980 with John Mills taking on the role of the good professor but a low budget and general lack of ideas contributed to the film's failure. The production covers similar ground to *Invasion of the Bodysnatchers*, but with less emphasis placed on the "alien takeover and more placed on the conspiracy of those in authority, and their willingness to enslave themselves and consequently their fellow men, an undercurrent that betrays the influence of George Orwell's *1984*, filmed only one year earlier in 1956.

Brian Donlevy, as Professor Quatermass, reprises his role from *The Quatermass Experiment* and, as ever, is angry at not having sufficient funds to finance a moon rocket project. He learns of a mysterious meteorite shower at Wynnerton Flats and an investigation finds that the whole area has been cordoned off. Strange pressure domes pierce the skyline in what looks like a moon base station on earth. Quatermass, unravelling the mystery, learns that the "fake" meteorites contain minute alien organisms that have the ability to take over humans. The zombiefied victims maintain the complex and its specially controlled environment, as the aliens cannot survive on earth's oxygen.

It is left to Quatermass to rouse village support and pump oxygen into the domes to kill the aliens. The authorities respond by blocking up the pipes, using the dead bodies of workers they have "bought off". The chilling portrayal here of the callous authority figures, brings home the message that here, it is the humans who pose the biggest threat to the future of mankind, as in *Invasion of the Bodysnatchers*. Even a skilled scientist such as Quatermass has difficulty in overcoming such powerful enemies as the Commissioner of Scotland Yard.

The film's climax provides an ironical twist as oxygen, our means of survival, acts as the grim reaper to the aliens, just as the common cold virus defeats the invading forces in *War of the Worlds* (1953). Despite the behind the scenes dispute over director Val Guest's rewrite of Kneale's screenplay, the film still plays as a coherent and thought-provoking essay into the foibles of the human character.

Not all the films of the period

Close Relations - Science Fiction Zombies

scrutinised alien occupation of human society so closely as the above films. Some were content to show a good old-fashioned struggle between good and evil, only updated from warfare to combating alien invaders. Typical of these were Edward L Cahn's *Invisible Invaders* (1959), which has the title creatures arriving from the moon to take over human corpses and embark on a conquest of the earth ! Horror stalwart John Carradine stars as a resurrected scientist leading an army of living dead across the countryside.

They wreak havoc as they kill anyone prepared to stop them, and it is left to John Agar to defeat them using high frequency sound waves to drive the aliens from their human shells. Despite the rather perfunctory direction and reliance on stock footage, the film is interesting for a number of reasons. The use of sound waves to eliminate the alien dead was itself repeated, albeit vice-versa in the later zombie epic, Jorge Grau's *The Living Dead At The Manchester Morgue*, only here, the soundwaves, in fact, reanimate the dead corpses within the confines of the scenic Lake District.

The sight of gaunt, gazing zombies roaming the Northern countryside is similar to numerous scenes from *Invisible Invaders*. The chalk-white faces and blackened eyes of the ghouls can also be seen in *Children Shouldn't Play With Dead Things*.

Invisible Invaders scenario of survivors trapped in an isolated farmhouse, was to be used to good effect in further zombie films such as *The Earth Dies Screaming* (1964) and *Night of the Living Dead* (1968).

Cahn's earlier attempt at a similar zombie subject, *Creature With The Atom Brain* (1955), featured an erratic plot that encompassed many diverse elements such as Nazism, atomic power and gangsters, but without being able to mould them into a cohesive shape. The imaginative screenplay from Curt Sidomak, writer of such horror classics as *The Wolf Man* (1941) and *Son of Dracula* (1943), has Karl Davis as a giant who injures his boss in a fit of rage.

Richard Denning plays the investigating police doctor who discovers that Davis' character has had his brain replaced by atomic power due to the handiwork of an ex-nazi scientist (Gregory Gay).

The operation involves removing the top of the victim's skull in order to replace the brain, the tell-tale signs of the victims being stitches jutting out around the skull that displays a non-too convincing skill in embroidery ! The finance for the surgery is provided by a gangster (Michael Granger), who uses the zombie creations with which to murder his enemies. The hectic finale has Davis rampaging his way through buildings and railways and a desperate Granger sending out his zombies only for them to be shot en masse by the police.

Despite the wealth of material here, no obvious parallels are drawn between zombieism and nazism for example, or to analyse the dangers of atomic power. Cahn is simply content to take a back seat and to let the action dominate. (In 1981 the singer Roky Erickson recorded a song based on the film, one of numerous compositions he has released using the horror genre as his subject matter. He also contributes to the soundtrack music for *The Return of the Living Dead*).

Another British entry into the science fiction zombie series was *The Earth Dies Screaming* (1964). It was director Terence Fisher's first, in a series of three sci-fi films made outside the auspices of Hammer, the others being *Island of Terror* (1966) and *The Night of the Big Heat* (1967), the latter living up to its name and creating a perspiring, cloying sense of claustrophobia that carries through the film's entirety.

The Dead Walk

In *The Earth Dies Screaming*, we see an American test pilot Nolan (William Parker) returning from a flight to discover that England has been devastated by an alien-controlled robot army. He joins with other survivors, horror luminaries Dennis Price and Thorley Walters among them, and travels to London with them. There, they are attacked by the robots who kill by touch and resurrect corpses to their cause, as mindless zombies.

The conclusion sees Nolan discovering the power source of the robots and destroying their transmitter station that is controlled by the aliens from their distant planet, a ploy reminiscent of *Daleks - Invasion Earth 2150 A.D.* (1966), one of the two films (thus far), featuring the popular Timelord Dr. Who. Fisher uses his usual no nonsense, straight forward directorial style to enhance the flow of the film, whose own eyeless zombies are an effective evocation of the living dead, together with their faceless robot masters.

Without doubt, the funniest film of the period was Ed Wood's space zombie "epic" *Plan 9 From Outer Space* (1956). The film's main claim to "fame" is its inclusion in Harry and Michael Medved's book "The Golden Turkey Awards", published in 1980 and featuring the 50 "worst" films ever made, voted for by members of the public. Wood's foray into the ridiculous involves two aliens (small budget here remember !) and their plans to take over the world by raising the dead. It is left to an intrepid pilot (Gregory Walcott) to conquer the aliens in their spaceship and rescue his own imprisoned wife in the process. The film ends as the spacecraft bursts into flames, killing the aliens as an excited narrator exclaims; "Can you prove it didn't happen ?" Well ,we can't but we can tell all too clearly how the film was made, with economy replacing authenticity.

Even today, the film stands as a monument to the totally unsophisticated manner in which Wood worked. Standard film conventions such as continuity are dispensed with as "day" and "night" scenes jostle with each other for attention even though they are supposed to be just one continuous scene. The studio floor peeks unceremoniously through the grass in the cemetery set, and cardboard tombstones flop easily to the ground.

The "special effects" at the conclusion consist of a paper plate being set on fire to simulate the enflamed spaceship, not exactly the work of George Lucas' Industrial Light and Magic team! The sheer

Steve Railsback as Colonel Tom Carlsen, getting to grips with the situation in Tobe Hooper's wildly entertaining Lifeforce

eccentricity of the film's production techniques are only matched by the extrovert nature of the film's cast and director. *Plan 9 From Outer Space* boasts a 400lb wrestler in the firm figure of Tor Johnson, a sultry, voluptuous siren in the shape of late night horror show hostess Vampira, and the weird and wonderful Criswell, who was Mae West's psychic adviser !

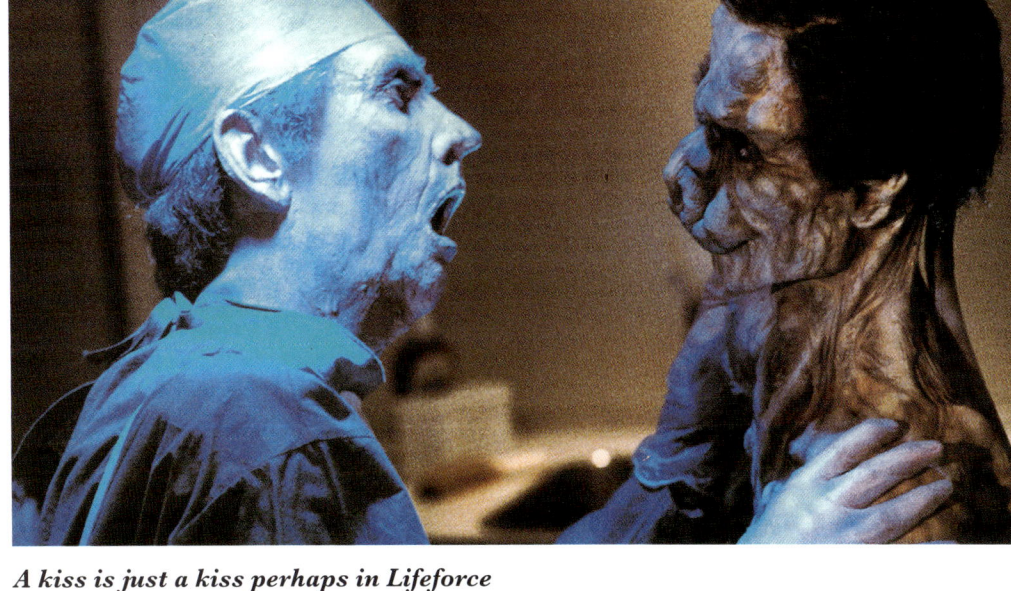

A kiss is just a kiss perhaps in Lifeforce

Also on view is the last film appearance of Bela Lugosi, even though he was in fact already dead when the film was made! Instead Wood used unseen footage from Lugosi's unreleased *Tomb of the Vampire*. For further scenes, Wood used a Lugosi "double", who was well over a foot taller than the world's most famous vampire, and whose face was so different he had to cover it up with his cloak for most of the picture!

Wood himself cut a bizarre figure, with his penchant for wearing women's clothing, often directing in high heels and stockings and sporting angora sweaters. A former soldier, Wood also courted notoriety by reputedly wearing a bra and panties under his uniform during a military landing in the Pacific ! He went on to film autobiographical work such as *Glen or Glenda ?* (1953), his tale about transvestites, and the "straighter" horror films such as *Night of the Ghouls* (1959).

After a comparative rest from extra terrestial zombies, the 1980's saw their return in two vastly different films.

1984's *Night of the Comet* is a subtle attempt to update Richard Matheson's "I Am Legend" to the modern day, with a few plot twists thrown in. Thomas Eberhardt's film has cinema usherette Regina (Catherine Mary Stewart) stuck in the projection booth with her boyfriend, pirating some old science fiction movies as outside a comet strikes the earth, turning all who see it into dust or bloodthirsty zombies. Regina's sister (Kelly Maroni), is one of the few fellow survivors as the two girls visit the local radio station, deserted clothes shops and generally have a good time. Later they run into some Devo-esque lunatics and narrowly escape, only to then fall into the hands of a scheming scientific research group.

One of the most interesting aspects of the film is its portrayal of the girls as being resourceful, pugnacious characters, roles typically reserved for men, especially so in the horror genre. The film also contains a fine dream sequence as the girls imagine they are being menaced by a zombie cop. Despite effective scenes such as this though, the film is a disappointment overall, in its cheap-skate creation of a deserted earth, and its low zombie count of only two - (count'em).

Night of the Comet is liberally sprinkled with references to other assorted genre films such as *Dawn of the Dead* and *The Day of the Triffids* (1963), and is very much a film promising greater things for the future from the various talents involved here, especially Catherine Mary Stewart, who previously appeared in the science fiction film *The Last Starfighter* (1984).

The same cannot be said of 1985's *Lifeforce* which employs already proven personnel to rather indifferent effect.

The film's source novel, Colin Wilson's excellent "Space Vampires", has been confusingly translated to the screen, the story submerged beneath a welter of admittedly superlative special effects and kinetic action scenes. Directed by Tobe Hooper, who had previously filmed the electrifying *The Texas Chainsaw Massacre* (1974), one of the most genuinely frightening horror films of all time, and the suitably scary (for TV anyway) adaptation of Stephen King's modern day vampire novel *Salem's Lot* (1979).

The intricacies of Hooper's direction are mainly lost in *Lifeforce* as most of the film's 26 million dollar budget has been spent on the special effects. Take the starkly realistic opening sequence as a group of astronauts make a strange discovery inside the tail of Halley's Comet - lovingly created for the film. The exploration team, led by Steve Railsback, take three crystal tombs containing the bodies of mysterious alien lifeforms to a London research establishment run by Frank Finlay.

Here, similarities to Hammer's *Quatermass and the Pit* and *Alien* take a back seat to the phenomenal special effects showcased here. The action picks up as one of the aliens, a very fetchingly naked Mathilda May, comes to life and literally sucks the lifeblood from one security guard and then proceeds to demolish the building upon leaving. The now dried husk of the hapless guard then returns to life and starts to create other zombies. A top SAS man (Peter Firth), is then called in to deal with the "D Notice" situation as reports flood in of a naked girl (May) wandering through the parks in central London.

Rapidly, the great city is reduced to rubble and civil war as the zombies begin to take over, all convincingly realised by the effects men as buildings burn and people die. Eventually, we learn that St. Paul's Cathedral is being used as a giant conduit for the collected "lifeforces" to be transported into space to other aliens. It is left to the ever-dependable Firth to rescue the earth.

Lifeforce is certainly a film that is difficult to take seriously, its inane script (from Dan O'Bannon, the writer of *Alien*), the perfect backdrop for the ludicrous plot that unfolds so spectacularly. The exemplary effects, nowhere as nerve-jangling as the autopsy where a jittery surgeon, about to cut into a zombie corpse, leaps back in horror as the newly animated cadaver begins pulsing with life again...

As it is, the frenetic action scenes and the very scale of the ensuing destruction, obliterate many of the film's deficiencies in other areas. However, much of the source material and spirit is lost to the screen and the definitive film version of "Space Vampires" remains to be made and seen.

Here, Hooper has only succeeded in creating cartoonish characters who jangle the funny bone as much as the nerves. *Lifeforce* appears almost to be a modern day *Plan 9 From Outer Space*, only with superlative rather than primitive effects. Hooper badly needs to recapture the

Close Relations - Science Fiction Zombies

highly-charged atmosphere and carefully drawn characterisations that are prevalent in his earlier films. That said, *Lifeforce* is incredibly entertaining and much more appealing than his other big budget work, including the rather too nicely commercial *Poltergeist* (1980) and his insipid remake of *Invaders From Mars* (1987).

"IT'S THEIR PLANET…WE ARE THE ALIENS."

In a similarly entertaining vein is John Carpenter's *Ghosts of Mars* which is set in the year 2176. The red planet has been colonised and 640,000 people work on Mars. A mining operation unearths a Martian artefact and unleashes long-dormant Martian warrior spirits, that systematically possess the human intruders. A disparate group of cops and criminals band together to stop them.

Mars, with it's matriarchal society, represents a return to the strong female characters of Carpenter's early films. *Ghosts of Mars* has a unique cast. Natasha Henstridge plays Melanie Ballard, the police officer given the task of transporting criminal Desolation Williams (Ice Cube)-named in the tradition of Carpenter anti-heroes like Snake Plissken (*Escape From New York*) and Nada (*They Live*). The cast also includes Pam Grier, Jason Statham, Clea Duvall, Peter Jason, Joanna Cassidy and Robert Carradine.

When the police officers arrive at the mining town of Shining Canyon, they find everyone is dead, except for the people in the town jail. A situation that harkens back to Carpenter's 1976 classic *Assault on Precinct 13*, a film heavily inspired by both Howard Hawks *Rio Bravo* (1959) and George A. Romero's *Night of the Living Dead*. Just as in *Ghosts of Mars*, in *Assault on Precinct 13*, a group of police officers and criminals must band together against a remorseless foe.

People under siege is a theme that fascinates Carpenter. Carpenter's world is one of Hawksian equality. A world so dangerous it is assumed nobody would enter it unless he or she has the "right stuff". In other words, it is up to the individual to rise to the occasion. In Carpenter's world, institutionalised authority has failed, survival depends on a combination of self-reliance and being able to work with others (the Hawksian team). While *Assault on Precinct 13* was not a financial success, it garnered a great reaction at the 1977 London Film Festival and helped put Carpenter on the map (so enamoured was Carpenter with *Rio Bravo* that he edited *Assault on Precinct 13* under the name John T. Chance, the name of John Wayne's character in *Rio Bravo*). Like Carpenter, Hawks often returned to the same well of inspiration, remaking *Rio Bravo* as *El Darado* (1966) with John Wayne and Robert Mitchum.

Carpenter's work often has a subtle theme or undercurrent. The paranoia of *The Thing* (1982), the extremism of the both the far right and the far left in *Escape From L.A.* (1996). *Ghosts of Mars* addresses colonisation

Natasha Henstridge as Melanie Ballard in John Carpenter's Ghosts of Mars

Big Daddy Mars (Richard Cetrone) surveys the destruction in Ghosts of Mars

and imperialism, with the Martains reclaiming their world and using the humans' own bodies to do it. *Ghosts of Mars* has the gritty feel of Carpenter classics like *Escape From New York* (1981) and *The Thing*. Production on *Ghosts of Mars* took place at a gypsum mine on the outskirts of Albuquerque, New Mexico, part of the Zia Pueblo, over 12,000 acres of sacred land that was settled by the Zia Indians almost 800 years ago. In respect of the Zia tradition, John Carpenter requested a tribal elder and medicine man of the Zia tribe to bless the production.

Carpenter has composed the music for the bulk of his films, giving them a highly distinct sound, a minimalist synthesised mood. His score for *Ghosts of Mars* is no exception, giving the film it's dark heartbeat, a sonic pulse, a feeling of desolation and isolation, of being trapped.

The idea of a supernatural defence system owes much to the aforementioned *Quatermass and The Pit*, the 1967 Hammer film based on a six part BBC T.V series scripted by Nigel Kneale (a major Carpenter influence) and broadcast in live 35 minute episodes broadcast between December 1958 and January 1959. *Quatermass and The Pit* (known as *Five Million Miles to Earth* in the U.S), concerns an artefact discovered on a building site in Hobb's Lane, in Knightsbridge in London. The artefact is of Martian origin and has the ability to possess humans, in effect to make them Martians. Directed by Roy Ward Barker and starring Andrew Keir as Quatermass, it's a worthy, thought-provoking picture.

Ghosts Of Mars was savaged by critics on release, yet on mature reflection, it's an intriguing and entertaining work, mixing the director's diverse influences to great effect. The idea of Mars being a matriarchy, with male and female roles largely reversed is sensible (and I like touches like the authorities being referred to as 'The Woman' rather than 'The Man' as in *Escape From New York*, and a female president on the dollar bills).

Using a flashback format, (unusual for Carpenter), an inquest is being held into an incident at the Shining Canyon mine. Lieutenant Melanie Ballard (Natasha Henstridge), the sole survivor of a police squad sent to escort prisoner Desolation Williams (Ice Cube) for trial in Cryse, Mars' capital city. Williams is accused of mass murder. The reverse chauvinism is a scream. They travel to Shining Canyon on a freight train captained by Carpenter favourite Peter Jason. On the train we learn how Martian society works, and also that Melanie takes a drug to kill the tedium of Martian life. "A years contract here equals two years earth time, gotta read the fine print." When they reach Shining Canyon, the streets are empty. The jails' inmates

Close Relations - Science fiction Zombies

are in their cells but there's no sign of the guards.

They check out a building with flickering lights. Inside there's blood everywhere. Mealnie and Jerico (Jason Statham) find a severed arm and some lethal looking sculptures made out of wire. The other police officers find another building resembling an abattoir, with headless bodies hanging from the ceiling (one of several fine effects from KNB). They open Desolation's cell, as well as the other prisoners, there's a women called Dr. Arlene Whitlock. She says she's a science officer but she clearly knows a lot more than she's telling. They find a survivor displaying zombie-like symptoms. "It was almost like she was possessed, like there was a force inside her." They also find a survivor in a truck who kills himself rather let something get him.

Desolation has escaped his cell in the meantime, holding an officer named Bashira (Clea DuVall) hostage. Melanie courageously offers to take her place. Melanie overpowers him. "Damn, girl, I like you already." He in turn overpowers her, and runs towards the clinic. Inside there are zombie-like humans. Desolation saves Melanie. She in turn saves him and disarms him. "I didn't say I was innocent. I didn't kill nobody." Desolation says he found the dead bodies just hanging from the station ceiling, so he took the payroll they had being guarding. He tells her she would have done the same. She retorts. "I'm a cop not a crook." He smiles. "There's a thin line between a cop and a crook these days."

Sergeant Jerico discovers that his commanding officer has been decapitated by the Martian zombies. He sees more of these Martian zombies, bodies mutilated, teeth filed to razor sharp points. They are culling those not like them (an idea taking from *Quatermass And The Pit*). Jerico wisely gets out of there, radioing Melanie. "Lieutenant, we've got a situation here. The commanders dead. Everyone in the mine has gone insane." Melanie gets more of the story from Whitlock. "Whatever used to live here, we woke it up. It takes us...a kind of possession."

Jerico has found three survivors, who say they "used to be miners, then everyone in this place lost their minds, running around chopping people's heads off." The three survivors saw red mist advance on the miners, who fell unconscious. Then, "some of them started to come round, walk around like they were confused...then they started changing. Act different. Stand different. Start cutting themselves for decoration. Filing their teeth. Making weapons. Killing the ones who hadn't changed." However,

Desolation (Ice Cube), Sergeant Butler (Jason Statham) and Bashira (Clea DuVall) in Ghosts of Mars

More devastation from Ghosts of Mars

the three men are really Desolation's partners in crime, and they disarm the cops. Melanie manages to trap them and Desolation. She makes a deal, she'll let them out if they agree to work with her. She deputises the other prisoners, save the one that's now a Martian zombie, mutilating his face. There is the weapons scene that also features in Carpenter's Snake Plissken film. There are a series of explosions as the Martian zombies blow up the town. There is a pitched battle. Desolation saves Melanie again. "Second time I saved your life." "Run a tab!" Desolation's brother (one of the three accomplices) gets possessed by a Martian spirit. The leader of the zombies, Big Daddy Mars, exhorts his troops on. Losing two men to the Martian zombies' lethal throwing discs, they barricade themselves into the jail (shades of *Assault On Precinct 13*, which itself was *Rio Bravo* meets *Night Of The Living Dead* with a dash of *Zulu* (1964) thrown in for good measure).

Whitlock explains she was called in for a find of scientific significance at the mine. A tunnel carved into the rock, by Martians, at the end of tunnel, a chamber sealed with hieroglyphics, Whitlock breaks the seal, allowing the Martian souls to escape. "I opened Pandora's Box. I let them out." Guilt-ridden, she brings to mind Father Malone in Carpenter's *The Fog* (1980). The whole concept is a reversal of the Martian 'colonisation-by-proxy' idea in *Quatermass And The Pit*.

The train is coming back for them, but firstly they have to survive the horde of Martian zombies outside. Melanie asks Desolation if he believes in anything. "Stick around and I might tell you." "When?" "When the tide is high and the water's rising." (This is very Howard Hawks in inspiration).

Bashira shoots the possessed prisoner, and it's spirit gets into Melanie. They leave her outside, giving her one of her drugs so she won't know what's happening. In another nod to *Quatermass*, Melanie sees into the memory of the Martian trying to possess her. She sees what Mars was like when they had their original forms. With the aid of the drug, she expels the Martian spirit and climbs the jail wall, trying to get back in. Jerico realises she's back in the driving seat. "..haven't heard any of those things speaking English." She says, "the tides getting high out here" and Desolation lets her back in. She tells him. "I had a glimpse of the Martians, of their minds, of what they want. They won't rest short of the destruction of any invading species. As far as they are concerned, we are the invaders."

Big Daddy has had a battering ram built and the Martians launch an all-out assault on the jail. Breaking the doors, they meet a spirited resistance. (This is an idea of survival taken from Howard Hawks-of survival through co-operation). They torch Big Daddy and escape to rendezvous with the

Close Relations - Science Fiction Zombies

train. But Melanie decides they must go back, and blow up the town's nuclear reactor in the hope of stopping the Martian zombie hordes. They set explosive charges at the town's power plant, but the Martians led by the now singed-looking Big Daddy launch an all-out attack on the train, killing everyone but Melanie and Desolation. Big Daddy and a few zombies make it onto the train. They fight them off and the reactor explodes, when Melanie comes to, Desolation is stitching her injury, he has also handcuffed her to her bunk. There's a stand-off, she could shoot him, but she doesn't - something she doesn't tell a sceptical inquest. "Is our statement to the cartel going to be that Mars is being overrun by ghosts?"

But they believe her story when Cryse comes under attack, the explosion only destroyed the Martian's host bodies. Desolation comes for her with weapons, "Tide is high. Time to survive." They have a very Hawksian exchange. "If you ever want to come over to the other aside, you'd make a hell of a crook" offers Desolation with "You'd make a hell of a cop" being Melanie's rapid response.

SOCIETY ZOMBIES

Besides the alien origins of zombiehood alluded to in the above films, film makers have also been continually fascinated by the idea of zombies being formed from within our own society, by other humans, with no alien connections.

One of the first films in this style came from one of the "new wave" directors of the 1960's, Frenchman Francois Traffaut, whose *Farenheit 451 oC* (1966) dealt with the suppression of free will in society as well as free thought. Taken from writer Ray Bradbury's novel of the same name, the title refers to the temperature at which books will burn. The film's premise delineates future society as being a restrictive state, governed by totalitarian rules that have banned all books as being subversive, and so, a threat to society and the authorities.

That being so, society is now divided into two camps; the "book-burners" who protect the ruling oligarchy and the "book people", who each memorise one book to keep alive the spirit of free thought and free will in society. The once proud firemen, eradicators of fire, are now transformed into book-burners. Oskar Werner's fireman, is one of the film's central characters, who leaves his wife for the literary teacher next door, both parts symbolically played by Julie Christie, showing the duality of human nature, mirrored in Werner's ability to transform from book-burner to book-reader later in the film.

Traffaut places before us a curiously sad film, rejecting the literary counterparts celebration of the liberated book people in favour of a more insular portrayal of them as mere zombies. They endlessly recite passages from their books, apparently neither learning nor understanding anything, as is shown by their continual propensity for walking around in circles upon the snow-laden ground. Werner's passage into book learning as opposed to book burning is shown as a pointless exercise, merely transferring from one regulated occupation to another.

There are many diverse elements of society that are under attack from Taffaut here. The usually heroic image of the fireman and of racing fire-engines is turned upside down, though paradoxically, one of the book's that is burned is Hitler's testament to nazism, "Mein Kampf". Traffaut also "succeeds" in somewhat "romanticising" the novel in that the film shows Christie's literary teacher as being not a threat to society, but instead a comfort to a lonely Werner. The film charts this progression from

The Dead Walk

isolation to companionship, sometimes at the expense of other areas of the story.

Probably the most visually memorable impressions left by the film are the various lingering shots of burning books, engulfed by flames, an image that was to provide further mileage for Lucio Fulci's *The Beyond* and Dario Argento's *Tenebre*. The often stirring visual compositions were mainly the work of cameraman Nicholas Roeg, who also shot such sumptuous costume horror's as Roger Corman's *The Masque of the Red Death* (1964) and the more overtly science fiction orientated vehicle, *The Man Who Fell To Earth* (1976).

The interesting cast included Anton Diffring, who also starred in such genre features as Hammer's *The Man Who Could Cheat Death* (1959) and *Circus of Horrors* (1960).

Nor does the horror connection end there, as the soundtrack was provided by Bernard Herrmann, composer of numerous Hitchcock film scores including *Psycho* (1960), *Vertigo* (1958) and other horrors, such as *It's Alive* (1974) and *Sisters* (1972), before turning full circle and scoring Brian De Palma's *Psycho* clone, *Dressed To Kill* (1980).

Farenheit 451oC was Traffaut's only excursion into science fiction, save for a cameo acting role as a French scientist in the staggeringly popular *Close Encounters of the Third Kind* (1977). His talents lay elsewhere, portraying, albeit in his own singular fashion, the contemporary world as found in films such as *Jules et Jim* (1962) and *The Bride Wore Black* (1969).

A far more celebrated film, concentrating on a similar subject is Stanley Kubrick's celluloid version of Anthony Burgess' chilling novel *A Clockwork Orange* (1971). The subject matter may be akin to Traffaut's film but there any similarities end as Kubrick's own interpretations and ideas offer a completely different emphasis, as this film positively celebrates free will, but also highlights the price that you inherently pay to have it. The film features a bravura performance from an utterly convincing "yob" Alex (Malcolm McDowell), the leader of a vicious gang of thugs called "Droogs" who live in a perpetual state of anarchy in a near future Britain.

We chart Alex's "progress" from a violent but free spirit, who beats up tramps and even his own droogs, his anger culminating with his rape and murder of a female fitness fanatic. He is convicted and after "rehabilitation" in a state prison, he undergoes a form of "aversion therapy" as he is forced to watch endless scenes of mutilation and torture, eyes bulging, straining against the metal pincers that hold them rigidly open, all of this to the accompaniment of classical music that is pounding in his ears.

Eventually, he is released back into society, a pale shadow of his former self, he has been "cured" of his violent tendencies, but only at the expense of being left a physically sick, pathetic figure, now repulsed by violence of any kind, he has simply passed from one extreme to another. The denouement sees him "bounced" to and fro between the government and the opposition parties until he is finally returned to his original moronic state, not for his own good but for political expediency.

Kubrick's film, like its literary source, lines up its "targets" before systematically destroying them in much the same way as Alex behaves. The soft underbelly of "civilised" society is exposed for what it really is - a haven for hypocrisy, the government populated by faceless automatons (clockwork oranges), who are more concerned with public relations than principled policies. The "therapy" that Alex undergoes, is itself, simply an orgy of sex and violence. Alex is

Close Relations - Science Fiction Zombies

"cured", but only by overdosing on the type of behaviour for which he was originally imprisoned.

There are many anomalies here, scenes of graphic violence are underscored with joyous classical music. The tests that Alex undergoes to prove the "success" of his treatment are both degrading and meaningless. He is forced to grovel at a man's feet and lick his soles, subjecting himself to all manner of verbal abuse. Like an obedient animal, Alex does as he is told, crawling and cowering to order. He also rejects the advances of a completely naked woman; he is left a neutered, whimpering figure, the very antithesis of his former self.

The futility of all this is no better illustrated than here, as the prison warder, sitting in the audience that are observing the "tests", betrays his "baser" human instincts by gazing lecherously at the disrobed female form in front of him. It is highly debatable if Alex has been cured and even if he has, the message firmly seems to be that there are countless others like him, ready to take his place as the warder clearly shows.

Alex's impotent actions here also signal the film's attitude towards sex. It is regarded as a purely perfunctory exercise, devoid of emotion or meaning. Cafes are decorated with outlandish furniture, moulded into the shape of female bodies, drinks are even drawn from sculptured breasts that adorn the interior. Alex himself refers to sex as a bit of "in and out" and when he does procreate, it is in a comically "speeded up" sequence so that the whole "act" is over in a matter of seconds. The act of loving is now just that, an "act", with no feeling or sincerity attached. It has become as regimented as washing the dishes and about as exciting. Women have now become a part of the furniture, literally, who can be pushed and pulled, kneaded and sat on at will.

Even Alex's murder of the fitness teacher earlier in the film, is a bizarre sexual act as he kills her with one of her own giant, phallic-shaped sculptures, Alex forcing the weapon in and out of her body suggestively and unambiguously.

The diminishing importance (impotence ?) of sex is equalled only by the diminishing integrity of the politicians in the film. The treatment they prescribe Alex is called appropriately, the "Ludrico technique", its name echoing its effects. When it is convenient for the government to arrest Alex, they do so, and when it is convenient to publicise his release, they do so, and when it is convenient to convert him back to his former self, they do so. All this in the interests of public opinion, any considerations on humanitarian

The Droogs indulge in some random violence in Stanley Kubrick's film version of A Clockwork Orange

grounds are swept away on a tide of political connivance and scheming.

The violence in the film (for which it has been heavily criticised), is shown as coming from all sides, not just from Alex. This is reinforced towards the end of the film when Alex is arrested again, this time by his former droog companions, who now act out their vile atrocities under the cover of their newly-donned police uniforms. They may have a more acceptable image now but beneath their veneer of respectability lies a still rotten centre.

Where the film does succeed is in the way that it shows how the "stylised" violence has become integrated into all areas of society, regardless of social class or status. It is all presented in a highly original way however, as brutal acts of aggression are continually underscored with moments of outre music - Patrick Magee's wife is raped by Alex to the strains of "I'm singing in the rain." Alex undergoes his aversion therapy watching Nazi concentration camps scored with Beethoven's 9th symphony, which paradoxically, had been his favourite piece of music when he had been his "old", violent self.

In Kubrick's world, all of our preconceptions are turned upside down, beautiful becomes ugly and good becomes bad. Music is used to a similar end in David Lynch's *Blue Velvet* (1986), as appalling acts of violence are accompanied by inane musical numbers.

Kubrick is a master at manipulating his audience as first we dislike Alex, then we sympathise with him, and yet all these differing responses are proved to be ultimately meaningless as Alex has his original characteristics restored to him. It is not just Alex but we the audience who have become victims of the authorities cynical betrayal of human integrity.

There is a poignant scene towards the film's conclusion that

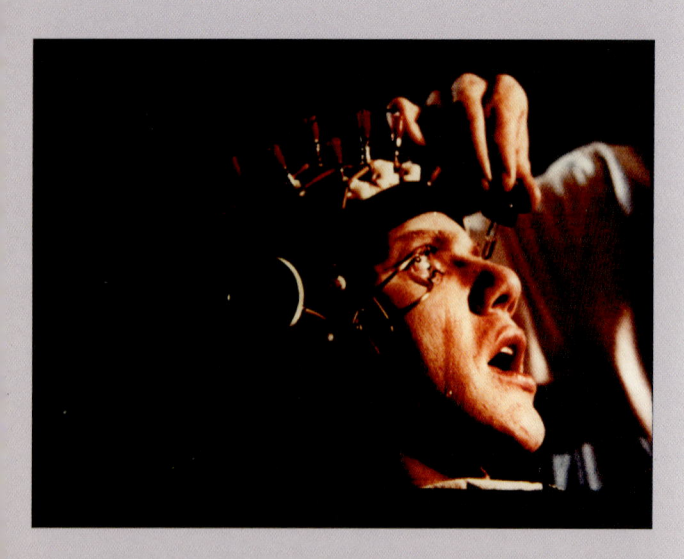

Images from A Clockwork Orange

Charlton Heston plays the sole human survivor in The Omega Man

concisely states the picture's morals as a maddened Magee - intent on revenge, forces Alex into a bungled suicide attempt, leaping through an upstairs window to the music of Beethoven's 9th Symphony, Alex's former favourite, that has now returned to haunt him. Free will is a basic human right, but with it comes the threat of violence. To deny one is to deny the other. Magee is free to use the "mental torture" of beautiful music to try and kill Alex who, because he has been denied free will, can only affect a negative response - his attempted suicide.

A Clockwork Orange seems to suggest that personal autonomy must be upheld whatever the cost, otherwise we become as zombies, denied both mental and physical freedom of expression. there are no easy solutions as society and its people are fraught with anomalies but such is the nature of life, and to deny life is to deny everything.

An intriguing variation on this theme can be found in 1974's *The Terminal Man* written by Jurassic Park author Michael Crichton, a real life doctor of medicine whose previous works, *Coma* (1978), *Westworld* (1973) and *The Andromeda Strain* (1971), all reflected his rather clinical nature. George Segal stars as the psychotic man of the title, who has a miniature computer implanted in his brain to control his aggressive instincts.

However, the process that calms him down is so "pleasurable" as to turn him into a homicidal maniac, killing solely to revel and luxuriate in the resulting restraining techniques. This concept is entirely different to that of *A Clockwork Orange* as here, the victim (Segal), actually "enjoys" the therapy that he is given by the authorities, in fact, it is that very therapy that is largely responsible for his murderous rampages. The marriage here between man and machine is seen as being potentially explosive, a theme covered in other films such as Joseph Sargent's *The Forbin Project* (1969) and Robert Wise's *The Andromeda Strain*.

Unfortunately, the gleaming antiseptic laboratory sets are the ideal background for the film's vapid characters. Segal as a hopeless, powerless guinea pig, is someone that we feel little sympathy for. His emotions are turned on and off at random by the scientific team who control him. His violence, including his sensationalist murder of his girlfriend stripper (Jill Clayburgh) on a water bed, and the nonchalance of the scientists callously experimenting with Segal, inciting him to make a play for Joan Hacket's frigid lady scientist, does not endear either to the audience.

The crudeness of the film's title pun and its simplistic dressing of drab characters in black, others in white, seems at odds with the film's use of classical music from Bach and literary quotations from T.S. Elliot's "The Waste Land".

For all the high tech gloss of the scientists' laboratories and their endless banks of equipment, they cannot cure their creation but instead kill him. The final image of Segal, crawling into his own grave, is a damning reflection on the ineffectual techniques of the scientists who have driven him to this state. Director Mike Hodges doesn't quite invest enough impact on the dual struggle between man (Segal) and man (scientists), combined with man versus machine. Hodges is better served in his more light-hearted recreation of *Flash Gordon* (1980).

The link between the loss of identity and the rise of Nazism alluded to in both *Farenheit 451oC* and *A Clockwork Orange* has helped to give birth to a brace of films which deal more exclusively with the subject.

The Boys From Brazil (1978),adapted from an Ira Levin novel, features an ingenious, if also unlikely plan to establish a Fourth Reich in the modern world using cells preserved from Hitler's body to produce clones. Levin had previously written a book on a similar theme that was filmed in 1974 as *The Stepford Wives*, (as well as being remade in 2004), also dealing with cloning, this time by scientists, of their wives and programming them into their "ideal" women.

The Boys From Brazil's rather starry cast, has Gregory Peck as the geneticist Dr. Mengele, the "Angel of Death" from Auschwitz concentration camp, now living in South America. He surgically experiments with local peasant children, assisted by a fellow Nazi (James Mason), and implants Hitler's cell tissue into the victims. The convoluted plot has them needing to kill the boys fathers in order to recreate the exact environment that Hitler had grown up in as a boy. Their plan is eventually defeated by Sir Laurence Olivier's nazi hunter (based on the real life figure of Simon Wiesenthal), and, in an enfeebled climax, the nazis' are overwhelmed by a pack of giant dogs.

Where the film impresses is in the luscious photography of the various locations, ranging from the Alps to Brazil, and to the forests of Connecticut. The central metaphor of young Hitler clones, characterless children, is a powerful indictment of the nazis and their philosophical dogma. The loss of personal pride and indeed life, suffered by so many Jewish people during the war years, is mirrored here in the equation of zombieism with nazism.

The once overladen procession of the innocent to their gas chamber genocide, is here replaced by the mindless followers of nazism whose own indoctrination leads them to their own mental suicide. It is a recurring theme that has been explored more realistically in Fredrick Forsyth's "The Odessa File" and more fantastically in James Herbert's "The Spear".

The conflict between Jews and Germans is also prevalent in the earlier *Hausers Memory* (1970), a TV film based on a Curt Sidomak novel. Similar in concept to the oft-filmed *Donovan's Brain*, the plot concerns the "takeover" of a living person by a dead one, making this a rather early forerunner in the "possession" film stakes.

David McCallum plays a Jewish scientist, who volunteers to receive an

Close Relations - Science Fiction Zombies

injection of DNA brain fluid from a dying nazi scientist called Hauser. The unwitting McCallum inherits the scientific secrets he wanted to, but also the dead man's memory, so he is a zombie of a rather different kind. He is literally "caught in two minds".

This intriguing variation is disappointingly realised however during the remainder of the film as it degenerates into a simple act of revenge for McCallum, who rejects Hauser's wife (Lili Palmer), who is still a nazi, and he goes in search of the SS guard who punished Hauser for his eventual defection from the nazis. The film is most notable for having won a Golden Asteroid award at the Trieste science fiction festival in 1971, and also features the versatile Leslie Nielsen, the star of the *Airplane* film series and of George A Romero's *Creepshow*.

Boris Sagal, the film's director, contributed a rather different film to the zombie genre a year later. His *The Omega Man*, the second screen version of Richard Matheson's novel "I Am Legend", loses much of the paranoia and chilling atmosphere of the source material, as had the earlier version in 1964. The sight of a strident Charlton Heston amidst the rubbish-strewn streets of Los Angeles, soon becomes tiresome as does his repeated viewing of the *Woodstock* (1970) music concert film, (something Heston loathed),in a deserted local cinema. Heston, a seemingly sole survivor of a Sino-Soviet germ war, acts less like the paranoid survivor of the novel than a minor Rambo, with his muscular gun-toting figure, his raison d'etre almost is to "mow down" the remaining zombies who are led by Anthony Zerbe.

When not indulging in such pursuits, Heston stays in his nightly-besieged apartment, listening to music and sipping wine with a decadence that belies his plight. The notion that the human survivor is in fact the real zombie compared to the mutations outside is lost here as the benevolent Heston finds an antidote serum to cure the zombies. The antidote to the protagonists' personal battle is far away though and Heston's eventual death has been made inevitable by his refusal to practise the peace ideals preached so obviously in his favourite film *Woodstock*.

In truth, Heston had already reached his own apex in the science fiction genre three years earlier in the excellent *Planet of the Apes* (1968), where his final realisation at discovering the buried "Statue of Liberty" amongst the rubble, is that the primitive "alien" planet he has landed on is in reality the devastated earth from the future. It is a discovery that is as awesome in its

Mutants abound in Boris Sagal's The Omega Man

The Dead Walk

magnitude and implications as it is in its chilling cinematic conception.

To complete a triumvirate of film adaptations of Richard Matheson's 1954 source novel, Francis Lawrence's *I Am Legend* (2007), at least retains the title if not all of the salient themes and darker nuances within the writer's work.

Perhaps not too surprisingly, given Will Smith's casting as the "lone" survivor Robert Neville, *I Am Legend* proved to be a major draw at the US box office. Indeed Matheson himself heartily approved of his casting in the role, commenting that "I think Will Smith is the perfect person to portray Robert Neville", continuing that "I've seen almost every film he has made and he is always totally convincing in whatever role he is playing. In this story, his character is the key, and, therefore, he is key."

It takes a special actor to basically "carry" an entire film upon his shoulders and it's fair to say that in the main, Smith accomplishes this – his only aid being Sam (a German Shepard dog called Abby in real life), and Smith's performance eclipses the efforts of his predecessors in the role, messrs Price and Heston.

Located in New York in 2012, what most elevates this *Legend* above the mundane is Smith's portrayal of the lonely, slightly loopy Neville, whose desperation for fellow human contact leads him to strike up "conversations" with the mannequins in a deserted video shop. Think Tom Hanks bravura solitary role as Chuck Noland in *Cast Away* (2001), only Neville has Sam for a real life companion rather than the volleyball Hanks christens "Wilson".

We learn that a British scientist Dr. Krippen (!), (played un-credited by Emma Thompson), has developed a cure for cancer, only with the unfortunate side-effect of unleashing a deadly airborne virus which is transmitted by physical contact amongst humans. The ensuing worldwide pandemic results in death to the fortunate one's but transformation into nocturnal, zombie-like "Dark Seekers" for those who are less so.

As well as being "apparently" the solitary human survivor, Neville is also a scientist and uses the basement of his brownstone house on Washington Square to continually strive to find a cure for the virus. Amidst this obsessive scientific odyssey, kudos are due to the film's

Will Smith as Robert Neville, with faithful companion Sam, in 2007's I Am Legend

production designer Naomi Shohan for the stunning visualisation of the post apocalyptic wasteland which forms the backdrop to Neville's explorations.

What we see is an evocative vision of Manhattan–littered with abandoned cars and decimated bridges, symbolising the collapse of society and its infrastructure. The streets are now overgrown with weeds and foliage, the city now literally a "jungle", complete with escaped lions from the zoo, and now chasing deer down a deserted Fifth Avenue.

Whilst the unnerving depiction of the eerily silent city is undoubtedly one of the film's master strokes, it is a similarly sweeping brush which also re-colours Matheson's novel and in effect dilutes its impact.

One of the major strengths of the novel, aside from Neville's characterisation, is in its original approach to the ancient curse of vampirism, as science is used to filter out fact from folk-lore. The creatures in Lawrence's film however, are most certainly not vampiric in appearance, owing more to the modern video game generation and the fast moving "infected" of *28 Days Later* (2002). Perhaps this is seen as a necessary modernisation, as by taking the vampire out of its historical, arcane milieu, the horror is dissipated. The creatures are rendered more frightening here due to their superior numbers rather than their intellect as Neville is generally able to outrun, out think and outfight them. There is perhaps just a seed of an evolving "intelligence" however, in the sequence where Neville inadvertently springs a trap the creatures have set for him, resulting in his narrow escape, but at the cost of the faithful Sam becoming wounded and infected.

Lawrence's film also considerably shifts the emphasis from the military to the the medical world here, as the blame for this avowedly man made plague is laid firmly at the door of the Health authorities, whilst in the source novel, the plague is carried on clouds of dust that have resulted from a nuclear war. In *The Omega Man*, there is also a militaristic explanation for the outbreak due to a chemical/biological weapons conflict between the USA and China.

The most damaging deviation though, is in the screenplay's departure from the novel's subtle suggestion that it is Neville who may be the *real* monster, so effectively does he destroy the creatures. Matheson's gloomy ending, which no doubt echoed the angst of the period, is sacrificed here in favour of a "Hollywood friendly" ending – New York can be convincingly destroyed on film but in no way can the film's A list star.

The tension and authentic horror contained in the film is greatly reduced upon the discovery that there are indeed other human survivors – a woman Anna (Alice Braga) and a young boy Ethan (Charlie Tahan). The idea of a man made plague and Neville's role as a scientist also opens up the possibility of finding a cure – again departing from Matheson whose far more disturbing idea suggested that the entire definition of "normal" had now changed. For Matheson, the real horror was embodied in the realisation that societal beliefs and values were an unconscious part of life, an artificial construct only held in place by society, so, when society collapses, so does everything in the cadre associated with it, leaving an unpalatable vacuum in its place.

The book's original ending, where Neville is destined to become a "Legend" in a new society of vampires – regarded with a combination of awe and fear by the creatures, is diametrically opposed to the film's conclusion where Neville, grenade in hand, launches himself into the amassed creatures invading his lab, leaving Anna with a vial containing his newly discovered antidote. "We are his legacy. This is his legend. Life over darkness" are the platitudes Anna gushes in an overly sentimental scene as she hands over the "cure" to the fellow survivors she has now discovered in a remote, countryside location.

So, instead of being lauded by the creatures, Neville is celebrated by humanity here for providing the panacea to mankind's ills. Given the limited number of creature's that Neville's martyrdom has killed and the previously imparted information that the humans are outnumbered by at least one thousand to one, it is debatable as to just how effective his actions will have been and likewise, as to the importance of any legacy he will leave behind.

In the risible alternative ending to the film, Neville instead releases the female creature he has been experimenting on in his lab, to the alpha male (Dash Mihok), her "mate", gingerly wheeling her out on an operating trolley and into the snarling, twitching ranks of the mutants.

As Neville proceeds carefully to inject her with the "cure", she then embraces her mate – an entirely unconvincing attempt at ascribing a new found "human" display of affection – but with little change in their physical appearance this is rendered as simply embarrassing. Neville's "hand-over" of his "patient" is simultaneously accompanied by him mouthing "Sorry" to the alpha male – perhaps a moment of realisation for Neville as the creatures think that it is *he* who is the monster, momentarily echoing Matheson's theme in the novel, although unlike the source novel, here, Neville kills as a consequence of his search for a cure.

It's a problematic coda – after all, if the female creature is returning to a "human" state then surely the other creatures will merely feed upon her? In this alternative ending, Neville, having seemingly given up hope of finding a universal cure, is content to drive out into the daylight with Anna and Ethan with the status quo of "us" and "them" simply reinforced. "You are not alone. There is hope" Anna broadcasts on the radio unit, in a message intended for any other survivors out there – not exactly a rousing or particularly inspiring ending.

The overwhelming impression from Lawrence's film remains the iconic image of the resourceful Neville, essentially alone and fighting against an unrelenting threat, but also of Hollywood's insistence in twisting events to conspire towards a contrived, "upbeat" ending, which only serves to negate the inventive flourishes which precede it and so stymie the potency contained within the source novel.

ROMERO IS LEGEND

Richard Matheson, one of the most influential horror writers, was born in 1926. He began his prolific writing career with the short *Tale Born of Man and Woman*, which appeared in The Magazine of Fantasy and Science Fiction. Matheson has managed to cross-pollinate several different genres of writing, and has been highly influential on a great many writers. Matheson was born to write, actually gaining a degree in journalism

His potent story-telling is highly visually charged and cinematic, a rich vein that film-makers have been eager to mine.

Mathson wrote the script for *The Incredible Shrinking Man* (based on his 1956 book - *The Shrinking Man*), the film won a Hugo award in 1958. He wrote screenplays for *The Twilight Zone* (including the classic Nightmare At 20,000 Feet), *The Alfred Hitchcock Hour*, and *Night Gallery*. (He also did the script for *Jaws-3D* (1983), but hey, we all have our 'will work for food' moments!). He wrote Steven Spielberg's first feature *Duel* (1971) and also worked on *Kolchak - The Night Stalker* (1974). One of the best Matheson works is the Christopher Reeve and Jane Seymour starring, doomed-romance story, *Somewhere In Time* (1980) (Based on the story *Bid Time Return*), a moving story of a man falling in love with a photograph of a woman taken in 1897, he manages to travel back to her, but alas, in the words of Shakespeare, "time is out of joint, oh cursed spite, that I was ever born to put it right."

Other novels include *Hell House* (1971, filmed as *The Legend of Hell House* in 1973), *Earthbound* (1982), *Ride The Nightmare* (1959), *What Dreams May Come* (1978, filmed in 1998) and *Journal Of The Gun Years* (1992).

Without a doubt, Matheson's most influential work is the classic *I Am Legend*, first published in 1954. The story concerns Robert Neville, the last living man on Earth, after a bio-plague has rendered the rest of the world undead. Visually exciting, poignant and thought-provoking, it is simply a masterwork. One that invited film-makers to immortalise it's dark beauty on celluloid.

In 1957, Matheson himself wrote an adaptation of *I Am Legend* for Hammer films. Word came back from the BBFC (scripts were scrutinised by the British Board of Film Censors before the films actually entered production in those days), so sadly Hammer didn't proceed with the project. It was the custom at the time for the cost-effective Hammer to submit their scripts to the BBFC in order to save money by cutting unapproved scenes before they were filmed. We can only wonder what it was about Matheson's script that provoked such an adverse reaction. This experience obviously didn't sour relations between Matheson and Hammer. He wrote a superb script for their production of Dennis Wheatley's *The Devil Rides Out* in 1968, starring Christopher Lee and Charles Grey, and directed by Terence Fisher. The film (known as *The Devil's Bride* in the US, for fear it would be mistaken for a western!), is such a classic, we can only imagine what might have been and mourn Hammer's lost *I Am Legend*.

The next attempt to capture *I Am Legend* on film was 1964's *The Last Man On Earth/L'Ultio Uomo Della Terra*. Filmed in Rome with the great Vincent Price in the title role and released by American International Pictures. This is believed to be a much-altered version of the script Matheson originally produced for Hammer, so widely divergent from his original vision, that Matheson adopted the pseudonym Logan Swanson for the films script credits. Interestingly, Matheson had scripted many classic Vincent Price films such as *House of Usher* (1960), *The Pit and The Pendulum* (1961), *Master of the World* (1961), *Tales of Terror* (1962), *The Raven* (1963) and *Twice Told Tales* (1963).

Vincent Price told Fangoria's Weekend of horrors in 1990; "Actually, I thought (*The Last Man On Earth*) wasn't too bad…The problem was that it was supposed to be set in Los Angeles, and if there's a city in the world that doesn't look like Los Angeles, it's Rome! We would get up and drive out at five o'clock in the morning to find something that didn't look like Rome. Rome had flat trees, ancient buildings-we had a terrible time." And I was never so cold in my life as I was on that picture. I had a driver and I used to tip him a big sum to keep the car running so I could change my clothes in the backseat."

The next attempt to film *I Am Legend* was *The Omega Man* in

1971, starring Charlton Heston and directed by Boris Sagal. Charlton Heston wrote of his character's dilemma in his autobiography *In The Arena*. "What would it be like to be always alone, day after day, yet threatened every night by murderously dangerous creatures maniacally intent on killing you?" Matheson himself was less than impressed with this version. "It was so far removed from my book, I don't know why I bothered."

After several failed attempts, a new version of *I Am Legend* emerged in 2007, directed by Francis Lawrence, and featuring a fine performance by Will Smith.

Interestingly, one of the most faithful interpretations of *I Am Legend* is George A. Romero's *Night Of The Living Dead* (1968). Romero has made no secret of his admiration of Matheson. "I like Matheson's books and was inspired by some of his novels. I had a similar idea. The old becomes the new and vice-versa, like the mentally disturbed becoming the rational ones instead. I decided that *Night of the Living Dead* was going to be a far more extravagant and fantastic plot, one step beyond the last human being in a society of vampires."

"Matheson's novel was never really treated well, from a cinematographic point of view, though the one with Vincent Price wasn't that bad…"

I Am Legend begins with the following line. "On those cloudy days, Robert Neville was never sure when sunset came, and sometimes they were on the streets before he could get back." Masterfully, in the space of a single sentence, the novel's first, Matheson establishes his hero's name and a nameless threat that arises with nightfall.

Matheson's description of the measures Neville has taken to defend his home are mirrored in *Night of the Living Dead*, when flight to a safer place would be a wiser option. "He checked each window to see if any of the boards had been loosened. After violent attacks, the planks were often split or partially pried off, and he had to replace them completely, a job he hated."

Security is an ingrained basic human desire. Better the devil you know. People so often suffer misery due to fear of the unknown, often putting up with horrible jobs or relationships for this reason. Even if such security is a chimera, waiting for the dawn to disperse it like mist, or in this case, nightfall. "He could still see them out there, the white-faced men prowling around his house, looking ceaselessly for a way to get at him. Some of them, probably, crouching on their haunches like dogs, eyes glittering at the house, teeth slowly grating together, back and forth, back and forth." This is a perfect description of the ghouls that surround the farmhouse in *Night of the Living Dead*.

"Outside they howled and pummelled the door, shouting his name in a paroxysm of demented fury. They grabbed up bricks and rocks and hurled them against the house and they screamed and cursed at him. He lay there listening to the thud of the rocks and bricks against the house, listening to their howling." *Night of the Living Dead* perfectly captures the horror of the protagonist's situation.

"He kept firing the pistols until they were both empty. Then he stood on the porch clubbing them with insane blows, losing his mind almost completely when the same ones he'd shot came rushing at him again", conveying the invulnerability of the undead.

"Everybody's got an idea. But they aren't worth anything.

Close Relations - Science Fiction Zombies

Everything from germ warfare on down." *I Am Legend*'s attempts at a rational explanation for the phenomenon are similar to those in *Night of the Living Dead*.

"He threw her body out the front door and slammed it against their faces. Then he stood there against the door breathing heavily. Faintly he heard through the soundproofing the sound of them fighting like jackals for the spoils." Romero perfectly captured the horror of bodily dismemberment described by Matheson. The description of 'men in canvas and masks' brings to mind *The Crazies*.

"Everyone without exception had to be transported to the fires immediately upon death. It was the only way they knew how to prevent communication. Only flames could destroy the bacteria that caused the plague…He couldn't use any of the cemeteries. They were locked and watched. Men had been shot trying to bury their loved one." This parallels the grim measures taken in *Night of the Living Dead* to deal with the emergency.

Neville's wife Virginia ("He couldn't even scream. He just stood rooted to the spot, staring dumbly.") returns to him undead in much the same manner as Johnny in *Night of the Living Dead* returns to Barbara (ironic when you think of his "they're coming to get you, Barbara" taunt at the beginning of *Night of the Living Dead*, now 'they really are coming to get her and now Johnny is one of 'them'.)

The line "a weird Robinson Crusoe, imprisoned on an island of night surrounded by oceans of death" sums up the monotony of despair in both *I Am Legend* and *Night of the Living Dead*.

In *I Am Legend*, the main character is at war with himself. In *Night of the Living Dead*, the characters are at war with each other.

The media in *Night of the Living Dead* and *I Am Legend* behave in similar fashion. "There was something grotesquely amusing in that; the frenctic attempts to sell papers while the world died."

"I buried her, but one night she came back. She looked like-like you did. An outline, a shadow. Dead. But she came back. I tried to keep her with me. I tried, but she wasn't the same anymore…you see." Both Romero and Matheson understand for horror to cut deep, it must be personal. "Suddenly he thought, I'm the abnormal one now. Normalcy was a majority concept, the standard of many and not the standard of just one man."

At the end of *I Am Legend*, as in *Night of the Living Dead*, 'good' does not triumph over 'evil'. The new order ("New societies are always primitive.") is no better than the human one it evolved from. Matheson sums it up perfectly. "Full circle. A new terror born in death, a new superstition entering the unassailable fortress of forever. I am legend."

UNSEEN LEGEND

The road to the Will Smith-starring *I Am Legend* was a long and rocky one. It began in 1996, with producer Lorenzo di Bonaventura at Warner Brothers, who began to develop *I Am Legend*.

Warners had optioned a script called *The Cell*, written by Mark Protosevich, who was subsequently offered the job of creating a script for *I Am Legend*.

His first draft script was set in San Francisco, in 2002 (then six years into the future), where a virus has turned the entire population into creatures called Hemocytes, save for Robert Neville. It bears some resemblances to the version of *I Am Legend* that was eventually filmed. Neville watches video tapes (also a story-telling device to explain what has happened), broadcasts radio messages in the hope of attracting other survivors. Watching video tapes of old TV programs, and hunting the Hemocytes, Neville eventually falls victim to one of his own mantraps and is trapped in the city as darkness falls. He manages to make it back home, but his dog is bitten by an infected dog and he is left with no choice but to leave it to it's own devices. At this stage Neville is ready to crack, when he encounters an uninfected woman named Anna. Anna is, however, addicted to morphine. They form an uneasy relationship. But she betrays Neville to the Hemocytes. They are holding her brother prisoner, along with other uninfected humans being harvested by the Hemocytes, a kind of living larder. The Hemocytes deal with Neville by crucifying him. He manages to escape, and attacks the Hemocytes lair with a subway train. He rescues Anna and her brother, and as many of the uninfected as possible, and they escape by sea.

Warner Brothers were pleased with this version of the script and decided to develop it further.

So, in the June of 1997, Arnold Schwarzenegger entered into negotiation to play Neville, with Ridley Scott slated to direct. Scott appointed Beau Marks to produce the film. More significantly for Protosevich, he also brought in John Logan (who would share an Academy Award for *Gladiator*) to re-write the script. Protosevich wasn't sacked for lack of talent, far from it, rather Scott regarded him as the studio's writer, so he was sacrificed.

Logan and Scott did extensive research on plagues, disasters, anything relating to that. In the first fifteen minutes of the film they showed the destruction and disintegration of human civilisation. (Logan for some reason, felt this to be a 'bold approach', but it's all been done before, *Mad Max 2* (1981) for instance, and in a much shorter and effective way). The next change they made (and this was bold, or stupid, depending on your opinion), they did away with anyone for Neville to interact with, including his dog, and there was to be no narration. Eventually, they realised that this would be too much, for both Neville and the audience, human beings are social animals, so they had Neville playing tapes his wife made while she was dying - it sounds like a laugh a minute.

Scott put together an art department consisting of Arthur Max on production design, story board artist Sylvian Despretz, and conceptual illustrator Tani Kunitake.

They rejected Prosevich's concept of setting *I Am Legend* in San Francisco for practical reasons and decided on Los Angeles. San Francisco has very distinct architecture wheras' Los Angeles is bland and many cities with cheaper production costs could substitute for it.

One good idea they came up with was that Neville lived in a modern fire station converted for his defence (Neville's house in *I Am Legend* isn't the most defensible and secure place, particularly not with an entire city to chose from). It had a moat filled with gasoline, weapons ports, and a perimeter of floodlights and landmines (one aspect retained for the filmed version). In a homage to *The Omega Man*, Neville had filled his home with art from the J. Paul Getty Museum.

They had the charming idea

Close Relations - Science Fiction Zombies

that in 2005 (by then seven years down the line) that there would be solar-powered phone booths. Now with the rise of mobile phones, it looks like there won't be any phone booths, which shows the perils of predicting the future.

They came up with a blood disease which affected the skin's resistance to ultraviolet rays. Scott wanted to use CGI to give the actors a skeletal appearance. These creatures were christened Hemocytes (a big improvement on 'dark seekers', the name used in the filmed *I Am Legend*).

The Hemocytes had their own hierarchy. The Caretakers at the bottom, to look after the wounded. The Drummers, who would create martial music. The Clerics-who were the religious group. Finally, there were the Warriors. There were two lieutenants, Christopher, who was in charge of the Clerics, and Eva, who was leader of the Warriors. The overall leader was a Hemocyte named Cortman, who was subject zero of the virus, one of the ten original experimental subjects who escaped from the research facility the virus was developed in, and from there to infect the population.

Scott and Logan kept changing their minds. Sometimes the Hemocytes could speak, other times they were like wild animals (why didn't they simply use the ideas from the book the film is supposed to be based upon?). They were to be pale and covered in bandages to keep their skin moist, and halos of flies would indicate their presence.

It was around this time that Mill Film, the special-effects company in London that the Scott brothers own, came up with a piece of software to computer-generate a deer for a scene where Neville hunts for food (another scene to survive in the filmed *I Am Legend*).

Some of the script changes had no logic. Neville, before he even knows of the Hemocytes, dynamites buildings! Why? (because there was nothing on TV?).

They came up with a sequence that survives in a form in the filmed version, with Neville capturing a Hemocyte and using his blood to create a serum (similar to in *The Omega Man*) to change her back.

But, budgeted at over $100 million, neither studio or creative people could see eye-to-eye. So original screenwriter, Mark Protosevich was brought back on board. Scott and Protosevich made the Hemocytes much more feral, they no longer spoke. The film was to end on a positive note, as Neville survives an all-out assault on his home and flees to a abandoned airfield, where he finds a small boy who has been hiding there with his mother.

This draft nearly got filmed, but budget continued to be a problem, as *Sphere* (1998), *Batman & Robin* (1997), and *The Postman* (1997) had all fared badly at the box office. So, *I Am Legend* needed it's budget reduced. The misfortunate Protosevich was fired again. Scott eventually quit, taking many of the team that would have made *I Am Legend*, writer Logan, production designer Max, and concept artist Despretz.

While this was the end of Scott's involvement, Warner Brothers appointed a new producer and brought Protosevich back yet again. Schwarzenegger was still attached to star, but Warner Brothers wanted to make the film for $70 million rather than $100 million. They hired Rob Bowman (who would go on to direct the excellent *Reign Of Fire* in 2002). Protosevich cut down the scale of the story, setting much of it indoors, and limiting the number of locations. The

The Dead Walk

characters of Anna and her nephew Ethan were increased in scope. This time, the problem in getting the film made was Schwarzenegger - his recent films had not struck box office gold as before, and his recent heart surgery may have affected Warner Brothers confidence.

They then considered Kurt Russell as Neville, who no doubt would have done a fine job but the failure of *Soldier* (1998) put a stop to this. It was around this time that Will Smith began to be connected to the role of Neville.

Eventually, in March 2002, Schwarzeneger became a producer of *I Am Legend*, with Michael Bay to direct and Will Smith to star. This was stopped however, due to WB president Alan F. Horn's dislike of the script. In 2004, Akira Goldman was asked by head of production Jeff Robinov to produce the film. Guillermo del Toro was originally approached to direct *I Am Legend* by Smith, but he turned it down to direct *Hellboy II: The Golden Army* (2008). *I Am Legend* eventually went into production in 2006, with Akira Goldman and Protosevich being credited with the script, and directed by Francis Lawrence, who insisted on changing the film's setting to New York. Despite criticism of the unconvincing CGI used for the Hemocytes, and the film's divergence from the source material (something addressed in the alternative cut of the film), there is a great deal to admire in the filmed *I Am Legend*. The devastated New York in the film is breath-taking, and until you actually see the Hemocytes, they are a very scary threat. Most importantly, Will Smith puts in a career defining performance as Neville, the scene where he has to kill his infected dog and only friend is truly poignant and heart-breaking, a performance to be applauded. Another *I Am Legend* film with Smith and Lawrence is planned, and, learning from their first film together, we expect great things.

Images from The Omega Man below

10
BANDAGED BUT UNBOWED – THE MUMMY LIVES!

The Mummy (1999)

The Dead Walk

Not many film genres have been spawned as the direct result of an insect bite. However, the mummy genre can shuffle forward to stake such a claim given the death of Lord Carnarvan over two months after the long lost tomb of Egypt's "child-king" Tutankhamun had been uncovered by English Egyptologist Howard Carter.

Before being able to shout "tabloid press", the curse of the mummy became the global headline courtesy of the feverish imagination of the newspaper hacks who erroneously attributed Carnarvan's demise to the romantic notion of the pharaoh's revenge upon the defilers of the tomb.

With the tombs of fellow Kings Ramses II, Meneptah and Ramses VI also discovered, plus the gold coffin of King Tut, now over 3000 years old, "mummy mania" spread asunder.

Although the French *La Momie du Roi/The Mummy of King Ramses* was the inaugural gauze-covered production to be mounted in 1909, followed by other offerings such as *Die Augen der Mumie/Eyes of the Mummy* (1918), it was one of the tabloid reporters, John L. Balderston, who helped to helm the first major mummy box-office hit, when his screenplay for Universal became the Boris Karloff vehicle *The Mummy* (1932).

Set in the Valley of the Kings in 1901, we see Edward Van Sloan, Arthur Bryan and Bramwell Fletcher as three members of an archaeology team discuss their latest finds; the mummified remains of Egyptian high priest Imhotep and an alabaster box.

It is the impatient Fletcher who secretly opens the box whereupon he discovers the legendary "Scroll of Thoth" and begins whispering the ancient incantation aloud. Here follows the film's most celebrated sequence as we see a solitary eye flicker open, hands twitch as one of them snatches the arcane parchment leaving us with only a hallucinatory glimpse of the putrifying bandage.

F.W.Murnau collaborator, german cameraman Karl Freund, directs this all with considerable elan, proving that the "less is more" adage can flourish as atmosphere rather than entrails permeate the scene, although this would later be reversed in the visceral excesses of the 1970's and onwards.

The action then jumps forward 11 years as the gnarled features of Ardath Bey (Karloff reprising his mummy guise) aids a new team of archaeologists to uncover the tomb of his ancient love, Princess Anck-es-en-Amon, before embarking on the pursuit of her modern day reincarnation, played by Zita Johann.

Karloff's is indeed the definitive performance, bringing subtlety to an outwardly crude and monstrous character and his (misguided) attempts to rekindle his unrequited love for the Princess, lends an air of nobility to his deeds - namely that he's not in it for the money but for the love of a "good" woman !

As Imhotep, buried alive for the sin of trying to revive the Princess by utilising the Scrollo of Thoth, he now stands before us intending to sacrifice her "modern" incarnation in Johann, in a forlorn attempt to rediscover his loved one.

If *The Mummy* remains at the apex of the genre, then its subsequent sequels (of a sort) flounder closer to the nadir of it, requiring the bandages in part to cover up the plot inadequacies and pedestrian pacing.

Thus, we have Christy Cabanne's Universal offering *The Mummy's Hand* (1940), which relies on its' ornate sets to cultivate a milieu approximating regal splendour and an air of mystery, courtesy of the temple set used in James Whale's *The Green Hell* the same year.

No Karloff this time and his

Bandaged But Unbowed - The Mummy Lives

Poster art for Universal's seminal 1932 entry, The Mummy, starring Boris Karloff

replacement is cowboy actor Tom Tyler delineating the mummy Kharis, resurrected by tana leaves as opposed to incantation this time, but still pusuing the same goals, the revival/reincarnation of his beloved priestess and revenge upon the desecrators of his tomb.

The rather brief running time of 67 minutes is padded out using "flashbacks" from the original films, some doctored so that Tyler and not Karloff is seen in *Hand's* flashback scenes of ancient Egypt, with its' one spark of imagination being Tyler's partially paralysed mummy - continually dragging one leg behind him as he stalks his victims due to a tana juice deficiency.

If the juice had begun to evaporate in *Hand* it all but dried up in *The Mummy's Tomb* (1942), probably the most mundane of all Universal's mummy series.

Relocating the action from history-steeped Egypt to contemporary New England probably wasn't the wisest move, nor was the casting of the rising star (or so Universal fervently hoped), Lon Chaney Jnr. as a rather portly mummy whose bandages are well and truly overstretched (unlike the imagination !) as he strives to find his reincarnated love (Elyse Knox).

Borrowing scenes liberally from not just *The Mummy* but *The Mummy's Hand* too, the film completes its plagiarism during the climax where villagers, brandishing burning torches, instantly recall the far loftier *Frankenstein* (1931).

Chaney Jnr. reprises his mummy role again in *The Mummy's Curse* (1944), only this time his beloved Princess Anaka rises unusually from a quicksand-covered coffin when a swamp is drained by engineers (utilising the evocative Louisiana bayou locale).

Chaney Jnr.'s Kharis on this occasion really does bring the house (or temple at least) down during the enfeebled "climax" when an ancient stone monastery collapses on the bandaged one.

The Dead Walk

After a hiatus of some eleven years, save for such oddities as Egypt's own entry *Haram Aleck* (1953), the mummy suffered the ignomy of a "comedy" intervention courtesy of *Abbott and Costello Meet The Mummy* (1955).

With stuntman Eddie Parker in harnass as the mummy, Klaris (sic), we are treated to a turbo-charged mummy, (in comparison), to what has preceded him as his large strides rapidly circle in on the would-be victims.

The duo's rather crass attempts at humour largely fail and although dynamite features heavily in defeating the mummy here, this is one denouement that is far from explosive.

The rather lesser-known *Pharaoh's Curse* (1957) helmed by Lee Sholem is far more inveigling, utilising Death Valley exteriors to lend some kind of atmosphere to his "Egyptian" locations.

In an inventive plot wrinkle, we see a British patrol on a mission to bring back an archeological expedition at the turn of the century. The mission is accomplished but only when a tomb has been discovered and one of the archaeologists becomes cursed and begins to stalk the others.

With secret chambers and hidden passageways, Sholem cranks up the tension for all its worth and if you prick this mummy does he not bleed ? Well, yes, and if you pull his arm... it will come off, as one protagonist discovers!

Whilst Mexico dabbled with the bandaged one in the likes of *The Aztec Mummy* (1957), *The Robot Versus The Aztec Mummy* (1959) and *Curse of the Aztec Mummy* (1959), before the inevitable "santo" entries such as *Santo y Blue Demon contra los Monstrous* (1971) and *Santo en la Vegenza de la Momia* of the same year, not to forget the equally prolific Spanish actor/director Paul Nashy who starred in such gems as *La Vegenza de la Momia* (1973), it was to be Hammer Films flirtation with the character which was to provide fresh

Christopher Lee as Kharis in Hammer Films 1959 version of The Mummy

Bandaged But Unbowed - The Mummy Lives

Kharis (Christopher Lee) fights to the finish with John Banning (Peter Cushing) in The Mummy

impetus, if not necessarily ideas, to the mummy cycle.

Having successfully revived both *Dracula* and *Frankenstein* previously, Hammer's first mummy film, Terence Fisher's *The Mummy* (1959), combined elements from Universal's *The Mummy's Hand* and *The Mummy's Tomb*, rather than being a straightforward remake of the original Karloff feature.

Christopher Lee and Peter Cushing are reunited, if only in opposition here, with Lee essaying the role of Kharis, an Egyptian high priest tortured and then executed for his love of the Queen Anaka (Yvonne Furneaux).

When the Queen's tomb is desecrated, Lee later recognises that Cushing's wife (also played by Furneaux) is the reincarnation of the Queen and so battle commences, or rather it doesn't, as the decidedly talky production is high on exposition but low on excitement, lacking the frissons Hammer injected into much of their *Dracula* and *Frankenstein* series.

That said, Fisher does manage to cultivate a moody swamp milieu which features heavily during the climax and the mummy's subsequent demise.

It was left to Michael Carreras to take over the reins in 1964's *The Curse of the Mummy's Tomb* which managed to infuse some new ingredients into the mix. Here, an American P T Barnum styled entrepeneur (Fred Clark) plans to take Ra-Antef's mummy (Dickie Owen) on tour despite the feverish warnings he receives advising against such a course of action.

Amidst a rather convoluted structure, much of the action is played out in "blighty" rather than Egypt, climaxing in London's sewers, where the mummy meets its untimely end courtesy of a sewer cave-in.

In the last of the Hammer films to be shot at Bray Studios, the cloth-wrapped feet shuffled into view again in John Gilling's *The Mummy's Shroud* (1966) where Prem (Eddie Powell again) plays the guardian mummy of a young pharaoh's tomb.

A lengthy pre-credits sequence set in ancient Egypt indicates the tone for the longuers which are to follow, momentarily enlivened when Powell, and a would-be victim, square up in a photographic dark room, dousing each other with corrosive chemicals.

As the mummy crumbles to dust a la *Dracula* (1958) during the conclusion, there is little of stand-out quality here, save for Catherine Lacey's scenery-chewing Haitian soothsayer

Excavation work begins in The Mummy's Shroud

and archaeologist Claire's (Maggie Kimberley) ample cleavage.

The death of the talented Seth Holt, during the making of Hammer's next entry, *Blood from the Mummy's Tomb* (1971), added an unfortunate appendage to the legend of the mummy's curse and provided Michael Carreras with a challenging role as he took over to helm this imaginative adaptation of Bram Stoker's "The Jewel of the Seven Stars".

Here, we find an Egyptian Queen Tera (Valerie Leon) who is entombed for practicing black magic. Thousands of years later, Egyptologist (Andrew Keir) unearths her body, simultaneously as his wife dies giving birth to a baby daughter back in England.

The child grows up to be Margaret (Leon again) who is in fact, possessed by Tera's spirit when she is given the Queen's ancient ring.

Utilising the assistance of one of her father's associates (James Villiers), she then embarks upon recovering the exact relics that will enable Tera to return to life.

Eschewing the conventionally blunt approach to the subject, *Blood* concentrates on the more cerebral aspects involved in constructing a cogent, clandestine world of evil and explores the moral issues raised in deliberately releasing such a nefarious power into the "real" world.

Leon excels in her dual role and the film successfully bucks the trend of male-dominated mummy films (!) by presenting a potent female version here.

Whilst Mike Newell's *The Awakening* (1980) proved to be embalmed rather than created such is the ennui it induces in the viewer, there is even less imagination on view in what is so far, one of the few "zombie" mummy film, 1981's *Dawn of the Mummy*. The Romero influences are present again here, even down to the derivative title. The opening

Queen Tera (Valerie Leon) in Blood From The Mummy's Tomb

Bandaged But Unbowed - The Mummy Lives

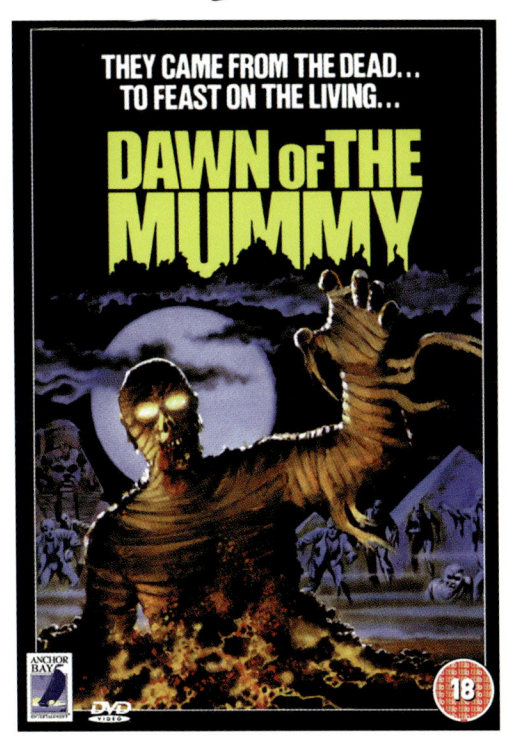

sequence shows an Egyptian royal being mummified in the year 3000 BC along with his attendant slaves.

In a plot that borrows heavily from the earlier Universal mummy films, three modern-day grave robbers desecrate the tomb and in doing so, reawaken the royal mummy and his flesh-eating acolytes. Caught in the middle of this, are a group of touring American fashion models, who soon become victims of the murderous zombies. The all too familiar climax sees the mummy and his followers burned to death.

It is a film long on zombie attacks and short on exposition, the acting never rising above the atrocious, even the picturesque Egyptian locations cannot compensate for a woeful lack of invention. Director Frank Agrama took over from Armand Weston, his previous films including *Queen Kong* (1976), so he simply exchanged a film about a beast for a beast of a film !

Aside from relatively minor entries such as *Time Walker* (1982) and *Bram Stoker's Legend of the Mummy* (1997), it is the triumvirate of modern mummy films which have belatedly breathed life once again into the forgotten genre; from the Hammer homage *Talos The Mummy* (1999), the more esoteric *The Eternal* (1999), to the high octane, mega-budget Universal remake *The Mummy* (1999),

Horror and fantasy pedigree is certainly not lacking with *Talos the Mummy*, given director Russell Mulcahy's previous works such as *Highlander* (1985) and *Razorback* (1984), together with a cast that includes such icons as Christopher Lee.

Fittingly then, given Lee's prescence, that *Talos* is very much a deliberate and affectionate throwback to Hammer's movie series, featuring a traditional plot but a mummy with some modern invention to keep things boiling.

So, we have the requisite prologue sequence set in 1948 when an archaeological dig in the Egyptian desert goes horribly wrong. Led by Professor Turkel (Lee), the team are as much interested in uncovering treasure as to uncovering the remains of any Egyptian gods, but when they discover an unmarked tomb, Turkel realises through his extensive knowledge that it is the tomb of Talos.

Whilst attempting to stop the desecration, Turkel and his party are buried alive in an explosion which

Brendan Fraser as Rick O'Connell - an all action hero in Universal's updated version of The Mummy (1999)

The Dead Walk

reseals the tomb.

Cut to 50 years later and a new expedition of scientists including the Professor's granddaughter, Samantha (Lousie Lombard), Brad (Sean Pertwee), Professor Marcus (Michael Learner) and Claire (Lysette Anthony). The group re-open the tomb and to their amazement - find a sarcophagus suspended from the ceiling of a vast chamber, "guarded" by an array of deadly spikes designed more to keep something in rather than to keep others out.

When Talos' bandaged remains

The High Priest Imhotep (Arnold Vosloo) leads out his acolytes in The Mummy

are shipped back to London for display, they mysteriously disappear, as a wave of gruesome murders begins to grip the entire city. Samantha, along with a street-wise cop Riley (Jason Scott Lee), then discover the truth behind the murders - the legend of Talos. In the spirit of Mulcahy's inventiveness, it is the bandages themselves which are revealed as having the power to entwine and crush their victims like a deadly snake, as well as being capable of transforming into the form of an eight foot tall demon.

In rather less capable hands this would spell disaster but Mulcahy manages to invest a sense of menace and evil into the scuttling tendrils of sackcloth which snake out to ensnare each new victim, and their kinetic movement certainly proves more cogent than the pedestrian ramblings of any typical mummy figure.

If Mulcahy is bravely toiling to inject new frissons into the mummy genre then perhaps arthouse "fave" Michael Almereyda is going one stage further in flouting genre conventions.

Following on from his offbeat vampire film *Nadja* (1995), Almereyda's unique take on the mummy mythos in *The Eternal/Trance*, he describes as being about "two cheerful alcoholics, a married couple and their son, who go to dry out."

However, this proves a bad move when in their musty, decaying ancestral home they discover a slew of dreadful secrets from their family's past awaits them - worst of which is the 2000 years old and perfectly preserved Niamh - unusually attractive for a mummy and a Druid witch to boot.

When Nora (Alison Elliott), the wife of the couple, succumbs to her addiction, this allows Niamh to be reborn and so she begins consuming Nora's identity.

Partly lensed in Ireland, *The Eternal* benefits from the unusual (for a mummy film!) local colour with Almereyda's directorial flourishes rendering it more poetic than scary and more erotic than horrific, as he accentuates the emotional and physical urges within the revived Niamh. As Almereyda himself commented on the character; "She comes to life, full of longing and rage."

Given the recent activity within the mummy genre these words serve not so much as an epitaph but as an ode to the welcome rejuveneation of this once dormant Egyptian legend, now once again ripe for re-discovery within the celluloid world.

In contrast, Stephen Sommer's *The Mummy* is essentially a *Raiders of the Lost Ark* (1982) "boys own" style adventure yarn into which some superlative special effects and the mummy legend are interwoven.

Certainly the frequent bursts of kinetic action make for a welcome change of pace, injecting some sorely-needed energy into the gagging corpse of the mummy film genre.

Under the authorship of Sommer, we find ourselves once more transported to 1920's Egypt, where an ex-Foreign Legionaire O'Connell (Brendan Fraser), having years before discovered the lost city of Hamunaptra, meets up with a librarian/Egyptologist Evelyn (Rachel Weisz) and the mercenary Jonathan (John Hannah). The trio set off in search of the buried treasure Hamunaptra conceals - themselves pursued by a group of American archaeologists come treasure hunters, as the film veers off into pure adventure territory.

Their endeavours flounder upon the mummified body of Imhotep, the evil high priest of Thebes, whose fate was sealed some 3000 years ago for his indiscretions with the pharoah's mistress Ank-Su, and who exacted his revenge by placing a curse upon the

Images from 1999's The Mummy

Jonathan Carnahan (John Hannah), Evelyn Carnahan (Rachel Weisz) and O'Connell (Brendan Fraser) in The Mummy

city of Hamunaptra as we discover in the elongated prologue.

Once Fraser and company have located and opened the tomb, Imhotep is reanimated and is found to be suitably pissed off!

ILM's superlative special effects include the revolting CGI mummy itself - a zombie-like mutation, an awesome sandstorm and a particularly abhorrent army of man-eating scarab beetles, who scuttle throughout the burial chambers at will, and herein lies one of the main weaknesses of Sommer's film.

Whilst the state of the art effects utilise modern cinema technology to the full and instantly surpass the more primitive mummy films which have gone before, the small matter of atmosphere and characterisation is rendered almost perfunctory here.

Despite the location shooting, the mystique of the whole mummy mythos appears strangely artificial rather than authetic here, not helped by the thinly-sketched leads who don't so much interact as merely act as signposts to the next conflagration.

Given that many major players in the horror genre had been linked to the film in its torturous pre-production period, including such luminaries as Clive Barker, Joe Dante and George A. Romero, perhaps they would have had more affinity for the genre and provided some much needed subtlety amidst the blood-soaked bandages.

Barely two years after the dust "settled" on *The Mummy*, Fraser's Egyptologist and Weisz's librarian were reunited in *The Mummy Returns* (2001), only this time as husband and wife,

Maria Bello as Evelyn in The Mummy 3 - Tomb of the Dragon Emperor

Bandaged But Unbowed - The Mummy Lives

some nine years on from the original and complete with eight years old son Alex (Freddie Boath).

"It is written that…" – "Where is all this written" being Rick's typically flippant response as his "Boy's Own" adventure style proceeds to cut a swathe through the trappings of tana leaves and papyrus scrolls. The "plot", as it is – the search for a mythical golden pyramid, signposted by the magical bracelet now adorning Alex's arm and which requires removal in seven days, lest the undead jackal army of Anubis and the legendary Scorpion King (The Rock/Duane Johnson) be unleashed against an unsuspecting world, merely acts as the skeleton for a plethora of flashy set pieces to augment the flesh against.

These include Evelyn's near ritual sacrifice in the bowels of the British Museum, the surreal sight of newly-revived mummies chasing the protagonists through the streets of London, the flight of a dirigible traversing mountainous terrain to find the fabled golden pyramid and the voracious pygmy skeletons secreted in the nearby undergrowth, who eagerly attack all who dare enter.

Amongst this surfeit of unremitting action lies the almost parallel issue of the eponymous mummy – High Priest Imhotep (Arnold Vosloo) once again returning from the tomb and seeking his eternal love Anck Su Namun – now reincarnated in the guise of Meela (Patricia Velasquez in dual roles).

With a whole raft of B-Movie styled accoutrements – be it hidden passageways, secret doors or mysterious treasure trove boxes, the relentless action becomes almost too overbearing and is at the expense of the first film's undoubted humour – hence the dearth of good natured verbal sparring between Rick and Evelyn here – there's simply no time!

Despite the evocative desert battles between Anubis' army – fearsome canine warriors, standing upright on their hind legs, ominously breaching the horizon as they descend the sand dunes, Sommer's sequel is somewhat deflated by the closing conflagration between Imhotep, the Scorpion King and Rick. With seemingly "rushed" special effects rendered not so "special" here, WWF icon "The Rock" suffers the indignity of merely having his head and torso morphed onto an unconvincing insect body, with the sting in the tail here appearing to be of the lobster variety rather than the intended scorpion!

At one stage in the action, young Alex amusingly infuriates his captors whilst undergoing a long journey by uttering the perennial child favourite (indeed it is written that children must say just so..), "Are we there yet?" You really begin to empathise with this sentiment by the

Zi Juan (Michelle Yeoh) & Lin (Isabella Leong) in The Mummy 3 - Tomb of the Dragon Emperor

end of the film as almost too many, often blistering), set pieces crave our attention, yet conversely also numb the senses by the climax.

In hindsight, perhaps the Scorpion King was just one major character too far, cluttering the already congested action scenes further and looking somewhat out of place in this film – no surprise then that his appearance begat a largely unrelated film with no mummies – *The Scorpion King* (2002).

Sommer's film is also noticeable for creating some kind of evolutionary history as at one point we are informed that the Scorpion King's resurrection will be "Starting a chain reaction that could start the next apocalypse." Obviously we all blinked and missed the first event?!!

There's also a kind of chain reaction at work in the third entry in *The Mummy* series, which returned after a brief hiatus with Rob Cohen's *The Mummy 3 – Tomb of the Dragon Emperor* (2008). Exchanging Egypt for China and more importantly, any mummies in favour of reanimated Terracotta warriors, Cohen wrings the changes here in an attempt to inject new life into the franchise, but meets with decidedly mixed results.

The film is ushered in on the back of a prologue which establishes the ancient China motif, delineating how the titular Emperor Han (Jet Li), betrays a sorceress Zi Juan (Michelle Yeoh), resulting in the death of her lover General Ming Guo (Russell Wong). Zi Juan exacts her revenge by transforming Han and his army into the aforementioned Terracotta army. It is some two thousand years later when the now teenage Alex (also transformed from British to Australian in the shape of actor Luke Ford), who stumbles upon the tomb. Enlisting the help of his, by now, bored parents yearning for another adventure – the returning Rick (Brendan Fraser) but with Evelyn now also "transformed" (are you still following?!), from Weisz into Maria Bello ! They are double-crossed into returning a mysterious relic to the Chinese people, which allows General Yang (Anthony Wong Chau-Sang) to resurrect the Emperor and his army.

Aside from the undoubted anomaly of having a "mummy" film without an actual mummy (!) it is also ironic how the first two films, self-styled *Indiana Jones* with mummy approach, happened to fill a void created as a result of no *Indiana Jones* films being on the horizon, yet Cohen's entry debuted almost simultaneously with a new Spielberg entry in his series – *Indiana Jones and the Kingdom of the Crystal Skull* (2008).

Both films feature the similar plotting device of a returning hero – only now slightly older and slower and sharing their new adventures with their now nearly "grown-up" sons. Cohen's film even includes a booby-trapped tomb and a scene with the hero being dragged along underneath a truck – scenes equally present in Spielberg's creations.

As well as living in the shadow of Spielberg's *Indiana Jones* series, Cohen's film is ultimately compromised by the uneasy "alliance" between East and West present here. Although the Terracotta Army is an important part of Chinese mythology, they are merely an expedient device here, shoe-horned into the film as a mummy "replacement" and as an adjunct to stage the all important battles between the two opposing undead armies, rather than any meaningful attempts at characterisation, or, indeed exploring this particular strand of Chinese history further. The nearest we get to any such insight is with the neat circular conceit of having the Emperor's army defeated by Zi Juan's army of skeletal slaves who lie buried beneath the Great Wall, having first constructed it before their own demise.

Cohen's ill-fated attempts to recreate the Hong Kong/ Martial Arts epics of fantasy, flounder given the absence of any real lyricism, poetry or romance in the filming, whilst the over reliance on CGI effects reduces both the impact of the action scenes and any audience empathy with the characters on show.

Most criminal of all here though, is the use of Li – undeniably a fine actor but unable to pierce the the stultifying amount of CGI he sinks under– (it is interesting to note that his most expensive Asian film to date, *The Warlords*(2007), cost in the region of $40 million whilst Cohen's opus is nearer the $150 million mark.

Likewise, with Yeoh's underdeveloped character and Isabella Leong's ass-kicking babe, Lin, the fight scenes remain strictly routine and uninspiring with an overcrowding of stars similar to the extraneous role of the Scorpion King in the first mummy sequel – there's even a Yeti, yes Yeti, fight scene elsewhere in the film! Bello, another talented actress is woefully miscast here, creating barely a zero chemistry rating with co-star Fraser, but most disappointing of all is the missed opportunity for an emotional climax as Zi Juang singularly fails to reunite with her dead lover. Only her subsequent sacrifice of her own immortality and that of her previously immortal daughter (Lin), offers any semblance of sensitivity towards the end.

Most frighteningly of all however – having exchanged Egypt for China in this film, is the threat/promise which provides a final hint in the direction of Peru as the location for another film? Aztec mummies again anyone?!

11
BRAVE NEW ZOMBIES

Zombie Strippers!

Brave New Zombies

The 1980's, 1990's and into the new millenium, have definitely become the age of the sequel as far as the film world is concerned. The *Rocky* series starring Sylvester Stallone is already punch-drunk from five bouts at the box office so far, not to mention *Rocky Balboa* (2006) and close behind, snapping at the bit is *Jaws: The Revenge* (1987), *Alien Resurrection* (1997) has even begat the hybrid *AVP:Alien vs. Predator* (2004), and lamentably *AVPR: Aliens vs.Predator - Requiem* (2007), whilst there have already been seven plus *Nightmare on Elm Street* entries and we've hit double figures in the *Friday the 13th* franchise with the inevitable remake scheduled for 2009. There's also been the obligatory meeting of maniacs (if not minds) with *Jason vs. Freddy* (2003).

The list of other sequels is endless, and some films appear to be in severe danger of disappearing up their own non-creative orifices! It is against this rather pessimistic climate that we have to look to see if the zombie film can still not only survive, but flourish, investing new impetus and ideas into a tired formula and to some extent it has been successful.

Contemporary film makers, unsure of producing completely serious horror films have attempted an artful dodge, or compromise, by fusing together manic humour with even crazier storylines to offset the horror in such films. To this end we have seen some exhilarating examples of this form such as *Reanimator* (1985), *The Return of the Living Dead* (1985) and *The Evil Dead 2-Dead By Dawn* (1987) - the latter, a sequel, but containing enough creativity to be considered as a total original. These films have all worn their horror mantles proudly and yet supplied sufficient humour along the way in an attempt to reach further than a purely horror-orientated audience.

Others have sought a more serious route in an effort to address some of the problems of modern society. In David Cronenberg's *The Fly* (1986), who can deny the resonance of Seth Brundle's (Jeff Goldblum) decaying scientist, his flesh rotting away as he becomes an insect, in this age of killer diseases such as cancer and Aids. It would be wrong to call the film a social metaphor of our times, as it is much more than that due to the depth of human emotions that the film contains, but it is a powerful allegory that can be drawn.

The modern zombie film has also appeared reluctant to return to its roots, its origins in Haitian voodoo. On the few occasions it has, the Caribbean form of voodoo has been submerged under a sea of Americanised voodoo and religious indoctrination; take John Schlesinger's *The Believers* (1987) and Alan Parker's *Angel Heart* (1987) as examples. Only Wes Craven's epic *The Serpent and the Rainbow* (1987) has in any way helped to redress the balance.

Craven's film, based on anthropologist Wade Davis' factual account of zombies in Haiti (see Chapter 1), returns to the very heart of voodoo country for its subject matter. The film has Dennis Alan (Bill Pullman) as the investigative scientist researching into voodoo in Haiti, in the hope of finding the elusive potion ingredients to create zombies. He finds himself taking an hallucinatory concoction that foretells his future as he becomes even more entwined in the voodoo ceremonies and customs that hold the island in thrall. Craven's experience from attending genuine voodoo ceremonies in Haiti contributes to the film's realism and there are some expertly staged shocks on view here, from the opening burial of a man, clearly still alive, to the repeated battles that Alan has with the island's living dead.

Unlike *Angel Heart* and *The Believers*, Craven has presented voodoo from its Caribbean origins as opposed to its American variations, and he considers his portrayal of voodoo as being a "well-rounded thing with both a light and a dark side". The film also shows the chief villain Mokae, to be not just a priest but a symbol of voodoo power and governmental terrorism in Haiti - a political aspect completely ignored in many other voodoo films. In fact, the zombie as political metaphor has been an idea only sparingly used. The growth and appraisal of America's war involvement in Vietnam, as well as Afghanistan and Iraq, may lead to some future investigation along this theme.

We are still waiting for the definitive "space zombie" film as well, as very little has been seen of zombies in an avowedly futuristic setting in space or on an alien planet. The closest yet has been the post-nuclear holocaust films that feature a collapsed society, left in turmoil from a nuclear strike. The greatest hope in this direction may once have been Charles Band's rapidly expanding film production company Empire, though the quantity of the films produced far outweighed the quality. Before the company's abrupt demise he had shown a willingness to experiment however, that had resulted in such diverse product as *Reanimator* (1985), *Zone Troopers* (1986) and *The Evil Clergyman* (1987).

Instead, the nearest film makers have come to creating alien zombies is from out of those symbols of twentieth century life, the television and video recorder. Like Band's *Terrorvision* (1986), the "monsters" of the piece in Lamberto Bava's *Demons 2* (1987) and Robert Scott's *The Video Dead* (1987) both emerge from out of the tv screen, though neither film goes much beyond its original premise, a fault not levelled at the heavy media theorising from Marshall Macluhan that punctuates David Cronenberg's more thought-provoking exercise into the terror of the tv screen in *Videodrome* (1983).

Fortunately, one director has been prepared to use a more overtly fantastical setting in order to create an intelligent zombie film that also addresses some of the wide range of emotions that are inherent within the complex human psyche.

Clive Barker's auspicious directorial debut *Hellraiser* (1987), adapted from his own novella "The Hell-bound Heart" is the film in question. It's an entirely assured debut that has Larry and Julia Cotten, played by Andy Robinson and Clare Higgins, returning to Britain from America to live in the house owned by Larry's brother Frank (Sean Chapman), who has mysteriously vanished. After accidentally cutting himself when moving furniture into the house, Larry's blood drops through the floorboards where it helps to reanimate Franks's corpse

Wes Craven's inveigling The Serpent and the Rainbow

which is trapped there. This is Frank's punishment for playing with a magical puzle box that unlocks the key to another dimension, populated by a master race of grotesquely-fashioned human monsters with sadistic tendencies - the Cenobites.

Julia discovers the barely recognisable, gelatinous skeleton that is Frank, and after overcoming her initial revulsion, agrees to help revive him, and their long-lost love affair. To this end, she lures a procession of vulnerable victims back to the house, before clubbing them to death with a claw hammer and serving them up for Frank to greedily devour and sap their lifeblood. Now, with his resurrection almost complete, Frank takes the ultimate step and takes over the body of his unsuspecting brother, Larry.

It is left to a tenacious step-daughter Kirsty (Ashley Lawrence) to capture the puzzle box and so recall the avenging Cenobites to mete out Frank's punishment. The denouement sees the house aflame, but under the watchful eye of a mysterious tramp, who is revealed to be the demon that tempted the Cenobites into perversion, and he is now ready to repeat the cycle again.

There is much to admire here, but what is most impressive is the way that the carefully-etched characters interact, to produce a powerful emotional undercurrent and raison d'etre for the more graphic violence that pervades the film. *Hellraiser* quite literally shows the breakdown of the now decidedly dysfunctional family unit we have been constantly warned against, leading eventually to Hell itself. It is on a purely personal, human level that the film works best however, unlike the "besieged" family in *Poltergeist* (1980) for example, where it is only the house possessions, the television set and the swimming pool that create the axis for the "ghostly" happenings to revolve around.

The iconic Cenobite, Pinhead (Doug Bradley), poised to inflict suffering in the imaginative Hellraiser

In *Hellraiser*, no possessions, only human emotions are considered. In this world, no one is content with their lot. Larry, who appears as a bland and boring figure, is a mirror image of the now sterile relationship he and Julia have, their move to England a futile attempt at reconciliation. Frank is the complete opposite of his brother, being a wild, impetuous adventurer whose pursuit of sensual fulfilment has led him straight into the unyielding hands of the Cenobites, who arrest such libidinous desires with their unsubtle torture methods.

Julia's willingness to escape her

stagnant bourgeois existence to find greater pleasure, is again a mirror image of Frank's impulsive nature. They both find their emotional release simultaneously, as each butchered victim brings Frank nearer his "rebirth" and replenishes Julia's love for him. This is reflected visually by her transition from a merely average woman at the beginning, to an increasingly attractive example of flourishing womanhood towards the end. The same can be said of Kirsty, though in purely emotional terms, as she matures throughout the film before finally condemning Frank to his ultimate fate.

The fact that Julia, despite being a villainous character, kills out of love (for Frank) rather than hate, endures her to the audience as she has a recognisable reason for killing, unlike the host of masked killers that cut their way through the casts of undistinguishable films such as the *Friday the 13th* series and its' would-be imitators. That Julia, and the reviving Frank, grow emotionally together, is underlined by the wonderfully romantic score from Christopher Young, that also reminds us of their earlier love, as well as highlighting their present love as Frank's resurrection is complete.

Where *Hellraiser* also departs from many other horror films is its treatment of the film's "monsters". Here, the Cenobites are thoughtful, intelligent creatures, who establish a legitimate viewpoint for their actions, unlike the snarling abominations that populate so many other genre films. Frank has trespassed into their world and now they seek justice, their own justice. Frank himself, though barely even a corpse, still wears a suit and smokes a cigarette, a symbol of "normality" despite his otherwise alarming appearance. Because both he and Julia have their own opinions and feelings, it is difficult for us to reproach

Images from Hellraiser & sequel Hellbound (bottom) & the Cenobites unique Lament configuration box (overleaf)

them for their actions, even though we think we must.

Here the monsters cannot simply be blasted into space and forgotten as in *Alien* (1979), the monsters are part of the texture of our own internal workings so we have to attempt to make peace with them or we are doomed. Thus the Cenobites must be appeased to restore the equilibrium. (In one of Barker's other filmed stories, *Rawhead Rex* (1986), the title monster is killed at the end, possibly explaining the failure of that film to sustain even a perfunctory level of interest.

In *Hellraiser*, fantasy is mixed with reality as far as the film's creation of horror is concerned. On the one hand we have the marvellously macabre Cenobite lair - a veritable charnel house full of torturous meat hooks and flailing chains, amidst the bloodied human flesh that lies strewn across the dank floor. Contrast this Lovecraftian imagery with the more conventional, as a Christ statue falls out of a closet, scaring the crouched figure of Kirsty who is hiding there a la *Halloween* (1978) style.

Barker's own vivid imagination comes to the fore in the film's picturesque camera style, as it fluidly tracks the interior of the house, traversing morbid delights ranging from the maggots that squirm on a plate of rotting meat, to the cracking walls that reveal monstrously scuttling scorpions. The slow motion tension, as the blood from Larry's cut hand drops below the floorboards and is magnified into exploding blood-bombs by the camera, betrays an accomplished guiding hand from Barker.

The nightmarish elasticity of the house also plays host to a number of pervading religious icons. Figurines of Christ abound, a precursor to Frank's later resurrection and crucifixion at the hands of the Cenobites. The actions of the Cenobites themselves almost seem to be a kind of "divine" retribution.

The fact that nearly all the scenes take place in cramped interiors, Frank's house, the Cenobites lair and a hospital where Kirsty stays, only serves to reinforce the tension and atmosphere of the piece. This is only momentarily shattered in the film in one disastrously judged scene where Kirsty is chased by a ferocious monster. Otherwise it is a compelling and cohesive descent into terror that unsurprisingly has spawned no less than seven (!) sequels so far, with even the promise of a big budget US remake slated for 2009.

Clive Barker undoubtedly unearthed new directions for the horror film with his innovative debut work here.

In the sincere hope that he is not alone in exploring this undoubted potential, the mantle for imagination and creativity has been (partially) at least, grasped by the hands of Argento protege, Michele Soavi, with his audacious zombie hymn *Cemetery Man/Dellamorte Dellamore* (1994).

Having cut his teeth aiding Argento on *Creepers* and playing bit parts in the likes of *Demons*, Soavi's directorial debut was the hyper-

Dellamorte (Rupert Everett) & She (Anna Falchi) in Michele Soavi's masterful Dellamorte Dellamore

charged *Stagefright* (1987) - a stylish psycho-slasher with more than enough directorial flourishes to indict a bright future. This initial promise hasn't quite flourished as yet but Soavi's gradually evolving ouevre - *The Church* (1989) and *The Sect* (1991) are eclipsed by the finery and maturity shown within *Cemetery Man*.

Soavi's main character here, cemetery caretaker Francesco Dellamorte (Rupert Everett), is captivated by the nubile temptress yet grieving widow, She (Anna Falchi), confiding that she is "the most beautiful woman I have ever seen."

The witch-like spell that She casts over Dellamorte perfectly compliments the prevailing air of sorcery and mysticism that permeates the nebulous confines of the cemetery. This is reinforced by the sight of the zombies or "returners" who are resurrected from Dellamorte's cemetery (including She), the elegiac tone accentuated as former Playboy centrefold Falchi's morbid fascination with the cemetery ossuary knows no bounds; "I have never seen anything so exciting" she drools, surrounded by walls of skulls, gushing that "I couldn't ask for anything more, it's like a dream."

The necrophilia laced atmosphere concludes with She kissing Dellamorte passionately - though only after having first wrapped his head in a red shroud - climaxing (literally) in their lovemaking upon her late husband's grave. Although the earth does indeed "move" it proves to be the corpse of her late husband "returning" as he witnesses the carnal chaos before him, ravenously biting a chunk out of his wife.

The zombie dead also take on

Dellamorte (Rupert Everett) & his faithful assistant Gnaghi (Francois Hadj-Lazaro) in Dellamorte Dellamore

an altogether more symbolic meaning following the startling materialisation of "death" when a burning phone book reassembles into the spectre of the Grim Reaper - "Stop killing the dead - they're mine!" he admonishes the zombie-killing Dellamorte, before offering his own advice that; "If you want to stop the dead returning to life then start killing the living."

Only for Soavi, the term "love" becomes combined with "life" as we see the returning She appear as an "angel" - complete with ivory shroud dress and wild foliage hair - her passion for Dellamorte rather too all-consuming as she bites a chunk from his shoulder. Here, She encapsulates the full cycle of life, love, death and rebirth.

It is left to the forlorn figure of Dellamorte to signify the existence of life and love - chiding that "Life goes on" at the very beginning of the film, after he has just shot down another "returner".

The ensuing dramatic tracking shot - past Dellamorte and beyond the door and leading into the rows of graves in the cemetery outside - immediately establishes that Dellamorte lives in a world of "death"; even his aforementioned sexual sparring with She takes place either in the ossuary or on a gravestone. As Dellamorte knowingly remarks later; "Hell, at a certain point in life you realise that you know more dead people than are living."

As Soavi himself has commented, the whole remit of the zombie genre he flirts with here, has been deliberately inverted. "The main character is not scared of zombies because killing them is a normal job to him. What is more scary, is living. Instead of being a horror film about being scared of death, it's more a film about being scared of life."

To this (literal) end, Soavi concludes the film fittingly, with Dellamorte and his loyal assistant Gnaghi (Francois Hadj-Lazaro) existentially poised upon an isolated precipice.

As they survey the dramatic but desolate scene before them, Dellamorte comments; "I should've known. The rest of the world doesn't exist" as snow flakes begin to fall, obliterating their increasingly distant figures as the snowflakes layer the landscape.

It is very much a case of *Cemetery Man* capturing the pessimistic mood of its own decade, reflecting the somewhat nihilistic forces of our own times. Perhaps because of this, that master of realism and drama, Martin Scorsese, declared *Cemetery Man* to be the best film of its year and a fitting testimony to the potency of the zombie film through the years.

Given his affinity for the genre and burgeoning talent, Soavi's subsequent career has proved to be a major disappointment for horror and fantasy fans, with his confinement to the sanitised creative vacuum of TV work. His series of drama's only recently enlivened by a return to film with *The Goodbye Kiss* (2006) and the recently complete *Il Sangue dei Vinti* (2008).

However, instead of acting as an inspiration to revitalise the zombie genre, what ultimately followed was as disappointing as Soavi's own career curve, with *Cemetery Man* effectively signalling a coda rather than a catalyst to herald any new zombie film boom.

This apparently lifeless genre body, in fact, lay dormant until two factors were to revive it in the new millennium. At first glance the words "computer" and "virus" would appear to be intrinsically related and yet, ironically, it was to be "computer" in the form of the video game/PC, digital era and a physical "virus" whether in animal or human shape, which would usher in a newly resurgent zombie film renaissance.

DIGITAL DEAD

The video game "inspiration" regarding the film world has thus far been anything but that, littered with a litany of moribund entries ranging from the likes of *Mortal Kombat* (1995), *Lara Croft: Tomb Raider* (2001), *Lara Croft Tomb Raider: The Cradle of Life* (2003), *Doom* (2005), *BloodRayne* (2005), *BloodRayne 2: Deliverance* (2007) and *Max Payne* (2008) – whether the forthcoming *Halo* film version due in 2009 will buck the trend remains to be seen, but don't hold your breath!

The major entries in the zombie genre reflect, rather than reject, this general malaise, although it must be noted that the *Resident Evil* franchise (thus far) – *Resident Evil* (2002), *Resident Evil: Apocalypse* (2004) and *Resident Evil: Extinction* (2007), offer more redeeming features than Uwe Boll's *House of the Dead* (2003) and Michael Hurst's *House of the Dead 2* (2005).

Most video game adaptations to film are doomed by the inherent artifice of attempting to graft conventional storylines and characters onto the purely sensory, arcade adrenaline rush induced by the original game format. In his "defence", Boll's film singularly ignores any "minor concerns" regarding story or character development, instead conjuring up a bombardment of actual arcade inserts within the film, taken from the Sega video game which spawned the film version.

The emaciated plot, such as it is, sees a group of college kids pleading with a wily old seadog, Captain Kirk (!), played by Jurgen Prochnow, to take them on his boat from Seattle to the "rave of the year" on the San Juan Island, ominously dubbed "Isla del Morte". Upon their arrival there, they find the rave site curiously abandoned and one of the girls, Cynthia (Sonya Salomaa) is left stranded, before becoming the first victim of the indigenous undead who appear.

Despite some partially effective scenes of zombie chases through the spooky, moonlit woods and grotesque zombies emerging from mist laden streams and open sea, any attempts at creating a cogent atmosphere of dread are instantly dismantled with Boll's child-like enthusiasm for lengthy fight scenes. A deflating mix of slow motion camera moves, uneasily juxtaposed with freeze frame backgrounds and foregrounds swirling into view, serve only to create a totally jarring experience.

These elongated sequences, besides dispersing the admittedly low level of tension created, also serve to underline the fact that Boll's raison d'etre here is not to augment the video game origins but simply underscore them.

Kirk's clandestine arms smuggling operation proves useful as there is no shortage of guns available to perpetuate the arcade style "shoot 'em up" approach and he also narrates the strangely effective, sepia-tinted flashback sequence which seeks to explain the history of how the island's zombies were first created. Otherwise, the lasting impression is not the zombies but the unedifying descent of Prochnow's career into the murky waters he once so triumphantly traversed as German U-Boat Captain in *Das Boot* (1981).

Perhaps having noted the creative dead end symbolised by Boll's film, Hurst's *House of the Dead 2*, simply dispenses with any connections to that film and ploughs its own furrow – this time revolving around a regeneration serum, developed by Sid Haig's goofy scientist and which is unleashed to spread havoc through an unsuspecting University campus.

It falls to a crack team of "AMS" troops to infiltrate the University, eliminate the outbreak and obtain a blood sample from the original, infected zombie or "generation zero" as they are known, in order to create an antidote. All this, while the "clock is ticking" with the military due to nuke the campus by the end of the day.

Apart from some tedious sequences where the troops painstakingly, (for us), search each room, corridor and basement in the campus – some judicious editing and jump cuts would have helped considerably here guys, this sequel benefits from forsaking its game origins in favour of concentrating on being a stand alone film in its own right.

With Emmanuelle Vaugier as Nightingale – a feisty, resourceful scientist in sub Sigourney Weaver mould and Ellis (Ed Quinn), as her tough but intelligent foil, the film doesn't take itself too seriously and coaxes some better than we should expect performances from both of them, and, from the scene-stealing Bart (James Parks) - an obnoxious "redneck" soldier whose sickly sense of humour in having his picture taken with a dead corpse using his mobile phone, becomes simply "sick" later when he is infected by a mosquito bite – a first in zombie film history!

It may not plagiarise its video game roots but it certainly drinks from the same well as a number of fellow zombie films – the hasty amputation of one infected soldier's arm is straight out of Romero's *Day of the Dead* (1985), whilst the sequence where the survivors crawl through ceiling vents above the teeming zombies below, is reprised from *Aliens* (1986) – an idea itself cannibalised in *Resident Evil* (2002).

There can sometimes be a

Uwe Boll's House of the Dead

thin dividing line between dumb and inventive and there is one scene here where Quinn smears himself with zombie intestines in order to traverse a room full of zombies, which operates as a kind of surreal, incidental delight. It's a shame though that the ambitious idea of a large scale University campus becoming overrun by zombies isn't matched by the decidedly small scale budget which constrains the film, resulting in a rather vapid ending where repetitive zombie attacks and attempts to obtain, lose, then obtain a blood sample again, dominate proceedings to the detriment of any further creative artistry.

In contrast, with the *Resident Evil* trilogy, the entire series *does* rest hugely on the more than capable frame of the gun-wielding, high kicking, action figure of Alice (Milla Jovovich) who truly does embody Nietzsche's ubermensch' philosophy – in *Resident Evil: Apocalypse*, her partial infection by the 'T-virus' leads to her development of 'superhuman' strength, as well as showing telekinetic powers in *Resident Evil: Extinction* as she levitates both giant rocks and an

The Dead Walk

off road bike to dramatic effect.

It is the ubiquitous Umbrella Corporation, which, as the name implies, now threatens to envelop the entire USA with its nefarious, experimental research, DNA cloning and related technologies. As the narrator in *Resident Evil* obligingly details; "At the beginning of the twenty first century, the Umbrella Corporation has become the largest commercial entity in the USA. Nine out of every ten homes contains its products. Its political and financial influence is felt everywhere. In public, it is the world's leading supplier of computer technology, medical products and healthcare. Unknown, even to its employees, its massive profits are generated by military technology, genetic experimentation and viral weaponry."

It is the genetic cloning aspect of the Umbrella Corporation's work (truly a shady company in both name and deeds), which unleashes the aforementioned 'T-virus' in their underground facility 'The Hive' – conveniently explained to us by the computer generated hologram the 'Red Queen' as being 'protean, changing from liquid to airborne to blood transmission, depending on its environment. It is almost impossible to kill,' continuing ominously that "Just one bite, one scratch from these creatures is sufficient. And then you become one of them."

Zombies attack in Resident Evil

It is instantly noticeable how the Umbrella Corporation reacts immediately upon the accidental release of the virus – summarily gassing their employees in order to contain the virus but also the inevitable bad publicity and ensuing corporate share meltdown, which is the implicit message here.

Ironically, as Romero was originally slated to direct the film, his influence is never doubted as Alice, resplendent in miniskirt and boots, aided by Matt (Eric Mabius) and an elite force (of course!) including Rain (Michelle Rodriguez), then proceed to shoot their way out of the subterranean locale and past all manner of rampaging zombies and resurrecting, in particular, the 'ghost' of Romero's *Day of the Dead*. This continual game of 'cat and mouse' encounters, evoking the film's game origins, whilst the films two most effective scenes are also responsible for eliciting some of the most pithy critical responses. Thus *The Guardian*'s Derek Malcolm was so moved by the rabid, zombie dogs Alice has to battle with, that he felt their flesh-tearing should have been expanded so that "Someone should have eaten the script and director as well." *The Observer* noted that "one unfortunate fellow is diced by a grid of laser beams, which would appear to rule out an open casket!"

The gung-ho, muscular militarism of Alice and her cohorts does have the unfortunate effect on diluting any tension, as we never truly feel that she in particular, is endangered enough, a theme expanded upon in the sequel *Resident Evil:Apocalypse*, the least successful of the series both thematically and aesthetically.

Although we do learn here that the 'T-virus' had an altruistic genesis – to revive dead cells to help people regain the use of damaged limbs, this is an isolated moment of innovation as the porous plot see Major Cain (Thomas Kretschmann) ordering The Hive to be reopened – why? Inevitably, the virus escapes again and contaminates all of Racoon City or the city of the dead as it has now become. Once again, Alice, together with mirror image – the gun-toting Jill (Sienna Guillory) and the obligatory elite forces leader Carlos (Oded Fehr), dodging zombies as they attempt to rescue the daughter of Umbrella Corporation scientist Dr. Ashford (Jared Harris), in return for him facilitating their safe exit from the city.

The course of truly dire plots does not run smoothly however, as the final conflagration involves pitting the superhuman powers of Alice against her literal nemesis – the robotic alter ego, Nemesis, (Matthew G. Taylor). Alice's speed and agility versus Nemesis' slower strength could have made for an interesting encounter, but director Witt shows a distinct lack of it, by favouring confusing close-ups and rapidly cut action where we can see nothing of consequence, rather than a more effective combination of mid range and crane shots. Their battle, an experiment for the purposes of the Umbrella Corporation's own agenda, as explained by Major Cain; "The two of you showed such promise, but we had to see you in action. And most impressive you've been. You're like brother and sister. Heightened speed, strength, agility, the same killer instincts. Parallel strands of research. And now…we discover which is superior."

The cramped interiors and urban sprawl of the first two films are replaced with the positively agoraphobic (by comparison) Nevada desert in *Resident Evil: Extinction*. As Jovovich explains on

Alice (Milla Jovovich) in Resident Evil

the ethos behind the move; "It's like a whole new world because we had the first one, which is very dark and claustrophobic. It was underground the whole time. And then in the second one you have this much bigger space, trying to escape the city. And here, it's really like the end of the world and it's all shot in daytime. It's all these very epic scenes. You've got these incredible desert sequences. It's got a completely different look, a completely different feel."

This 'different look' becomes a kind of *Night of the Living Dead* meets *Mad Max* (1979) 'car crash' in effect as Alice is rejoined by Carlos, LJ (Mike Epps), plus new survivors

Claire (Ali Carter), K-Mart (Spencer Locke) and Betty (Ashanti), travelling the desert wastes in convoy to escape the zombies.

There are some incidental delights – the surreal sight of Las Vegas now all but reclaimed by the shifting desert sands, the partially buried casinos and faux Eiffel Tower emerging, barely visible, (courtesy of Oscar winning Production Designer, Eugenio Caballero, for *Pan's Labyrinth* in 2006), but elsewhere, the sporadic, lacklustre battles with the zombies in the sand fail to muster much of a lasting impression.

Equally, the much vaunted zombie crows only serve to show how little the special effects here for such creatures have improved since the primitive titular stars in Alfred Hitchcock's *The Birds* (1963), with one characters' lame 'self sacrifice' of slamming shut the bus doors of her vehicle to contain the attacking crows and save her friends, rendered futile by the smashed windows she is surrounded by!

The only partially imaginative plot wrinkle here remains the Umbrella Corporation scientists shift in emphasis now in concentrating on trying to 'domesticate' the zombies rather than simply extirpate them (shades of *Day of the Dead* again). Their covert reasoning being to use them as 'slave labour' for the Umbrella corporation, an ironic self fulfilling prophecy when considering the real life Sony Corporations plundering of both the game and film series revenue streams to boost their own profits.

It may be a might churlish but you do have to wonder how such a global, multi-million dollar company comes to rely only on a loosely constructed chain link fence for security in the film!

A rather stronger link in the chain is provided during the opening

The all action Alice (Milla Jovovich) reprising her role in Resident Evil: Extinction

moments however, as Alice awakes, trying to escape the Hive laboratory only to be 'killed' by one of many booby traps awaiting her and she is revealed, in a neat plot conceit, to be just one of many such clones who've met their deaths whilst searching for a way out – effectively Alice is killed repeatedly only to rise again in homage to the game play origins of the film series.

Ultimately, the *Resident Evil* series relies on a formulaic, evil corporate with evil scientists manipulating the masses, combated by barely dressed fugitives from zombiefication, utilising military weaponry together with some superhuman powers in order to survive.

There is absolutely no doubting that Jovovich can perform the physical aspects of the Alice role with some considerable élan, but as far as any emotional subtext is concerned, this characteristically remains as submerged as the Vegas landscape lying buried beneath the sand.

There may be no actual desert in Danny Boyle's *28 Days Later* but there is the explicit statement that the sands of time may have now run out for humanity. Taking on board the national and international hysteria spawned by viral outbreaks, *28 Days Later* spearheaded this particular, ahem, strain of films, complete with its own sequel *28 Weeks Later* (2007), before *Doomsday* (2008) and *The Vanguard* (2008) both riffed on the same theme.

Whilst strictly speaking, the 'infected' in Boyle's universe are not 'undead' and therefore not technically zombies as the director is at pains to point out, one feels that he does protest *too* much. So much of his iconography here betrays echoes of Romero's *The Crazies* (1973), and his (then) living dead trilogy – witness the impromptu shopping/shoplifting spree a la *Dawn of the Dead*, to the discarded newspaper, buffeted open by the wind to reveal a headline of 'Evacuation" (it is 'The Dead Walk' in *Day of the Dead*), to quote but two examples.

We are firmly rooted within the realms of Darwinism from the film's opening sequence as a group of animal rights activists emancipate a number of apes from their Cambridge laboratory, 'experimental prison' but only succeed in unwittingly unleashing a 'rage' virus upon the unsuspecting populace, who are all but annihilated within a month.

A bike courier who is injured and taken to hospital, awakens from a coma several days later to find the hospital deserted. As Jim (Cillian Murphy) slowly regains consciousness he begins to investigate the outside world, only to find the London streets eerily derelict as he traverses rubbish strewn roads, overturned buses and empty houses. The deafening sound of silence in what is ordinarily such a bustling cacophony of noise and vibrancy is startlingly effective. To see landmarks such as Piccadilly Circus and Westminster Bridge totally abandoned, devoid of any semblance of life, is truly disquieting.

Having survived his first encounter with the 'infected' in a nearby church – no sanctuary here, merely savagery instead, Jim is 'rescued' by two street-wise survivors, Selena (Naomie Harris) and Mark (Noah

Jim (Cillian Murphy) runs for his life in 28 Days Later

Huntley). When Mark is then bitten by one of the infected, Selena reacts instantly – brandishing a machete and decapitating him without hesitation. Selena's bleak 'sermon' being that "He (Mark) was full of plans. Have you got any plans Jim? Do you want us to find a cure and save the world or just fall in love and fuck? Plans are pointless. Staying alive's as good as it gets."

By hooking up with a cab driver they meet called Frank (Brendan Gleeson) and his young daughter Hannah (Megan Burns), the quartet escape the sprawling anarchy of London, encouraged by sporadic radio broadcasts, optimistically advising survivors to head north to Manchester where a surviving army battalion has set up base camp. This must be the first time ever that the typically 'grim' M6 has signposted the way to 'sanctuary' rather than suffering some hellish road congestion.

Eschewing the urban confines

of the capital – there's an incredibly tense (if improbable) scene where the group hurriedly change the cab's tyre in a dark tunnel, barely managing to escape from the rapidly closing infected by driving the cab 'over' a series of abandoned vehicles, to the relative safety of the light outside. There is a vivid contrast with the new rural, countryside location.

This verdant sense of agoraphobia is one which although effective, is rarely alluded to in the zombie genre – evoking the memory of Jorge Grau's surreal extravaganza *The Living Dead at the Manchester Morgue* (1974), where the picturesque Lake District becomes home to all manner of outlandish gore and crimson coated carnage. (Interestingly, in Fresnadillo's sequel, *28 Weeks Later,* there's an equally effective sequence when Donald (Robert Carlyle) flees a zombie attack on an isolated farmhouse, racing across the lush fields before dramatically affecting his escape in a speedboat, conveniently moored at the bank of a nearby river.

Unlike many films in this genre, Boyle also manages to convey a small fraction of the emotional angst within the decaying world, especially when related to a family environment. There is a haunting scene where Jim returns to his parents home only to discover them both lying dead together – finding a handwritten note from his mother, "With endless love, we left you sleeping. Now we're sleeping with you. Don't wake up." We identify with Jim here, our empathy begging the question of just what would you do, how would you react in such an unbearable situation?

In another sequence on their journey, Jim experiences a nightmare – fearing he has been abandoned by his new friends – Frank hears him and comforts him whereupon Jim replies "Thanks Dad" in his fitful sleep, conveying the need for family, for friends and for interpersonal and social connection as a counterbalance to perhaps our more violent tendencies. Jim knows this innately, but it appears to be something that Selena will have to relearn, having become desensitised by all the violence erupting around her. She does comment poignantly on Frank and Hannah's bond – "All the death. All the shit. It doesn't really mean anything to Frank and Hannah because…well, she's got a Dad and he's got his daughter. So, I was wrong when I said that staying alive is as good as it gets."

It is ironic that the rural idyll they seek under Major West's (Christopher Eccleston) leadership at the army base proves to be even more dangerous than the infected – filled streets of the capital. This is where the film transmogrifies from the realms of an effective sci-fi orientated chiller into a more visceral, action shoot-out towards the end – a dramatic change in pace and style a la *From Dusk Till Dawn* (1996). The dawning truth that it is the soldiers, mankind, who as much

London in chaos - 28 Days Later

The Dead Walk

as the infected, pose the greatest threat to civilisation, is an ominous portent for the drama which unravels. As West comments; "This is what I've seen in the four weeks since infection. People killing people. Which is much what I saw in the four weeks before infection, and the four weeks before that, and before that and as far back as I care to remember. People killing people. Which to my mind, puts us in a state of normality right now."

The Darwinian themes inherent in the opening ape experiments and the dangers posed to civilisation by mankind, reinforce the fact that the rage virus is a man made disease – we are the architects of our own doom. Given that the virus is effective within twenty seconds of transmission, according to Darwinian theory, the virus will not be an efficient survivor, the host population will soon be dead. Ditto, the virus and yet significantly, it is the probable genetic manipulation carried out in the lab which completely changes this structure.

West and his slavish troops seem to subscribe to the Herbert Spencer dictum that it will be the 'survival of the fittest' or as our friend Nietzsche would have it – back to the 'supermen' as civility is stripped away in favour of the laws of the animal kingdom to ensure survival. There's also a risible 'discussion' around the dinner table where the human race's propensity towards violence is debated, but the thinly drawn West is the only soldier even partially developed, so the chances for any enlightened opinions or profound comments are extremely remote.

Despite the waves of attacking rage victims outside the barracks, the most extensive threat to Selena and Hannah is the soldiers inside as they discover their intended fate, not only as the 'objects' of desire for the men, but also the means to an end, albeit this 'end' being the continuation of the species. It poses an unpalatable question as to what is the most frightening proposition – the end of the world or a surviving world populated by animalistic humans? There's a pathos inducing scene as Selena offers Hannah some valium as the soldiers wait expectantly outside the bedroom – "Are you trying to kill me" the vulnerable young girl asks, with Selena's pragmatic response being, "No sweetheart. I'm making you not care. Okay?"

Jim's behaviour towards the end, as he gets angrier and angrier, resorting to killing in order to ensure his own survival, leads to Selena beginning to suspect that he too has become a victim of the virus. The ambiguity is continued as a bloodied Jim tries to console a confused Selena before Hannah hits him over the head with a bottle. "Hannah,

Don (Robert Carlyle) evading the "infected" in 28 Weeks Later

it's ok. He's not infected" Selena explains. "But I thought he was biting you" the child exclaims. "Kissing. I was kissing her. Are you stoned?", a bemused and recovering Jim replies, as the close link to our innate tendency to violence is reinforced. Jim's personal journey is now complete – from his earlier 'rebirth', awakening in hospital to the dawn of a new world, alone and vulnerable, to the conclusion where he is an embodiment of necessary violence to protect himself and his friends as well as becoming very much a realist.

Up close and personal - 28 Weeks Later style

His odyssey is vital to the film as Boyle prefers to concentrate on the human survival instinct as opposed to the how's and why's of the virus outbreak, which owes its identity to the numerous diseases to have plagued the world over the last decade and beyond – be they AIDS, SARS, Foot and mouth, MRSA or Blue tongue.

At one point Jim questions rather naively; "What do you mean there's no government? There's always a government, they're in a bunker or plane somewhere!" This distinct lack of authority present throughout the film, aids the vacuum for uncontrolled violence which occurs in its wake, with the resulting anarchy causing the characters to speculate regarding the kind of world they will be (hopefully) living in. Any such existential thoughts, as Selena ponders with Jim – "You were thinking that you'll never hear another piece of original music ever again. You'll never read a book that hasn't already been written or see a film that hasn't already been shot", are jettisoned due to the frantic pace during the second half of the film. This also deprives us of any opportunity to fully explore the military/civilian divide with so many characters to concentrate on (or not, as the case may be). It's also worth noting that Boyle and scriptwriter Alex Garland originally intended to focus on the original four protagonists but this would have left too close a similarity to Romero's *Dawn of the Dead*.

Boyle's somewhat controversial use of digital camera's gives the film a punchy immediacy as well as a rather grainy, ugly hue in parts – with a dystopian grime permeating the closing scenes, played out almost entirely against a (typically?!) Mancunian backdrop of incessant rain. In contrast, the upbeat coda which sees Jim, Selena and Hannah welcoming a plane flying overhead to their new coastal retreat, is shot on film as if to reinforce the euphoric effect.

With Boyle handing over the directorial reins to Fresnadillo for the sequel *28 Weeks Later* – London, or more specifically the Isle of Dogs is now a US army controlled quarantine zone, a kind of Ballardian refuge colony if you will.

There is a bravura opening

sequence set in a remote farmhouse which undergoes a frenzied attack from the infected. The haunting image where Don (Robert Carlyle) manages to flee, but only by leaving behind his wife Alice (Catherine McCormack) to a bloody 'demise', is undoubtedly the film's highpoint.

The remainder defies credibility as Don's two children manage to escape the heavily guarded Wharf area, find their mother still alive in the family home but now infected, before Don's 'lowly' caretaker character, gains access to the lab where his wife is now being held, by using only a swipe card?! After an impromptu exchange of all manner of bodily fluids, Don now joins the ranks of the infected, continuing to pop up like a pantomime villain when you least expect him.

With trite dialogue, proliferated with 'code reds' and 'green zones' the height of military intellect leaves the considered opinion to be to call in an air strike and raise the entire area to the ground – infected and innocent victims alike. The one shred of interest here is the notion that Don's children may indeed contain a 'cure' for the rage virus within their genetic make up, so their safety becomes paramount amidst the numerous chase sequences and graphic carnage which ensues.

The tension and intrigue of Boyle's opus are all but forgotten save for some effective moments with the survivors escaping the infected and a good use of several London locations including the new Wembley Stadium for the finale.

London is now a necropolis once again, it survived everything life could throw at it but not the Rage virus, defeated as HG Wells said of the Martians, 'by the humblest things that God, in his wisdom, has put on this Earth." (Save that the Rage virus was very much the work of man). The survivors fly out of the devastated city, over the white cliffs of Dover. 28 Days Later…Paris is infected by the Rage virus.

Ably directed, Juan Carlos Fresnadillo, *28 Weeks Later* nevertheless misses the hand of *28 Days Later* director Danny Boyle, and particularly that of writer Alex Garland. On the positive side, there are new ideas displayed, some of individual performances are good, but the dialogue isn't up to the standard of the first film.

While racking up the action is welcome, the level of violence spoils the effect, and loses the subtle atmosphere of menace established in the previous film. In fact, the proof of this, is the opening ten minutes of the film, are far superior to what follows. Also there are huge lapses in logic. Why does Flynn decide to bring the children? How were they allowed into France, when the whole world has seen what the Rage virus did to Britain. The quarantine and evacuation are never explained, this would have been a superior story in itself. If there are so many British evacuees, why are there no signs of British police, government, army,(many of which would have been serving abroad anyway). Why are the Americans there?

None of these questions are answered much to the film's detriment. We aren't stupid, we see these things. Nevertheless, it is to be praised for not following the same pat as it's predecessor and is a franchise that has more to offer in the future, preferably with greater involvement from Alex Garland and Danny Boyle.

Originally there were ideas of making a film called "29 Days Later" set in London after Cillian's Murphy's character Jim leaves. Another idea of Alex Garland was that the virus went everywhere and the world had ended. His idea was to do a film from the local point of view like a "28 Days Later Dublin", "28 Days Later Japan", Australia, or America. The Rage isn't over yet!

ZOMBIE VIRUSES

We're all familiar with the viruses that make zombies in the movies from The T-Virus in *Resident Evil* to the Rage Virus in *28 Days Later* (Not to mention such killer virus films as *The Omega Man*, and *The Andromeda Strain*). But what about the real killer viruses out there?

A virus is a microscopic organism that lives in a cell of another living organism. They are the tiniest and most basic form of life…and a huge cause of infection and diseases. Some infect humans with diseases like measles, other infect animals, plants and even bacteria.

Amazingly, viruses are so primitive that many scientists regard them as both non-living and living (a similarity to the state of the zombie itself!). By itself, a virus is a lifeless particle, it cannot reproduce (like a zombie). However, inside a living cell, a virus can become an active organism, capable of multiplying (like a zombie bite, carrying the infection to it's victim and hence to other victims).

Viruses are shaped like rods or spheres and range in size from .01 to .3 microns (A micron is .001 millimetre). Most viruses can only be observed by electron microscope. The largest virus is about one-tenth as big as a bacterium of average size.

The study of viruses began in 1898, when a Dutch botanist named Martinus Beijerinck discovered that something smaller than bacteria could cause disease. He christened this particle a virus, the Latin word for poison. In 1935, Wendell M. Stanley, an American biochemist, discovered that viruses contain protein and can be crystallised. This led to the development of vaccines for such diseases as poliomyelitis and measles.

Viruses, unlike other organisms, are not made up of cells. Therefore, they lack some of the substances needed to live on their own. To obtain these substances, a virus must penetrate the cell of another living organism. It can then use the cell's materials to live and reproduce. A virus has two basic parts, a core of nucleic acid and an outer coat of protein. The core consists of either DNA (deoxyribonucleic acid) or RNA (ribonucleic acid). The DNA or RNA enables the virus to reproduce after it has penetrated a cell. The coat of the virus consists of individual proteins that give the virus its shape. It protects the nucleic acid and helps the DNA or RNA to get inside a cell. Some viruses have an outer membrane that provides additional protection.

Most viruses reproduce in specific cells of certain organisms. For example, viruses that cause colds reproduce in the cells of the human respiratory tract. Viruses cannot live outside their particular cells. They must be carried into the organisms by air currents or some other means, to be transported by body fluids into the cells. When a virus comes into contact with a cell it can enter, it attaches itself to the cell at areas called receptors. Chemicals in the receptors bind the virus to the cell and help bring it or it's nucleic acid inside. The nucleic acid then takes control of the cells' protein making process. Prior to the viral invasion, the cell only made the proteins specified by it's own genes. The genes are the cell's hereditary structures and they consist of nucleic acid. A cell that has been infested by a virus begins to produce proteins that are called for by the nucleic acid of the virus. These proteins enable the virus to reproduce itself thousands of times over.

As new viruses are produced,

they are released from the cell and infect other cells. The new viruses become lifeless as soon as they are released, but they return to life after entering another cell. The viruses then start to reproduce and spread infection to more cells. When a virus reproduces, it changes the chemical make-up of a cell. This change usually damages or kills the cell, and disease results. A few kinds of virus change a cell only slightly because they do not reproduce.

Viral diseases in human beings, include cold sores, mumps, chicken pox, rabies, measles, yellow fever, colds, poliomyelitis, and hepatitis. The body protects itself from viruses and other harmful substances by several methods, all of which combine to form the immunity system. For example, white blood cells called lymphocytes produce substances called antibodies, which cover a virus's protein coat and prevent the virus from attaching itself to the receptors of a cell. Other lymphocytes destroy cells that have been infected by viruses and thus kill the viruses before they can reproduce. Lymphocytes do not start to produce antibodies until days after a virus has entered the body.

However, the body has additional methods of fighting viral infections. For example, the body produces a high fever to combat such viral diseases as measles and chicken pox. The high fever limits the ability of the viruses to reproduce. To fight colds, the body forms large amount of mucus in the nose and throat. The mucus traps many cold viruses, which are expelled from the body by sneezing. The body also makes a protein substance called interferon that provides some protection against all types of viruses.

The outside treatment of a viral infection consists mainly of controlling its symptoms. As an example, physicians prescribe aspirin to bring down a high fever. Doctors often cannot attack the cause of the disease itself because most drug able to kill or damage a virus also damage healthy cells.

The best way to deal with viruses is vaccination before a viral disease strikes. Vaccination causes the body to produce antibodies that resist a virus when it enters the body. Doctors use vaccines to prevent such viral diseases as polio and influenza.

A few viruses are called slow viruses because they reproduce more slowly than the others. Diseases caused by slow viruses include Creutzfeldt-Jakob disease and Kuru, both of which gradually destroy the cells of the brain.

Viruses cause hundred of diseases in animals. These diseases include distemper in dogs, foot-and-mouth disease in cattle, and Newcastle disease in chickens. Most viral diseases in animals occur in certain species, but some of the diseases spread to other species, and a few of them infect human beings. For example, dogs can give people rabies, which destroys nerve cells.

Viruses infect all kinds of plants and can cause serious damage to crops. Plant cells have tough walls that a virus cannot penetrate. But insects penetrate the cell walls while feeding on a plant, enabling viruses to enter. Plant viruses may infect one or two leaves or an entire plant. They produce billions of viruses which are then carried to other plants by insects or air currents.

Viruses that attack bacteria are called bacteriophages. The word bacteriophage means bacteria eater. Bacteria, like plants, have tough cell walls. To penetrate these walls, most bacteriophages have a structure that resembles a hypodermic needle and works in a similar manner. This structure consists of a sphere-shaped

Brave New Zombies

head that contains a nucleic acid, and a hollow, rod-shaped tail made of protein. When a bacteriophage enters a bacterium, the tail first penetrates the cell wall. Then the nucleic acid in the head moves through the tail and into the cell.

Virologists study viruses, chiefly to learn how they cause disease and how to control these organisms. Scientists also use viruses for such purposes as insect control, cell research, and vaccine development.

Insect-control - certain viruses cause fatal diseases in insects. Virologists are seeking ways to use these viruses to kill insects that damage crops. The use of such viruses may one day replace insecticides, which kill insects but also may harm plants as well as other animals.

Cell-research - Viruses are such simple organisms that scientists can easily study them to gain more knowledge about life itself. Research on bacteriophages has helped biologists understand genes, DNA, and other basic cell structures.

Development of vaccines - Scientists produce vaccines from either dead or live viruses. Those used in dead-virus vaccines are killed by chemicals and injected into the body. They cause the body to produce antibodies and other substances that resists viruses. For live-virus vaccines, virologists select very mild forms of living viruses that stimulate the body's immunity system but cause no serious harm.

Real-life dead viruses include Marburg, a fast acting virus that causes haemorrhagic fever (named after the German town where there was an outbreak in the 60s), West Nile Fever, which is spread by mosquitoes, and causes fever and sometime death. Avian Influenza. Ebola, which causes haemorrhagic fever also, and death in over 50% of the infected. And, of course, the biggest killer virus of all, HIV, killing over 25 millioon since 1981. Who knows what virus will arise next to threaten humanity.

A bleak future portrayed in **28 Days Later**

Eden (Rhona Mitra) in the wildly entertaining Doomsday

Two of the most recent entries within the pantheon of virus-focused films choose vastly differing styles to approach the subject. Whilst Matthew Hope's *The Vanguard* (2008) offers a more deliberately paced, almost reflective approach to a post apocalyptic world, Neil Marshall's *Doomsday* (2008) is a high octane mix of tribal warfare and explosive action scenes, which fuel an already potent, (if not original), brew.

In fact, given the audacious manner in which he tackled the werewolf mythos in *Dog Soldiers* (2002) and the verve exhibited in delineating the dark recesses of humanity with *The Descent* (2005), *Doomsday* is very much a "cut and paste" effort by Marshall, reflecting his intent on making an offbeat, "time-travel film, veering between eras and genres" – what remains is a somewhat confused but admittedly entertaining romp.

The intriguing premise sees the outbreak of the killer "Reaper" virus and the erection of a giant, metallic, Hadrian's Wall structure, to isolate all the infected victims in Scotland – a rather extreme route to "Independence" methinks! We see the main protagonist Eden Sinclair (Rhona Mitra) as a young girl, one of the last people to be whisked away by helicopter to "safety" – yet agonisingly, her freedom is at the expense of her mother who is left behind.

Fast forward to 2033 and the now grown up Eden – all leather and attitude, is selected to lead an exploratory force into the "forbidden zone" to locate Dr. Kane (Malcolm McDowell), a scientist working on a cure for the virus prior to the wall being installed, and, to investigate rumours that a magical vaccine exists there. The mission is all the more urgent as the virus has now erupted in London – the aftermath of a drugs war.

However, Eden's attempts at obtaining tissue samples from apparently "immune" survivors are severely impeded by the discovery of all manner of battling tribes who now populate the area – the main obstacle being the cannibalistic "Visigoths" led by Sol (Craig Conway), with an equal penchant for leather and 80's music of variable quality.

Although some of Marshall's independent spirit, and undeniable talent, prevails, his creative aesthetic is roundly compromised as his perceived homage to 80's exploitation films is devoid of any real humour, whilst the most memorable scenes are generally cribbed from the objects of his affection. It's as if the relatively sumptuous budget

Brave New Zombies

here – reputedly four times that of *The Descent*, has stymied the creative vision as multiple set pieces are thrown at the screen. That said, all of the budget is undeniably all on screen and the action is directed with such verve and gusto as to positively shame many of the prosaic (in comparison), multi-million dollar action films made in the States these days

A whole gamut of diverse influences collide before us as salivating ghouls, tooled-up punks, bravura motorcycle & climactic car chases, a medieval castle and armoured knights evoke a plethora of earlier films including *Escape From New York* (1981), *Mad Max 2:The Road Warrior* (1981), *Excalibur* (1981) and *Army of Darkness* (1992) to name but a handful.

As if this deluge of influences wasn't enough to chew over, Marshall incorporates a number of often intriguing sub-plots which are generally left to wither on the vine. McDowell revels in the role of Kane – now set up as a "King" in an ancient castle – having renounced modern technology in favour of a return to a medieval, feudal lifestyle – natural selection rather than medical science being his new raison d'etre. The subsequent revelation that Sol, is in fact his son, having been introduced, is then summarily ignored.

Eden's repeated attempts to reconnect with the memory of her mother, are similarly neglected and her quest for Kane echoes Captain Willard's (Martin Sheen) hellish odyssey to locate Colonel Kurtz (Marlon Brando) in *Apocalypse Now* (1979), but any further investigation of this doppelganger motif is submerged beneath the welter of heavyweight action sequences.

Most tantalising of all perhaps, is the conspiracy theory expounded when the British Prime Minister (Alexander Siddig), acquiesces to the suggestion of his machiavellian adviser Canaris (David O'Hara), that they utilise the Reaper virus to reduce the overpopulated country, before taking advantage of any cure that Eden may discover – (a similar conceit is alluded to in *The Vanguard*).

For every energised sequence – Eden's arena battle with a mace-swinging gladiator and the closing car carnage, there are a number of relative duds. The use of primitive spears and arrows to defeat the high tech vehicles in Eden's modern day convoy springs to mind, as does the somewhat risible scene where one victim is boiled alive and served up to Sol's cannibalistic clan – amidst chaotic scenes of pole dancers and can-can acolytes who patently can't-can't – ironic given the amount of films similarly cannibalised by *Doomsday*! Even here though, you've got to admire the way Marshall whips

The effects of the Reaper virus in Doomsday

up the enthusiasm of the baying masses, complete with bursts of Adam and the Ants, Fine Young Cannibals (of course!) and Siouxsie and the Banshees

A deliberately ambiguous denouement, which rejects any form of "closure" and indeed, suggests this as a mere prelude to a much bigger battle for Eden to face, is completely inspired and in total keeping with the spirit of the film, also acting as a reminder of the enterprising scale and vision present in *Doomsday*, only to be dissipated by some ribald dialogue spoken by one dimensional characters. This is surprising considering Marshall's utterly compelling, highly credible realisation of close-knit groups in both *Dog Soldiers* and *The Descent*, with the inherent camaraderie, petty jealousies and human dynamics they bring, but there again, the avowed aim in *Doomsday* is exhilarating combat scenes coupled with some highly evocative designs, ranging from a decaying Glasgow to the imposing Hadrian's Wall - itself a spectacular creation here.

Whilst Eden's troops are rendered disposable with her being seemingly unaffected by their demise – she may be fashioned by Marshall in the image of Kurt Russell's Snake Plissken in *Escape From New York* and Sigourney Weaver's Ripley from *Aliens* (1986), but that is where any true similarity or impact ends. In Marshall's defence however, it should be noted that having been effectively orphaned at the tender age of six, Eden is probably entitled, (and required by her job), to be pretty hard nosed now.

Eden's character may also have an eye-patch like Snake Plissken but it's all part of an ingenious plot twist. Rhona Mitra plays Eden with great subtlety and restraint, something we sadly see too little of in films these days and something it would be good to see more of. One of the all-time great performances in cinema is Robert Mitchum in *Rio Bravo* (1959).

Images from Doomsday

One sincere gesture means more than any all too typical scene of overacting. Thus, the scene at the end where Rhona's Eden finally sheds a tear when she finds a photo of her mother is genuinely moving.

Amongst the dystopian view of London – with delicious irony the Millenium Dome now reduced to the role of an internment camp, the problematic factor for *Doomsday* and films of its ilk, is that our fear of nuclear Armageddon has now changed. Our previous concerns over Cold War/Super-power posturing has now been supplanted by the primal fears over nature – the spectre of global warming, of natural, finite resources running out, overpopulation, mass immigration and the harbinger of evil being overtly medical now, in the form of viruses and disease.

Indeed, it is ironic given the gas-guzzling gamut of motorbikes and assorted vehicles in *Doomsday*, that more mention of sustainable fuel sources (and the lack of) isn't highlighted!

This particular aspect is certainly brought to the fore in Matthew Hope's inveigling *The Vanguard*. Set in the year 2015, the world has reached a fundamental "tipping point" – the oil supply is now exhausted and a labyrinth company "The Corporation" has taken charge of controlling the overpopulation in society. Their master plan – to create a disease, to kill the poor and enable the rich to have a (less crowded), better way of life (a potential panacea for many governments one feels!). As the assorted populace unknowingly lines up to take their "vaccine", the ploy goes awry – designed to kill the

Max (Ray Bullock Jnr) using his axes to good effect in The Vanguard

recipients within one month, the shot only succeeds in transforming them into zombie-like creatures or Biosyns, as they are referred to here.

Their simian-like movement and primitive actions, lend these feral creations an intended lineage to our primordial ancestors, with director Hope admitting that the idea came from watching the apes in Stanley Kubrick's *2001 – A Space Odyssey* (1968). Hope explains that the Biosyns, "fit perfectly into the story, that everything has been reduced to a primal state; not only the humans turned into Biosyns, but the survivors too."

In relation to the main protagonist, the mute Max (Ray Bullock Jnr.) – apparently one of the "last men on earth" and eeking out an existence in the wilderness of the woods, with only a bicycle and an armoury of mini-axes for "company", in order to fight off the sporadic Biosyn attacks he faces. Hope elucidates that this "idea was about a young man from an industrial society trying to survive as a hunter gatherer after the end of the world."

Noting literary nods to James Dickey's *To the White Sea* and David Morell's *First Blood*, where the protagonists are hunted through the wilderness, and, with cinematic nods to Akira Kurosawa's *Throne of Blood* (1957) samurai epic and the anticipated zombie classics such as *Dawn of the Dead*

The Dead Walk

(1978). Max's solitary existence is disturbed with the appearance of a resistance fighter, Zac (Steve Weston) and a scientist, Rachael (Emma Choy) – whose presence causes further friction, given the revelation that she was one of the scientists who (innocently) carried out the mass injection program.

The appearance of The Corporation's "Tracker" – Jamal (Shiv Grewal), in the woods – supposedly Max's nemesis with a "seek and destroy" mission, Jamal instead, undergoes a seismic change of heart when he realises Max's potential for "saving" humanity – Max's blood revealed to be the antidote to cure the infected in a rather predictable plot wrinkle.

The role of both The Corporation and the Trackers, the antipathy between the characters and the overt political tensions dominating the world are an intrinsic part of the film's continual projection of contemporary fears, now extrapolated into a bleak and uncertain future.

Hope adds insight to this particular theme, explaining that "Part of what I was interested in was a quote by Mussolini. 'Fascism should more properly be called corporatism because it is a merger of state power and corporate power...' The Tracker's are based on child soldiers in places like Uganda where they were forced to fight. They were made to kill their parents so if they escaped they had nothing to return home to."

Max, in effect, becomes a cipher for the existential ruminations and the political invective permeating the film – "Our armies plundered the East for oil to preserve our way of life. Our bombs rained down from the sky and two billion Easterners perished", being one of his many inner monologues. He anxiously questions his own place in this collapsed society, "Is there a world outside of my own? Or has God already forsaken me?"

Seeking not just divine but patriarchal intervention, Max observes that, "When nature took her revenge I had a rifle; the last symbol of a mechanised world. But that was five years ago. Now nature laughs at me. The savages are Her gift to us, the walking dead. I am at Her mercy, the primitive man. She knows my sins, has seen the things I have done, the acts of murder, of cannibalism, of madness. Will God ever forgive me? I miss my rifle, father..."

One of the feral Biosyn's from The Vanguard

Whilst Hope admirably cultivates a sense of real isolation from the almost expressly rural locations, often eerily silent before being punctuated by distant sounds of Biosyn screams, there is little visual evidence offered as to the collapse of society – no billowing smoke effusing from disintegrating cities to delineate the hellish aftermath.

Max is the only "roundly" developed

Max battling with a Biosyn in The Vanguard

character here with the obligatory "resistance" and "antidote" motifs thrown into the mix, along with the white-orbed, open-mouthed Biosyns lacking the fear factor or immediacy of the similarly infected creatures in *28 Days Later* (2002).

Given Max's overtly hirsute appearance, he becomes a "dead ringer" for Ray Lovelock's bearded lead in *The Living Dead At The Manchester Morgue* (1974). Like Grau's film, *The Vanguard* shares the same verdant iconography – all expansive, wide open plains, with only the darkened woods and the bluish green hues of an effective sequence, shot in a desolate, supposedly "deserted" farmhouse, with lugubrious huts and outbuildings full of shadows and menace.

Geysers of crimson erupt across the screen – bloody arterial spray coating the camera as Max summarily dispatches one zombie, expertly wielding mini-axes, whilst the low angled shot of him silhouetted against a dark sky and red-hued fields, emphasises his utter isolation against the landscape - a miniscule dot on the horizon as if a character from a Thomas Hardy novel.

As Max pointedly observes; "I have sacrificed my humanity in all this bloodshed. Am I strong enough to fight to the last breath?"

His valedictory address suggests that he realises that it is he who represents mankind's only chance of survival in such desperate times; "There is a war being waged against us. A war we did not start. A war we did not ask for. But a war we will have to fight. I know what I must do. I know there is a world outside of my own. I know we here, are the Vanguard."

If this clutch of neo-viral, post apocalypse zombie film's have avowedly concentrated on horror rather than any humour, a brace of films have reversed this emphasis with the accent on chuckles as much as chills, mirth as much as malevolence.

Leading the way quite gloriously in its own particular "vanguard" of this genre is Edgar Wright's marvellously judged zombie homage, *Shaun of the Dead* (2004). Straight from the off, with its' "punning" title, *Shaun* is a particularly British take on the zombie genre, but it is realised with such affection, not to mention invention, that the humour traverses all boundaries, so finely judged are the japes.

Focusing on terminal underachiever Shaun (Simon Pegg) and his slothful best friend, Ed (Nick Frost), their idea of an "aspirational" lifestyle is how many visits they can fit in to The Winchester – their local pub. As Shaun's flat mate Pete (Peter Serafinowicz) chides him over Ed; "Stop defending him, Shaun, all he does is hold you back. Does it make your life easier having someone who's even more of a loser than you?" Shaun also runs the gauntlet of his stepfather

> "AN INSTANT CULT CLASSIC, THIS IS THE SMARTEST, FUNNIEST BRITISH COMEDY FOR AGES"
> ★★★★★
> HEAT

SHAUN OF THE DEAD
A ROMANTIC COMEDY. WITH ZOMBIES.

★★★★★
GQ

is then promptly "dumped" by Liz. Having resorted to type upon realising that their "relationship" is now over, Shaun awakes the next day in a hung over state, vaguely registering his hastily scrawled note on the fridge to "Sort life out".

Typically though, it is not the dawning of a new found maturity and sense of responsibility which shakes Shaun from his stupor, but the dawn of the newly dead who now populate Crouch End, London and give Shaun a new found purpose in life – namely, to save his now ex-girlfriend and his mum! This encapsulates the film's grounding in realism rather than fantasy and is a neat inversion on the typically lofty genre ambitions to "save the world".

The real genius of Shaun is in how it avoids merely trying to squeeze some comedy into a horror film premise, the fate which befalls most "intended" horror comedies. Instead, it is as if we are intruding upon a private sit-com where the zombies are portrayed as an almost incidental irritant, an inconvenient diversion from the constantly arguing characters and their complex personal lives. This makes for some great comedic moments as farce replaces fear and the soap opera characters and situations supplant horror genre conventions. (Wright and Pegg's similarly zany mock TV sit-com, *Spaced* very much lays the groundwork for the droll creations on screen here).

Phil (Bill Nighy), who, reminding him of his fortnightly visit to see his mother Barbara (Penelope Wilton), also wastes no time in prompting him to bring flowers this time – and "not some cheap posy from a garage forecourt" – happy families eh?!

Amongst this motiveless, directionless malaise that is Shaun and Ed's "marriage" of inertia, emerges the final part of this unique "love" triangle – Liz (Kate Ashfield), Shaun's "get ahead" girlfriend whose life ethos is the very antithesis of Shaun's.

Having singularly failed to book "Fulci's" restaurant (!) for a meal, Shaun

Emulating the traditions of some of the most compelling

zombie films, the characters in Shaun universally ignore the repeated TV news broadcasts, warning of an epidemic of violence, Shaun and Ed preferring to either channel surf for the latest football match or head to their "spiritual" home, The Winchester. Most glaring of all is Shaun's walk, in a drunken reverie, to get a fizzy drink which betrays the true zombie-like nature of this particular aspect of life. Cadaver's lurch past him across the street only to go unnoticed by Shaun. His visit to the corner shop continues his somnambulistic state as he ignores the bloody handprints plastered all over the drinks cabinet and even manages to slip on the floor – failing to notice the pool of blood lying there!

The humour continues unabated back at the flat when a zombie girl invades their back garden and tries to chew on Shaun's face – Ed's initial response is to grab his camera as he thinks Shaun is "necking" with her! When they finally realise something is horribly wrong, their very British response is to throw a mug tree at the zombie. As they search the garden shed for makeshift weapons to use, the "patriotic" theme continues as all they can find are a cricket bat and garden spade. The last resort is to hurl the contents of their vinyl record collection at her – even this leads to arguments as to what albums from the "classic collection" can be jettisoned – "Dire Straits? Throw it!"

As Shaun hatches his rescue plan to get Liz and his mum – the irony is not lost as Liz's earlier ultimatum, "me or the pub" is ignored as Shaun intends to lead everyone to the "sanctuary" of The Winchester to escape the zombie hordes and "wait for all this to blow over" – typifying the film's low key approach to what is potentially a global crisis. "I've come to take you somewhere safe", announces Shaun as he arrives at Liz's flat. We were perfectly safe before you arrived" is the pithy reply. "It's not about you and me. It's about survival..we're going to The Winchester" is Shaun's considered response. Likewise, Ed's "We're coming to get you, Barbara" promised to Shaun's mum over the phone is a delicious reference to the mock warning issued at the beginning of Romero's *Night of the Living Dead* (1968).

Aside from the burgeoning ranks of the undead now gathering in the streets, the biggest threat Shaun faces is Liz's irksome flatmate David (Dylan Moran), who himself harbours his own nascent designs on Liz, to the resigned disapproval of his own girlfriend Di (Lucy Davis). "Do you think his master plan is going to amount to anything more than sitting and eating peanuts in the dark?" David hisses, instantly goading Shaun.

Having eventually made it to The Winchester, the group are then holed up, *Assault on Precinct 13* (1976) style, as the zombies muster in front of the pub. Even this journey is fraught with danger (and laughs) as Di, playing an actress here, ironically hatches a scheme whereby the group all pretend to shuffle like zombies in order to safely reach the pub. True to form, it is Ed who manages to take a call on his mobile phone in the midst of all this and almost sabotage the plan. Once inside The Winchester, it is Ed again who shatters the intended silence by firing up the jukebox – Queen's "Don't Stop Me Now" riotously blasting out to highlight their presence in the pub to those outside.

Bertram Russell is quoted; "The only thing that will redeem mankind is co-operation" but this is unlikely, given the friction within the group already, reinforced as David, callously hands Shaun the pub's eponymous rifle, to dispatch his mum who has now been bitten. Even when faced with this dilemma of whether to shoot his own mum or not, there remains the irony

Shaun (Simon Pegg), coming out to bat in Shaun of the Dead

(and running joke) of Shaun's woeful shooting thus far, coupled with Ed being the sole person to have used a gun before – when he accidentally shot his sister in the leg!

As the zombies invade, eventually only Shaun, Liz and Ed are left alive, retreating down to the cellar *Night of the Living Dead* style, with Shaun contemplating them killing each other but recoiling – "I don't think I've got it in me to shoot my flatmate, my mum and my girlfriend, all on the same evening." In a moment of rare selflessness, Ed, suggests to Shaun and Liz; "Think you two should make a go of it – I'll only hold you back." As the couple proceed to burst outside and take their chances in the expected battle, the cavalry (or army, such as it is), arrive to speedily expunge the remaining zombies.

Fast forward six months later and the TV screen playing informs us that the end result of "Z Day" as it has now been termed, is for the zombies to be used as mindless slaves in the service/labour industries (as when they were living) and to appear on reality TV shows (as when they were living). We also glean that "claims the virus was caused by Rage-infected monkeys have now been dismissed" in a subtle aside at the *28 Days Later* "we're not zombies" protestations given by director Danny Boyle upon that film's release.

With Shaun and Liz now happily ensconced in domestic "bliss" having survived the ordeal, and Ed, now officially a zombie rather than an inferred one, residing happily in their garden shed, "normality" appears to have returned.

Besides any wider observations on the mindless, selfish automatons we can become within an increasingly brutal and impersonal society, Wright's film also skilfully explores the fear of change and its inevitability as the disparate thirty-somethings are forced to cast aside their youth and gain a greater sense of purpose in life, with the incumbent responsibilities that this brings. Only for Ed of course, his life has probably changed immeasurably for the better as zombiehood has saved him from confronting the responsibilities in real life he has thus far avoided.

With believable, likeable characters, the humour effuses naturally from the cast and their situation, rather than from any crude style of forced slapstick and there's certainly a high degree of audience empathy with the characters as a result, not to mention a vestige of pathos, particularly in Shaun's fractured relationships.

Of special note is the poignant chord sounded in Shaun's latent bond with his stepfather Phil. In addition to upholding the quintessentially British, middle-class values in the face of adversity – "You do realise this is a 20 miles an hour zone?" he exclaims as they attempt a rapid escape in his car from the zombie-strewn streets and, his typically reserved response to being bitten on the hand and informed he is facing a certain zombie future – "It's ok. I ran it under the tap."

His "death-bed" confession to Shaun is both revealing and emotive; "Being a father is not easy. You were already twelve when I met you…grown up so much. I just wanted you to be strong and not give up because you lost your dad. I always loved you, Shaun. I always thought you had it in you to do well, you just needed motivation, someone to look up to and I thought it could be me. Just take care of your mum. There's a good boy."

An ambitious mixture of *Dawn of the Dead* (1978) with the British comedy foibles of the loveable rogues Gary and Tony in the long-running TV series *Men Behaving Badly* (1992-1999), *Shaun* really does hit the spot, substantially raising the bar for this kind of film. It's a captivating collision of horror and humour, yet retaining a vibrant heartbeat all of its own, underscored by its ironic "life's wasted on the living" mantra.

For both Wright and Pegg, they relinquished the "living" to join the "dead" as extras in Romero's return to the zombie genre with *Land of the Dead* (2005), before collaborating again with Frost to garner equally impressive results in the TV cop/police satire *Hot Fuzz* (2007).

Following in the zombie comedy (or "zom-com") vein established by *Shaun*, director Andrew Currie brings (or should that be "fetches"), yet more imagination to the genre, if not exactly the vigour or bad taste humour of *Shaun*, with *Fido* (2006)

Establishing a kind of "retro-future" where radioactive dust has fallen from space and subsequently reanimated the dead, Currie creates a heavily stylised, kitsch, 50's satire where the ubiquitous ZomCom Corporation reigns supreme.

It transpires that this rather sanitised, conservative community in a town called Willard, are now protected by ZomCom, which maintains electrified fences in order to keep the "wild" zombies out, whilst simultaneously, the Corporation oversees the creation of "domesticated" zombies who now replace low income workers and illegal immigrants. These "worker" zombies (almost a throwback to the class divide in Hammer's *Plague of the Zombies*), are kept restrained by the electronic dog collars they wear and which inhibit their now natural cannibalistic tendencies. Now these cobalt coloured zombies are left to put out the rubbish, mow the lawns and similar menial tasks.

In this picture perfect setting, it is now regarded as de rigueur to have your own servant displaying rigour mortis – to keep up with the Joneses' you need to keep a zombie. Flustered by the thought of ZomCom's Head of Security, Mr Bottoms (Henry Czerny) living opposite, Bill and Helen Robinson (Dylan Baker and Carrie-Anne Moss) decide to buy the latest lifestyle accessory – in the form of Fido (as he is later christened by their son Timmy (K'Sun Ray), in an understated performance from Scottish comedian Billy Connolly).

Whilst Bill is decidedly reluctant to welcome Fido, (later explained in the personal trauma he experienced in having to kill his own father, who had caught the zombie infection), Helen and Timmy however, are far more enthusiastic. For Timmy especially, Fido is a boon – the boy having previously been friendless, bullied in class and ignored by his father. Fido, almost instantly becomes Timmy's best friend – useful for playing "fetch" in the park, but equally adept at snarling menacingly in order to frighten his enemies away.

When Fido's collar malfunctions, causing him to attack one of their more cantankerous elderly neighbours, she "returns" as a zombie and starts her own spate of killings. Aided by their freakish neighbour, Mr Theopolis (Tim Blake Nelson), Timmy endeavours to cover up the murders and keep Fido safe from the clutches of ZomCom who would recall him.

What is most impressive here is how the veneer protecting the artificial, glossy 50's milieu, is gradually peeled back to uncover a plethora of dark motives beneath this apparently "wholesome" setting.

Satirising the social stereotypes of this period and revelling in the bold, art deco inflections of the time, is nothing new – a number of films have sought to investigate this era, be it the black humour of *Parents* (1989) and *Pleasantville* (1998), to the surrealism of *Edward Scissorhands* (1990) or the dark secrets affecting a "perfect" family in *Far From Heaven* (2002), but Currie manages to unify some of these disparate strands, but without carrying the courage of his convictions to follow

The Dead Walk

key motifs through to their logical conclusion.

One of the most salient, not to mention resonating themes here is the omnipresence of ZomCom's prevailing mission statement – "Better living through containment" – overtly symbolised in the slave/master society and the literal zombie "blue-collar" workers.

The notion that "containment is king" is highly appropriate here, just as the collar signifies a very physical form of social control for the zombies, the threat of the "zombie menace" renders the human populace as equally fettered. The immense stranglehold which the ZomCom Corporation exerts over society, effectively "zombifies" the humans also. Emotions and social friendships are frowned upon in this sanitised atmosphere – after all, anyone could become a zombie the community are warned.

The parallel drawn with today is inevitable – just as with the zombie threat, so too are western governments utilising the "war on terror" debate as a means of increasing their own power base and influence through fear, seeking to legitimise their position and give "meaning" to their actions. In the same way in *Fido*, Mr Bottoms carries out his role with zeal – it allows him the necessary trappings of power and sense of superiority, instantly giving his life purpose as well as massaging the ego.

Ultimately, the collars which so restrict their zombie charges, also serve to confine the ambition of the ending – instead of a more logical, apocalyptic conclusion in the manner of *Dawn of the Dead*, the imagination is rained in rather than unleashed, and consequently the closing stages portray a safe, comparatively gentle state of affairs where the emphasis is on improving the treatment of zombies in general. If anything, this serves to continue, if not amplify, the "domesticity" thread running through Romero's *Day of the Dead* with Bub.

It is the foibles and frailties of the human condition which are also acutely observed in *Fido*. In comparison to the sterile, emotionless figures of Bill and Mr Bottoms, Fido's close, "natural" friendship with Timmy merely highlights

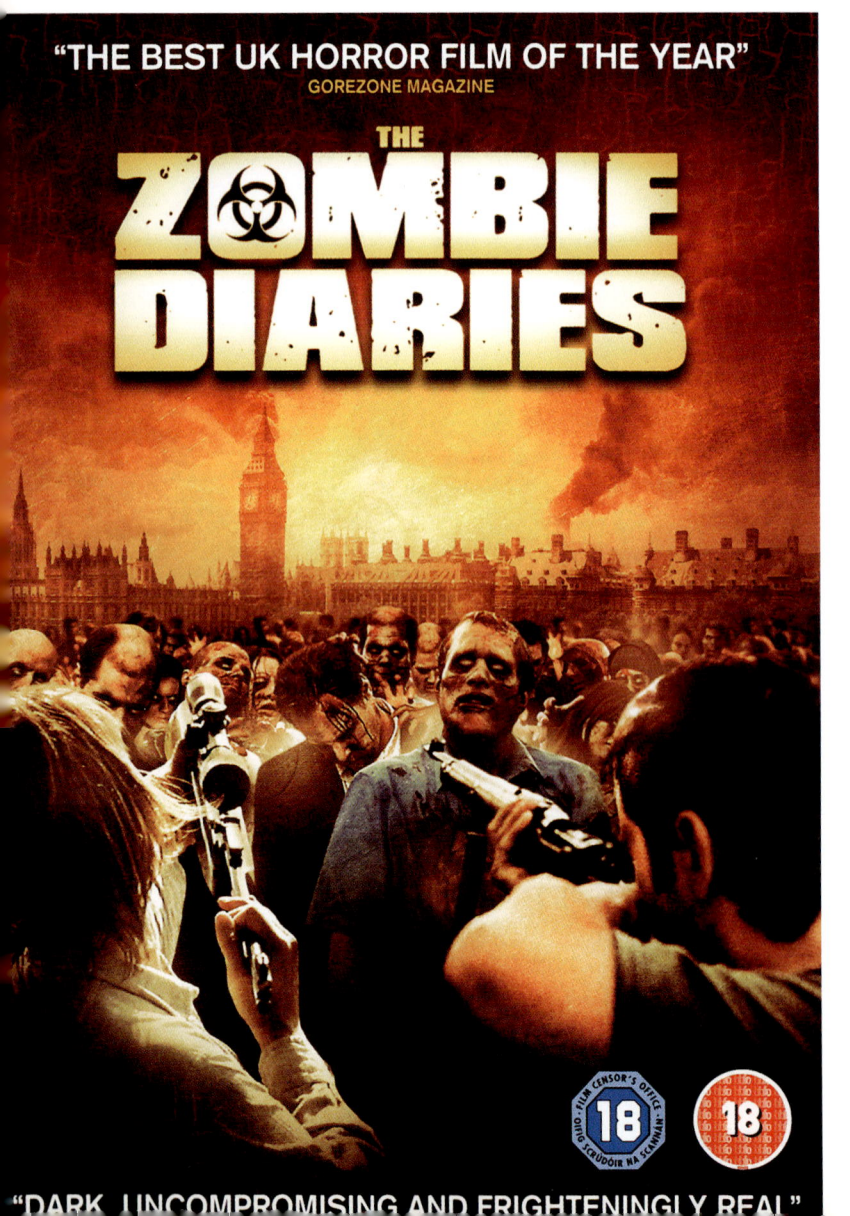

Bill's failings as a father to Timmy. Similarly, the affection between Fido and Helen largely fills the void in her apparently empty, loveless marriage. Hell, even when Fido's collar malfunctions, he still manages to show a discerning side to his nature by only killing victims who would be regarded as "irritants" in any case.

It's all kicking off in the superior [REC]

So, zombies are better friends, better lovers and seemingly, more demonstrative than at least some of their human counterparts. To reinforce this unsettling motif, we also have Mr Theopolis' bizarre relationship with his "voluptuous" zombie Tammy (Sonja Bennett) – his very own sex doll, so, even better sex with zombies?!!

It's certainly high concept, audacious at times and has (against all odds), a convincing relationship at its core with the friendship between a boy and his zombie, yet one can't help feeling that the thirteen years spent in development with British Columbia as reputedly, their highest budgeted independent film, perhaps compromised the final vision.

From high concept to high velocity, a brace of recent films have turned almost full circle from the spectacular impact of Romero's *Night of the Living Dead* some forty years ago now, utilising the same raw, cine verite approach and documentary style realism to generate a palpable sense of dread.

Michael Bartlett and Kevin Gates *The Zombie Diaries* (2006) coupled with Jaume Balaguero and Paco Plaza's *[REC]* (2007), take on the appearance of a low budget *The Blair Witch Project* (1999) in the case of the former and the kinetic energy of *28 Days Later* (2002) in the case of the latter – all cocooned within a quasi-documentary aesthetic.

The near future premise in *Diaries* revolves around a triumvirate of video diaries which are discovered after a virus outbreak has triggered reports of strange attacks. The first of these, "The Outbreak", shows a group of young film makers (Craig Stovin, Anna Blades, Victoria Nalder and Jonathan Ball), drive out into rural Hertfordshire and to the blighted rural farmhouse that the reports have emanated from. Their search of the property only uncovers the "strange dead things running around" as they flee to the nearby woods.

"The Scavengers" centres around a married couple (Kyle Sparks and Alison Mollon) and a combative traveller with a video camera (Jonnie Hurn), who drive around the small town of Southgate looking for food supplies and a working radio signal. The final segment, "The Survivors" features a besieged group comprising (Russell Jones, James Fisher, Imogen Church, Sophia Ellis, Will Tosh and Ralph Mondi), who have kept the zombies at bay for a month until one member becomes infected and what little camaraderie remaining, rapidly begins to unravel. A suitably bleak coda even reveals that one of them

The Dead Walk

may indeed be far more hideous, not to mention dangerous, than the zombies they are fleeing from.

Emerging from the shadows of films exhibiting a similar cadre, based upon the "home movie/found footage" aesthetic – think *Cannibal Holocaust* (1979), *My Little Eye* (2002) and *The Collingwood Story* (2002), Bartlett and Gates' film does, however, pre-date Romero's own *Diary of the Dead* (2007) and the Hollywood hit *Cloverfield* (2008).

Whilst the jerky, hand held footage shot "on the fly" retains a certain frisson with its immediacy, the multi-plotting story device the directors opt for here, is certainly ambitious but a difficult contrivance to pull off effectively a la Quentin Tarantino's masterful *Pulp Fiction* (1994), for example. As a consequence, the fractured nature of the disparate storylines being gradually interwoven has the ultimate effect of slowing down the action with the non-linear conceit becoming somewhat confusing at times.

Riding on the coat tails of *28 Days Later* (2002) success, *The Zombie Diaries* nonetheless offers an intriguing mediation on a society in meltdown – all manner of causal effects are referenced here from 9/11 to rural livestock culls, to avian flu panics. The film also sets the tone for luminaries such as Romero's *Diary of the Dead* by highlighting our obsession with documenting every aspect of modern life, no matter how mundane it may be. This minutiae readily served up for public consumption to satiate the media-savvy, YouTube generation.

In the same way, the opening sequence, which includes the film crew carrying out interviews with the public, raises concerns that if schools are infected with the virus and displayed online for speed, how will those unfortunates with no internet access be informed? Contrast this (over) reliance on technology with an effective sequence where a family is forced to deal with one of their own becoming infected – what would any of us do in such a fraught situation? How will mankind adapt to such a catastrophic situation with events unfolding rapidly, way beyond our control?

What *The Zombie Diaries* increasingly underlines is an apocalyptical view of societal collapse from the "ground up" – no military or governmental solutions are provided here, with the lugubrious finale offering up the prophetic coda that perhaps surviving the zombie hordes may be the "easy" part – surviving the dark tendrils of the human soul may prove to be considerably harder.

The flaunting of this repellent recess of the human psyche jars somewhat

The terrified face of Angela (Manuela Velasco) stares out from the abyss in the chilling [REC]

with the avidly documentary style approach, whilst the film's modus operandi involving "video jockeys" to carry on filming the onrushing zombies, whilst simultaneously trying to run away and escape, is perhaps, a necessary narrative flaw within the ferocious vignettes *The Zombie Diaries*, at times, depicts.

What danger lurks in the shadows for Angela in [REC]

The lineage of the Spanish zombie film may not exactly be long and illustrious, but for directors Juame Balaguero and Paco Plaza, it proved mightily fertile ground for their superior *[REC]* (2007) - a taut, stylish foray into a contemporary world of urban nightmares, with zombies lurking from seemingly every shadow. As Philip French memorably noted in The Observer, "The film comes at you with the ferocity of a Spanish Inquisitor with a branding iron and holds you there to the bitter end."

An intriguing premise sees an intrepid TV reporter, Angela (Manuela Velasco) and her tenacious cameraman Marcos (Pablo Rosso), on location recording the nocturnal work of the Barcelona Fire Service, whilst filming for a late night TV news programme "While You Sleep". The duo shadow the fire crew as they are called out to attend a disturbance in an apartment block, where an old lady is found screaming.

When they arrive, they find her covered in blood and she attempts to bite one of the firemen. In the ensuing chaos, the residents, firemen and TV crew are all effectively quarantined inside as the exits are closed and the entire building sealed off. The inherent tension and claustrophobia arising from this, together with the increasing hysteria of the confused tenants, immeasurably heightens the impact of the macabre discovery that the dead are now walking…

Balaguero and Plaza betray a masterful guiding hand here – the natural, unhurried build up establishing the relaxed approach and camaraderie of the firemen at the station, before scrambling to a seemingly banal incident involving an old woman, then, careers into overdrive as the confined milieu and palpable air of paranoia, conspire to create an escalating atmosphere of malevolence.

The genius of this central conceit lies in its deliberate confinement of the zombie outbreak to one, quickly isolated, urban tower block. It's not depicting global domination, it's diametrically opposed to such an approach. It is just this insular rather than expansive aesthetic which propels *[REC]* into playing out as a real tour de force for the directorial team.

Their most audacious deviation from zombie film convention is that the zombies aren't outside the building trying to get in, because here, they are already inside. The natural performances from the residents and their descent into hysteria – arguing

Angela discovers the grim truth during the nihilistic coda in [REC]

and seeking to apportion blame rather than joining forces to boost their survival chances, evokes the spectral influence of Romero's *Night of the Living Dead* (1968). The tension is ratcheted up considerably with the realisation that any of them could be the next to die, with suspense emanating from trying to second guess who will be next – (it's a cerebral counterpoint to the "physical" blood test the survivors in *The Thing* (1982) undergo, in order to try and discover who the next infected victim is).

As with the aforementioned *The Zombie Diaries*, one could be churlish and argue over whether such endangered figures would really still have the presence of mind to continue filming the resulting carnage and yet it's a concept which sits far more easily here as it reinforces Angela and Marcos' professional commitment and integrity in keeping the camera rolling under any circumstances – Angela's virtual epitaph proving to be; "We have to tape everything Marcos for fuck's sake!"

Given this journalistic bravura – similar to the "film at all costs) mantra which war reporters espouse when in the battle arena, the jolting, hand held camera is more integral to the plot here than its slightly forced used in the likes of *Cloverfield* or *The Blair Witch Project*, and considerable tension is derived from it.

As we join Angela and the ever present (but entirely unseen) Marcos, there's a voyeuristic intimacy to the proceedings – long, unbroken takes adding to the suspense as the roving camera prowls through empty corridors, records ethereal sounds, culminating in one extraordinary shot as the lens spirals down the central stairwell, only to uncover zombies emerging from almost every recess, before a heart-stopping moment as one ghoul's face bursts into view in ultra close-up.

With no weapons to defend themselves, the sheer scale and hopelessness of the situation becomes ever more apparent, with the fast spreading contagion and economical glimpses of the zombies adding to the effect – the camera continually cutting out, jerking away or even dropping to the floor to disorientate us.

Angela anchors the whole piece, being virtually ever present on screen. She is attractive, yet believable, professional and practical – in one scene she stems the flow of blood from a fireman's neck wound by compressing her jacket against it.

The hellish nightmare which unfolds is experienced through her eyes and the camera lens becoming as one and the sense of paranoia is almost unbearable as the authorities (shown in silhouette outside), proceed to vacuum pack the entire building with "biohazard plastic". Frantic, tantalising last glimpses of the outside world, of "normality", show only the flashing blue lights and neon street lamps beyond – authority figures cast only as vague shadows as the final rays of light ebb away to render the building a virtual coffin.

This theme of events beyond our control and left to watch as "outsiders" looking in, is accentuated as Angela and Marcos secretly film the newly arrived health inspector- himself a monstrous apparition, clad in gas mask, lurid yellow suit and carrying a black medical case, trying to administer a serum to the infected in a locked room he commandeers.

The inevitable happens, as an injured policeman, handcuffed to a table, proceeds to bite the inspector – not before he has explained that they believe the virus has emanated from an infected dog and is carried on its saliva.

Not one to neglect her journalistic duties, her immediate response is to shout to Marcos; "Get this on tape", when one girl, Jennifer (Claudia Font), is infected and handcuffed to the bottom of the stairwell.

Adding greatly to the tension in *[REC]* is the "characterisation" of the apartment block where all the action unfolds. Besides being rendered a literal "tomb" with its very own incumbent zombie residents, its labyrinth passageways and shadowed recesses signify an architectural motif which manifests itself as a parallel creation to Dante's *Inferno* - as we spiral ever upwards from the bowels of the basement, in ever decreasing circles to the impenetrable reaches of the attic eerie, which ultimately harbours an even greater horror.

With only Angela and Marcos left as "survivors" now, their plans to escape via the basement and into the sewers, are thwarted by a veritable army of zombies now inhabiting the stairwell. Having momentarily lost Marcos, adrenaline supplants fear as, now reunited, the duo embark on a frantic bid to reach the attic – struggling to find the right keys to enter the locked room with the chasing zombies now in rapid pursuit.

Once "safely" inside, we reach the truly harrowing conclusion as they discover newspaper cuttings everywhere, delineating the story of the demonic possession of a Portuguese girl Nina Medeiros, as well as a rather risible tape recorded message they listen, to explaining the origins of the virus, in a similar plot device to *The Evil Dead* (1982).

Discovering a trap door leading up into the attic space. Marcos climbs up and swings it open to investigate with the camera – his 360 degree pan abruptly halted as he fixes upon the grotesque features of Medeiros' (Javier Botet) snarling, demonic face – who, hits out wildly at the camera and breaks the light.

Switching to "night vision" mode on the camera, the room is bathed in a spectral, incandescent green hue, (akin to a similarly suspenseful climax in *The Silence of the Lambs*, 1991).

Almost unbearable tension is created here as whilst we, the viewer, and Marcos, can see the emaciated, skeletal figure of Medeiros now in the room with them via the night vision lens, Angela cannot.

Armed with a hammer, the ghoul repeatedly attacks Marcos, raining blows upon him before proceeding to devour his near lifeless body. With the camera now grounded, our final images are of Angela screaming and being dragged by her feet away from us, before the screen reduces to black – an unremittingly nihilistic coda.

Whether the actual device of somewhat "clumsily" attempting to explain the origins of the virus actually works is open to debate – perhaps leaving things unexplained would have added a further aura of mystique and menace here?

Whatever your viewpoint, with a US remake *Quarantine* (2008) due later this year and the idea of a sequel directed by Balaguero and Plaza again also being muted, their edgy, vibrant reinterpretation of the zombie mythos looks certain to continue – with the same compelling terror, energised élan and authentic scares, we hope.

FILMOGRAPHY

EXPLANATORY NOTES:

Title of the film/Foreign language title (if known or applicable)
Year of release / Country of origin
D - Director
S - Stars
Synopsis

A

ABBOTT AND COSTELLO MEET THE MUMMY - (1955) (US)
D - Charles Lamont
S - Bud Abbott, Lou Costello, Marie Windsor, Eddie Parker, Michael Ansara, Dan Seymor, Kurt Katch.

THE ALIEN DEAD (1980) (US)
D – Fred Olen Ray
S – Buster Crabbe, Ray Roberts, Linda Lewis, George Kelsey, Mike Bonavia, Dennis Underwood
The swamps of Florida are the unlikely (and only original) aspect to this entry from direct to video, softcore porn merchant Ray. A crashed aircraft carrying toxic substances is the cause of the zombie outbreak here, but the pedestrian pacing is as slow as the zombies themselves.

ANCIENT EVIL:SCREAM OF THE MUMMY (2000) (US)
D – David Decocteau
S – Jeff Petersen, Trent Latta, Ariauna Albright, Russell Richardson, Michele Nordin, Brenda Blondell, Michael Lutz
Better than most of DeCocteau's other offering such as *Creepozoids* (1987) and yet still utterly average. Blondell's Professor Cyphers unearths an Aztec mummy only for one of her students to steal an ancient amulet in order to revive the mummy. The whole mummy revenge on campus motif here was done much better in *Tales From The Darkside: The Movie* (1990).

ARMY OF DARKNESS - (1992) (US)
D -Sam Raimi
S - Bruce Campbell, Embeth Davidtz, Bridget Fonda

ASTRO ZOMBIES - (1968) (US)
D - Ted V. Mikels
S - John Carradine, Wendell Corey, Rafael Campos, Tom Pace.
From the director of *The Corpse Grinders* (1972), Astro

Zombie Filmography

Zombies is made on rather less than a shoestring, featuring only one set around which the tiresome "action" occurs. Carradine, in the umpteenth abysmal film of his career is the evil Dr. De Marco who utilises a constant stream of human body organs to create a master race of omnipotent men, the "Astro Zombies" of the title.

ATTACK OF THE MAYAN MUMMY - (LA MOMIA AZTECA) - (1957) (MEX)
D - Rafael Portillo
S - Ramon Gay, Rosita Arenas, Crox Alvarado, Luis Aceves Castaneda, Arturo Martinez.
Portillo's series is most probably the best known of the Mexican mummy genre, which generally targets its historical conquerors Spain, as opposed to Egypt, as the "enemy". Here we see Dr. Almada (Gay) utilising his regression and hypnosis theories on his lover Flor (Arenas), who, we learn was once the Xochitl, executed for an illicit affair. It is Xochitl's lover, the warrior Popoca who returns as the mummy in order to stop Gay and his helper (Alvarado) from stealing the treasure which is buried in his tomb. The unique conclusion sees some cross-monster fertilisation as a crucifix (normally associated with repelling the vampire), and sticks of dynamite are used to kill off the mummy.

THE AWAKENING - (1980) (UK)
D - Mike Newell
S - Charlton Heston, Susannah York, Jill Townsend, Stephanie Zimbalist, Patrick Drury, Bruce Myers.

B

BANGKOK ZOMBIE CRISIS (2004) (Thailand)
D – Taweewat Wantha
S – Suthep Po-ngam, Supakorn Kitsuwon, Phintusuda Tunphairao, Lene Christensen, Andrew Biggs, Naowarat Yuktanan
Dubbed as a "SARS Wars" saga with Tunphairao as the kidnapped daughter of a wealthy businessman, mixed with a plot revolving around a SARS infected cockroach (!) from Africa, finding its way to a Thai airport to spread the infection. With a giant zombie snake, soft core animated sequences and featuring conventional, as well as light saber swordsplay, Wantha's film may not be logical but you can't accuse it of being dull.

BATTLE GIRL (1991) (JAP)
D – Kazuo Komizu
S – Kenji Otsuki, Cutey Suzuki,

THE BEYOND - (1981)(E TU VIVRAI NEL TERRORE ! L'ALDILA) (IT)
D - Lucio Fulci
S - Catriona MacColl, David Warbeck, Sarah Keller, Antoine Saint John, Veronica Lazar, Giovanni de Nava, Michele Mirabella.

BEYOND REANIMATOR (2003) (SP)
D – Brian Yuzna
S – Jeffrey Combs, Tommy Dean Musset, Jason Barry, Barbara Elorrieta, Elsa Pataky

BIO ZOMBIE (1998) (HK)
D – Wilson Yip
S – Jordan Chan, Emotion Cheung, Sam Lee, Yiu-Cheung Lai
A rip roaring, gory zombie comedy where a couple of video bootleggers manage to unleash an Iraq-engineered contaminate onto an unsuspecting shopping metropolis with predictable results.

BLACK DEMONS - (DEMONI 3) - (1991) (IT)
D - Umberto Lenzi
S - Keith Van Hoven, Joe Balogh, Sonia Curtis, Philip Murray, Juliana Texeira, Maria Alves.
An unofficial sequel to Lamberto Bava's Demons series, Lenzi's film sees Van Hoven, Curtis and her boyfriend (Balogh) holidaying in Rio de Janeiro and falling foul of the local voodoo lore. Living off the corpse of *Zombie Flesh Eaters* (1979) Lenzi has his tourists' jeep conveniently break down near a graveyard whereupon the ground heaves and spews forth the attendant negro zombies. Their sole intent is to slaughter any white people they can find in revenge for those who had sent them to their early graves - a rare glimpse of social comment within the genre.

THE BLACK PIT - (1958) (MEX)
D - Fernando Mendez
S - Gaston Santos, Rafael Bertrand, Mapita Cortes, Carlos Anciea, Antonio Raxel.
Two doctors working, appropriately in an asylum, agree to a "death pact" whereby when one dies he will return to tell the surviving partner about the "afterlife". It is Dr. Aldama (Raxel) who dies leaving the remaining doctor (Bertrand) to arrange a seance to make good the bargain. Instead he is only informed by Raxel of his own impending death, which occurs 3 months later when Bertrand is executed for murder. He rises again to seek revenge by killing Raxel's daughter (Cortes), but is then himself set alight in the climax by the girl's boyfriend (Santos). Most notable sequences here are the corpse rising from the grave and later playing the violin !

The Dead Walk

BLACK ROSES - (1988) (US)
D - John Fasano
S - John Martin, Sal Viviano, Ken Swofford, Carmine Appice, Paul Kelman, Julie Adams.
The adage that "the Devil has all the best tunes" comes true here as a heavy metal band Black Roses, breeze into an American town and really do play the Devil's music. Soon their ghoulish concerts are sending the local kids wild, literally, as they begin to slay their parents in gruesome fashion. There are some impressive special effects sequences on show as the band members are transmogrified into grotesque zombies, and the film also marks the first genre appearance of Adams since *The Creature From The Black Lagoon* (1954).

BLOODEATERS - (1979) (US)
D - Chuck McCrann
S - Charles Austin, Beverly Shapiro, Dennis Helfend, Harriet Miller, John Amplas.
Shot in Romero country, Pittsburgh, the film also features one of his regulars, Amplas from *Martin* (1976) and *Day of the Dead* (1985). The plot concerns a group of youths who are busy harvesting a marijuana crop in an isolated forest that has been the scene of previous herbicide spraying experiments. Needless to say, this chemical residue transforms the youngsters into zombies who then set about attacking anyone in sight with machetes. The picture was originally shot on 16mm film.

BLOOD FROM THE MUMMY'S TOMB - (1971) (UK)
D - Seth Holt (Uncredited), Michael Carreras
S - Andrew Keir, Valerie Leon, James Villiers, Hugh Burden, Rosalie Crutchley, Aubrey Morris.

BLOOD OF GHASTLY HORROR - (1971) (US)
D - Al Adamson
S - Regina Carol, Roy Morton, Tracey Robbins, Kent Taylor, John Carradine, Tommy Kirk.
Adamson is on familiar territory with this exploitation film, having previously been responsible for *Dracula's Castle* (1967) and *Horror of the Blood Monsters* (1970). The film was actually started in 1965, undergoing various changes before its eventual release. As it stands, the plot revolves around a mad doctor, Carradine, who unleashes his zombies onto an unsuspecting world to avenge the death of his own son who died at the hands of another doctor. The film is most notable for the scene where Kirk opens a box that contains a severed head, and it also stars the beautiful Carol, Adamson's real wife.

BLOODSUCKING PHARAOH'S IN PITTSBURGH - (1990) (US)
D - Alan Smithee, (Dean T. Schetter)
S - Veronica Hart, Jane Hamilton.
Actually filmed in Pittsburgh as the title suggests, this was announced as a remake of H G Lewis' *Bloodfeast* (1963). The perfunctory plot sees two cops and a detective's daughter pursuing a chainsaw killer as the whole gamut of black humour and gore is visited upon the screen, complete with decapitations and cat fights in the "Egyptian" part of Pittsburgh (!), enlivened with ex-porno star Hart's presence.

BODYSNATCHERS (1993) (US)
D – Abel Ferrera
S – Gabrielle Anwar, Terry Kinney, Billy Wirth, Christine Elise, R. Lee Ermey, Meg Tilly, Reilly Murphy

THE BOYS FROM BRAZIL - (1978) (US)
D - Franklin J. Shaffner
S - Gregory Peck, Laurence Olivier, James Mason, Lilli Palmer, Uta Hagen, Denholm Elliot.

BOWERY AT MIDNIGHT - (1942) (US)
D - Wallace Fox
S - Bela Lugosi, John Archer, Wanda McKay, Tom Neal, Dave O'Brien, J. Farrell MacDonald.
Lugosi in slightly above-average form leading a dual life as both a professor of psychology and owner of a food kitchen helping out vagrants. The disguised atrocities are all perpetrated in the basement by Lugosi, complete with its own cemetery and graves together with an ante-chamber populated by zombies.

BOY EATS GIRL (2005) (UK/IRELAND)
D – Stephen Bradley
S – Samantha Mumba, David Leon, Tadhg Murphy, Laurence Kinlan, Sara James, Mark Huberman, Sarah Burke, Paul Reid, Jane Valentine
Part of a mini Irish invasion along with 2004's *Dead Meat*, Bradley's film restores the voodoo motif back to the zombie film to good effect - using ancient lore to revive her son Nathan (David Leon) following his untimely suicide. A vegetarian, Nathan is most definitely a reluctant "returner" and his reticence, is coupled with a good evocation of High School life in leafy Ireland. Samantha Mumba as Jessica - the object of his desires, gives a decent performance but the show is stolen by Sara James as Cheryl, the class slut whose short skirts and literally "killer" heels, as she stabs one zombie with them, leave a lasting impression.

Zombie Filmography

Teen angst, bullying, the role of peer pressure, social awkwardness and some lively black humour, all conspire to generate an above average, low budget entry of some promise.

BRAIN DEAD - (2007) (US)
D - Kevin Tenney
S - Joshua Benton, Sarah Grant Brendecke, David Crane
Pretty decent return to zombies from the director of *Night of the Demons*, has a group stranded in a log cabin facing zombies created by meteor landing nearby.

BRAIN DEAD - (1992) (NZ)
D - Peter Jackson
S - Tim Balem, Diana Penalver, Liz Moody, Brenda Kendall, Stuart Devenie, Ian Watkin.
The third feature from zany New Zealander Jackson, after the appropriately-titled *Bad Taste* (1988) and the "Sluppet Show" of *Meet The Feebles* (1990). This zombie "slapstick" sees the ranks of the walking dead swell courtesy of the infectious bite of an evil rat monkey, from the mountains of Sumatra. Lashings of gore and outrageous humour populate a film not to be taken too seriously! A sign of the talent later to helm the awesome *Lord of the Rings* (2001-2003) trilogy and lavish *King Kong* (2005) remake.

THE BRIDE OF RE-ANIMATOR (1989) (US)
D - Brian Yuzna
S - Jeffrey Combs, Bruce Abbott, David Gale.

BUBBA HO-TEP (2002) (US)
D – Don Coscarelli
S – Bruce Campbell, Ossie Davis, Ella Joyce, Heidi Marnhout, Bob Ivy, Edith Jefferson, Larry Pennell, Reggie Bannister
A spoof horror which tells us what "really" happened to Elvis Presley (played with relish, not to mention sideburns, by *Evil Dead* icon Bruce Campbell), as the "King" battles an Egyptian mummy, aided by former President John F Kennedy (Ossie Davis), only now he's back and decidedly black in colour!
The zany premise of a mummy stalking the corridors of a Texas nursing home - "Shady Rest" is original to say the least and Campbell gives a bravura performance amidst the gags, with a surprisingly subtle subtext on the rigours of old age thrown in for good measure.

BURIAL GROUND - (ZOMBIE 3) (LE NOTTE DEL TERRORE) (1981) (IT)
D - Andrea Bianchi
S - Karin Weil, Maria Angela Giordan, Peter Bark, Gian Luigi Chrizzi.
An extremely gory film that sees zombies emerging from an Etruscan tomb to invade a weekend party that is taking place in a country mansion. Some of the guests escape to a nearby monastery but are soon devoured by the carnivorous zombies. Fulci regular, Gianetto de Rossi, handles the gruesome effects which include eyeballs being skewered, one zombie kid biting its' mother's nipple off and one victim being crucified and then beheaded with a scythe. The film lacks the visual imagination found in Fulci's more inspired works that this film tries so hard and unsuccessfully to emulate.

C

CANNIBAL APOCALYPSE - (APOCALISSE DOMANI) (1980) (IT,SP)
D - Antonio Margheriti
S - John Saxon, Elisabeth Turner, Cindy Hamilton, May Heatherly, Cinzia Carolis, Tony King, Giovanni Lombardo Radice.

CEMETERY MAN - (DELLAMORTE DELLAMORE) (1994) (IT)
D - Michele Soavi
S - Rupert Everett, Francois Hadji-Lazaro, Anna Falchi

THE CHILD - (1977) (US)
D - Robert Voskanian
S - Laurel Barnett, Rosalie Cole, Frank Janson, Richard Hanners, Ruth Ballan, Blossom Bing Jong.

THE CHILDREN - (1980) (US)
D - Max Kalmanowicz
S - Martin Shakar, Gil Rogers, Gale Garnett.
Any film that relies on fingernails turning black for its "special effects" is in serious trouble as this comical exploiter shows. The story concerns a contaminated cloud escaping from a nuclear plant turning a bus load of school kids into zombies. They generally make a nuisance of themselves; setting fire to their parents, and the only way that they can be killed is by cutting their hands off ! This gives rise to the ludicrous spectacle of the distraught children caught amidst a sea of recently severed hands. This is certainly a case of thumbs down though, despite the musical score that is provided by Henry Manfredini of *Friday the 13th* fame.

CHILDREN SHOULDN'T PLAY WITH DEAD THINGS - (1973) (US)
D - Bob Clark
S - Jeffrey Gillen, Paul Cronin, Roy Engleman, Bob Filep

The Dead Walk

A CHINESE GHOST STORY - (1987) (HK)
D - Ching Siu Tung
S - Leslie Chum, Woo Mar.

A CHINESE GHOST STORY 2 - (1990) (HK)
D - Ching Siu Tung
S - Leslie Cheung, Joey Wong, Jacky Cheung, Ma Wu, Waise Lee.

Following on from the universal acclaim the original film garnered, once again we find our tax collector protagonist in trouble, being held captive in prison before embarking on a tug of war between an Imperial Wizard and a corrupt general as the outre special effects take hold, together with the bizarre characters ranging from high-kicking heroines to fake Buddhas, to pedantic trolls.

A CHINESE GHOST STORY 3 - (1991) (HK)
D - Ching Siu Tung, Tsui Hark
S - Jacky Cheung, Tony Leung,, Chiu Wai, Nina Li Chi, Joey Wong.

Very much a retread of the original movie as we see the return of the evil Tree Spirit along with the requisite assortment of ghosts and swordsmen to conclude the series.

CHOPPER CHICKS IN ZOMBIETOWN - (1988) (US)
D - Dan Hoskins
S - Don Calfa, Ed Gale, Catherine Carlen, Jamie Rose, Vicki Frederick.

A slightly above-average release from the Troma stable with female bikers pitted against zombies with Calfa starring as a mad mortician a la his turn in *Return of the Living Dead* (1985) and who turns the townsfolk into zombies. The biker heroines save a bus full of blind orphans, who then help them to decapitate the attacking zombies and lure them into a church using raw meat. Bizarrely, Rose was previously seen in the US TV soap *Falcon Crest*.

CITY OF THE DEAD - (1960) (UK)
D - John Moxey
S - Christopher Lee, Patricia Jessel, Betta St. John, Dennis Lotis, Venetia Stevenson, Valentine Dyall, Ann Beach.

CITY OF THE LIVING DEAD - (PAURA NELLA CITTA DEI MORTI VIVENTI) (1980) (IT)
D - Lucio Fulci
S - Christopher George, Janet Agren, Catriona MacColl, Carlo de Mejo, Daniela Doria, Giovanni Lombardo Radice, John Morghen, Antonella Interlenghi.

CITY OF THE WALKING DEAD (INCUBO ULLA CITTA CONTAMINATA) (1980) (IT)
D - Umberto Lenzi
S - Hugo Stiglitz, Laura Trotter, Mel Ferrer, Francisco Rabal, Maria Rosaria Ommagio, Sonia Viviani.

A CLOCKWORK ORANGE - (1971) (UK)
D - Stanley Kubrick
S - Malcolm McDowell, Patrick Magee, Michael Bates, Adrienne Corri, Miriam Karlin, John Clive, Warren Clarke.

CONDEMNED MEN - (1940) (US)
D - William Beaudine
S - Mantan Moreland, Dorothy Dandridge, Niel Webster.

A typical zombie film from the 1940's cycle, this one including a negro cast amongst whom Moreland is best known for his role of Birmingham Brown in the long running "Charlie Chan" films. Beaudine was a prolific director making over 300 films including the infamous "western horrors" *Billy the Kid v's Dracula* (1966) and *Jesse James Meets Frankenstein's Daughter* in the same year.

THE CORPSE BRIDE (2005) (UK/US)
D – Tim Burton, Mike Johnson
S – Johnny Depp, Helena Bonham Carter, Emily Watson, Tracey Ullman, Paul Whitehouse, Joanna Lumley, Albert Finney, Richard E. Grant, Christopher Lee, Michael Gough, Jane Horrocks

An exquisite, animated film featuring a stellar cast (of voices) which sees Burton regular, Johnny Depp's Victor destined to marry Victoria (Emily Watson) in an arranged marriage. Whilst enunciating his vows in the forest to a fallen tree, the corpse bride (Burton's wife, Helena Bonham Carter) is summoned to claim his hand instead.
With acutely observed irony, Victor finds more colour, life and vitality when journeying into his bride's undead world, than in the muted, stifling pretension of the supposedly "living" world above.
With masterful puppetry and an even finer vocal cast, Burton recovers some of the gothic flair and disquieting edge distinctly missing from his forays into the mainstream (by his standards at least!), with *Planet of the Apes* (2001) and *Big Fish* (2003).

CORPSES (2004) (US)
D – Rolfe Kanefsky
S – Jeff Fahey, Tiffany Shepis, Stephen W. Williams, Robert Donovan, Melinda Bonini, Khris Kaneff, Lorielle New

Zombie Filmography

Playing as a kind of *Re-animator* reworking this sees a mortician find a way to bring people back from the dead, but for only sixty minutes in the most original aspect of the story. After that, the zombies need an hourly "fix" just to stay "alive". It may not be the height of social commentary but the plot wrinkle of the funeral parlour being closed down to make way for a shopping mall is something of a first, as is the relative absence of flesh on display from Shepis. New, as a living junkie hooker turned undead zombie, remains a junkie, only for the zombie serum now, in an eye-catching turn.

THE CRAZIES - (1973) (US)
D - George A. Romero
S - Lane Carroll, W.G. McMillan, Harold Wayne Jones, Lloyd Hollar, Richard Liberty, Lynn Lowry.

CREATURE WITH THE ATOM BRAIN - (1955) (US)
D - Edward L. Cahn
S - Richard Denning, Angela Stevens, John Launer, Michael Granger, Gregory Gay, Karl Davis.

CREEPSHOW - (1980) (US)
D - George A. Romero
S - Leslie Nielsen, E.G. Marshall, Adrienne Barbeau, Ted Danson, Hal Holbrook, Fritz Weaver, Carrie Nye, Viveca Lindafors.

CULT OF THE DEAD - (LA MUETRE VIVIENTE) (1968) (MEX)
D - Juan Ibanez
S - Boris Karloff, Julissa, Carlos East, Raphael Bertrand. One of Karlof's last films (he made four of these Mexican "quickies" in five weeks), and despite his star-billing his screen time is so short as to be virtually just a cameo - no doubt a result of his own ill health during the making of the picture. The plot, as it is, calls on Karloff to play both a doctor, Van Molder and Damballah, the evil priest who lordes it over the voodoo-fearing natives on a remote island. Despite the gothic trappings of mist laden caves, the film rarely rises above the cheap titilation provided by endless scenes of writhing female victims about to be both zombiefied and violated by libidinous snakes ! I'll leave you to decide which fate is worse!

THE CURSE OF THE AZTEC MUMMY - (LA MAL DICION DE LA MOMIA AZTECA) - (1957) (MEX)
D - Rafael Portillo
S - Ramon Gay, Rosita Arenas, Crox Alvarado, Luis Acevas Castaneda, Arturo Martinez, Emma Roldan.

Featuring the same cast and crew, this entry was shot immediately after *Attack of the Mayan Mummy* and once again, we see the "good" doctor (Gay) opposing the "evil" Dr. Krupp (Castaneda) who attempts to claim the Aztec jewels from Xochitl's corpse, still guarded by the warrior Popoca. Treading much the same ground as the first film with the mummy once again bizarrely repelled by a crucifix, the most engaging scene sees the mummy lock Krupp in a room containing hundreds of vipers - well before such similar scenes in the *Indiana Jones* film series.

CURSE OF THE DOLL PEOPLE - (MUNECOS INFERNALES) (1960) (MEX)
D - Benito Alazraki
S - Elvira Quintana, Ramon Gay, Roberto G. Rivera, Quintin Bulnes.
A voodoo curse is placed on those people responsible for stealing a Haitian doll and consequently they begin to die, despite warnings from an occult expert (Quintana). The murders are perpetrated by miniature demonic dolls and a zombie, controlled by a malevolent voodoo priest (Bulnes), who dresses in black robes embroidered with serpents. The climax sees him traced to his underground lair and frightened by Quintana's crucifix. The best scenes are those featuring the dolls stalking their victims, an idea replayed in the above average Amicus anthology *Asylum* (1971).

CURSE OF THE MAYA (2004) (US)
D - David Heavener
S - David Heavener, Amanda Baumann, Joe Estevez, Todd Bridges, Steven Bracy
With a UK release title of *Dawn of the Living Dead* in 2008 there's no attempt to bask in the reflected glory of George A Romero's resurgence is there guys?! Estevez and Baumann are the married couple looking for solitude in a new house, only to find it has been built on the site of a Mayan graveyard. Cue, unleashed zombies in a reasonably enjoyable romp spoilt by low quality film stock.

CURSE OF THE MUMMY'S TOMB - (1964) (UK)
D - Michael Carreras
S - Terence Morgan, Ronald Howard, Fred Clark, Jeanne Roland, George Pastell, Dickie Owen.

D

THE DARK POWER (1985) (US)
D – Phil Smoot
S – Lash La Rue, Anna Lane Tatum, Cynthia Bailey, Mary Dalton, Paul Holman, Cynthia Farbman
When a native American Indian dies, his house, built

The Dead Walk

over the graves of four sorcerers, is rented out by a group of teenagers, who, unwittingly release them. After a slow start, the visualisation of the zombie quartet is well realised, as is their appropriation of weapons which suitably reinforce their identities, be it tomahawks or bow and arrows.

DAWN OF THE DEAD - (1978) (US)
D - George A. Romero
S - David Emge, Ken Foree, Scott H. Reininger, Gaylen Ross, David Crawford, David Early.

DAWN OF THE DEAD (2004) (US)
D – Zack Snyder
S – Sarah Polley, Ving Rhames, Jake Weber, Mekhi Phifer, Ty Burrell, Michael Kelly, Kevin Zegers, Lindy Booth

DAWN OF THE MUMMY - (1981) (US, IT, EGYPT)
D - Frank Agrama
S - Brenda King, Barry Sattels, George Peck, John Salvo, Joan Levy, Dianne Beatty.

DAY OF THE DEAD - (1985) (US)
D - George A. Romero
S - Lori Cardille, Terry Alexander, Joseph Pilato, Jarlath Conroy, Antone Dileo Jnr, Howard Sherman, Richard Liberty.

DAY OF THE DEAD (2008) (US)
D – Steve Miner
S – Mena Suvari, Nick Cannon, Michael Welch, AnnaLynne McCord, Stark Sands, Matt Rippy, Pat Kilbane, Ian McNeice, Ving Rhames

DAY OF THE DEAD 2 – CONTAGIUM (2005) (US)
D – Ana Clavell, James Glenn Dudelson
S – Laurie Baranyay, Stan Klimecko, John Freedom Henry, Justin Ipock, Julian Thomas
Commits the worst crime for any film, particularly a zombie film, by being simply boring. The use of the title is the only tentative link to any of Romero's works other than using the release of an airborne virus contained in a flask and dating back to 1968. The resulting mayhem occurs in a modern day mental institution and leaves the overriding impression as being to question the sanity of anyone unfortunate enough to want to watch the film in its entirety!

DAYS OF DARKNESS (2007) (US)
D – Jake Kennedy
S – Tom Eplin, Sabrina Gennarino, Travis Brorsen, Roshelle Pattison, John Lee Ames, Eric Stuart
A surprisingly effective *Day of the Dead* meets *Night of the Comet* hybrid, with likeable leads and a serviceable (if not original) premise. A group of diverse characters are secured inside an old bunker, whilst the rest of the world struggles to survive a zombie-like infection brought to earth by a crashed meteorite. Given the added concept of alien life forms harboured within the infection, zombies are not the only concern here in an imaginative picture.

DEAD AND BURIED - (1981) (US)
D - Gary Sherman
S - James Farentino, Melody Anderson, Jack Albertson, Dennis Redfield, Nancy Locke Hauser.

DEAD AND DEADER (2006) (US)
D – Patrick Dinhut
S – John Billingsley, Dean Cain, Colleen Camp, Susan Ward, Greg Collins, Ellie Cornell, Affion Crockett, Esteban Cueto, Peter Greene
Cain is the army officer bitten by an insect whilst on an an abortive seek and destroy mission. The bite leaves him in a state of limbo - half human, half zombie, whereupon he endeavours to help stave of the imminent zombie invasion in a rare act of altruism within this genre.

THE DEAD DON'T DIE - (1975) (US)
D - Curtis Harrington
S - George Hamilton, Ray Milland, Ralph Meeker, Reggie Nalder, Yvette Vickers, John Blondell, Linda Cristal.
A madcap 1930's influenced yarn about a group of West Indians in Chicago who plan to rule the world using a zombie army. The most notable aspect is the all-star cast featuring Hamilton who later starred in *Love at First Bite* (1979), Milland who later appeared in *Frogs* (1972) and the gnarled features of Nalder who graced both Hitchcock's *The Man Who Knew Too Much* (1956) and Tobe Hooper's *Salem's Lot* (1979). Harrington went on to direct future horrors such as *Ruby* (1977) and *Devil Dog - Hound of Hell* (1978).

THE DEAD HATE THE LIVING - (1999) (US)
D - Dave Parker
S - Benjamin Morris, Rick Irwin, Kimberly Pullis, Matt Stephens, Wendy Speake, Matt McGrory
With a theme song provided by punk band Penis Flytrap (!) and a zombie henchman (McGrory) who was also one of the main performers in Marilyn Manson's controversial "Coma White" music video, there is a strong music strand here as well as a homage to Fulci in the the hospital setting a la *The Beyond* and Stephen's character being

Zombie Filmography

named Eibon. The plot wrinkle here concerns a group of renegade filmmakers who decide to shoot a zombie epic in an abandoned hospital. Before you can shout *Children Shouldn't Play With Dead Things*, they stumble across an actual corpse and do what any right-minded person would - include it in their movie! When they accidentally revive the corpse using the hospital's decaying equipment, it becomes a real rather than "reel" battle between life and death.

DEAD HEAT - (1988) (US)
D - Mark Goldblatt
S - Joe Piscopo, Toru Tanaka, Vincent Price, Treat Williams, Darren McGavin, Lindsay Frost, Keye Luke.
An interesting idea has two detectives (Piscopo) and Williams), attempting to solve a series of bank robberies and discovering that the perpetrators of the crimes are in fact dead, though very much living zombies. All in all, it's an outrageous mixture of comedy and gore; in one scene Piscopo is attacked by a gutted pig and in another a zombie is sliced in half after being hit by a car. Genre favourites present include McGavin, star of the successful *Night Stalker* TV series from the 1970's and Price, reportedly making his "last" horror appearance - now where have we heard that before ?!

DEAD MEAT (2004) (IRELAND)
D – Conor McMahon
S – Marian Araujo, David Muyll Aert, Eoin Whelan, David Ryan, Amy Redmond, Kathryn Toolan
The surreal image of zombies stumbling through verdant Irish countryside instantly recalls such luminaries as *The Living Dead At The Manchester Morgue*, as an outbreak of infected cattle leads to the rapidly expanding zombie plague which develops. Araujo gives a good performance, attempting to evade the undead along with local gravedigger (!) Ryan. There are definite signs of promise here from McMahon - his use of ruined castles and the protagonists gingerly picking their way through ranks of "sleeping" zombies, recalling the *Blind Dead* series, but some obnoxious, antagonistic characters somewhat stymie the final impact.

THE DEAD NEXT DOOR - (1988) (US)
D - J.R.Bookwalter
S - Pete Ferry, Bodgan Pecic, Michael Grossi, Jolie Jackunas, Robert Kokai, Floyd Ewing Jnr.
After an epidemic leaves the world run amok with living corpses a group of survivors head for Ohio to try and discover a cure for the epidemic. Ferry, Grossi and Jackunas are amongst the group who run into trouble in the unusual form of a cult of zombie lovers who believe it is God's will to preserve the zombies and form a new world.

THE DEAD ONE - (1961) (US)
D - Barry Mahon
S - John Mackay, Linda Ormond, Monica Davis, Clyde Kelley, Darlene Myrick.
The ad' lines give this one away; "See the voodoo princess call on the dead ones to Kill! Kill! Kill!" The story sees Mackay and his bride (Ormond), honeymooning on their family plantation. A cousin (Davis) is left furious as the marriage means she loses her rights to the plantation, so she summons up voodoo powers to revive her dead brother (Kelly). The plan goes awry as the zombie kills Myrick in mistake for Ormond and then disintegrates in the sun as the authorities shoot the voodoo priestess. Mahon also directed a number of "skin-flicks" as well as acting as Errol Flynn's agent.

DEAD PEOPLE - (1972) (US)
D - William Huyck
S - Michael Greer, Marianna Hill, Joy Bang, Anitra Ford, Royal Dano, Elisha Cook.
From the writers of *American Graffiti* (1973), this uninspired tale has Hill visiting a Californian town in search of her painter father only to unearth a colony of zombies. The usual bloodletting is restrained here, but so is the imagination as the film's advertising lines; "When there's no more room in Hell" (Taken straight from Romero's *Dawn of the Dead*) exemplifies. Not surprisingly Romero sued the film makers.

THE DEAD PIT - (1989) (US)
D - Brett Leonard
S - Cheryl Lawson, Jeremy Slate, Stephen Gregory Foster
Shades of Fulci's *The Beyond* (1981) here with shuffling zombies invading a hospital, only this time the ensuing cranium-cracking, by "mental" patients, is all in aid of brain worship ! Their plight is caused by the evil Dr. Ramzi, who, having used lobotomised patients for his own Frankenstein-esque experiments, proceeds to throw his victims into the formaldehyde-filled chamber of the title. The good doctor himself is later banished to the pit upon the discovery of his unorthodox practices. The arrival, 20 years later, of a hallucinating amnesia patient acts as the catalyst for an earthquake to re-open the sealed pit and so again release the victims - not quite the medicine the doctor ordered !

DEATH BECOMES HER - (1992) (US)

The Dead Walk

D - Robert Zemeckis
S - Meryl Streep, Goldie Hawn, Bruce Willis, Isabella Rossellini, Ian Ogilvy, Adam Storke, Sydney Pollack.

DEATHDREAM - (1972) (US)
D - Bob Clark
S - Richard Backus, Lynn Carlin, John Marley, Henderson Forsythe, Anya Ormsby, Jane Daly.

DEATH HOUSE - (1989) (US)
D - John Saxon
S - John Saxon, Michael Pataki, Dennis Cole, Ron O'Neal, Anthony Franciosa.

Riding on the coat-tails of a plethora of "prison" horror films released in the late 1980's comes *Death House*, about a group of prisoners who are injected with CIA-financed experimental drugs and turned into toxic zombies as a result. The film's director Saxon, is more familiar with the other side of the camera having starred in numerous horror's from *A Nightmare on Elm Street* (1985) to Dario Argento's *Tenebre* (1982), whose co-star, Franciosa, he is reunited with here.

DEATH WARMED UP - (1985) (NZ)
D - David Blyth
S - Michael Hurt, Margaret Umbers, William Upjohn, Norelle Scott, David Letch, Gary Day

DEMONS - (1986) (IT)
D - Lamberto Bava
S - Natasha Hovey, Urbano Barberini, Fiore Argento, Karl Zinny, Bobby Rhodes.

DEMONS 2 - (1987) (IT)
D - Lamberto Bava
S - David Knight, Asia Argento, Nancy Brilli, Bobby Rhodes.

Beginning where *Demons* left off, as the title creatures burst through into a party that is being held in a high rise block of flats, via a television screen. The random plotting and accompanying absurdities present in the original, still apply here but are similarly whisked away with the roller-coaster pace of the film. Once again, Sergio Stivaletti's gruesome special effects steal the show as numerous victims transmogrify into razor-toothed, snarling demons, only here, tearing down the corridors of the flats as opposed to the cinema aisles of the former film. Zombies burst asunder from victim's stomach's in true gut-churning fashion and the film is also graced with an excellent score, courtesy of The Cult and Simon Boswell to name just two.

DEMONS 3 - THE OGRE - (1988) (IT)
D - Lamberto Bava
S - Paolo Malco, Virginia Bryant, Sabrina Ferilli, Stefania Montorsi, Patrizio Vinci, Alice Di Giuseppe, Davide Flosi.

This, the third instalment in the *Demons* series features the most insipid climax of all. The cliched story of a horror writer trying to confront her own childhood fears - here embodied in the flesh by a living demon, is embalmed beneath the listless pacing of the film. The rampaging demon hordes of the earlier entries are lost here as the budget runs to only one demon.

The conclusion, as the demon perishes beneath the wheels of a car, is embarrassingly inept. It is even more disappointing when considering the potential talent that is on display here. Bava's ever tracking camera supplies a certain gothic flair as it glides through cobwebs and railings before prowling through the opulent interiors of the Arsoli Castle that dominates the luscious Italian mountain scenery, all ravishingly captured by Bava's lens. Numerous crane shots embellish the vapid script but too often Bava is guilty of robbing filmic graves; from the *A Nightmare on Elm Street* influenced dream sub-plot to the writer's subterranean nightmare as a tableau of corpses rise to frighten her, a direct steal from his father's scene in Dario Argento's *Inferno* (1980).

THE DEVILS CROSS - (1975) (SP)
D - John Gilling
S - Carmen Sevilla, Adolfo Marsillac, Emma Cohen, Fernando Sancho.

A welcome return to the zombie genre for Gilling who previously directed Hammer' *Plague of the Zombies* (1966) so effectively. Marsillac is a writer who delves into the old folk legends of Spain and eventually believes himself to be possessed by the Devil. Not even his love for Sevilla, his perfect woman, can save him as she is partly the cause of his problems. Gilling again relies on a dream sequence, this time showing a medieval sect as he had also done in his earlier zombie film. It's an extremely evocative piece considering that it was his first film since *The Mummy's Shroud* (1967), also for Hammer, and also the first he had made in Spain.

DIARY OF THE DEAD (2007) (US)
D – George A. Romero
S – Josh Close, Philip Riccio, Michelle Morgan, Shawn Roberts, Amy Lalonde, Joe Dinicol, Scott Wentworth, Tatiana Maslany

DISCIPLE OF DEATH - (1972) (UK)

Zombie Filmography

D - Tom Parkinson
S - Simon Raven, Marguerite Hardiman, Ronald Lacey, Virginia Wethrell, Nicholas Amer.

Utilising most of the cast from *Crucible of Terror* (1971), the film is set in 18th century Cornwall showing the resurrection of a stranger (Raven), who is a demon from Hell, by two lovers spilling blood on his grave. His continual search for a virgin who will sacrifice herself willingly and spend eternity with him leads to numerous gory killings as when Wethrell's heart is torn out from her spread-eagled body, the blood being wrung out into a conveniently placed cup. Wethrell herself is put to better use in Kubrick's *A Clockwork Orange* (1971). The music from none other than Bach, also seems glaringly out of place.

DR. BLOOD'S COFFIN - (1960) (UK)
D - Sydney J. Furie
S - Kieron Moore, Ian Hunter, Hazel Court, Kenneth J. Warren, Paul Stockman.

An incredibly crude shocker which like Furie's *Revenge* (1971) simply records gruesome butchery, only here, it is set against some picturesque Cornish locations. Moore stars as the synonymous doctor who, in his underground laboratory lair set amongst the old tin mines, practices experimental heart surgery on local villagers. He attempts to "win" Court's affections by resurrecting her now dead husband, which he does in a grisly climax, courtesy of some effective make-up from Les Bowie, to create the rotting cadaver.

Furie's own rather self-conscious direction is better employed in the Michael Caine spy vehicle *The Ipcress File* (1965) adapted from Len Deighton's Harry Palmer novel of the same name. Court was better served by Terence Fisher's *The Curse of Frankenstein* (1957) and Roger Corman's *The Masque of the Red Death* (1964).

DOCUMENT OF THE DEAD - (1978) (US)
D - Roy Frumkes
S - Various

Not so much a film as a documentary by Frumkes about Romero's much vaunted 1978 opus *Dawn of the Dead*. The documentary is presented as an intimate study of Romero both as a film maker and as a person, including hitherto unseen footage from behind the scenes on some of Romero's films. Almost as interesting is the documentary's own protracted release date. Amidst frantic searches for missing cans of film it was eventually premiered in America in 1981, but not released generally onto video until 1989 !

DOOMSDAY (2008) (UK/US/S.AFRICA)

D – Neil Marshall
S – Caryn Peterson, Adeola Ariyo, Emma Cleasby, Christine Tomlinson, Vernon Willemse, Rhona Mitra, Jeremy Crutchley

DRACULA VS FRANKENSTEIN - (EL HOMBRE QUE VINO DE UMMO- (1969) (SP,IT,GER)
D - Tulio Demichelli
S - Michael Rennie, Karen Dor, Craig Hill, Paul Naschy (Jacinto Molina), Paty Shephard.

Rennie plays Dr. Odo Warnoff, an alien from Ummo who is living in a Transylvanian castle where he plans to conquer the earth by unleashing the most fabled monsters on the world, including Dracula, Frankenstein, a werewolf and a mummy.

DRUMS OF THE JUNGLE - (1935) (US)
D - George Terwilliger
S - Fredi Washington, Sheldon Leonard, Philip Brandon, Marie Paxton, Winifred Harris.

Love does not conquer all in this potboiler which sees a voodoo priestess (Washington), fail to inveigle the white man she desires (Leonard). Hell indeed hath no fury like a woman scorned as she orders her zombie followers to kidnap Leonard's fiancee and offer her up to the gods as a voodoo sacrifice. Leonard manages to save her and there was also to be new life for the film as it was remade in 1939 as *Pocomania*, filmed in Jamaica like the original and featuring a script by that film's director Terwilliger.

DRUMS O'VOODOO - (1934) (US)
D - Arthur Hoerl
S - J. Angustus Smith, Laura Bowman, Gus Smith, Morris McKenny, Edna Barr, Lionel Monagas.

An obscure voodoo thriller based on an Augustus Smith play "Louisiana" and starring the original Broadway cast. The action revolves around a voodoo priestess who uses her special powers to control the local negro community and also a saloon bar owner who she sees as guilty of "corrupting" the natives inhabiting the swamp locale.

E

THE EARTH DIES SCREAMING - (1964) (UK)
D - Terence Fisher
S - Willard Parker, Virginia Field, Dennis Price, Thorley Walters, Vanda Godsell, David Spencer, Anna Falk.

EROTIC NIGHTS OF THE LIVING DEAD (LA NOTTE EROTICHE DEI MORTI VIVENTI) - (1979) (IT)
D - Aristide Massaccesi

The Dead Walk

S - Luigi Montefiore, Laura Gemser

Hiding under his favourite pseudonym of "Joe D'Amato", this is Massaccesi's unofficial remake of Lucio Fulci's *Zombie Flesh Eaters* (1979), only with soft-core porn accentuated rather than the horror. Massaccesi, a prolific film maker, also produced the glorious *Stagefright* (1987) with Monefiore supplying that films script. Gemser is a Massaccesi regular appearing in the likes of 1976's *Emanuelle and the Last Cannibals*, whereas Montefiore's moment of "fame" occurs during *Anthrophagus* (1980) as he munches his way through his own guts - a literally stomach-churning experience !

THE ETERNAL - (1999) (US)
D - Michael Almereyda
S - Christopher Walken, Alison Elliott, Jared Harris.

EVIL CLUTCH - (1988) (IT)
D - Andreas Marfori
S - Coralina C. Tassoni, Diego Ribon, Luciano Crovato, Elena Cantarone, Stefano Molinari.

This film almost plays as an *Evil Dead* homage with its roving camera lensing some diverse scenes - a young boy's sex organs being ripped away by a witch, and the French kiss between two young lovers that goes drastically wrong as the girl turns into a zombie. The climactic scenes, as the heroes defeat a very small zombie "army" are uninspired. Tassoni however, chose better by also appearing in both Argento's *Opera* (1988) and Lamberto Bava's *Demons 2* (1987).

THE EVIL DEAD - (1982) (US)
D - Sam Raimi
S - Bruce Campbell, Ellen Sandweiss, Betsy Baker, Hal Delrich, Sarah York.

EVIL DEAD 2 - (1987) (US)
D - Sam Raimi
S - Bruce Campbell, Sarah Berry, Dan Hicks, Kassie Wesley, Theodore Raimi, Denise Bixler.

EVIL UNLEASHED:THE MUMMY (2003) (US)
D – Joe Castro
S – Serena Morales, Heather Chase, Perrine Moore, Jelani Gibson, Brian Guest, Liisa Evastina

Four college students grappling with the age old problem of a lap dancing mummy/priestess whose pendulous cleavage is probably as much of a danger as the dagger she randomly wields, much as the plot randomly weaves...

EYES OF THE MUMMY (DIE AUGEN DER MUMIE) - (1918) (GER)
D - Ernst Lubitsch
S - Emil Jannings, Pola Negri, Max Laurence, Mararete Kupfer.

One of the first ever mummy films, this German silent is unique in one aspect at least - the lack of a mummy in it !

F

FACE OF MARBLE - (1946) (US)
D - William Beaudine
S - John Carradine, Claudia Drake, Robery Shayne, Maris Wrixon, Willie Best, Rosa Rey.

A typically cheap "quickie" from Monogram which has Carradine as a doctor (again)! - attempting to raise the dead. He only partially succeeds - by reviving a dog, but he cannot perfect the process on his wife (Drake) or a drowned sailor he experiments on. Besides these zombies, Rey also contributes as a voodoo-practising housekeeper. As one critic succinctly remarked; "Laughs are apt to come at periods where a tense moment was designed."

FACE OF THE SCREAMING WEREWOLF - (1959) (MEX)
D - Gilberto Martinez Solarz
S - Ann Taylor, Lon Chaney Jnr, Yerye Beirute, German Valdez.

Chaney Jnr dons the bandages again here as one of the mummies present, along with a growling Mexican mummy as Taylor is hypnotised and her subsequent regression reveals her to be hosting a Mayan ceremony in a pyramid. With a nonsensical "plot" and a running time of barely an hour, Solarz' film fails to deliver any original chills, save for the sequence where Chaney Jnr is trapped inside a wax museum and miraculously turns into the screaming lycanthrope of the title!

THE FACULTY (1998) (US)
D – Robert Rodriguez
S – Jordana Brewster, Clea DuVall, Laura Harris, Josh Hartnett, Salma Hayek, Famke Janssen, Piper Laurie, Robert Patrick, Bebe Neuwirth

An above average film which riffs almost exclusively on *Invasion of the Bodysnatchers* (1956) and *The Thing* (1982) - including lifting an entire scene from the latter as we try to discover who on the college campus setting, has been infected by the alien parasite which populates the film, but which lacks the suspense of its superior predecessors. That said, a willing cast give it more than it probably deserves by fleshing out their sterotypical characters

Zombie Filmography

somewhat. A pre *Lord of the Rings* Wood is the geeky student, DuVall the ugly duckling, Hartnett the rebel, Harris the newcomer and so it goes. Patrick is in fine form as the already infected coach, whilst Hayek, Janssen and Neuwirth, in particular, as Principal Drake, add considerable eye candy to a heady brew, only to be nullified by an overlong finale with a jarring parasitic apparition.

FARENHEIT 451 oC - (1966) (UK)
D - Francois Truffaut
S - Julie Christie, Oskar Werner, Cyril Cusack, Anton Diffring, Jeremy Spenser, Bee Duffell.

FEAR NO EVIL - (1981) (US)
D - Frank La Loggia
S - Stefan Arngrim, Elizabeth Hoffman, Kathleen Rowe McAllen, Frank Birney, Daniel Eden, Jack Holland.
A promising debut from La Loggia whose ingenious premise here has Andrew (Arngrim) as a student who also happens to be the Devil's incarnate, doing battle with two adversaries named Julie (McAllen) and an old woman (Hoffman), who are the angels Gabrielle and Mikhail - sent to earth to defeat the Devil. The dazzling, effects-laden conflict between them climaxes as Andrew unleashes his zombie acolytes onto the angels, the ghouls being culled from a community passion play (!). The film is graced with a new wave soundtrack and La Loggia has since gone on to direct the haunting *The Lady in White* (1988).

FIDO (2006) (CAN)
D – Andrew Currie
S – Billy Connolly, David Kaye, Lyn Pendleton, Henry Czerny, Aaron Brown

FIEND (1980) (US)
D – Don Dohler
S – Don Leifert, Richard Nelson, Elaine White, George Stover, Greg Dohler, Del Winans, Kim Dohler
Dohler, founder of the Cinemagic Magazine in the 1970's directs here as a erubescent energy forces falls from the sky to land in a graveyard and reanimate the dead, complete with their very own "Ready Brek" glow!

FLESHEATER - (1989) (US)
D - Bill Hinzman
S - None !
Talk about robbing your own grave ! Hinzman produced, directed and stars in this ferrago - his previous single claim to fame being as the first ghoul in Romero's seminal *Night of the Living Dead* (1968). This is nothing more than a formularised replay but without the panache as ravenous zombies decimate the obligatory tennage-fodder on Halloween night.

FLIGHT OF THE LIVING DEAD:OUTBREAK ON A PLANE (2007) (US)
D – Scott Thomas
S – David Chisum, Kristen Kerr, Kevin J O'Connor, Richard Tyson, Erick Avari, Todd Babcock, Siena Goines, Mieko Hillman
Perhaps with the title as the best thing going for it, Thomas' film is no where near the worst you'll ever see, but ultimately, is just plain average with the requisite "scares" and "chills", together with leaden attempts at humour. Yes, there are hot hostesses, a nun, a sports star, a mysterious container down in the hold, a mad doctor, newlyweds and a pilot on his last flight before retirement. There are some good effects once the action gets going but nothing you won't have seen before.

THE FOUR SKULLS OF JONATHAN DRAKE - (1959) (US)
D - Edward L. Cahn
S - Eduard Franz, Valerie French, Henry Daniell, Grant Richards, Paul Cavanagh, Paul Hexler.

FROM BEYOND (1986) (US)
D – Stuart Gordon
S – Jeffrey Combs, Barbara Crampton, Ken Foree, Ted Sorel, Carolyn Purdy-Gordon, Bunny Summers

FROZEN SCREAM (1975) (US)
D – Frank Roach
S – Renee Harmon, Lynne Kocol, Wolf Muser, Thomas Gowan, Wayne Liebman, Lee James, Sunny Bartholomew
A mad doctor (James), and his equally deranged assistant (Harmon) attempt to reverse the ageing process by experimenting on their continual stream of tied-up captives, obligingly supplied by sythe-wielding henchmen - I kid ye not!

G

GHOSTBREAKERS - (1940) (US)
D - George Marshall
S - Bob Hope, Paulette Goddard, Richard Carlson, Paul Lukas, Willie Best, Anthony Quinn, Noble Johnson.

GHOSTS OF MARS (2001) (US)
D – John Carpenter
S – Natasha Henstridge, Ice Cube, Jason Statham, Clea

The Dead Walk

DuVall, Pam Grier, Joanna Cassidy, Richard Cetrone

GHOST TOWN - (1988) (US)
D - Richard Governor
S - Jimmie F. Skaggs, Franc Luz, Catherine Hickland,
An example of that rare hybrid - the zombie western ! Even stranger is the fact that the film is from the Empire Pictures stable, but directed by an Australian (Governor), who also lends the picture a strong, visual gothic flair, not qualities immediately associated with Empire! Skaggs stars as a zombie gun fighter who eventually battles it out with the *Ghost Town* sheriff, Luz. It's a film refreshingly free of gore for gore's sake, that still encompasses some authentic frissons such as the zombie gunslinger who bursts through the arid earth from his desert grave.

GORE-MET - ZOMBIE CHEF FROM HELL - (1986) (US)
D - Don Swan
S - Theo Dupuay, Kelley Kunicki, C. W. Casey, Alan Marx, Michael O'Neill, Jeff Pillars, Jeff Baughn.
Full marks for the title, but that's about the only thing "cooking" here as the creative juices have been boiled dry. The demonic chef of the title is Goza, who has been reincarnated from a dead philosopher, banished in the 14th century to forever roam the earth. Now he is the owner of "Goza's Beach Club & Deli". The special ingredient needed to sustain his immortality is blood, which is provided in abundance by his unwitting diners. Besides puzzling at where all these new diners to the slaughter come from, viewers can also marvel at the non-too-special "special effects" (all off camera !), the background music (so loud it's in the foreground), and the appearance of Chris Martel, who starred in *The Gruesome Twosome* (1966). As the ad' lines have it; "Dining out can be a permanent experience!"

GRAVEYARD DISTURBANCE - (1987) (IT)
D - Lamberto Bava
S - Gregory Lech Thaddeus, Lino Salenne, Lea Martino, Beatrice Ring, Karl Zinny.
A lamentable effort featuring a group of teenagers who, after some petty shoplifting, discover a tavern where they are challenged by the weird bartender to spend the night in the ancient crypt below and so win copious amounts of treasure. Once underground, endless shots of the labyrinth corridors are repeated, as rotting zombies emerge from every crevice. The solitary scene of any note occurs as the group gatecrash a ghoul's feast. The most horrific aspect of the film is that its director, Bava, has sunk to such low depths after his previous works such as *A Blade in the Dark* (1983) and *Demons* (1986).

H

HAUSER'S MEMORY - (1970) (US)
D - Boris Sagal
S - David McCallum, Susan Strasberg, Lili Palmer, Leslie Neilsen, Helmut Kautner, Herbert Fleishmann

HARD ROCK ZOMBIES - (1984) (US)
D - Krishna Shah
S - E.J. Curcio, Geno, Sam Mann, Mick McMains.
Much touted but little seen offering merging heavy metal music with the zombie genre. The natural affinity between the two has been reinforced with other additions such as *Trick or Treat* (1986) and *Black Roses* (1987).

HELLGATE - (1989) (US)
D - William A. Levey
S - Ron Palillo, Abigail Wolcott, Carel Trichardt, Pedtrea Curran, Evan Klisser.
A woeful effort that never aspires to transcend its' tired storyline and painfully inept acting. The gang murder of a young woman Josie (Wolcott) devastates the mining town of the title. The victim's grieving father, Lucas (Trichardt) then discovers a magical crystal that can raise the dead - which he duly uses to maximum effect. A group of travellers are caught up in the ensuing melee as, in the film's only worthwhile scenes, an army of zombies pour out of every conceivable hiding place in the town. Even with the reasonable special effects on show here *Hellgate* is not another *Hellraiser* (1987), despite New World's attempts to market it as such, even down to the film's glaringly similar title.

HELLRAISER - (1987) (UK,US)
D - Clive Barker
S - Andrew Robinson, Clare Higgins, Sean Chapman, Ashley Laurence, Oliver Smith.

HELLRAISER 2 - HELLBOUND - (1988) (US)
D - Tony Randel
S - Ashley Laurence, Kenneth Cranham, Imogen Boorman, Sean Chapman, Oliver Smith, Clare Higgins.
Immensely disappointing sequel to *Hellraiser* (1987), substituting the original's highly-charged emotional subtext with random chase scenes that take place in an all too studio-bound vision of Hell. Cranham (of "Shine on Harvey Moon" TV fame), is excellent as the misguided Dr. Channard, and the scene where he resurrects Julia's corpse from a blood-stained mattress is one of the film's better moments. Impressive too are the whirlwind history

of Pinhead's creation and the first appearance of the Cenobites - entering from all four corners of a room, Pinhead bathed in a shimmering light, a virtual horror icon. Unfortunately, these moments are all too brief set amidst a backdrop of self-conscious direction, pedantic pacing and lack of genuine frissons, for which Randel must shoulder the blame. A missed opportunity.

HELLRAISER 3 - HELL ON EARTH - (1992) (US)
D - Anthony Hickox
S - Doug Bradley, Ashley Laurence, Terry Farrell.
Much like Wes Craven's runaway baby, the *A Nightmare on Elm Street* series, creator Clive Barker has negligible involvement here as his incomparable Cenobites are let loose again - this time in downtown Los Angeles and under the directorial reins of Anthony Hickox. The blood and humour of his earlier *Waxworks* (1989) and *Sundown - The Vampire in Retreat* (1990) are jettisoned here as Pinhead (Bradley) reprises his role of chief cenobite and torturer - this time engaged in some severe "soul-tearing" with the decorative Farrell's prying news journalist.

HELLRAISER BLOODLINE - (1996) (US)
D - "Alan Smithee" (Kevin Yagher)
S - Bruce Ramsay, Valentina Vargas, Doug Bradley, Kim Myers, Charlotte Chatton, Mickey Cottrell.
It is year 2127 as Yagher's spin on the *Hellraiser* series attempts to cross three generations as we find Pinhead on board a space station in outer space, run by a scientist Dr. Merchant. The good doctor attempts to close the gates to hell forever as his ancestor - an 18th century toy maker, built the evil puzzlebox which opens the gates. All efforts at fusing the past, the present and the future fail totally due to the lack of cohesion present, although the period scenes which detail the Cenobites genesis carry a certain appeal. Yagher's vision of creating both prequel and sequel is ultimately undone by studio interference, hence the use of the dreaded pseudonym, Smithee, Hollywood's own kiss of death.

HELLRAISER:INFERNO (2000) (US)
D – Scott Derrickson
S – Craig Sheffer, Nicholas Turturro, James Remar, Doug Bradley, Nicholas Sadler, Noelle Evans, Lindsay Taylor
With Sheffer as a hard-boiled, unlikeable lead and Pinhead only contributing two brief appearances to book end the film (and justify the title), this is could have been a serviceable film as a supernatural detective yarn, but fails miserably with the seemingly tacked on *Hellraiser* "connection".

HELLRAISER:HELLSEEKER (2002) (US)
D – Rick Bota
S – Dean Winters, Ashley Laurence, Doug Bradley, Rachel Hayward, Sarah-Jayne Redmond, Jody Thompson, Kaaren de Zilva, William S. Taylor
The sixth entry in the series reunites Bradley's Pinhead with old adversary Kirsty (Laurence), albeit in mainly flashback mode, but singularly fails to rediscover the flair or frissons present in the original.

HELLRAISER:DEADER (2005) (US/ROM)
D – Rick Bota
S – Kari Wuhrer, Paul Rhys, Simon Kunz, Marc Warren, Georgina Rylance, Doug Bradley, Ionut Chermenski
Wuhrer is the headstrong reporter who picks up the magical box to unleash the Cenobites, intertwined with a snuff tape story and with Pinhead's obligatory role here reduced merely to a cameo.

HELLRAISER:HELLWORLD (2005) (US)
D – Rick Bota
S – Stelian Urian, Katheryn Winnick, Anna Tolputt, Khary Payton, Henry Cavill, Christopher Jacot, Lance Henriksen, Doug Bradley, Magdalena Tun
A group of friends browse the "Hellworld" web site and are able to explore a computerised version of the Lament Configuration box in a token effort at updating what is now the fourth direct to video/disc instalment in the series.

HORROR EXPRESS - (PANICO EN EL TRANSIBERIANO) - (1972) (SP, UK)
D - Eugenio Martin
S - Christopher Lee, Peter Cushing, Telly Savalas, Silvia Tortosa, Jorge Rigaud, Albert de Mendoza.

HORROR OF THE ZOMBIES - (EL BUQUE MALDITO) - (1974) (SP)
D - Amando de Ossorio
S - Maria Perschy, Jack Taylor, Carlos Lemos, Blanca Estrada, Barbara Rey, Margarita Merino.

HORROR RISES FROM THE TOMB (EL ESPANTO SURGE DE LA TUMBA) - (1972) (SP)
D - Carlos Aured
S - Jacinto Molina, Emmas Cohen, Victor Alcazar, Helga Line, Betsabe Ruiz, Maria Jose Cantudo, Christina Suriani, Luis Ciges.
A rather convoluted tale beginning with the grisly demise of a knight (Molina) who is decapitated whilst his wife "splits" literally. The appearance of four descendants at

their ancestral home acts as the catalyst for the knight to revive - all in one piece this time, along with his wife (Suriani) and wreak havoc amongst the rest of the cast. We are then "treated" to numerous decapitations, zombies filing out of a watery grave and a particularly gruesome moment where Suriani tears the skin off her lover's back. A skin-full indeed!

HOUSE - (1986) (US)
D - Steve Miner
S - William Katt, Mary Stavin, George Wendt, Kay Lenz
A patchy horror comedy that has a writer (Katt) suffering from a mental block in his work and other personal problems such as his ex-wife's comparative success as a TV soap star and his son's mysterious disappearance. He is also plagued by memories of his past war service in Vietnam. His attempts to remedy these problems are hampered when he moves to his aunt's house (she has just committed suicide there), as soon he is being chased by flying objects, bodies that will not lie down and a particularly ferocious fish that adorns one wall.

The film's only moments of inspiration are supplied in the episodes Katt has with a decaying Vietnam zombie who inhabits a parallel world to the writer's, that can be accessed through the house. In the end we are left to watch the antics of ex-Miss World (Stavin) and "Cheers" TV show star (Wendt) and rue the mediocrity of the whole debacle, remembering from one of producer Cunningham's other films (*The Last House on the Left*) that; "It's only a movie... it's only a movie...".

HOUSE 2 - THE SECOND STOREY - (1987) (US)
D - Ethan Wiley
S - Jonathan Stark, Ayre Gross, Royal Dano
This lame sequel plays down the attempted horror of the first film in favour of attempted humour. The idea that the house is an opening into different dimensions is expanded on as doors open to reveal steaming prehistoric jungles, wild west towns and ancient Egyptian settings. The action is set in motion when two friends (Stark and Gross) dig up their 970 year old grandpa (Dano) in order to obtain the translucent blue skull that is buried with him and is rumoured to contain special powers. As he bursts into life, the remainder of the film deals with various people's efforts to capture the skull as Stark and Gross repeatedly win it back. The good moments are even more infrequently visible than in the original film - a common failing with the third entry in the series which followed.

THE HOUSE BY THE CEMETERY - (QUELLA VILLA ACCANTO AL CIMITERO) - (1981) (IT)
D - Lucio Fulci
S - Catriona MacColl, Giovanni de Nava, Dagmar Lassander, Anja Pieroni, Daniele Doria, Carlo de Mejo, Giovanni Frezza, Silvia Collatina.

HOUSE OF THE DEAD (2003) (US)
D – Uwe Boll
S – Jonathan Cherry, Tyron Leitso, Clint Howard, Ona Grauer, Ellie Cornell, Will Sanderson, Enuka Okuma, Kira Clavell, Sonya Salomaa, Jurgen Prochnow.

HOUSE OF THE DEAD 2 (2005) (US)
D – Michael Hurst
S – Emmanuelle Vaugier, Ed Quinn, Sticky Fingaz, Steve Monroe, Victoria Pratt, Dan Southworth, Billy Brown, Nadine Elazquel, Ellie Cornell, Sid Haig

I

I AM LEGEND (2007) (US)
D – Francis Lawrence
S – Will Smith, Alice Braga, Charlie Tawan, Salli Richardson, Willow Smith

THE INCREDIBLY STRANGE CREATURES (WHO STOPPED LIVING AND BECAME CRAZY MIXED-UP ZOMBIES) - (1964) (US)
D - Ray Dennis Steckler
S - Cash Flagg, Brett O'Hara, Carolyn Brandt, Sharon Walsh, Atlas King.
Besides containing the longest horror film title ever, this is also the "first monster musical", featuring song and dance numbers such as "The Mixed Up Zombie Stomp", which are the results of the combined efforts of three choreographers hired to promote the film and secure finance for its' meagre $20,000 budget.

The zany plot has a gypsy fortune teller hypnotising patrons at an amusement park, disfiguring them with acid before imprisoning them as circus freaks in cages. Director Steckler stars in the film with his wife (Brandt), having previously made title such as *The Thrill Killers* (1964) and *The Lemon Grove Kids Meet The Monsters* (1966). He exhibits the same showmanship qualities as William Castle and even had to change the title of this film to avoid confusion (!) with Stanley Kubrick's similarly subtitled Dr. Strangelove which was released in the same year.

The professional crew who worked on Steckler's film included cameraman Lazlo Kovak's who also shot *A Reflection of Fear* (1971) amongst others and Vilmos Zsigmond who photographed *Close Encounters of the Third Kind* (1977).

Zombie Filmography

I EAT YOUR SKIN - (1964) (US)
D - Del Tenney
S - William Joyce, Heather Hewitt, Walter Coy, Robert Stanton, Betty Hyatt Linton.
Originally an unseen black and white feature *I Eat Your Skin* was later released on a double-bill by producer Jerry Gross with *I Drink Your Blood* (1971). Tenney, who made the infamous *Horror of Party Beach* in the same year fares only marginally better here as Dr. Biladeau (Stanton) experiments with a serum derived from the plant life on his tropical island to cure cancer. The unfortunate side-effects produce zombies whom the island's plantation owner (Coy) plans to use to conquer the world, in similar vein to your archetypal James Bond villain, though here on a fraction of the budget. The film's title is itself luridly misleading as no cannibalistic urges are encouraged.

THE INVASION (2007) (US/AUS)
D – Oliver Hirschbiegel, James McTeigue (uncredited)
S – Nicole Kidman, Daniel Craig, Jeremy Northam, Jackson Bond, Jeffrey Wright, Veronica Cartwright

INVASION OF THE BODYSNATCHERS - (1956) (US)
D - Don Siegel
S - Kevin McCarthy, Dana Wynter, King Donovan, Carolyn Jones, Larry Gates, Jean Willes, Whit Bissell.

INVASION OF THE BODYSNATCHERS - (1978) (US)
D - Philip Kaufman
S - Donald Sutherland, Brooke Adams, Leonard Nimoy, Veronica Cartwright, Jeff Goldblum, Art Hindle, Kevin McCarthy.

INVASION OF THE ZOMBIES - (1961) (MEX)
D - Benito Alzaki
S - Santo.
Santo, an incredible Mexican phenomenon, is the silver-masked wrestling hero who has appeared in over forty films to date. This time out he has to defeat an army of zombies that have been unleashed by a mad scientist planning to conquer the world with them.

INVISIBLE INVADERS - (1959) (US)
D - Edward L. Cahn
S - John Agar, Jean Byron, Robert Hutton, John Carradine, Paul Langton, Eden Hartford.

ISLE OF THE DEAD - (1945) (US)
D - Mark Robson
S - Boris Karloff, Ellen Drew, Marc Cramer, Katherine Emery, Helene Thimig, Alan Napier, Jason Robards.

IT CAME FROM OUTER SPACE - (1953) (US)
D - Jack Arnold
S - Richard Carlson, Barbara Rush, Charles Drake, Russell Johnson, Joseph Sawyer, Alan Dexter.

I WALKED WITH A ZOMBIE - (1943) (US)
D - Jacques Tourneur
S - Francis Dee, Tom Conway, James Ellison, Christine Gordon, Edith Barrett, Sir Lancelot, Darby Jones.

I ZOMBIE - CHRONICLES OF PAIN - (1998) (UK)
D - Andrew Parkinson
S - Ellen Softley, Giles Aspen, Dean Siplin
A young man gets infected during a field trip and gradually begins to transform into a zombie. With his girlfriend leaving him and by moving into his own place, Parkinson attempts with partial success to portray the alienation the zombified Mark (Aspen) feels and sense of moral degeneration he feels in having to kill people and devour their flesh to feed his illness.

J

J'ACCUSE - (1937) (FR)
D - Abel Gance
S - World War 2 Veterans.

JASON AND THE ARGONAUTS (1963) (UK/US)
D – Don Chaffey
S – Todd Armstrong, Nancy Kovack, Gary Redmond, Laurence Naismith, Niall MacGinnis, Michael Gwynn, Douglas Wilmer, Jack Gwillim, Honor Blackman, Patrick Troughton, Nigel Green

JUNK:SHIRYO-GARI (2000) (JAP)
D – Atsushi Muroga
S – Nobuyuki Asano, Shu Ehara, Tate Gouta, Yuji Kishimoto, Miwa, Natsuki Ozawa, Kaori Shimamura

K

THE KILLING BOX (1993) (US)
D – George Hickenlooper
S – Corbin Bernsen, Adam Pasdar, Ray Wise, Cynda Williams, Roger Wilson, Jefferson Mays, Billy Bob Thornton, Martin Sheen, David Arquette
An intriguing curio set in the American Civil War with Pasdar as a Union soldier investigating a series of crucifixions by a renegade band of Confederate soldiers. Bernsen, is enlisted from his prison "home" to apprehend

the criminals, only to find that they are his former charges - deceased, but now very much alive, thanks to an African curse which has revived them.

KING OF THE ZOMBIES - (1941) (US)
D - Jean Yarbrough
S - Dick Purcell, Joan Woodbury, Henry Victor, Mantan Moreland, John Archer.

The caped figure of Victor (the strongman in *Freaks* - 1932) creates an army of black zombies on a remote island for other foreign powers to use. Comic relief here is provided by Moreland's petrified black servant.

KISS ME QUICK - (1964) (US)
D - Bethel Buckalew
S - Max Gardens, Frank A. Coe, Natasha. Bibi

Also known as *Emmanuelle Meets Frankenstein* and with a title in *Kiss Me Quick* which apes Billy Wilder's *Kiss Me, Stupid* released during the same year. As you will gather, humour is a strong element here as Coe portrays a camp alien, Sterilox who visits the castle of the mad Dr. Breedlove (!) in order to find women for his planet. As well as finding Frankenstein and Dracula, he also discovers a weird female mummy as well as a whole host of nubile women the camera instantly pursues as they sing, dance, strip and frolic unfettered!

L

LAND OF THE DEAD (2005) (US)
D – George A. Romero
S – Simon Baker, John Leguizamo, Dennis Hopper, Asia Argento, Robert Joy, Eugene Clark, Shawn Roberts

THE LAST MAN ON EARTH - (L'ULTIMO UOMO DELLA TERRA) - (1964)(IT, US)
D - Sidney Salkow and Ubalda Ragona
S - Vincent Price, Emma Danieli, Franca Bettoia.

The first film version of Richard Matheson's novel "I Am Legend" loses much of its' source's chilling atmosphere when translated onto screen. The emphasis switches to repetitive scenes of violence as Price, the sole human survivor from a world wide plague, battles against the vampire mutations the disease has created. The film's attempt at infusing a science fiction angle to the theme flounders as Price is shown collecting garlic and sharpening stakes, regalia more closely aligned to the requirements of traditional gothic horror than any futuristic fantasies.

The denouement sees the film's one saving grace as Price himself is considered the "vampire" by the mutants. Price's oddly restrained performance shows how much better suited he is to the period costume horror as in *Witchfinder General* (1968) which found him at his most impressive in his chilling portrayal of the real life witchfinder Matthew Hopkins.

LAST RITES AKA 48 WEEKS LATER (2006) (US)
D – Duane Stinnett
S – Enrique Almeida, Howard Alonzo, Reggie Bannister, Stephen Basilone, James C. Burns

Gang warfare between black and Latino gangs is the unlikely setting for this zombie pic, as their petty rivalries are interrupted by the old meteorite crashing routine causing a zombie outbreak in Los Angeles - from the City of Angels to the City of Angst indeed.

THE LAUGHING DEAD - (1989) (US)
D - Somtow Sucharitkul
S - Somtow Sucharitkul, Gregory Frost, Time Sullivan, Wendy Webb, Ed Bryant.

We have all seen literary excursions into the film world before - such as the already established novel adapted to the cinema screen, but not a film almost exclusively starring authors as opposed to actors. *The Laughing Dead* was written, co-produced, directed, scored and even stars science fiction/fantasy author Sucharitkul. his rampaging story concerns a party of amateur archaeologists, including more members of the literary alumni, who, fascinated by Mayan and Aztec rituals, are intent on observing the "Dea de los Muertos" (the Mexican Festival of the Dead).

The equilibrium is shattered when a young boy is kidnapped and the group must then descend into the bowels of the earth and do battle with the incumbent zombies to decide the fate of all mankind. This almost Lovecraftian scenario is punctuated with bouts of gory activity as one girl rips out her own heart and buries it in a priest's chest, whilst another scene has a victim lose his own arm - only for it to be then stuffed down his throat, whereupon the still-twitching fingers burrow out of his neck. Not for the squeamish !

LEGEND OF THE MUMMY - (1997) (US)
D - Jeffrey Obrow
S - Louis Gossett Jnr, Amy Locane, Eric Lutes, Mark

No "Jewel With Seven Stars" here, merely a mummy with seven fingers and the likely cause of a series of mysterious deaths, leaving Margaret (Locane), the daughter of an Egyptologist, to solve the murders. Aside from being one of the few female mummy films and attmpting to recreate some of the period atmosphere of a Hammer film, Obrow's work remains strictly "low brow" as opposed to "high brow".

Zombie Filmography

THE LEGEND OF THE 7 GOLDEN VAMPIRES - (1973) (UK, HK)
D - Roy Ward Baker
S - Peter Cushing, David Chiang, Julie Edge, Shih Szu, Robin Stewart, Robert Hanna, John Forbes-Robertson.

LIFEFORCE - (1985) (US)
D - Tobe Hooper
S - Steve Railsback, Peter Firth, Frank Finlay, Mathilda May, Nicholas Ball.

LIVE AND LET DIE - (1973) (UK)
D - Guy Hamilton
S - Roger Moore, Yaphet Kotto, Jane Seymour, Clifton James, Geoffrey Holder.

LIVING A ZOMBIE DREAM - (1996) (US)
D - Todd Reynolds
S - Amon Elsey, Michelle White, Mike Smith, Frank Alexander.
A shoestring indie feature from Reynolds which sees sibling rivalry rear its ugly head as two brothers fight over one girlfriend, leading to some rough justice and a spot of zombification - "..it's gonna get messy, real messy" as the tagline so rightly states.

THE LIVING DEAD GIRL - (LA MORTE VIVANTE) - (1982) (FR)
D - Jean Rollin
S - Marina Pierro, Francoise Blanchard, Mike Marshall, Carina Barone, Fanny Magier, Dominique Treillou.

THE LIVING DEAD AT THE MANCHESTER MORGUE - (NO PROFANAR EL SUENO DE LOS MUERTOS) - (1974) (SP, IT)
D - Jorge Grau
S - Ray Lovelock, Christina Galbo, Arthur Kennedy, Aldo Massaso, Giorgio Trestini, Roberto Posse, Jeanine Mestre.

THE LIVING GHOST - (1942) (US)
D - William Beaudine
S - James Dunn, Joan Woodbury, Minerva Urecal.
An attempted horror/comedy from Monogram which ends up as neither, concerning a man who is transmogrified into a zombie killer.

LONDON VOODOO - (2004) (UK)
D - Robert Pratten
S - Doug Cockle, Sara Stewart, Michael Nyqvist
American yuppies Cockle and Stewart move into an expansive London home with their baby daughter. The discovery of skeletons beneath the floorboards, (makes a change from closets perhaps!) and Stewart's possession by an African priestess transforms her beyond recognition, in a well shot effort.

M

THE MAD GHOUL - (1943) (US)
D - James P. Hogan
S - George Zucco, Evelyn Ankers, David Bruce
One of the better "B" pictures to emerge from the period, featuring the prolific Zucco - his other credits include *The Mummy's Hand* (1940) and *House of Frankenstein* (1945), as an evil professor who has rediscovered a gas used by the ancient Egyptians as an elixir of life. Anyone exposed to it becomes a zombie, a fate that befalls Bruce who loves the same girl, Ankers, as Zucco. Eventually Zucco himself is shot whilst attempting to procure a heart from an undertaker's coffin (he needs a heart transplant to stay alive). Ankers, who plays a singer in the film is herself no stranger to the horror genre as her appearance in *The Wolf Man* (1941) will testify.

THE MANCHURIAN CANDIDATE - (1962) (US)
D - John Frankenheimer
S - Frank Sinatra, Janet Leigh, Angela Lansbury, Henry Silva, Whit Bissell.
A political "hot potato" that has only recently resurfaced after years without being seen. The contentious plot has Communists brainwashing a loyal American and turning him into a zombie assassin who will murder on suggestion. Truth proved stranger than fiction with later events leading up to President J. F. Kennedy's assassination. An all-star cast includes Sinatra, Leigh from *Psycho* (1960), and Bissell, *I Was A Teenage Werewolf* (1957). Frankenheimer also directed *Seconds* (1966), another film full of claustrophobic tension and paranoia but appears to be losing his touch of late given his inneffectual handling of Richard Stanley's *The Island of Dr. Moreau* (1996).

MONSTROSITY - (1964) (US)
D - Joseph Mascelli
S - Frank Gerstle, Judy Bamber, Erika Peters, Marjorie Eaton.
Directed by the cinematographer of *Incredibly Strange Creatures* (1964), this has an old woman dreaming of immortality by having her brain transplanted into a beautiful European girl's body. The impromptu operation, performed by a bogus surgeon, fails and leaves the the girl and later victims as zombies. One unfortunate even has a cat's brain implanted into her head ! The film's

The Dead Walk

electrical effects were handled by Ken Strickfaden who also provided the elaborate laboratory pyrotechnics for *Frankenstein* (1931).

MORBUS - (1982) (SP)
D - Ignasi P. Ferre Serra
S - Joan Borras, Carla Day, Mon Ferrer, Victor Israel, Montse Calvo, Irene Rives.
Soft-core sex and eye popping gore mix as a scientist develops a serum to raise the dead. The predictable results involve the flesh-eating zombies attacking prostitutes and their clients in a forest. In this particular case, the warning "don't go into the woods" proves to be prophetic.

THE MUMMY - (1912) (UK)
D - A.E.Coleby
S - ?
An early silent.

THE MUMMY - (1932) (US)
D - Karl Freund
S - Boris Karloff, Zita Johann, David Manners, Arthur Byron, Edward Van Sloan, Bramwell Fletcher

THE MUMMY - (1959) (UK)
D - Terence Fisher
S - Christopher Lee, Peter Cushing, Yvonne Furneaux, Eddie Byrne, Felix Aylmer, George Pastell, Raymond Huntley.

THE MUMMY - (1999) (US)
D - Stephen Sommers
S - Brendan Fraser, Rachel Weisz, John Hannah, Arnold Vosloo, Jonathan Hyde, Kevin J. O'Connor.

THE MUMMY AND THE CURSE OF THE JACKAL - (1969) (US)
D - Oliver Drake
S - Anthony Eisley, John Carradine.
An obscure oddity which never received a full theatrical release, has Eisley starring as David, a theorist who talks about Atlantis and other mysteries in the hope he will become famous. He insists on being locked in a house overnight with the body of an ancient princess and transforms into a cartoon-like werewolf with three big claws on each hand. Into this chaos enters the rather rotund, glaring mummy, who fights the titular jackal on the streets of Las Vegas (!) and whose victims include a stripper and a belly dancer, whilst horror icon Carradine turns up as a professor who spends countless screen time attempting to explain things - no doubt he gave up when it came to making sense of the plot !

THE MUMMY:TOMB OF THE DRAGON EMPEROR (2008) (GER/CAN/USA)
D – Rob Cohen
S – Brendan Fraser, Jet Li, Maria Bello, John Hannah, Luke Ford, Liam Cunningham, Albert Kwan, Isabella Long, Michael Yeoh

MUMMY'S BOYS - (1936) (US)
D - Fred Guiol
S - Bert Wheeler, Robert Woolsey, Barbara Pepper, Moroni Olsen.
An awful attempt to parody *The Mummy* (1932) with Wheeler and Woolsey on a mission (unusually in such films), to return treasure to the tomb of Pharaoh Maitime - avoid as if one of the fabled Egyptian plagues !

THE MUMMY'S CURSE - (1944) (US)
D - Leslie Goodwins
S - Lon Chaney Jnr, Peter Coe, Virginia Christine, Kay Harding, Martin Kosleck, Kurt Katch.

THE MUMMY'S GHOST - (1944) (US
D - Reginald Leborg
S - John Carradine, Lon Chaney Jnr, Ramsay Ames, Robert Lowery, Barton Maclane, George Zucco.

THE MUMMY'S HAND - (1940) (US)
D - Christy Cabanne
S - Dick Foran, Peggy Moran, Wallace Ford, Eduardo Cianelli, George Zucco, Tom Tyler.

THE MUMMY LIVES - (1993) (US)
D - Gerry O'Hara
S - Tony Curtis, Leslie Hardy, Greg Wrangler, Jack Cohen, Mohammed Bakri, Mosko Alkalai
"Bound by destiny. Consumed by sin. His vengeance is eternal" the tagline trumpets for this entry.

THE MUMMY'S KISS (2003) (US)
D – Donald F. Glut
S – Mia Zottoli, Sasha Peralto, George Thomas, Aysia Lee, Richard Lynch, Arthur Roberts, Katie Lohmann, Regina Russell
Not arousing enough to be a soft core epic, nor horrific enough to be an effective genre film, Glut's entry sees a beautiful mummy awoken from its sacrophagus in a University campus.

THE MUMMY'S KISS:2nd DYNASTY (2006) (US)

Zombie Filmography

D – Donald F. Glut
S – Mark Bedell, Stacy Berk, Tony Clay, Belinda Gavin, Paul Guay, Joan Marlowe, Jonas Neal
Soft core sequel to *The Mummy's Kiss* and equally void of the intended eroticism - the movie certainly sucks but not in the way intended!

THE MUMMY RETURNS (2001) (US)
D – Stephen Sommers
S – Brendan Fraser, Rachel Weisz, John Hannah, Arnold Vosloo, Oded Fehr, Dwayne Johnson, Patricia Velasquez, Alun Armstrong

THE MUMMY'S SHROUD - (1967) (UK)
D - John Gilling
S - John Phillips, Andre Morell, David Buck, Elisabeth Sellars, Maggie Kimberley, Michael Ripper, Dickie Owen, Catherine Lacey, Eddie Powell.

THE MUMMY'S TOMB - (1942) (US)
D - Harold Young
S - Lon Chaney Jnr, Dick Foran, Elyse Knox, John Hubbard, Turhan Bey, Wallace Ford, George Zucco.

THE MUMMY'S VENGEANCE - (LA VENGANZA DE LA MOMIA) - (1973) (SP)
D - Carlos Aured
S - Paul Naschy (Jacinto Molina), Jack Taylor, Maria Silva, Helga Line, Eduardo Calvo.
Aured's feature begins in ancient Egypt as the sadistic Pharaoh Amen-Ho-Tep (Molina) and his vivacious queen (Line) slash the throats of young women in order to drink their blood. Having been mummified alive as punishment for such crimes, an English Egyptologist (Taylor) and a mysterious Arab, Bey (Molina again) disturb their tombs and revive the Pharaoh. There then follows a litany of gratuitous gore scenes as the bloodthirsty mummy simply stalks victim after victim as heads are smashed and throats cut before the mummy's final flame-filled demise.

N

NEITHER THE SEA NOR THE SAND - (1972) (UK)
D - Fred Burnley
S - Susan Hampshire, Frank Finlay, Michael Petrovitch, Jack Lambert.
A rather unsavoury mix of love and necrophilia from the novel by former British newscaster Gordon Honeycombe. It has Hampshire and Petrovitch as the protagonists in an affair during a holiday in Jersey. He dies from a heart attack and his brother (Finlay) holds Hampshire responsible. He himself is then killed in a car crash leaving the two lovers (Petrovitch is still alive as far as Hampshire is concerned), to wade into the sea at the conclusion. This image may faintly recall *I Walked With A Zombie* (1943) but there is very little else to commend this overblown, melodramatic shocker.

NIGHTMARE WEEKEND - (1985) (US, UK, FR)
D - Henry Sala
S - Preston Maybank, Wellington Meffert, Kim Dossibn, Andrea Thompson, Kimberly Stahl.
A weekend holiday in a country house turns to horror as three girls are experimented on and turned into zombies by a scientist and his evil acolytes.

NIGHT OF THE COMET - (1984) (US)
D - Thom Eberhardt
S - Catherine Mary Stewart, Kelly Maroni, Geoffrey Lewis, Mary Woronov, Sharon Farrell, Robert Beltran.

NIGHT OF THE CREEPS - (1986) (US)
D - Fred Dekker
S - Jason Lively, Steve Marshall, Jill Whitlow, Tom Atkins, Dick Miller.

NIGHT OF THE DEMONS - (1988) (US)
D - Kevin G. Tenney
S - Linnea Quigley, William Gallo, Hal Hayins, Cathy Podewell.
A non too original "frightener" that has a group of teenagers holding a Halloween party in a derilict funeral parlour - a certain recipe for disaster, which is what strikes via the evil spirits that inhabit the place and infect the revellers. The film piles cliche upon cliche as the group split up and search the labyrinth corridors, eventually turning into demons themselves. Only some visceral special effects enliven this rather lame *Demons* (1986) retread, along with some good music ("Stigmata Martyr" from Bauhaus) and an eye-catching performance from Quigley, the like of which can also be glimpsed in *The Return of the Living Dead* (1985).

NIGHT OF THE DEMONS 2 (1994) (US)
D - Brian Trenchard Smith
S - Cristi Harris, Darin Heames, Bobby Jacoby, Merle Kennedy, Amelia Kinkade, Christine Taylor, Rod McCary.
This sequel sees the return of Angela (Kinkade) as her sister Mouse (Kennedy) is taken to a party at Hull House once again, by her bullying school friends and before long, everyone is once more transformed into snarling demons. Amongst the ensuing chaos are some brief standout

The Dead Walk

moments such as the demon who plays basketball using a head and an ass-kicking ninja nun (!), whilst much of the party music is suitably provided by Morbid Angel. Also includes an appearance by *Brady Bunch* movie star Taylor.

NIGHT OF THE DEMONS 3 - (1997) (US)
D - Jim Kaufman
S - Larry May, Amelia Kinkade, Kris Holdenried, Gregory Calpakis, Tara Slone, Christian Tessier.
Absolutely dire retread to (hopefully) conclude this particular series which once again has Kinkade reprising her role as the demonic Angela and performing her requisite mayhem on Halloween night as a group of kids seek shelter in Hull House, but only succeed in summoning up Angela as the gore begins. Released as *Demon House* in the UK.

NIGHT OF THE GHOULS - (1959) (US)
D - Edward D. Wood
S - Criswell, Tor Johnson, Keene Duncan, Valda Hansen, Maila "Vampira" Nurmi.
The unique Ed Wood carries on where only he can from the wreckage of *Plan 9 From Outer Space* (1956), with this equally inept/incredible effort featuring most of that film's cast. Criswell plays a TV prophet rising from his coffin to warn of monsters who are to be both pitied and feared. Duncan, playing a bogus medium aided by a fake "ghost" (Hansen) and a lumbering monster (Johnson), deceives people into thinking that he can contact the dead. This he indeed does and in the resulting melee, is buried alive by the revived cadavers. The suitably sinuous Nurmi appears as a "real" ghost, otherwise the film's lack of inventiveness is best illustrated in the name of Duncan's character-Dr. Acula !

NIGHT LIFE - (1989) (US)
D - David Acomba
S - Scott Grimes, Ken Davis, Lisa Fuller, Cheryl Pollac.
A less humour-filled variation on *The Return of the Living Dead* (1985) as four schoolkids are zombiefied after inhaling toxic gases from a chemical truck and then proceed to run around and wreak mayhem, drinking, stealing cars and killing any who get in their way. The film stars the young lead from *Critters* (1986) Grimes, and the gore-soaked zombies are provided by Ed French of *Breeders* (1986) and *Rejuvenator* (1988) fame, and Craig Reardon, whose own credits include *Poltergeist* (1982) and the effectively creepy *The Funhouse* (1981).

NIGHT OF THE LIVING DEAD - (1968) (US)
D - George A. Romero

S - Judith O'Dea, Duane Jones, Karl Hardman, Keith Wayne, Marilyn Eastman.

NIGHT OF THE LIVING DEAD - (1990) (US)
D - Tom Savini
S - Tony Todd, Patricia Tallman, Tom Towles, McKee Anderson, William Butler, Kate Finneran.

NIGHT OF THE LIVING DEAD 30TH ANNIVERSARY EDITION - (1999) (US)
D - George A. Romero, John Russo
S - Duane Jones, Judith O'Dea, Karl Hardman, Keith Wayne, Marilyn Eastman, Kyra Schon, Russell Streiner.
A new re-edit of the zombie classic which found little favour with critics and fans alike. As well as replacing much of the original score with some cheap synthesiser music, Russo has also added new material and deleted some scenes from the original, including the bravura opening sequence in the cemetery - sacrilege or what ?! In addition to this "heresy", a new ending, some extra gore and a whole new religious theme are included here, to the detriment of the original. Why tamper with an undisputed classic if only for the lure of the filthy lucre perhaps ? - not for nothing has this been called the "worst rape of a classic film since the colourisation of *Casablanca*."

NIGHT OF THE LIVING SCARECROWS - (1989) (US)
D - William Wesley
S - Ted Vernon, Michael Simms, Richard Vidan.
First-time feature from Wesley that mixes other "straw-epics" such as *Children of the Corn* (1984), and *Dark Night of the Scarecrow* (1981) with *Night of the Living Dead* (1968), as cadaverous scarecrows attack a military thief who parachutes into their territory. General carnage then ensues as the thief's criminal cohorts track him down only to be axed, sawed and knifed by the straw-ridden zombies, and finally hung up on crosses.

NIGHT OF THE SEAGULLS - (LA NOCHE DE LOS GAVIOTAS) - (1975) (SP)
D - Amando de Ossorio
S - Victor Petit, Maria Kosti, Sandra Mozarowsky, Julie James, Julia Saly, Jose Antonio Calvo.

NIGHT OF THE ZOMBIES - (1981) (US)
D - Joel M. Reed
S - Jamie Gillis, Joel Reed, Ryan Hilliard, Samantha Grey.
A shoestring budget only accentuates the film's numerous flaws as a group of nazi soldiers from World War 2 are

Zombie Filmography

found to be still living, fighting and eating each other, near Munich. Reed is revealed to be the culprit here as he is the supremo masterminding the zombies in an elaborate nazi plot. Gillis, a CIA agent here, is more renowned for appearances in porn films and, similarly, Reed is also the director of the infamous *The Incredible Torture Show* (1977).

NO MERCY NO FUTURE - (DIE BERUEHRTE) - (1981) (GER)
D - Helma Sanders-Brahms
S - Elisabeth Stepanek, Hubertus Von Weyraunch, Imgard Mellinger.
One of the rare German entries into the zombie genre, it is also singularly original in its' treatment of the theme. Stepanek is a woman undergoing a mental breakdown, her psychological disintegration reflected physically in her dreams which are of gory deaths and a visceral zombie world. It's an unusual film containing some painterly images which are in stark contrast to some of the events that are portrayed in the film.

NUDIST COLONY OF THE DEAD (1991) (US)
D – Mark Pirro
S – Forest J. Ackerman, Bea Lindoren, Rachel Latt, Braddon Mendelson, Darwyn Carson, Dan Hartel
Sheer lunacy, Pirro's horror musical comedy mixes bible-bashing groups with the titular fig-leaf wearers at The Sunny Buttocks Nudist Camp (!) That said, the songs are a higher quality than you'd have any right to expect....

O

OASIS OF THE ZOMBIES - (1981) (FR)
D - Jess Franco
S - Manuel Gelin, France Lomay, Jeff Montgomery
An expedition searching for nazi treasure buried in the desert during World War Two only succeeds in unearthing the zombie soldiers who guard it. Suffering from Franco's customary budget restraints the film does however, offer up an effective climax as the worm-eaten cadavers slowly encircle their tomb raiding prey as night falls to cloak the desert in an eerie gloom.

THE OMEGA MAN - (1971) (US)
D - Boris Sagal
S - Charlton Heston, Anthony Zerbe, Rosalind Cash, Paul Koslo, Lincoln Kilpatrick, Eric Laneuville.

ORGY OF THE DEAD - (1965) (US)
D - Ed Wood
S - Criswell, Pat Barrington, Fawn Silver.
This must be an Ed Wood film as it was shot in Astravision and Sexicolour ! The story, as such, concerns a horror novelist and his girlfriend (Barrington), who crash their car and find themselves captives of the undead Criswell, a ghoul, a mummy and a werewolf. Their mortal souls are only mentally not physically threatened as they are forced to endure a succession of "eternally damned women", stripping and dancing in the nearby graveyard - good work if you can get it !

OUTPOST (2008) (UK)
D – Steve Barker
S - Ray Stevenson, Julian Wadham, Richard Brake, Paul Blair, Brett Fancy, Enoch Prost, Julian Rivett
The latest in a lengthening line of war inflected horror movies -think *The Keep* (1983), *The Bunker* (2001 and *Death Watch* (2002), Barker's opus sees a group of grizzled mercenaries led by Stevenson, hired to protect a mysterious engineer (Wadham) as he searches an underground bunker in Eastern Europe. Riffing on the bad vibes of the location as portrayed in the likes of *Hostel* (2005) and *Severance* (2006), they guess Wadham is looking for Nazi gold left over from the war but the McGuffin here is a " unified field machine". Developed near the end of the war, it transpires that this secret machine is able to alter time and space in order to create an army of invincible "zombie" soldiers.

The eerie exteriors and nebulous interiors create their own supernatural aura, punctuated only by the glow sticks used to illuminate the gloom and the climactic visualisation of the undead nazi army silhouetted against the night sky as explosions clatter all around. Aside from the pure hokum of the quantum physics-straining machine and the pedestrian build up before action-packed climax, Barker has crafted a superior offering here, showing great promise as well as a disquieting mediation on the timeless nature and repetition of mankind's capacity for cruelty and conflict.

P

PANIC - (1981) (SP)
D - Tonino Ricci
S - David Warbeck, Janet Agren, Robero Ricci, Eugenio Benito, Maria Bianchi.
Fulci alumni Warbeck and Agren feature here as a scientist is accidentally transformed into a crazed zombie after being exposed to a germ warfare virus.

PET SEMATARY - (1989) (US)
D - Mary Lambert
S - Dale Midkiff, Fred Gwynne, Denise Crosby, Brad Greenquist, Michael Lombard, Miko Hughes

The Dead Walk

The eagerly anticipated collaboration between writer Stephen King and director George A. Romero remains a mere ghostly memory here as *Pet Sematary* surfaces under the direction of the relatively unknown Lambert. Despite the much vaunted use of King's own script the film largely jettisons the supernatural elements of the book in favour of a more "realistic" psychological approach to horror. Unfortunately, this serves only to detract from the "horror" as Doctor Louis Creed (Midkiff) sees his pet cat die, only to resurrect it by burying it in the "Pet Sematary" of the title. Emotions then overtake his rationale as he attempts to similarly revive his son Gage (Hughes), killed in a road accident, and then culminates in the "rebirth" of his dead wife Rachel (Crosby).

As such, it is the emotional core of the film that succeeds most as family traumas are convincingly enacted - the startling appearance of Rachel's disfigured sister provides the film's most horrifying moment and also signals *Pet Sematary*'s biggest failing. As the psychological weaknesses of the film's rather one dimensional characters overshadows all else. The film provides no genuine terror in the traditional sense, it simply does not frighten. Only the autumnal colours of Maine and the suitably eerie "Pet Sematary" lend any atmosphere to an otherwise vapid picture. There is, admittedly, a willingness to confront a contentious issue - childhood death, and the downbeat ending is in many ways courageous, but we are still left with a "hollow" film.

The single most resonant image being of the grieving father cradling his dead son and walking the pebble-lined path to the burial ground, itself faintly recalling Jacques Tourneur's superior *I Walked With A Zombie* (1943), a film which did manage to explore a gamut of emotions and authentic horror.

PET SEMATARY 2 - (1992) (US)
D - Mary Lambert
S - Edward Furlong, Anthony Edwards, Clancy Brown, Jared Rushton, Sarah Trigger.

Furlong is the alienated teen' moving to Maine after his actress mother has died in an on-set accident. When the local sheriff (Brown) kills one kids dog, it is revived by Furlong in the Indian burial ground from the first film. As the "hell-hound" violently kills Brown, the sheriff is then brought back to life by the kids as a sadistic zombie, whereupon Furlong also revives his own mother for a decidedly gory climax.

PESTICIDE - (1978) (FR)
D - Jean Rollin
S - Marie-Georges Pascal, Serge Marquand, Patricia Cartier, Felix Marten, Mirella Rancelot, Evelyn Thomas.

PHANTASM - (1978) (US)
D - Don Coscarelli
S - Angus Scrimm, Michael Baldwin, Bill Thornbury, Reggie Bannister, Kathy Lester, Ken Jones, Terry Kalbus.

PHANTASM 2 - (1988) (US)
D - Don Coscarelli
S - Reggie Bannister, Angus Scrimm, James LeGros, Paula Irving, Samantha Phillips, Stacy Travis.

The more major league star LeGros essays the role of Mike this time around with Scrimm returning as the predatory Tall Man, in this remake rather than sequel as most of the major scenes from the first film are restaged, only with a chainsaw and flamethrowers included here for even greater (intended) impact.

PHANTASM 3 - (1994) (US)
D - Don Coscarelli
S - Reggie Bannister, Michael Baldwin, Angus Scrimm, Gloria Lynn Henry, Kevin Connors.

Once again we see Reggie (Bannister) and Mike (Baldwin) returning from the original film to once again do battle with Scrimm's mysterious Tall Man. Connors sports a killer frisbee whilst Rocky (Henry) complains that "This kickin' zombie ass just ain't my thing" but still indulges in a cat fight in a mausoleum and a topless sex scene amongst the other assorted happenings, which include laughing zombies, nightmares and the ever-present metal balls.

PHANTASM IV - OBLIVION - (1998) (US)
D - Don Coscarelli
S - Michael Baldwin, Reggie Bannister, Bill Thornbury, Bob Ivy, Angus Scrimm.

The fourth instalment in the *Phantasm* series divided critics and fans between those who feel it a worthy entry and those who find it just plain awful. Although the Tall Man's identity is finally revealed as Jebediah Morningside, the reason for his supernatural powers is never explained, nor the presence of the obligatory metal spheres which zoom around. With footage from Coscarelli's original film arbitrarily worked into the new feature, the result is an incomprehensible mish-mash rather ominously leaving the way open for a fifth film.

PHARAOH'S CURSE - (1957) (US)
S – Mark Dana, Ziva Rodann, Diane Brewster, George N. Neise, Alvaro Guillot, Ben Wright, Guy Prescott

PIRATES OF THE CARIBBEAN: THE CURSE OF

Zombie Filmography

THE BLACK PEARL (2003) (US)
D – Gore Verbinski
S – Johnny Depp, Geoffrey Rush, Orlando Bloom, Keira Knightley, Jack Davenport, Jonathan Pryce, Mackenzie Crook, Kevin McNally
First film in the incredibly successful trilogy and, as you would expect from a film based on an amusement park ride, is laced with all out action. Depp is excellent as the loveable rogue and lead pirate, Jack Sparrow and is given fine support, especially from Rush as the cursed ancient mariner turned zombie, Captain Barbossa. His zombie pirate crew offer suitably creepy, skeletal support as Verbinski unashamedly concentrates on style and action over story - no doubt with an eye on setting up the future films in the series.

PIRATES OF THE CARIBBEAN: DEAD MAN'S CHEST (2006) (US)
D - Gore Verbinski
S – Johnny Depp, Geoffrey Rush, Orlando Bloom, Keira Knightley, Jack Davenport, Jonathan Pryce, Mackenzie Crook, Kevin McNally, Bill Nighy, Naomie Harris
Even more outlandish than the first film, with almost too much action and too many disparate plot lines going on, *Chest* is notable for the grotesque gallery of creations emanating from the ghost ship and for the mist shrouded lair of Harris, full of voodoo inflected paraphernalia and mystique.

PIRATES OF THE CARIBBEAN: AT WORLD'S END (2007) (US)
D - Gore Verbinski
S – Johnny Depp, Geoffrey Rush, Orlando Bloom, Keira Knightley, Jack Davenport, Jonathan Pryce, Mackenzie Crook, Kevin McNally, Yun-Fat Chow
The central premise of pirates banding together here to stave off the threat of being hunted to extinction is a good one but somewhat submerged beneath the welter of buccanneering deals and double-crossing that results, together with the contrived events which unfold simply to provide a convenient end. Most ironic of all is Keith Richard's cameo, which despite his requisite, cadaverous image, injects more vitality into the proceedings than the remainder of the cast on this occasion!

PLAGUE OF THE ZOMBIES - (1966) (UK)
D - John Gilling
S - Andre Morell, Diane Clare, Jacqueline Pearce, John Carson, Brook Williams, Michael Ripper.

PLANET TERROR (2007) (US)
D – Robert Rodriguez
S – Rose McGowan, Freddy Rodriguez, Josh Brolin, Marley Shelton, Jeff Fahey, Michael Biehn, Bruce Willis, Stacy Ferguson, Nicky Katt, Naveen Andrews, Quentin Tarantino

PLAN 9 FROM OUTER SPACE - (1956) (US)
D - Edward D. Wood
S - Bela Lugosi, Tor Johnson, Lyle Talbot, Joanne Lee, Gregory Walcott, Duke Moore, Tom Keene.

PSYCHOMANIA - (1972) (UK)
D - Don Sharp
S - George Sanders, Beryl Reid, Nick Henson, Mary Larkin, Robert Hardy.
A stylish amalgam of zombie/motorbike films from the director of *Kiss of the Vampire* (1962). Henson is the leader of a bike gang who, having learned the secret of immortality, kills himself only to revive and see the other members of the gang follow his example. The "living dead" bikers then proceed to roam the countryside wreaking as much havoc as possible. The film's main attributes are the bizarre scenes such as when Henson, buried with his bike, revs the machine and rides it up and out of his grave or, the other bikers, careering off bridges to die and be resurrected. Sanders, a devil-worshipping butler here, killed himself soon after completing the film.

Q
QUATERMASS 2 - (1957) (UK)
D - Val Guest
S - Brian Donlevy, William Franklyn, Tom Chatto, John Longden, Percy Herbert, Sidney James, Brian Forbes.

R
RAIDERS OF THE LIVING DEAD - (1986) (US)
D - Samuel M. Sherman
S - Scott Schwartz, Robert Deveau, Zita Johann.
A risible time-waster that has one teenager called upon to fight against the dead bodies that are now walking the earth again, these are the zombies of the title that noticeably apes Steven Spielberg's *Raiders of the Lost Ark* (1981).

REANIMATOR - (1985) (US)
D - Stuart Gordon
S - Jeffrey Combs, Bruce Abbott, Barbara Crampton, David Gale, Robert Sampson, Peter Kent.

[REC] - (2007) (SP)
D – Jaume Balaguero, Paco Plaza

The Dead Walk

S – Manuela Velasco, Javier Botet, Manuel Bronchud, Maria Lanau, Vincente Gil, Ferran Terraza, David Vert, Claudia Font, Pablo Rosso

REDNECK ZOMBIES - (1988) (US)
D - Pericles Lewnes
S - Lisa De Haven, W.E. Benson, William W. Decker, James Housely, Tyrone Taylor.
A below par offering from an unlikely named director (and cast), but from a likely stable of exploitation - Troma. It features "Tobacco chewin', Gut Chompin', Cannibal kinfolk from Hell (?!) -a sort of *Deliverance* (1972) with zombies, all filmed in "Entrail Vision" !

RESIDENT EVIL (2002) (UK/GER/FR)
D – Paul W.S. Anderson
S – Milla Jovovich, Michelle Rodriguez, Eric Mabius, James Purefoy, Martin Crewes, Colin Salmon,

RESIDENT EVIL:APOCALYPSE (2004) (UK/GER/FR/CAN)
D – Alexander Witt
S – Milla Jovovich, Sienna Guillory, Oded Fehr, Thomas Kretschmann, Sophie Vavasseur, Jared Harris, Mike Epps, Sandrine Holt, Iain Glen

RESIDENT EVIL:EXTINCTION (2007) (UK/GER/FR/US/AUS)
D – Russell Mulcahy
S – Milla Jovovich, Oded Fehr, Ali Larter, Iain Glen, Ashanti, Spencer Locke, Matthew Marsden, Mike Epps, Linden Ashby

REST IN PIECES - (1987) (SP)
D - Jose Ramon Larraz
S - Scott Thompson Baker, Lorin Jean Vail, Dorothy Malone, David Rose.
The creator of the sanguinary, not to mention erotic, *Vampyres* (1974) directs this tale of "un-neighbourly" actions as a young couple discover a clan of zombies are living next door to them (as opposed to "Alice" !).

THE RETURN OF DR. MABUSE - (1961) (WG, IT, FR)
D - Harald Reinhl
S - Gert Froebe, Lex Barker, Daliah Gavi, Wolfgang Preiss, Rudolph Forster.
Poor sequel to the more illustrious series of films by Fritz Lang. Mabuse (Preiss), plans to enslave Munich with an army of zombies created at a local prison using a drug invented by Forster. It is left to the detective Froebe and Barker, together with a reporter (Gavi), to prevent this catastrophe.

THE RETURN OF DR. X - (1939) (US)
D - Vincent Sherman
S - Humphrey Bogart, Rosemary Lane, Dennis Morgan, Wayne Morris.
Combines Bogart in his only horror appearance with first time director Sherman. The sometimes stylish production is let down by a sagging script and mediocre acting as Bogart returns from the dead, a walking zombie. Even his own triumphant first appearance, chalk-white face and streaked hair, fail to save this sequel (in name only), to Michael Curtiz's *Doctor X* (1932).

THE RETURN OF THE EVIL DEAD - (EL ATAQUE DE LOS MUERTOS SIN OJOS) (1973) (SP)
D - Amando de Ossorio
S - Tony Kendall, Esther Ray, Fernando Sancho, Lone Fleming.

THE RETURN OF THE LIVING DEAD - (1985) (US)
D - Dan O'Bannon
S - Clu Gulager, James Karen, Don Calfa, Miguel Nunez, Brian Peck, Linnea Quigley.

THE RETURN OF THE LIVING DEAD PART 2 - (1987) (US)
D - Ken Wiederhorn
S - Thom Matthews, James Karen.
Unfortunately, the kinetic drive and outrageous humour that characterised the original film have been completely lost here. Not even the re-appearance of Karen and Matthews from the first film can raise this above the atrocious. Widerhorn wastes his previous horror film experience (he directed the above-average *Shock Waves* - 1977), and the idea of killing the zombies through electrification fails to add any extra "spark" to the proceedings. The catch-phrase of "more brains" utilised so effectively in the original is now aimed in the direction of this film's creators and their moribund script.

RETURN OF THE LIVING DEAD 3 - (1993) (US)
D - Brian Yuzna
S - Kent McCord, James T. Callahan, Sarah Douglas, Mindy Clarke, Abigail Lenz, J. Trevor Edmond.
Yuzna's spin on this series is a firm departure from the previous zombie films before it as he constructs a genuinely thought-provoking thriller with an unusual Romeo and Juliet sub-plot as Curt (Edmond) uses military

Zombie Filmography

re-animation gas to revive his girlfriend Julie (Clarke) after she is killed in a road accident. His attempts to still love her despite her mental and physical deterioration, provide welcome substance to the material as well as some pointed observations on the body scarification which Julie indulges in - now given a renewed sense of irony given the current popularity and acceptance of body piercing in society.

RETURN OF THE LIVING DEAD:NECROPOLIS (2005) (US)
D – Ellory Elkayem
S – Aimee-Lynn Chadwick, Cory Hardrict, John Keefe, Jana Kramer, Peter Coyote, Elvin Dandel, Alexandru Geoana
The "More brains" cry from the original film is never more appropriate than here - only this time for the vapid cast and plodding direction. A teenager injured on his motorbike is taken to an experimental facility instead of the local hospital, run by a clandestine organisation (doubling for the Umbrella Corporation in *Resident Evil* methinks). When the boy's friends break in to release him, they only succeed in releasing a new outbreak of zombies.

RETURN OF THE LIVING DEAD:RAVE TO THE GRAVE (2005) (US)
D – Ellory Elkayem
S – Aimee-Lynn Chadwick, Cory Hardrict, John Keefe, Peter Coyote, Jenny Mollen, Claudiu Bleont, Sorin Cocis, Cain Manozi, George Dimitrescu, Maria Dinulescu
The fifth entry in the series has a stash of chemicals discovered in an attic, analysed, found to contain "party chemicals" & sold on by a drug dealer as a designer party drug "Z" to be used at the forthcoming Halloween rave with predictable results.

REVENGE OF THE DEAD - (1984) (IT)
D - Pupi Avati
S - Gabriele Lavia, Anna Canovas, Bob Tonelli, John Stacy.
The sometimes interesting Avati diects this tale about an author who searches for the "K Zones" where the dead are said to walk. Stylish, atmospheric, though decidedly slow-paced, this is an engaging film despite lacking the artistry of Avati's previous gem, *The House With The Windows That Laugh* (1976).

REVENGE OF THE LIVING DEAD - (1986) (FR)
D - Pierre B. Reinhard
S - Veronique Catanzaro, Sylvie Novak, Catherine Gourladuen, Anthea Wyler.
Three young women die after drinking poisoned milk - (shades of *Rebecca* ? - I think not !), only to later rise from the grave, presumably with a lot of bottle, to brutally slay unwilling victims inbetween some frequent soft-core couplings.

REVENGE OF THE ZOMBIES - (1943) (US)
D - Steve Sekely
S - John Carradine, Robert Lowery, Veda Ann Borg, Gale Storm, Mantan Moreland.
Carradine here, in one of his best roles excels as Dr. Max Heinrich von Altermann - a mad doctor on a remote island in the Louisiana swamplands. There he produces a zombie army for Hitler, simultaneously attempting to cure his wife (Borg) who has also been turned into a zombie. It is she who finally leads the zombies against their creator. There are some good moments, such as Borg's corpse wandering through the night. For Carradine, this was a dry run for *Shock Waves* (1977), another nazi-zombie film he appeared in.

REVENGE OF THE ZOMBIES - (1981) (HK)
D - Horace Menga
S - ?
From the producers who brought us *The Legend of the 7 Golden Vampires* (1973), this is a bizarre mixture of oriental culture with the zombie genre. The story has an evil sorcerer, who lives on human breast milk, creating an army of zombies by driving spikes into their heads. Alongside this is typical exploitation fare ranging from a shaved female crotch, used to create a potion, to alligators, kung-fu and cannibalism.

REVOLT OF THE ZOMBIES - (1936) (US)
D - Victor Halperin
S - Dorothy Stone, Dean Jagger, Roy D'Arcy, Robert Noland, George Cleveland.
The director of the seminal *White Zombie* (1932), tries to repeat that film's success here, even down to re-using shots of Lugosi's mesmeric eyes from that picture. The story has a French planter using zombies to fight for France in the Franco-Prussian war, but the ensuing melee cannot match Halperin's more illustrious predecessor.

THE ROBOT V'S THE AZTEC MUMMY - (LA MOMIA AZTECA VS EL ROBOT HUMANO) - (1957) (MEX)
D - Rafael Portillo
S - Ramon Gay, Rosita Arenas, Crox Alvarado, Luis Aceves Castaneda, Arturo Martinez.
The third and final entry in Portillo's Aztec mummy series

The Dead Walk

was shot straight after the first two films. Having escaped the nest of vipers from the previous film, Dr. Krupp appears again to hypnotize Flor (Arenas) into revealing the location of the treasure-laden tomb guarded by Popoca. In order to defeat Popoca, this time Krupp constructs a robot with a human brain and metal limbs but all to no avail as Popoca destroys the robot and retires back to his pyramid along with the requisite jewels.

S

SANTO EN LA VENGANZA DE LA MOMIA - (1971) (MEX)
D - Rene Cardona
S - Santo, Caesar Del Campo, Amada Zumaya, Eric Del Castillo
The second entry in the Santo mummy series, the infamous masked wrestler is enlisted for help with an expedition to the lost tomb of an Aztec warrior, Nonoc. When the party arrives at the tomb, an ancient scroll explains that by now entering they are officially cursed. Soon after, the group are stalked and killed off by the avenging mummy, or so we are led to believe.

SANTO Y BLUE DEMON CONTRA LOS MONSTROUS - (1969) (MEX)
D - Gilberto Martinez Solares
S - Santo, Carlos Ancira, Heidi Blue, Alejandro Cruz, Jorge Rado.

SCARED STIFF - (1952) (US)
D - George Marshall
S - Dean Martin, Jerry Lewis, Lizabeth Scott, Carmen Miranda, George E. Stone, Dorothy Malone, Jack Lambert.
A rather tame remake of *The Ghostbreakers* (1940) with Lewis and Martin taking over the roles of Hope and Crosby from the original. They play two nightclub owners on the run and Scott is the inheritor of a spooky castle in the Caribbean. The jokes and the scares are less worthy this time round, needing the brief guest appearances from Hope and Crosby to revive it along with Lambert's menacing zombie. Lewis gets to sing with Carmen Miranda.

THE SECRET OF DR. ORLOFF - (1964) (SP)
D - Jesus Franco
S - Agnes Spaak, Hugo Blanco, Marcelo Arroita-Jauregui, Perla Cristal, Pastor Serrador.

THE SECRET OF THE MUMMY (O SEGREDO DA MUMIA) - (1982) (BRZ)
D - Ivan Cardoso
S - Tania Boscoli, Regina Case, Felipe Falcao, Wilson Grey, Evandro Mesquita, Jos Mojica Marins.
A manic Brazilian comedy with a mummy and a mad scientists' assistant called Igor (of course), who is both horny and deranged in equal measures. In the heady overdose of exploitation here we find stock footage of a Miss Brazil contest, cannibalism, nudity and copious amounts of sex. Director Cordoso was also assistant director to Marins - the ubiquitous star of many such films revelling under the name of Coffin Joe.

THE SERPENT AND THE RAINBOW - (1987) (US)
D - Wes Craven
S - Bill Pulman, Paul Winfield, Zakes Mokae, Cathy Tyson, Michael Gough.

LES SEXANDROIDES - (1987) (FR)
D - Michel Ricaud
S - The Company "Le Petit Mescal".
Very weird ! Three (mercifully) short stories laden with graphic violence and nudity and featuring voodoo, a hideous zombie monster and a living dead girl dancing to what sounds like an asthmatic Tina Turner (!) whilst her vampiric lover awaits in the nuptial coffin.

SHADOWMAN - (1973) (FR, IT)
D - Georges Franju
S - Jacques Champreux, Gayle Hunnicutt, Gert Froebe, Clement Harrari, Ugo Paglial, Josephine Chaplin.
Taken from an eight part TV series and featuring the same cast, *Shadowman* revolves around the exploits of Champreux who plays a red-masked super criminal who searches for the long lost treasure of the Knights Templar. He is assisted by Hunnicutt and the evil Harrari, together with an army of zombies. The accent is on fantasy here, coupled with some effective set designs such as Champreux's laboratory with its gallows style torture devices. Champreux wrote the script himself and the director is the man who helmed the disturbing *Eyes Without A Face* (1959).

SHATTER DEAD - (1994) (US)
D - Scooter McCrae
S - Stark Raven, Flora Fauna, Larry "Smalls" Johnson, Marina Del Rey, Robert Wells, Candy Coster.
With a tagline of "There's No More Room In Heaven Either" a Romero influence is all too apparent, as debut director McCrae fashions his own take on the zombie genre. Considering that the film was made for barely $4,000 McCrae manages to imbrue his film with some

Zombie Filmography

arresting images which belie the budget constraints as one resourceful woman Susan (Raven) strives to survive the gun-toting vigilantes and the mysterious religious leader known as "The Preacher Man" (Wells) in a post-apocalyptic world full of anarchy and chaos. With something approaching a budget at his disposal, McCrae could well be one to watch.

SHAUN OF THE DEAD (2004) (UK/FR)
D – Edgar Wright
S – Simon Pegg, Kate Ashfield, Nick Frost, Lucy Davis, Dylan Moran, Nicola Cunningham, Bill Nighy, Martin Freeman

SHOCK WAVES - (1977) (US)
D - Ken Wiederhorn
S - Peter Cushing, John Carradine, Brooke Adams, Fred Buch, Jack Davidson, Luke Halpin.

SPOOKIES - (1986) (US)
D - Felix Ward, Brendan Faulkner
S - Thomas Doran, Frank M. Farel, Dan Scott, Alec Nemser.

STACY - (2001) (JAP)
D – Naoyuki Tomomatsu
S – Norman England, Tomoka Hayashi, Yukijiro Hotaru, Natsuki Kato, Shiro Misawa, Masayoshi Nogami, Kenji Otsuki

SUGAR HILL - (1974) (US)
D - Paul Maslansky
S - Marki Bey, Robert Quarry, Don Pedro Colley, Richard Lawson, Betty Anne Rees, Zara Culley.

THE SUPERNATURALS - (1985) (US)
D - Armand Mastroianni
S - Maxwell Caulfield, Nichelle Nichols, Scott Jacoby, Levar Burton.

T

TALES FROM THE CRYPT - (1972) (UK)
D - Freddie Francis
S - Peter Cushing, Robin Phillips, David Markham.
Another Amicus anthology in the style of *Dr. Terror's House of Horrors* (1964), based on the EC comics of William Gaines. The one zombie segment, "Poetic Justice", is also the best as a shy, neighbourly old man (Cushing), is victimised by a selfish property mogul (Phillips) who wants to buy the house for future development. The kindly old man is driven to suicide by all this but exacts his revenge by rising from the dead to rip out the heart of his "emotionally heartless" persecutor, appropriately on Valentine's Day. The sight of Grimsdyke (Cushing), with skeletal face and darkened eye sockets, is directly attributable to the fine make-up skills from another Hammer regular, Roy Ashton.
The stylish direction of Francis betrays his own affinity for the genre having previously directed *The Skull* (1965) and *Dracula Has Risen From The Grave* (1968), as well as being equally adept behind the camera lens, witness the superbly photographed *The Innocents* (1961) and *The Elephant Man* (1981).

TALES FROM THE DARKSIDE - THE MOVIE - (1990) (US)
D - John Harrison
S - Christian Slater, Steve Buscemi.
A trilogy of tales within this compendium format of which "Lot 249" taken from an Arthur Conan Doyle story has an enfeebled college geek gaining revenge on his persecutors by using a re-animated mummy.

TALOS THE MUMMY - (1999) (US)
D - Russell Mulcahy
S - Jason Scott Lee, Louise Lombard, Christopher Lee, Sean Pertwee, Michael Lerner, Shelley Duvall

TEENAGE ZOMBIES - (1957) (US)
D - Jerry Warren
S - Don Sullivan, Katherine Victor, Steve Conte, Paul Pepper, Nan Green, Chuck Niles, Mike Concannon.
As mad as it sounds, featuring four water-skiing teenagers who are taken prisoner on an apparently deserted island by an ape man who delivers them into the hands of a crazed doctor (Victor). She is working on a nerve gas that will turn humans into zombies and so ensure her domination of the world. The local sheriff, (Concannon) is also revealed to be part of the conspiracy and it is left to a zombie (Niles), to destroy the laboratory as the teenagers escape.

THE TERMINAL MAN - (1974) (US)
D - Mike Hodges
S - George Segal, Joan Hackett, Richard A. Dysart, Jill Clayburgh, Donald Moffat, Matt Clarke, Michael C. Gwynne.

TERROR CREATURES FROM THE GRAVE (CINQUE TOMBE PER UN MEDIUM) (1966) (IT, US)
D - Massimo Pupillo

The Dead Walk

S - Barbara Steele, Walter Brandi, Mirella Maravidi, Alfredo Rizzo, Riccardo Garrone.

TIME WALKER - (1982) (US)
D - Tom Kennedy
S - Ben Murphy, Nina Axelrod, James Karen, Shari Belafonte-Harper, Melissa Prophet.
A somewhat unique spin on the mummy genre, Kennedy's film has an alien mummy visiting California after jewels are stolen from a sarcophagus.

TOKYO ZOMBIE - (2005) (JAP)
D – Sakichi Sato
S – Tadanobu Asano, Sho Aikawa, Erika Okuda, Arata Furuta, Hina Matsuoka
The accent is decidedly more on humour than horror here as two friends working at a fire extinguisher warehouse (!) accidentally kill their boss. They decide to dispose of his corpse at a man made refuse mountain on the outskirts of Tokyo. As chemicals and bodily fluids combine, the resulting toxic mixture begins to reanimate the dead. With more than a passing nod to *Shaun of the Dead* (2004) and wrestling scenes straight out of *Land of the Dead* (2005), originality is not the film's trump card.

TOMBS OF THE BLIND DEAD (LA NOCHE DEL TERROR CIEGO) - (1971) (SP)
D - Amando de Ossorio
S - Oscar Burner, Lone Fleming, Maria Silva, Jose Telman, Maria elena Arpon, Juan Cortes.

TOMB OF THE UNDEAD - (1972) (US)
D - John Hayes
S - Duncan McLeod, John Dennis, John Dullaghan, Lee Frost, Lewis Sterling, Susan Charney.
One of a plethora of title aimed at emulating the success of *Night of the Living Dead* (1968) through plagiarism. A group of prisoners are killed in an abortive jail-break attempt and are turned into zombies by formaldehyde that is spilt on their mass grave. The enfeebled climax sees the zombies attack on the prison foiled by the beauty of Charney, who transfixes them whereupon they are shot.

TOOTH AND NAIL - (2007) (US)
D – Mark Young
S – Nicole DuPort, Rider Strong, Michael Kelly, Alexandra Barreto, Robert Carradine, Emily Catherine Young, Michael Madsen, Vinnie Jones
A low budget, post apocalyptic thriller where the world has ground to a halt, literally, in the year 2012 having run out of fuel. With most US inhabitants having left for the warmer south, a group of twenty-somethings are holed up in a high rise Philadelphia hospital, only to be attacked by a rampaging gang known as "Rovers" with a cannibalistic bent to boot. The single inventive element is the climax as the attackers are hampered by the effects of the drug-riddled victims they have feasted upon.

28 DAYS LATER - (2002) (UK)
D – Danny Boyle
S – Cillian Murphy, Naomie Harris, Noah Huntley, Brendan Gleeson, Christopher Eccleston, Megan Burns

28 WEEKS LATER - (2007) (UK/SP)
D – Juan Carlos Fresnadillo
S – Robert Carlyle, Catherine McCormack, Rose Byrne, Jeremy Renner, Harold Perrineau, Idris Elba, Imogen Poots

U

UNDEAD - (2003) (AUST)
D – Michael Spierig, Peter Spierig
S – Felicity Mason, Mungo McKay, Rob Jenkins, Lisa Cunningham, Dirk Hunter, Emma Randall, Steve Grieg, Noel Sheridan
Aliens are invading earth and turning Aussies everywhere into zombies, elevating them above the clouds on beams of light before returning them to earth as the walking dead. Former Beauty Queen Mason and a local woodsman (McKay) are the only vaguely memorable characters as the Spierig brothers directorial team seem most intent on raiding the tomb of their near neighbour in New Zealand, Peter Jackson and his *Bad Taste* (1987).

V

VALLEY OF THE ZOMBIES - (1946) (US)
D - Philip Ford
S - Robert Livingstone, Adrian Booth, Ian Keith, Thomas Jackson, Charles Trowbridge.
Keith plays an undertaker Ormond Munks who replenishes himself on a formula discovered in the "valley of the zombies". Helped by the hypnotised heroine (Booth), he embalms victims who supply the fresh blood he requires, resulting in blood-drained bodies as opposed to zombies.

THE VANGUARD - (2008) (UK)
D – Matthew Hope
S – Karen Admiraal, Jack Bailey, Ray Bullock Jnr. Emma Choy, Terry Cole, Rob Cooper, Bahi Ghubril

THE VENETIAN AFFAIR - (1966) (US)
D - Jerry Thorpe

Zombie Filmography

S - Robert Vaughn, Karl Boehm, Elke Sommer, Felicia Farr, Boris Karloff, Ed Asner.

Mundane spy story set in picturesque Venice locations about a nerve destroying drug that turns people into zombies. Adapted from famed espionage author, Helen Macinnes novel, the film boasts a starry cast headed up by Karloff, Vaughn from the popular spy series *The Man From U.N.C.L.E.*, Boehm from *Peeping Tom* (1960), and the sultry Sommer from *Baron Blood* (1975).

VENGEANCE OF THE ZOMBIES (LA ROBELLION DE LAS MUERTAS) - (1972) (IT, SP)

D - Leon Klimovsky

S - Jacinto Molina, Victoria Alcazar, Maria Kost, Mirta Miller.

The vengeance centres around a young English woman living in Benares who has recurring nightmares in which she sees people being killed. It is later revealed to be the result of a curse inherited by her family and dating back to colonial times. The psychologist heroine (Alcazar), helps her to defeat the vengeful zombies that have been raised by the evil leader of a mysterious Krishna cult.

VERSUS - (2000) (US/JAP)

D – Ryuhei Kijamura

S – Tak Sakaguchi, Hideo Sakaki, Chieko Misaka, Kenji Matsuda, Yuichiro Matsumoto, Hoshimi Asai

THE VIDEO DEAD - (1987) (US)

D - Robert Scott

S - Roxanna Augesen, Rocky Duvall, Michael St. Michaels, Jennifer Miros.

A genuine oddity this, featuring some rather inconsistent performances but making up for it with some inventive plotting. The story has the zombies of the title appearing in a fictitious black and white film "Zombie Blood Nightmare" that plays continually on a TV set that is wrongly delivered to a suburban house instead of the Institute for Studies of the Occult. The reason for their involvement becomes clear as the zombies emerge from the TV screen itself and set about mauling the cast. Despite the liberal helpings of gore, most of the scenes are played for laughs as one zombie receives a steam iron in the head for his pains and one victim is pushed head first into a spin dryer. *The Video Dead* would have benefited from some tighter editing but the promise is certainly here.

THE VINEYARD - (1989) (US)

D - James Hong, Bill Rice

S - James Hong, Karen Witter, Michael Wong, Lars Wanberg, Cheryl Madsen, Rue Douglas.

A mad-cap yarn starring and directed by Hong - obviously a "step-up" from manufacturing eyeballs in *Blade Runner* (1982) ! He plays chief brewer Dr. Elson Po whose own elixir of eternal life has human blood and wine amongst its ingredients. He also utilises the magical powers contained in an ancient amulet, stolen from his mother who he now keeps locked up in a room. His island stronghold, whose vineyard plays host to Po's legion of zombie experiments, is eventually rumbled by a persistent young journalist. Possibly a case of sour grapes.

VIRGIN AMONG THE LIVING DEAD (UNE VUERGE CJEZ LES MORTS VIVANTS) (1972) (SP)

D - Jess Franco

S - Christina Blanc, Britt Nichols.

One of Franco's numerous zombie films but sadly not his best. The lacklustre story has the alluring Blanc returning to her family mansion only to experience ghastly dreams of being chased by zombies. We have to decide whether this is a dream or reality, but most of the fantasy here revolves around Blanc who for the most part is clad only in her night gown.

VOICES FROM THE DEEP (VOCI DAL PROFONDO) - (1990) (IT)

D - Lucio Fulci

S - Duillo Del Prete, Karina Huff, Pascal Persiano, Lorenzo Flaherty, Bettina Giovannini.

VOODOO DAWN - (1989) (US)

D - Steven Fierberg

S - Raymond St. Jacques, Theresa Merritt, Gina Gershon, Kirk Baily, Billy "Sly" Williams, Tony Todd, Georgie Albrecht.

A low-budget voodoo offering where Todd, prior to his *Candyman* (1992) lead role, plays the chief zombie priest in a Southern plantation, who turns one student (Albrecht) into a zombie whereupon his friends, Baily and Williams learn to use the power of voodoo themselves in order to defeat the evil priest.

VOODOO ISLAND - (1957) (US)

D - Reginald Leborg

S - Boris Karloff, Rhodes Reason, Elisha Cook, Beverly Tyler, Muryn Nye.

Filmed in Hawaii, this has Karloff investigating the island of the title only to see his comrades turned into zombies. If this was not enough he also discovers the island to be inhabited by carnivorous cobra plants. Not one of Karloff's most memorable vehicles.

The Dead Walk

VOODOO MAN - (1944) (US)
D - William Beaudine
S - Bela Lugosi, John Carradine, George Zucco, Wanda Mckay, Louise Currie, Ellen Hall.

W

THE WALKING DEAD - (1936) (US)
D - Michael Curtiz
S - Boris Karloff, Edmund Gwenn, Ricardo Cortez, Marguerite Churchill, Barton Maclane, Warren Hull.
Features Karloff as an ex-con framed for a murder he did not commit and ending up in the electric chair. He is electronically brought back to life by Gwenn, as a piano-playing zombie ! Karloff, complete with white-streaked hair, then proceeds to murder his enemies in a violent rage.

WAR OF THE ZOMBIES (ROMA CONTRA ROMA) - (1963) (IT)
D - Giuseppe Vari
S - John Drew Barrymore, Susy Anderson, Ettore Manni, Ida Galli, Mino Doro.
Barrymore lords it up here as a crazy, bloodthirsty magician called Aderbal, clad in black robes and paying service to a sanguinary goddess. He sets about creating an army of zombiefied Roman soldiers to help him conquer the world. He fails, as the eye of the giant idol he worships is put out, but the film remains a visual treat due to the numerous underground caves on show, almost permanently shrouded by an ever-swirling mist.

WHITE ZOMBIE - (1932) (US)
D - Victor Halperin
S - Bela Lugosi, Madge Bellamy, John Harron, Robert Frazer, Joseph Cawthorn, Clarence Muse.

WILD ZERO - (1999) (JAP)
D – Tetsuro Takeuchi
S – Guitar Wolf, Drum Wolf, Bass Wolf, Masashi Endo, Kwancharu Shitichai, Makoto Inamiya, Haruka Nakajo

THE WRESTLING WOMAN VS THE AZTEC MUMMY (LAS LUCHADORAS CONTRA LA MOMIA) - (1964) (MEX)
D - Rene Cardona
S - Lorenza Velazquez, Elisabeth Campbell, Armando Silvestre, Maria Eugenia San Martin.
The las Luchadoras of the title - a group of nubile female wrestlers headed up by Loreat (Velazquez) and Rubi (Campbell) take on a gang of criminals in search of hidden Aztec treasure. The ensuing melee results in them facing a showdown at the tomb of Xochitl, the Aztec Princess, only unlike Portillo's series, guarded by the mummy of a warrior named Tezomoc. As the criminals attempt to steal a medallion from Xochitl's body, Tezomoc kills them all in his rage, as well as destroying the pyramid.

Z

ZOMBIE ARMY - (1991) (US)
D - Betty Stableford
S - Betty Stableford, Michelle Anderson, Jack Armstrong
A low budget romp which has the Army taking over a former asylum only to discover that some of the inmates still inside have become bloodthirsty zombies.

ZOMBIE 3 - (1988) (IT)
D - Lucio Fulci
S - Deran Serafian, Beatrice Ring, Olli Reinthaller.
Filmed in New Guinea (where life and extras are cheap !), this long awaited follow up to *Zombie Flesh Eaters* (1979) is ultimately disappointing, and not even a part of Fulci's oeuvre, strictly speaking, as the majority of the film was directed by Bruno Mattei of *Zombie Creeping Flesh* (1981) infamy due to Fulci's ill-health. This is indeed highly evident given that the theme from Mattei's earlier film; chemical contamination resulting in green, blood-lusting zombies, is also present here. The military response to this consists of cliched battles and reconaissance missions - the birth of a zombie baby is the nearest the film gets to displaying any originality. Beatrice Ring can also be seen in Lamberto Bava's *Graveyard Disturbance* (1988).

ZOMBIE 90-EXTREME PESTILENCE - (1990) (GER)
D - Andreas Schnaas
S - Matthias Kerl, Ralf Hess, Christien Biallas.
The absolute nadir of the zombie genre, an amateurish debacle awash with gore at the expense of invention. This won't be playing (ever) at your local multiplex.

ZOMBIE BRIGADE - (1988) (US)
D - Carmelo Musca, Barrie Pattison
S - Geoff Gibbs, John Moore, Leslie Wright.
Unbelievably from "Smart Egg Productions", a zombie picture that mixes shades of *The Return of the Living Dead* (1985) into its plot about the undead taking over America - sound far-fetched ? Well say hello Ronald Reagan, Bill Clinton and even more so, George Bush !

ZOMBIES ON BROADWAY - (1945) (US)
D - Gordon Douglas
S - Bela Lugosi, Wally Brown, Alan Carney, Anne Jeffreys, Darby Jones, Sir Lancelot.

Zombie Filmography

RKO trying to repeat the success of *I Walked With A Zombie* (1943), even down to including Jones and Lancelot from that film in the cast. The comedy duo of Carney and Brown play a pair of New York press agents who dream up a publicity stunt for a new show at Ace Miller's Nightclub, involving the appearance of a zombie. Miller threatens the pair when he finds himself in danger of attracting adverse radio publicity if the zombie used is found to be a fake.

The action switches to the duo's search of the Carribean for a "real" zombie serum. There they find Lugosi as Dr. Renault, who injects Carney with zombie serum. Unfortunately, the effect wears off before he can be pushed onstage, culminating with Miler being given a dose of the serum instead. This is one of a series of RKO comedies starring Carney and Brown.

ZOMBIE CREEPING FLESH (INFERNO DEI MORTI VIVENTI) - (1981) (IT,SP)
D - Bruno Mattei
S - Margi Evelyn Newton, Franco Giraldi, Selan Karay, Robert O'Neal, Gaby Renom.

THE ZOMBIE DIARIES - (2006) (UK)
D – Michael Bartlett, Kevin Gates
S – Russell Jones, Craig Stovin, Jonnie Hurn, James Fisher, Anna Blades, Imogen Church, Kyle Sparks, Alison Mollon, Victoria Nalder, Jonathan Ball, Sophia Ellis

ZOMBIE FLESH EATERS - (1979) (IT)
D - Lucio Fulci
S - Tisa Farrow, Ian McCulloch, Richard Johnson, Auretta Gay, Olga Karlatos, Luigi Conti, Stefania D'Amario, Monica Zanchi.

ZOMBIE HIGH - (1988) (US)
D - Ron Lind
S - Virginia Madsen.
An inappropriately titled film as this is a rock-bottom addition to the zombie genre. Madsen, as student Andrea Miller, enrolls at the prestigious Ettinger Academy only to find that the whole school is populated by lobotomised zombies, devoid of emotion. The low gore count and sanctimonious posturing - kids are turned into zombies in order to stop them becoming embroiled in sex, drugs and rock music, makes one think that this is a secret foray into the horror genre by the US Moral Majority! However, it is more awful than Falwell, and those seeking moral or cinematic enlightenment need not apply here for it.

ZOMBIE HOLOCAUST (LA REGINA DEI CANNIBAL) - (1980) (IT)
D - Marino Girolami
S - Ian McCulloch, Sherry Buchanan, Alexandra Delli Colli, Peter O'Neal, Donald O'Brien, Walter Patriarca, Linda Fumis.

ZOMBIE HONEYMOON - (2004) (US)
D – David Gebroe
S – Tracy Coogan, Graham Sibley, Tonya Cornelisse, David M. Wallace, Neal Jones
A a zombie film with a difference and way better than expected eschewing the conventional chewing for a pathos inducing portrayal of a doomed relationship with a difference. As newlweds Sibley and Coogan's marital bliss is soon shattered when the former is infected. The film deviates from the norm as instead of eating everyone in sight, Sibley attempts to control his "illness" whilst Coogan's unyielding love for him leads her to turn a blind eye to the killings which do occur. An unexpected, minor gem, especially with the performances from the leads.

ZOMBIE ISLAND MASSACRE - (1985) (US)
D - John N. Carter
S - David Broadnax, Rita Jenrette, Tom Cantrell.
Some exquisite Jamaican locations cannot disguise the paucity of ideas here in a film that owes more to the slasher genre than the zombie genre. The arbitrary inclusion of shots featuring the partially clothed Jenrette, a former congressman's wife and porn magazine star, only serves to underline the film's total lack of invention.

ZOMBIE LAKE (EL LAGO DE LOS MUERTOS VIVIENTES) - (1980) (SP, FR)
D - Jean Rollin
S - Howard Vernon, Robert Foster, Pierre Escourrou, Marcia Sharif, Anouchka, Nadine Pascal.

ZOMBIE NIGHTMARE - (1987) (US, CAN)
D - John Fasano
S - John Mikl Thor, Adam West, Billy Graham, John Fasano.
The most interesting aspect of this film is the assorted cast which includes Thor - a singer in a heavy rock band, Graham, a professional wrestler and West, who made the "Batman" role his own during the 1960's. The director, who makes a cameo appearance here, has another zombie film release besides this; *Black Roses* (1987).

ZOMBIE STRIPPERS - (2008) (US)
D – Jay Lee
S – Jenna Jameson, Robert Englund, Roxy Saint,

The Dead Walk

Joey Medina, Shamron Moore, Penny Drake, Jennifer Holland

Part of a mini new wave of "fleshed out" zombie epics, along with *Zombies! Zombies! Zombies!* (2007), this is actually quite an audacious film despite its low rent premise. Set in the near future during George Bush's fourth term(!), and with American forces spread thinly across the globe, the government's secret solution to the problem - zombie soldiers of course. When a soldier is accidentally infected he visits Rhino's strip club in Nebraska and proceeds to contaminate the star performer, Cat (porn star Jenna Jameson), turning her into a zombie.

Amidst the ensuing gore as the goggle eyed patrons become gooey zombies, there's a number of incidental delights to savour here. From the pithy one liners - "I'm running out of cliches" complains one character to Cat's comment on reading Nietzsche, whilst upside down, and that he "Makes so much more sense now", to the bravura "dance off" between Jameson and Moore using ping-pong balls!

There's some interesting side issues here - Cat's popularity proportionally increases as she visibly decomposes drawing a disturbing correlation between the still drooling customers, their lust verging on being close to necrophilia. The gender divide here also provides an intriguing dichotomy as the female zombies retain their intelligence, whilst their male counterparts, predictably revert to neanderthal type. Scariest of all however, is the thought that Jameson's pre-zombie, plasticised face may be more frightening than her undead visage - a biting metaphor for our slavish pursuit for the "perfection" of plastic surgery perhaps? Imagine *The Return of the Living Dead* meets *Showgirls* and you're somewhere near there with these "Stripping Yarns".

ZOMBIES AKA WICKED LITTLE THINGS - (2006) (US)

D – J.S. Cardone

S – Lori Heuring, Scout Taylor-Compton, Chloe Moretz, Geoffrey Lewis, Ben Cross, Craig Vye, Chris Jamba, Julie Rogers

A better than average entry, but without enough originality or standout moments to elevate it to classic status, Cardone's film is nevertheless an effective chiller. The returning souls of child coal miners killed during a mining accient in Pennsylvania in 1913, rise up to haunt the newly arrived family (Heuring, Taylor-Compton and Moretz), now residing in their ancestral family home in the mountains. The night shots of the spooky woods and the bizarre image of the antagonists here being children, dressed in the clothes of the period, is a captivating one. Beyond the tension of these scenes however, Cardone struggles to wrestle anything else meaningful from the script, with the introduction of an industrialist villain being a somewhat hackneyed conceit.

ZOMBIES OF MORA TAU - (1957) (US)

D - Edward L. Cahn

S - Gregg Palmer, Allison Hayes, Autumn Russell, Joel Ashley, Morris Ankrum.

ZOMBIES OF THE STRATOSPHERE - (1952) (US)

D - Fred C. Bannon

S - Judd Holdren, Aline Towne, Lane Bradford, Leonard Nimoy.

One of the better films to emerge from Republic Studios, despite an overly confusing premise of Martians destroying earth to enable their own planet, Mars, to move in and benefit from the earth's orbit space. Notable as one of Nimoy's early films. He later donned the now famous "pointed ears" to become Mr. Spock in *Star Trek*.

ZOMBIES! ZOMBIES! ZOMBIES! - (2007) (US)

D – Jason Murphy

S – Jessica Barton, Hollie Winnard, Lyanna Tumaneng, Sean Harriman, Anthony Headen, Tiffany Shepis, Juliet Reeves

A trio of sexy strippers (Barton, Tumaneng and Winnard), are left stranded in The Grindhouse club as it is besieged by zombies infected with a serum that has been smuggled out of a nearby research facility. Whilst the strippers are certainly easy on the eye and the sight of Tiffany Shepis sending herself up is amusing, the low budget production values and pedantic pacing ultimately stall the film. As director Murphy comments however, when comparing the film to other Hollywood epics; "I guess the main difference would be that our movie doesn't take itself too seriously...Besides, how serious can you be when the story is about strippers vs zombies?" Indeed!

ZOMBIETHON - (1986) (US)

D - Ken Dixon

S - Various artists.

A compilation of scenes from various zombie pictures. Choice clips from the likes of *Zombie Flesh Eaters* (1979), *Oasis of the Zombies* (1980) and *Zombie Lake* (1980) are all featured here, together with new footage set in a movie theatre.

Index of Films

INDEX OF FILMS (page number in bold indicates an illustration)

Abbott and Costello Meet the Mummy 204
A Blade in the Dark 158
A Clockwork Orange 186, **187**,**188**, 189, 190
A Company of Wolves 137
Airplane 191
Airport 142
Airport '77 142
A Letter To Brezchnev 137
Alien 118, 169, 180, 219
Alien Contamination 156
Alien Resurrection 215
Aliens 119, 223, 238
A Lizard in a Woman's Skin 90
Amityville Horror, The (1979) 99
An American Werewolf In London 137
Andromeda Strain, The 189, 233
Angel Heart 215
A Nightmare on Elm Street 119, 157, 215
Apocalypse Now 115, 237
Army of Darkness-The Medieval Dead 107, **108**, **110**, 123, **124**, **125**, 237
Assault on Precinct 13 (1976) 181, 184, 243
Asylum 21
Attack of the Fifty Foot Woman 20
AVP: Alien vs. Predator 215
AVPR: Alien vs. Predator - Requiem 215
Awakening, The 27, 206
Awful Dr. Orloff, The 151
Aztec Mummy, The 204
Back to the Future 131
Barbarella 161
Batman and Robin 199
Battle Girl 165, 166
Bay of Blood 84, 158
Beastmaster, The 117
Beguiled, The 171
Believers, The 215
Beyond, The 91, 95, **96-98**, 102, **103**, 186
Beyond The Door 111
Birds, The 39, 170, 226
Black Cat, The (1981) 21, 93
Blacula 111
Blair Witch Project, The 81, 247, 250
Blood and Black Lace 158
Blood from the Mummy's Tomb 27, **206**
BloodRayne 222
BloodRayne 2: Deliverance 222
Blow Up 90, 169
Blue Velvet 188
Body Double 18
Bodysnatchers 172

Boy Eats Girl 7
Boys from Brazil, The 190
Brain Damage 113
Breakheart Pass 139
Bride of Frankenstein 128
Bride of ReAnimator 128
Bride Wore Black, The 186
Bring Me The Head Of Alfredo Garcia 172
Cabinet of Dr. Caligari, The 17, 25, 172
Cannibal Apocalypse 157, 167
Cannibal Ferox 20, 36, 154
Cannibal Holocaust 20, 248
Carnival of Souls 70
Carrie 113
Cassandra Crossing, The 139
Cast Away 192
Castle Freak 62
Cat and the Canary, The 24
Cat O' Nine Tails 160
Cat People (1942) 18
Cat People (1982) 112
Cemetery Man 219, **220**, 221
Ceremonia Sangrienta 153
Child, The 111
Children Shouldn't Play With Dead Things 111, **112-114**, 177
China Syndrome, The 153-154
Chinese Ghost Story, A 163-165
Chinese Ghost Story 2, A 164
Church, The 220
Circus of Horrors 186
Citizen Kane 58, 170
City of the Dead 21, 23
City of the Living Dead 15, 31,,**89**, 91, 93, **94-95**, 97, 99
City of the Walking Dead 154-155
Close Encounters of the Third Kind 186
Cloverfield 81, 248, 250
Collingwood Story, The 248
Coma 189
Corpse Bride, The 7
Count Yorga, Vampire 31, 111
Crazies, The **40-41**, 42, 228
Creature with the Atom Brain 177
Creepers 219
Creepshow 40, 46, **47**, 191
Curse of the Aztec Mummy 204
Curse of the Dead 158
Curse of the Mummy's Tomb 205
Cut and Run 102
Dagon 128
Daleks - Invasion Earth 2150A.D 178
Das Boot 222

The Dead Walk

Dawn of the Dead (1978) 7, 40, **43-46**, 53, 65, 67, 75, 79, 84, 91, 92, 118,
Dawn (1978 cont) 130, 153, 154, 159, 180, 228, 231, 239, 244, 246
Dawn of the Dead (2004) 65, **66-69**, 70, 87
Dawn of the Mummy 206, **207**
Day of the Dead (1985) 7, 33, **47-51**, 52, **53-54**, 55-56, **57**, 58-59, **60**, 61-62, **63**, 70, 79-81, 166, 223-224, 226, 228, 246
Day of the Dead (2008) 85, **86-88**
Day of the Triffids, The 120, 180
Dead and Buried **118-120**
Death Becomes Her **131**, 132
Deathdream 11, 115-116
Death in Venice 90
Death Proof 132
Death Warmed Up 160
Deep Red 154
Deliverance 33
Demonia 101, **102**
Demons 7, 24, **136**, **158-160**, 219
Demons 2 160, 216
Descent, The 236, 238
Diary of the Dead 7, 52, 65, 80, **82-85**, 248
Dirty Harry 171
Dr. Jekyll and Sister Hyde 143
Dog Soldiers 236, 238
Doomsday 6, 74, 228, **236-238**, 239
Donovan's Brain 190
Don't Torture A Duckling 90
Door To Silence 101, **103**
Dracula (1931) 17
Dracula (1958) 121, 205
Dressed To Kill 186
Driller Killer, The 172
Duel 195
Dust Devil 169
Earth Dies Screaming, The 177-178
Eaten Alive 154
Escape From L.A. 181
Escape From New York 74, 181-182, 237-238
Eternal, The 207-208
Evil Dead, The 24, 36 ,119, **121-122**, 126, 159, 164, 167, 251
Evil Dead 2 - Dead By Dawn 121, **123**, 215
Exorcist, The 24, 111
Eyes of the Mummy 202
Eyes Without A Face 162
Faculty, The 169
Fahrenheit 451oC 185-186, 190
Fantastic Voyage 36
Fido **245**, 246
Fog, The 118, 184
Forbin Project, The 189
Four Skulls of Jonathan Drake, The 20

Four Weddings and a Funeral 137
Frankenstein (1931) 139, 203
Freaks 25
Friday the 13th 169, 215, 218
Fright 31
Frissons des Vampires, Les 161
From Beyond 114, **127**, 128
From Russia With Love 15
Full Metal Jacket 115, 174
Ghost Breaker, The 24
Ghostbreakers, The (1940) 24
Ghostbusters 21
Ghosts of Mars, The **181-184**
Glen or Glenda ? 179
Gorgon, The 23
Graduate, The 40
Green Hell, The 202
Halloween (1978) 114, 219
Hamlet 23
Harem Aleck 204
Hauser's Memory 190
He Knows You're Alone 114, 169
Hellboy 169
Hellboy 2: The Golden Army 169, 200
Hellraiser 137, 216, **217-219**
Hellraiser 2: Hellbound **218**
Hills Have Eyes, The (1977) 33, 120
Horror Express 7, **138-139**, 140-142, **143**
Horror of the Zombies 146, **147**
Hot Fuzz 245
House 85, 113
House By The Cemetery, The 21, 91, 98, **99-101**, 152
House of the Dead 222, **223**
House of the Dead 2 222
Howling, The 113
I Am Legend 70, **192**, 197-200
Invaders From Mars (1987) 181
Invasion, The **171-175**
Invasion of the Bodysnatchers (1956) 169, **170**, 171, 176
Invasion of the Bodysnatchers (1978) **168**, 172
Invisible Invaders 31, 70, 177
Island of Terror 177
Isle of the Dead **21**, 23
It Came From Outer Space 169, 172
I Walked With A Zombie 17-18, **19**
J'Accuse 25
Jack's Wife 40
Jason and the Argonauts 6, **104-109**, 125, 165
Jaws 92, 162
Junk **165**, 166
Knightriders 46

Index of Films

Land of the Dead 7, **35**, 52, 54, 65, 69-70, **71-81**, 245
Last Days of Pompeii 90
Last House on the Left 36
Last Man on Earth, The 70, 195
Last Starfighter, The 180
Last Wave, The 161
Last Year in Marienbad 161
Legend of the Mummy 207
Legend of the 7 Golden Vampires 31, 143, **144**
Levres de Sang 161
Lifeforce 7, **178-179**, 180-181
Little Shop of Horrors (1960) 113
Live and Let Die 8, 15, **137-138**
Living Dead at the Manchester Morgue, The 101-102, 151, **152-154**, 177, 229, 241
Living Dead Girl, The **162-163**
Long Hair of Death, The 84
London Voodoo **11**, **13**
Lord of the Rings 161
Macabre 158
Macunba Sexual **10, 14, 16**
Mad Max 225
Mad Max 2 198, 237
Malpertuis 96
Manhattan Baby 96, 101
Man Who Could Cheat Death, The 186
Man Who Fell To Earth, The 186
Martin **42**, 43, 161
Mask of Satan, The 158
Masque of the Red Death, The 186
Meaning of Life, The 137
Mummy, The (1932) 27, 202, **203**
Mummy, The (1959) 27, **204-205**
Mummy, The (1999) **201**, **207-210**
Mummy of King Ramses, The 202
Mummy Returns, The 210
Mummy 3: Tomb of the Dragon Emperor, The **210-213**
Mummy's Curse, The 203
Mummy's Hand, The 27, 202-203, 205
Mummy's Shroud, The 205, **206**
Mummy's Tomb, The 27, 203, 205
Murder By Decree 112
Murder Rock 101, **103**
New York Ripper, The 101, **103**
Night of the Big Heat, The 177
Night of the Comet 179-180
Night of the Creeps 113
Night of the Demons 130
Night of the Ghouls 179
Night of the Living Dead (1968) 6, 36, **37-39**, 40, 43-45, 48, 53, 64, 68, 70, 82, 85, 92-93, 111, 146, 151, 153, 161, 166, 177, 181, 184, 196-197, 225,

Night of the Living Dead (1968 cont.) 243-244, 247, 250
Night of the Living Dead (1990) **64-65**
Night of the Seagulls 147
North By North-West 239, 70
Nosferatu (1922) 91
Nosferatu (1979) 91, 159
Omega Man, The 23, 70, **189**, **191**, 195, 198-199, **200**, 233
Omen, The 111
Pesticide 161
Phantasm **116-117**
Pharaoh's Curse, The 204
Picnic At Hanging Rock 161
Pirates of Blood River, The 28
Pirates of the Caribbean 7, 79, 111
Plague of the Zombies, The 7, **26**, **28-34**, 70, 143, 145, 245
Plan 9 From Outer Space 178-180
Planet of the Apes (1968) 23, 191
Planet of the Lifeless Men 157
Planet of the Vampires 158
Planet Terror **132-135**
Poltergeist 21, 181
Poseidon Adventure, The 161
Psycho 23, 39-40, 186
Purple Rose of Cairo, The 159
Quarantine 252
Quatermass and the Pit **176**, 180, 182-184
Quatermass Experiment, The 176
Quatermass 2 176
Raiders of the Lost Ark 54, 209
Rawhead Rex 219
Razorback 207
Reanimator 125, **126**, **128-129**, 215, 216
Rear Window 170
[REC] 6,7,81, **247-250**, 251
Reign of Fire 199-200
Reptile, The 28
Requiem pour un Vampire 161
Resident Evil 88, 166, 222-223, **224-225**, 233
Resident Evil: Apocalypse 222-224
Resident Evil: Extinction 222-225, **226-227**
Return of the Evil Dead 145, **148-149**
Return of the Living Dead, The 119, 129, **130-131**, 166, 177, 215
Return of the Living Dead 2 115, 131
Return of the Living Dead 3 131
Rio Bravo 181, 184, 238
Robot v's the Aztec Mummy, The 204
Rocket to the Moon 169
Salem's Lot 23, 180
Santo en la Vengenza de la Momia 204
Santo y Blue Demon contra los Monstrous 204
Scanners 160

The Dead Walk

Scarecrow 160
Scared Stiff 24
Scarlet Blade, The 28
Schizoid 90
Scorpion King, The 212
Secret of Dr. Orloff **151**
Sect, The 220
Serpent and the Rainbow, The **9**, **12**, 16, 215, **216**
Seven Samurai, The 163
Seventh Victim, The 23
Shadow of Doubt 111
Shaft 111
Shaun of the Dead 6-7, 241, **242-243**, 244-245
Shining, The 98
Shivers 113
Shock 158
Shock Waves 114, **115**
Silence of the Lambs 169, 251
Sisters 186
Son of Dracula 177
Southern Comfort 33
Spookies 113
SS Experiment Camp 115
Stacy 166
Stagefright 220
Star Wars 169
Straw Dogs 172
Stepford Wives, The 33, 190
Sugar Hill 111
Supernaturals, The 114
Suspiria 95, 154
Tales From The Crypt 16
Talos the Mummy 207
Tarantula 169-170
Tenebre 154, 186
Terminal Man, The 11, 189
Terror Creatures From The Grave 21
Texas Chain Saw Massacre, The (1974) 33, 180
There's Always Vanilla 40
They Live 181
Thing, The (1982) 52, 115, 139-140, 165, 181-182, 250
Thing From Another World, The 139-140
Threads 153
300 69
Three Sovereigns for Sarah 23
Throne of Blood 239
THX 1138 33
Times Are Hard For Vampires 90
Time Walker 207
Tombs of the Blind Dead 144, **145-146**
Towering Inferno, The 161

28 Days Later 6,7,65, 70, 193, 227, **228-229**, 232-233, **235**, 241, 244, 247-8
28 Weeks Later 228-229, **230-231**, 232
Twins of Evil 137
Two Evil Eyes 75
2001 - A Space Odyssey 239
Vanguard, The 228, 236-237, **239-241**
Vampire Lovers, The 143
Vampyr 18
Vegenza de la Momia, La 204
Venus in Furs (1969) 151
Versus **167**
Vertigo 186
Video Dead, The 216
Videodrome 151, 216
Virgin Among The Living Dead 151
Voices From Beyond 101
Voodoo Man, The 24
War of the Worlds (1953) 176
War of the Worlds (2005) 169
Warlords, The 213
Warlords of Atlantis, The 165
Wax Mask 102
Weekend 161
Westworld 189
White Zombie 6, 8, 10, **18**, 19
Wild Bunch, The 172
Wild Zero 166
Wolf Man, The 177
Woodstock 191
Zombie Creeping Flesh 156
Zombie Diaries, The 85, **246**, 247-250
Zombie Flesh Eaters 36, **90-93**
Zombie Holocaust 156, **157**
Zombie Lake **161**, 162
Zombie Strippers! **214**
Zombie 3 100
Zombies of Mora Tau 20
Zombies on Broadway **22**, 24
Zone Troopers 216
Zoo Warriors From The Magic Mountain 165
Zulu 184